In the Philippines and Okinawa

In the Philippines and Okinawa

A Memoir, 1945–1948

William S. Triplet
Edited by Robert H. Ferrell

University of Missouri Press
Columbia and London

Library of Congress Cataloging-in-Publication Data

Triplet, William S., 1900–

   In the Philippines and Okinawa : a memoir, 1945–1948 /
William S. Triplet ; edited by Robert H. Ferrell.

      p.   cm.

   Includes bibliograhical references and index.

   ISBN 0-8262-1335-9 (alk. paper)

   1. Triplet, William S., 1900–   2. United States. Army—Officers—
Biography.   3. Soldiers—United States—Biography. I. Ferrell, Robert H.
II. Title

U53.T75 A3 2001

355'.0092—dc21

[B]   2001027551

⊚™ This paper meets the requirements of the
American National Standard for Permanence of Paper
for Printed Library Materials, Z39.48, 1984.

Text designer: Vickie Kersey DuBois
Jacket designer: Susan Ferber
Typesetter: BOOKCOMP, Inc.
Printer and binder: Thomson-Shore, Inc.
Typefaces: Officina Sans, Veljovic

The Press gratefully acknowledges the contribution made by the
Hulston Family Foundation toward the production of this book.

Contents

Preface

The present volume of the memoirs of the late (d. 1994) Colonel William S. Triplet completes a trilogy that sets out the colonel's military service in the two World Wars of the last century and, with the pages that follow, three fascinating years in the Far East after World War II. This last book deals with duty in the Philippine Islands and in Okinawa and does not cover a subsequent assignment after the Korean War when he advised the First Korean Division in 1953–1954. He wrote a short account of his experiences in Korea that lacks the proportion and interest of his earlier writing.

As set out in the two preceding books of his memoirs, *A Youth in the Meuse-Argonne* and *A Colonel in the Armored Divisions,* Triplet took interest in the military in 1917 because the United States had declared war on Imperial Germany. Then seventeen years old and a high school student in Sedalia, Missouri, he believed that he could enjoy himself in the army and also take advantage of a promise by the superintendent of the Sedalia public schools who allowed that every volunteer for military service could finish out his junior year without duties and not have to take a senior year of classes, receiving a diploma for military service alone. One thing then led to another. The attraction of service put Triplet into the Thirty-fifth Division of Missouri and Kansas National Guard troops. That division became one of the starting divisions in the Battle of the Meuse-Argonne, which proved to be the greatest battle in all of American history, both in numbers of men involved (one million) and in casualties (twenty-six thousand men killed). Triplet's experiences with his fifty-man platoon—he was a platoon sergeant without supervision by a second lieutenant, for second lieutenants were in short supply to the American Expeditionary Forces—so impressed him with army life that upon the end of the war and mustering out he arranged for a high school diploma somehow (the superintendent's promise was disavowed by the Sedalia school board) and obtained an appointment to West Point.

Graduating with the West Point class of 1924, the still youthful if veteran soldier from Sedalia spent the following years in a variety of posts. Most of his appointments were of the usual sort, in dusty wind-blown places in Arizona or sun-drenched camps in the Canal Zone, or with the Reserve Officers' Training Corps at Purdue University in West Lafayette, Indiana, or with troops assigned to housekeeping duties.

He served two years, 1936–1938, with the regiment then stationed at Tientsin, China, and afterward wrote four hundred typescript pages about his work with the regiment. Those pages could have been of historic importance—as are those on the Philippines and Okinawa—and much worth publishing, perhaps within the present volume on his Far Eastern service, except that for some reason, and it may have been the Tientsin regiment's entirely adequate training as he measured it, his account is of only passing interest. He regaled his family members (he appears to have written all of his accounts for members of his family, not for publication) with stories about local customs and of servants, hunts, and almost humdrum social entertaining by officers of the regiment.

At last his assignments turned toward importance; in 1940 he went to Fort Benning, Georgia, for duty with the Infantry Board, a group of select officers who tested weapons and vehicles for use by the rapidly expanding army. As participation in World War II loomed and then became a matter of fact, he discovered that his work of testing the board's prototypes was far more important than he could have imagined when initially assigned. He asked for and obtained reassignment only after Pearl Harbor and the army's involvement in a shooting war both in Europe and the Far East offered special attraction for again serving with troops.

At the beginning of American involvement in World War II and for nearly three years thereafter Triplet found himself in training missions, which led to an intense frustration, fear that the war was going to pass him by, with his not having heard a shot fired in anger since November 1918. He asked for service with armored units, as his experiences at Benning involved testing of tank armor and guns and before that he had been in several armored assignments. As a result he was assigned first to the Thirteenth Armored Division, an unhappy experience because the division commander did not desire advice from the colonel—Triplet became a full colonel in December 1942. Escaping the Thirteenth when it changed its table of organization (dropping its regiments in favor of separate battalions) he received a novel assignment as commander of a training group for amphibious tanks and troop carriers. After two years with the Eighteenth Armored Group (Amph.) he was posted to Europe through the intervention of a friendly general.

During the last half year of World War II, Colonel Triplet served with the Second Armored Division and then with the Seventh Armored, commanding a regiment in the Second and—his favorite assignment of his entire military service—Combat Command A of the Seventh Armored. From January until May 1945 he took his big four-thousand-man task force of tanks, troops, and artillery through Belgium and Germany in one engagement after another. His battalions were almost all reservists or enlisted or drafted men, an exhilarating group, everything he could have asked for, willing to push through anything, forests or light roads or at one point down an autobahn, thereby taking part in the destruction of the Wehrmacht. The end of the war found CCA on the Baltic, confronting the advancing forces of the Soviet Union.

He sought to take part in the Pacific war, but arrived in the Philippines only after V-J Day, to receive occupation duties in Luzon and Okinawa. The duties proved far from prosaic, what with dealing with demoralized occupation troops, bringing in Japanese holdouts, controlling renegade Philippine guerrillas, and organizing a Philippine Scout regiment for occupation tasks on Okinawa and transporting it there. He ended his Okinawa duty as deputy U.S. Army commander and chief of staff to the commanding general.

After more service in the continental United States, and in Korea, Triplet retired in 1954.

His next forty years, a longer time than his military career, he spent in retirement, in West Germany and Florida and finally in a small house near Leesburg, Virginia, that overlooked the scene of fighting a century before—he could not escape wars, wherever he went. He spent these years composing the memoirs that he gave to his family members or deposited at the Army War College at Carlisle Barracks, Pennsylvania, where the present writer, working on a book about the Meuse-Argonne, came upon them, admired them for their literary flair and military sagacity, and undertook to edit the thousands of pages, written laboriously with what appears to have been an old manual typewriter, into the volumes now at hand.

Acknowledgments

As in the previous volumes I again am indebted to the Triplet family, especially the colonel's daughter Elizabeth T. Hennig, whose description of family moments and her father's unfailing good humor made an outsider understand what a wonderful parent he must have been. My thanks also to the colonel's son-in-law, husband of his late daughter Catherine, Colonel Byron Fitzgerald, who shared memories.

The staff of the U.S. Army Military History Institute, a part of the Army War College at Carlisle Barracks, Pennsylvania, helped in every way: Lieutenant Colonel Edward M. Perry, director; Richard J. Sommers, assistant director; David A. Keough, head of the search room; and Pamela Cheney and James Baughman. All photos reproduced in this volume were provided by the Institute.

A thank-you to historian friends—Brigadier General James L. Collins, Jr., John K. Hulston, John Lukacs, and Russell F. Weigley. With their assistance an editor should make few mistakes.

Another to the University of Missouri Press: director and editor-in-chief Beverly Jarrett, whose interest in the manuscript was unfailing from the moment the big folders marked "Philippines and Okinawa" made their appearance in the files at Carlisle Barracks; managing editor Jane Lago, who keeps everything in order; and editor John Brenner, who has an eye for editorial error and makes his points gently if firmly.

Betty Bradbury once again, for the third time, put a long and complicated manuscript on computer disk—with great patience and courtesy; it is such a pleasure to work with her. And with John M. Hollingsworth, the skilled cartographer.

Lila and Carolyn make all tasks easier.

A Note on the Editing

As in the preceding volumes, so again in this one Colonel Triplet wrote in vignettes, and the principal task of an editor was to assemble them in chapters. The colonel was a skilled writer and this helped. In the 1930s he published several dozen articles in the *Infantry Journal* about the military adventures of two mythical brothers, Terry and Horry (for Horace) Bull, their tactical experiences and use of new as well as old weapons. But the task was not as easy as it sounds, for chapters needed structure, that is, unity, and required subsections that held together—two or three of the latter. In the vignettes Triplet could wander or get into detail and this sort of material needed to come out. Some of it went into notes, identifiable because of being in quotation marks. For the rest it is gone, without ellipsis points. There are no excisions within sentences, except in chapter 18 where for some reason, in a few instances, the colonel was off his usual wondrous style, or so it seemed.

The smaller portion of the editing consisted of virtual copyediting. It involved changing "which" to "that" if a comma did not precede, lower-casing capitals, sometimes introduction of semicolons, turning dashes to commas. Exclamation marks usually were unnecessary—the colonel's writing stood on its own. Dates appear uniformly, percentages in arabic, numbers written out to 101 and round numbers thereafter. Accents do not appear in Filipino names; a tilde does.

Readers may inquire about the provenance of this book, what it was based upon. In World War I the then platoon sergeant had his hands full with duties large and small and yet kept a voluminous diary, later lost, well remembered by one of the colonel's daughters. For World War II diary keeping was much more difficult because of command of regiments and eventually CCA of the Seventh Armored, but times of leisure allowed write-ups of the immediate past—some diary, some contemporary narrative. Such also appears to have been the basis of this singular memoir of duty in the Philippines and on Okinawa.

In the Philippines and Okinawa

One

The 342d Infantry Regiment

The Seventh Armored Division attached to the XVIII Airborne Corps as the cutting edge of the British Second Army crossed the Elbe near Bleckede on May 2, 1945, and raced fifty-five miles to the Baltic Sea in five hours. Combat Command A gathered in seventeen thousand Nordic supermen during this dash. The next few days we spent in organizing PW camps, combing the woods for the vaunted Werewolves (and a pitiful, scrawny lot they were),[1] and halting the surging flood of displaced persons. This last chore was particularly disagreeable but the Russians had moved up to our lines and there was an international agreement that the wall, later built in concrete and barbed wire, be stabilized at once.

All Europe seemed to be on the move. Thousands of East Prussians who had been driven west by the Russian advance were trying to return to their homes. Countless thousands of liberated Russian, Polish, Baltic, and Finnish PWs and slave laborers were trying to go east, and French, Belgians, Danes, and Dutch wanted to go west. Held immobile by the Allied road blocks, they slowly starved in place.

So when the war in Europe came to a long overdue end on May 8, I applied for a transfer to the Pacific front where there was an active war still going on. My request was thoroughly ignored until after V-J Day. Then, faced by the problem of returning and replacing MacArthur's war-worn veterans, a personnel clerk in the Pentagon unearthed my dust-covered letter in the hold file and chortled, "Oh, goody, look at this. Here's some damned fool that wants to go to the Pacific front." And I was belatedly on my way.

After a month of rest and recuperation leave with my family in Carmel, California, I landed in the Fifth Replacement Depot in Luzon where Dutch and Australian as well as American veterans were being rested, re-cuperated, rehabilitated, and repatriated. American replacements fresh from the States were growing bored awaiting reassignment. I was lucky; my orders were waiting for me. I was assigned to the Eighty-sixth Division as a regimental commander.

When I cheerfully stated at the mess that evening that I would be on my way to the Eighty-sixth Division next morning I noted an amazing reaction. The Dutch general gave me a china-blue Teutonic stare and remarked, "Ahhh sooo." The Australian brigadier, our ally, an affable, responsive type, merely fixed me with a pale-blue Anglo-Saxon stare and commented, "Hmmm." Some of the Americans were more informa-tive. All of them offered their sympathies and condolences. Each then followed up with his particular rumor or yarn about my new outfit.

The Eighty-sixth had been briefly employed in Europe and after V-E Day had been returned and given a month of home leave in the States, then had been reassembled and transported to the Philippines. It appeared that the principal occupation of the men of the division was writing sad and complaining letters to their friends, families, congressmen, newspapers, and especially to the more unscrupulous columnists.

The military police captain told of a group of the Eighty-sixth in Manila who asked one of his MPs where they could get a ride toward their camp.

"Where is your camp?" asked the MP.

"Eighty-sixth Division in Marakina."

"Oh, so you're the Black Hawks. Well, I'll tell you. Each one of you get all your friends to write ten letters to Congress and you write twelve. That'll make an even dozen. Then Congress will probably send you a fleet of plush-lined limousines to haul you back and forth from your nursery. But I don't know of any trucks that will haul you."

The quartermaster colonel contributed his poisonous gem. "I overheard a conversation one day when we were putting out surplus equipment that was free as air. One of your supply sergeants drove up. My men said, 'All right, back your truck in here and load up. You want 540? OK, wait a minute. Aren't you guys from that Black Buzzard Division?'

" 'We're from the Eighty-sixth Black Hawks.'

" 'Well, you'll have to get a requisition signed by Drew Pearson and approved by Congress before you get anything out of this dump.' "[2]

Then a brilliantly beribboned infantry lieutenant of the Ninety-sixth told of an Eighty-sixth truck driver who picked up soldiers of his battle-worn company.

" 'What outfit, chum?' one of them asked the driver.

" 'The Eighty-sixth Black Hawk Division,' said the driver, with unwarranted pride.

" 'Hold it. Stop right now and let us out. We ain't going to ride with any malingering sonofabitch from that home guard outfit.' "

I had been able to take care of the MP, the quartermaster, and a trio of general staff officers by very obviously reading their ribbons and inquiring about their combat experience. But the battlefield-promoted lieutenant had me stopped. He had collected as many Purple Hearts and other ribbons in two years as I had managed in two wars.

Then the nurses got into the act.

"I've never known a group of officers before that talked so much about going home," remarked the pretty brunette captain.

"But they're such nice boys," said the luscious blonde lieutenant in consoling rebuttal. "They're no trouble at all."

It was a full minute before I perceived the lethal barb in that remark. It is a great boost to a girl's ego to have to actively defend her virtue a bit on a date and she just doesn't care for the nice boys who never give her any trouble.

So I left the replacement depot next morning in a very thoughtful mood and arrived at the Eighty-sixth Division camp at Marakina heartily wishing I was back in Germany with CCA of the Seventh Armored or any other outfit I could be proud of.

First Impression

I was welcomed at division headquarters by Major General "Count" Melasky, whom I had known as chief of the test section of the Infantry Board at Fort Benning. I had spent more than a year working for him and was delighted to be with him again.[3] After lunch and pleasant reminiscences of our test section days he told me that I would take command of the 342d Infantry Regiment and briefed me on my missions to be performed in my sector, the southern half of Luzon.

Surrender points were to be maintained at such locations as would be convenient to known groups of Japanese who might wish to surrender. All Japanese pockets of resistance were to be eliminated by propaganda, persuasion, and judicial pursuit. But in dealing with the Japanese, I was to incur no casualties (and that would be a neat trick if possible).

I was to take charge of all Filipino guerrilla units in my area, nine thousand men in a dozen or more regiments, battalions, and squadrons. These recognized guerrillas were to be disarmed, paid for their services, and discharged in the near future. In the meantime I would be responsible for their maintenance and conduct.

I would supervise the activities of twelve hundred Japanese PWs in cleaning up the island of Corregidor.

I would maintain guards on the Philippine Treasury and on the Rizal cement plant.

Most important, I would make every effort to keep the morale of the regiment up.

"They've had a mighty rough deal," said Melasky, "fighting on the European front and then sent over here."

That remark surprised me. I had never heard of the Eighty-sixth except the scurrilous stories of my messmates of the night before and thought that they were practically an unblooded division that had nothing to be unhappy about. And at least they had had a month of home leave before being sent to the Pacific. I was amazed to see that General Melasky had the same complaining, self-pitying attitude as was alleged of the troops.

I jeeped over to my new command where I was met by the executive, Lieutenant Colonel Holt, West Point class of 1939. "They're sure making them younger or better nowadays," I thought. "He's made light colonel in less time than it took me to make first lieutenant."[4] Holt was a soft-appearing light-heavyweight, round-faced, easy-going, and wearing a customary smile that displayed his prominent front teeth.

He showed me about the headquarters area and pointed out the main features of the regimental area. It was basically a tent camp with a few prefabricated Butler buildings and quonset huts for kitchens, mess halls, and regimental and battalion headquarters. Tents for the troops were the general purpose type designed for twenty men, framed and floored, with an average occupancy of ten men. The poorly patronized Red Cross service occupied a circus tent of the type used by corps and army headquarters. All officers were in wall tents. My office next to the headquarters quonset was a framed 14 x 14 Sibley pyramidal tent.[5] Water and electricity had been installed throughout the camp.

The area was superficially clean due to the work of Japanese PWs who were drawn daily from the division stockade. A horde of Filipinos were also employed for carpentry, brush cutting, drainage digging, kitchen police, and orderlies. Filipino women were seen throughout the camp taking up or delivering laundry.

Three companies of the second battalion were on detached missions. E Company was guarding the Philippine Treasury, G Company was in charge of the cleanup of Corregidor, and H Company was the security force for the Rizal cement plant near Manila.

The service company drew and delivered rations to the numerous guerrilla units and the intelligence platoon of headquarters company manned the Japanese surrender points.

A few men in the first battalion attended a halfhearted educational program.

The rest of the troops did nothing, that is, nothing useful or constructive. They ate, slept, sunned, patronized native dives in Manila or neighboring villages, wore their hair long and their shirttails out, complained, and wrote letters to politicians and columnists while waiting for repatriation on their very scanty store of rotation points.

"The men are very dissatisfied," explained my exec. "We're the only division to be sent over here after fighting in Germany."

"What battles were you in, Colonel Holt? I can't remember hearing anything about the Eighty-sixth in Europe."

"We fought in the battles of the Rhine, the Ruhr, and the Redoubt."

"I never heard of the Redoubt, and the skirmishes of the Rhine and the Ruhr are included in the Battle of Central Germany. What was your casualty rate?"

"Why this regiment alone lost forty men killed."

"Hmmm, about 1 percent, probably a total casualty list of 4–5 percent counting scratches. In my opinion this outfit hasn't been through much more than a realistic infiltration course. And now please inform the battalion and special unit commanders and the regimental staff that I would like to see them at my office at 1600."

Such was my introduction to the poorest rabble with which I was ever associated. The men and many of the officers were dispirited, malcontent, hopeless, homesick, duty-dodging, shiftless, and undisciplined. The 342d was not the worst in the division; the Black Hawk Division was in toto simply the worst I had ever seen and the 342d was merely a representative regiment.

The officers I'd called for arrived as scheduled and were introduced by Colonel Holt. They seemed to be a decent, capable lot, with the exception of one battalion commander who may have started the cocktail hour too early or ended the last one too late. Three officers were wearing long-billed caps of native manufacture, exaggerations of the types normally affected by air corps mechanics and eccentric admirals, one of them an eye-catching scarlet. I decided that the situation required a gloves-off, bare-knuckle treatment.

"Gentlemen, I have just been redeployed from CCA of the Seventh Armored Division in Germany and have been assigned to command this regiment. I have been here three hours and in that time have seen enough to be thoroughly dissatisfied with the standards you maintain. I am particularly impressed with the level of your morale.

"I have been informed that this division was in contact with the enemy for twelve days in Germany and had a total of 716 casualties, a 3.9 percent loss including lightly wounded and missing. You were then withdrawn from the European theater, each man was given a thirty-day leave at home, the division was reassembled in San Francisco, and you were shipped over here too late for combat.

"Actually this regiment had fewer casualties in twelve days of skirmishing than my battalion suffered during a fight in the Meuse-Argonne in 1918. We had 82 percent killed and wounded in five days.[6] The Second and Seventh Armored Divisions have lost 30 percent each in Europe and they consider themselves fortunate. The First Infantry Division had a casualty list of 200 percent.

"So I am not impressed by your combat record. Remember that these divisions in Europe after taking a much heavier loss than you are still in Europe waiting for rotation on points just as you are and they have had no home leave as you have had.

"Therefore I don't want to hear any more about how you have been badly treated.

"Starting at 0800 tomorrow I will walk through the special units and the second, third, and first battalions in that order. As a concession to the heat your men may wear T-shirts or strip to the waist at work or games. Otherwise shirts will be worn, properly. All officers will be in uniform."

I looked them over. Most of them looked startled, aghast is a better word. The inebriated battalion commander was making a heroic attempt to appear sober and alert and the three lads wearing baseball caps seemed to be embarrassed so I decided to hold none of them for further discussion.

"That is all, and thank you very much, gentlemen."

So began the hardest battle of my military service. The walk-through next morning was a horror to everyone in the regiment. The orders had not been obeyed, apparently no orders were obeyed except at the convenience of the addressee. Two lieutenants hadn't gotten the word and, wearing baseball caps, lost their smarmy welcoming smiles when I informed them that they would forfeit twenty-five dollars each on their next paychecks for this first offense.

I had each company commander take the name of each of his NCOs who were wearing their shirts in Filipino fashion. When the inspection of the company was complete I reviewed the list of names and directed the immediate reduction of the senior NCO to basic private. I could not reduce all of the offenders; we would have lost most of our NCO strength.

There was enough dirty clothing lying about on tables, shelves, and in corners of kitchens, mess halls, and storerooms to clothe completely the half-naked kitchen force. The Filipino kitchen police were mostly engaged in squatting on their heels, languidly fanning the swarming flies, or eating, or both.

Thanks to the Japanese the camp areas were fairly clean but the outer fringes of each battalion area were strewn with beer and Toddy cans distributed at varying distances, the distance probably depending on the strength, accuracy, and sobriety of the thrower.

Toddy was a disgustingly sweet chocolate drink that I was told was in a great favor with the troops. It occurred to me that one of these newfangled psychiatrists could probably make something of that preference. Toddy was apparently a strengthening brew since the Toddy cans had generally been thrown farther than beer cans. One thing the cans had in common: those that had landed with the openings up were full of water and were swarming with the larvae of anopheles mosquitoes.

Beds were unmade or shoddily pulled up; some men were still in bed, many were unshaved, and most were out of uniform. Military courtesy was poor to nonexistent and military bearing was worse. But it was too early to start work on the privates; I had to get the officers straightened out first.

At the end of this miserable four hours I had another meeting with the commanders and gave them my opinion of their units in considerable detail.

"I shall continue the practice," I went on, "of hitting every officer I see in improper uniform with a twenty-five-dollar fine under the 104th Article of War for the first offense—sorry I can't make it more—unless he appeals and requests a court-martial. For a second offense I shall provide the court-martial without option. I shall also reduce the senior shirttail-showing NCO I see in each company area.

"The labor officer will reduce the Japanese and Filipino labor forces by 50 percent as of tomorrow. This will give you and your men the opportunity to do something useful for themselves.

"I shall conduct a similar inspection in three days. At that time I shall start a file on any officer who appears unable to cope with the problems in his command and as soon as feasible begin proceedings to reclassify and separate him from the service as unsatisfactory.

"That will be all. Thank you."

Corregidor, the Treasury, and the Cement Plant

The following day I borrowed an L-5 artillery observation plane and flew out to visit C Company on Corregidor. It was a thrilling trip, in a way. The engine was clucking and sputtering as the carefree baseball-capped lieutenant swung the plane into line at the end of the carabao-pasture runway; while he throttled for full power he remarked, "Hope this crate gets off the ground—sounds like a couple of burnt valves."

I hoped so too, because we were still on the ground at what I feared was the point of no return and a row of trees was coming up fast. But he whipped the plane up and over like a high jumper and leveled off immediately to prevent a stall. I observed that the engine didn't sound right yet but he reassured me.

"Oh, we're all right now. Even if the engine quits I can set her down anywhere. May not be able to get off again but I can set her down easy. By the way, colonel, there ought to be a couple of Mae Wests back there."

There were, underfoot. As we cruised out over Manila Bay, I fished them out of the debris of maps, tools, and stale sandwiches on the floor and blew them a quarter full with the mouth tube, just in case.

There was no usable landing strip on Corregidor and the landing had to be made on a straight stretch of the gravel road that led up from the dock area to "topside" on the head of the tadpole-shaped island. Again the pilot gave me a shot of adrenaline.

"Bad side wind, colonel, but I reckon we can make it." He was a cheerfully optimistic type.

We were crabbing fifteen degrees to the right into the wind between the sea at the foot of the steep slope on the right and the brush-covered slope rising sharply to the central ridge on our left. Angled like that, as soon as our wheels touched we would probably shoot off the road and down the slope into the breakers or if we straightened out before touching down we would doubtless hang our left wing in the brush and pinwheel. So I tightened my belt, fingered the release for the plexiglass hood, and planned on how to get out of the wreck most efficiently.

"Well, if you think you can do it so can I except I don't get flying pay for such damnfool stunts."

A moment later he touched, whipped the nose to the left, right wing down and tail up, swerved from edge to edge, then tail down. We'd made it. Well, he'd reckoned we could. No doubt about it, those artillery flyers do a wonderful job in handling their underpowered kites. But as I climbed out and tried to control the quiver in my fear-weakened legs I vowed that my next trip to Corregidor would be by boat.

I found G Company to be the only reasonably contented unit that I'd seen so far in the Black Hawks. The reason—they had a full-time job. The men who were sleeping, sunbathing, fishing, or swimming among the wreckage of sunken landing craft were the night shift of the guard required on the PW compound. The rest were supervising the gangs of Japanese who seemed quite cheerily content in their job of clearing up the wreckage of the island.

The major part of their work was in the Malinta tunnel where two thousand sons of heaven had barricaded themselves when the Americans were landing and as a last defiant gesture had blown themselves and a goodly part of the tunnel to bloody bits. Removal of the debris and bodies, aside from being disagreeable, was a hairy operation, due to the frequent rockfalls from the weakened roof. Light explosive charges were fired from time to time to jar loose earthfalls, rocks, and slabs of concrete that were on the verge of falling, but the danger was never completely eliminated. In spite of precautions twelve prisoners had been killed in the tunnel to date and many more injured.

On topside the wreckage was fantastic. The twelve-inch mortars were all dismounted from their shattered carriages in the crumbled concrete gun pits and one had been blasted sideways through the five-foot concrete wall of the ammunition magazine at the rear of the pit. Barracks and quarters were in complete ruin. The ship's mast that had served as a flagpole, its supporting members shot through or chipped and weakened, had a heavy list and seemed ready to collapse in a light breeze.[7] Overlapping bomb and shell craters reminded me of Verdun. The entire island except for the areas cleared by the work force was covered with a mass of bushes, small trees, and vines that had sprung up during three years of neglect. Live ammunition, unexploded shells and bombs, and Japanese skeletons were still being recovered from this jungle.

I spent a very instructive day observing the work of G Company and was most favorably impressed by the attitude of the men. The guards who were supervising the various details were alert and obviously proud of themselves and their labor gangs. I was pleased that several of them introduced their Japanese honchos who also seemed to take pride in the efficiency of their crews.

I was so deep in a study of the contrast between G Company and the rest of the regiment that I had seen that I forgot to be terrified until our return takeoff was well underway. Downhill, sidewind, left wing down, slewing, skidding, ripping twigs off bushes, kicking gravel over the edge into the surf below, then a sharp yank to port over the breakers when airborne. But my carefree birdman made it again.

Next day I visited the two companies in and near Manila. E Company was charged with the security of the Philippine Treasury building and had a full-time job. Their duties included not only normal security measures but also plans and preparation for the defense of the treasury against organized armed forces. Of course I wondered why we were required to guard the treasury; why shouldn't the Philippine Army take care of their own? I'm glad that I didn't ask; it would have exposed my total ignorance about Filipinos and their army. But again I was pleased to see a group of clean, sharp-looking soldiers who were living decently in their floored tents in a well-kept compound. Naturally they were looking forward to repatriation but in the meantime they were doing an important job well.

The Rizal cement plant, operating at full capacity in those days of reconstruction, was probably of more genuine value than the treasury, and H Company was stationed on the plant grounds to guard against thieves, vandals, and saboteurs of the Hukbalahap. While not as sharp and alert as the men of E and G companies, the members of H Company still appeared to be in good mental health.

While mulling the situation over during the return to camp I reached the conclusion that the outstanding difference between these three companies of the second battalion and the rest of the regiment was work, something to do—important, useful, instructive, or interesting missions to occupy their minds and hands while they were awaiting their return under the point system.

The point system was good, infinitely better than the return by unit that worked such injustice to the individual in World War I. Each man was credited with a certain number of points for months in the service, months overseas, for battles, decorations for valor, service, or battle wounds. But the Black Hawks had been formed of a late draft, had been sent to Europe late in the war, had seen very little combat, and consequently had received few medals, so they were at the bottom of the list for repatriation. It was up to me to find something constructive to keep the men busy until their embarkation numbers came up.

At division headquarters I called on Colonel Yale, chief of staff. After brief social preliminaries and the first sip of the thrice-boiled coffee he was pushing I made my proposition.

"We don't have enough to do in the 342d, Yale. I'd appreciate it if you'd pass on any detail that requires a company or more to us."

He seemed startled by this request. Commanders never ask for additional duties for their troops and usually try to protect their units from extra details.

"Why, for God's sake? You're doing your full share now."

"Because I've found that my working outfits are in good physical and mental health while the men in this camp on the rest and recreation program are bored, discontented, and going to hell fast. So I'd like to have four times as much duty as we have now. I want to get every man in the regiment on a useful job."

"Well, you've come to the right place at the right time. We've just got a warning order that we may have to send a battalion to Mindanao. The Philippine intelligence people say that there's going to be a lot of trouble with the Moros, they're talking up revolution and independence from the Christians. AFWESPAC intelligence says it's doubtful but possible. There are some Japanese holdouts in the hills, too.[8] And of course there's the usual trouble with unrecognized guerrillas, bandits, and common thieves. There are large supply dumps on the Del Monte plantation guarded now by service troops that we'll probably take over, good place to set up a base camp. As I said, it's not firm yet and I was planning on giving the job to the 341st but do you want it if it shapes up?"

I have seldom had my prayers answered so completely and suddenly. No further thought was required. I grabbed at it.

"I sure do. I'll get a reconnaissance party off on the next plane."

"By the air corps schedule there's one leaving at 1000 day after tomorrow."

"I'll have a party of three. Can you schedule three spaces for us?"

"Three it will be."

On returning to the regiment I discussed the Mindanao detail with Colonel Holt. The prime consideration was the selection of the battalion to send on the job.

"The second is already engaged on a broad front," he pointed out, "and the first battalion has a heavy educational program going on. So I recommend that we plan on using Colonel Ward's third battalion."

I played the devil's advocate. "But I've been told by Ward that a number of his men are also attending the classes. And what about the third battalion men on construction projects, and regimental athletic teams?"

After fifteen seconds of furious thought Holt came up with the answers. "We can do some transferring. Those men in the third who are taking a real interest in education, I mean those attending classes and working at it, we can transfer to the first battalion. I'll check with the information and education people on the men who qualify. Those who are on regimental athletic teams, very few of them, can be transferred to the special units. I'll see athletics and recreation about the men they want. About construction projects, Colonel Ward will need some handymen in settling into his new camp, so aside from the top men on special projects he should keep all those who are handy with tools. Finally we ought to replace the strength he loses with nonspecialists from the first battalion and if necessary from special units."

He had covered all bases and done it well.

"Good. Plan it that way. In the meantime I'd like to have you, Colonel Ward, and a surgeon fly to Mindanao and look the situation over. There are three spaces reserved for you on the plane at 1000 day after tomorrow. Look over the dumps and pick a centrally located campsite. The Japanese-Moro-guerrilla situations will change daily but the dumps and thieves will always be with us."

Major General Melasky

Next morning General Melasky jeeped over for a visit.

"How are you getting along, Bill?"

"Very slowly, general. There's a lot to be done and it looks like I'm going to have to start at the top and work down."

"Well, take it easy, Bill. By the way, I understand that you busted a sergeant in F Company for being out of uniform."

"That's right, sir, I did. Shirttail out. I reduced one sergeant in every company during my announced inspection of the area. And I fined two officers under the 104th AW and started them on their way to Class B boards unless they shape up fast."

"But you've got to remember that this is a civilian army, Triplet, and they're veterans too. You can't treat them like Regular Army recruits."

"Well, general, I've dealt with veterans in 1918 and had a damned fine outfit of civilian veterans in Europe before I was sent here and as long as I am in command of an outfit any sergeant who wears his shirttail out will get busted. And any officer who—"

"You just can't do it, colonel. You can't deal with a civilian army like that without trouble. You'll have the newspapers all over us and a congressional investigation within a month."

"Within a month, sir, I will have the 342d in shape for an investigation."

"I'm warning you, colonel, you can't do it." And the wheels of the general's jeep spurted dust and gravel as he drove off.

Odd, I thought, what a change a star or two could make in a man's outlook. But I'd seen it before; a man who had been a tower of strength as a line or field officer would pale, concede, and conciliate on receipt of a questioning or complaining letter from some politician after he had been promoted to brigadier. Naturally every general wants to be selected for another star and those who make waves or cause complaints just aren't selected.

After cooling down a bit I was amazed that he hadn't relieved me of command. If our positions had been reversed I certainly would have relieved him on the spot.

I was, however, in the very comfortable position of having no fear of punishment nor hope of reward. The war was over and I was forty-six years old. I would never be promoted. But due to my service in World War I, I had the privilege of retiring at any time with three-fourths of my current pay.[9] Like a lame duck politician I could now do what I believed was right and to hell with private or public opinion. So I decided to continue my present course of soldiering until I was relieved, which would probably be very soon.

On my way to the mess I was joined by Colonel Holt.

"Just talked to the general, Holt, and he seemed to be concerned about the reduction of that sergeant in F Company yesterday. Now why should a division commander get all steamed up about a sergeant in one of my companies?"

"I'm not sure, sir, but this might have a bearing. There's a soldier in F Company, Folsom, Fosdick, or something like that, who claims that his family are great friends of the Melaskys. We've gotten word from the company commander about this man making a nuisance of himself by bragging about being a close pal of the general and the rest of the men resent it."

"Ah yes, that's probably it. He carried the news. Please see S-1 right after lunch and have this man transferred to division headquarters company today."

"Transferring him like that might have repercussions, sir, but I think F Company will be delighted."

The general paid me another visit next morning.

"Triplet, Private Farquar complained to me last night that you had transferred him from F Company to division headquarters. Is that so?"

"Yes sir. I was informed that he and his family are close friends of yours and I thought that he should be in your headquarters area. Now he won't have so far to walk when he wants to see you."

I thought "this is it." But in spite of his turning light lavender and harrumphing three times I was amazed at the mildness of his reply.

"Well, he's been in F Company for two years and all his friends are there. We shouldn't take him away from them like that. So I'd like to have you take him back."

I saw that he had gotten the message and would probably pass it on the next time Private Farquar made a social call, so I agreed at once. F Company would be unhappy about it but all his friends could take care of him if they really put their minds to it.

My second inspection was made in company with all battalion and special unit commanders. I wanted each of them to see all of the unit areas in order to pick up the good ideas that any of the others might have developed.

There was a superficial improvement in all respects. The officers all looked sharp and I ordered only one sergeant and seven corporals reduced to the ranks for unsoldierly appearance. The senior NCOs reported as we entered quarters or offices. Some reported sullenly, awkwardly, or with embarrassment, but a surprising number gave their identity and responsibility in a soldierly clear and firm manner. We were making just a little headway toward getting their heads up again.

After the inspection I had another talk with the commanders.

"Gentlemen, I compliment you on the improvement that you have made in your commands in this short time. We will continue to work along these lines.

"I shall take a daily walk through your areas and shall expect the senior officer or NCO in each area or in charge of each activity or detail to report properly and inform me regarding his project.

"I shall continue to reduce any NCO and fine or court-martial any officer I find in improper uniform. Please see that they get the word.

"I expect them and you to start working now to get the privates in shape.

"If any officer feels that he cannot or does not wish to follow out this program I want him to let me know. I shall immediately transfer or reassign him to duties that are more commensurate with his preference or inability.

"Thank you."

Two.

Morale Building

Laundries

During my first inspection I was favorably impressed by the laundry that had been developed by a mechanical genius of headquarters company. At first glance it resembled one of Rube Goldberg's dizzier creations, but it worked. The genius proudly explained.

A Japanese Zero wing tank was mounted on a scaffold and kept filled with reserve water to be heated by the sun, and solar heat in Luzon is a formidable heating agent. A pipe with a valve led into a lower tank, into which the initially sun-heated water could be fed as needed. An open vat of used crankcase oil rigged with twisted and wired cloth wicks burned under the second tank, bringing the water to near the boiling point. This hot water was then fed into a salvaged quartermaster laundry drum that was rotated by a one-cylinder field generator engine.

The rest of the operation was more conventional. One Filipino woman (Filipina) took in the bundles, kept the books, and took in the cash. Another fed the clothing, soap, and water into the drum, emptied it, and refilled for the rinse. A third dipped the uniforms in a tub of starchy water, hung the clothes on lines, and delivered the dried clothes to the three Filipinas who were ironing. It appeared to be a most effective operation, of which the genius was justly proud.

The genius introduced me to his bookkeeper-cashier, a pretty, well-shaped, muscular, and very cheerful Filipina who was obviously pregnant.

"Colonel, this is Miss Anete Alvarez."

"Delighted to see you, Miss Alvarez."

Miss Alvarez smiled winningly, dropped an Old World curtsy, and sweetly responded:

"Eeef you don' lak me bananas don't shak me tree."

After I had left the laundry and was looking over the supply tent nearby I overheard the outraged genius instructing Miss Alvarez in the finer points of military etiquette.

"Goddamnit Annie, you don't never say that to a colonel, just to lieutenants and captains."

During the rest of the inspection I noted that several of the companies had a mélange of various tubs, washboards, irons and ironing boards, and that there were two more washing machines improvised with a paddlewheel and a churn, both powered by salvaged motors of varying efficiency.

But most of the regiment was doing its own laundry using privately

14

or company-owned equipment. Many patronized freelance lavanderas who solicited work from tent to tent. These ladies took the clothes home and let their husbands, brothers, and cousins wear them if they were anywhere near the right size. Many were "lost" or "stolen." If the Filipina was honest she washed the items in any available water, usually muddy. She would then beat the seams open and the bottoms off on a plank or rock with a wooden paddle and iron the uniforms without starch. Eventually the uniform might come back at a cost of one peso (fifty cents) or preferably two packs of cigarettes. Underwear, socks, and bed linen were also laundered at exorbitant prices.

With the efforts of the regimental scrounger, the engineer, an additional trio of mechanical geniuses, and the labor officer, three more highly efficient washing machines were developed, one per battalion. The headquarters laundry thrived with the additional patronage of the other special units, and the roving lavanderas were barred from the post.

The most reliable of the erstwhile freelance laundresses were hired to operate the plants under the supervision of the geniuses. The ladies seemed pleased with the soap and clean, hot water, and delighted with the pay. After the first few obviously overstuffed women had been stopped at the gate at quitting time, searched by the hancha lavandera, stripped of excess clothing, and discharged, the remaining Filipinas turned out to be a fairly reliable crew who turned out two complete outfits and had linen per man per week for the very reasonable cost of sixty cents.

There was incidentally a considerable reduction in theft and the surgeon reported a slight decline in the rate of social diseases among the troops once the lavanderas were restricted to the vicinity of their working areas.

Through the process of survival of the honest (or uncaught), Annie, "the pride of headquarters company," rose to the position of chief hancha of lavanderas and became a personage in the regiment. She was fascinated by baseball and would spend her lunch hour watching soldiers play catch. One day she asked a couple of the men to let her play and showed remarkable aptitude. She would throw like a man and learned to handle a fielder's glove like a veteran in minutes. Her subsequent application for the position of "shirtstop" on the regimental team was reluctantly disapproved because the surgeon, Captain Morris, pronounced her pregnancy too far advanced. She was not satisfied with her position as mascot—she brooded and plotted vengeance. She attended the next Sunday game with her best mestiza costume bulging a bit at the seams. As she waddled along in front of the bleachers toward her reserved seat behind home plate some irreverent recruit yelled, "Hey, Annie, who did that?" patting his belly. "Capitan Marris," she giggled in vengeful glee, pointing at our blushing surgeon and proudly patting her protuberance. It was rumored that after this public announcement of his approaching paternity was made Captain Morris required three of his corpsmen present as witnesses before he would even enter the surgery to treat one of our ailing lavanderas.

Battalion Clubs

We were having a constant casualty rate among the men who visited Manila. The division policy was that unlimited passes should be granted to all men who were off duty so practically any man who was not on guard, a duty cook, a charge of quarters, or on other rostered duty was at liberty to use the service company truck shuttle or civilian bus line to haunt the native night spots in the big city.

Marseilles had a reputation as the toughest city for the American soldier in Europe, even worse than Naples. But I will back Manila as being the outstanding sink of iniquity in the known world during 1945 to 1947. Americans were swindled, rolled, robbed, maimed, and killed nightly, and the American high command, the U.S. commissioner, and the State Department could not or would not do anything about it.

The Filipino police approved of any robbery or swindling of an American, since the loot added to the gross national wealth of the soon to be independent Philippine nation. If the police interceded in any disagreement, confrontation, or conflict between Americans and Filipinos, the Americans were jailed and fined as much as the traffic would bear.

As a veteran centurion of Caesar's legions remarked, "Milite non fornicatum non pugnatum," so venereal disease was epidemic. The surgeons were busy with their needles, even though the modern penicillin cure for gonorrhea was simple and fast. The old adage that a dose of clap was no worse than a bad cold had become a fact.[1]

To combat this situation we had to make night life in the camp as attractive as the fleshpots of Manila, an impossible requirement. I thought briefly of copying General Pershing's well-regulated bordellos in Mexico, or the three houses full of Oriental wit and beauty on Foochow Road in Tientsin that were so successfully held under exclusive contract by the Fifteenth Infantry Regiment.[2] With sanitation and health maintained by the surgeon such an installation would be the answer to the problem.

But conditions were not what they were in Mexico or China and I wasn't General Pershing. Officially sponsored bordellos would be Pulitzer Prize copy for the buzzards of the press. Mothers, wives, and sweethearts would doubtless prefer that their young heroes return slightly burnt and cured than to learn that they were possibly patronizing the 342d female entertainers. Illogical but realistic, so I dropped the idea at once and accepted the disadvantage we would have to work under.

We had a magnificent regimental club, well furnished and nicely floored but poorly patronized. It was too near headquarters and there was no activity except beer, soft drinks, gossip, and griping.

The Red Cross club was worse—chairs, tables, and writing paper, but no beer and no girls. The beer was forbidden and the Red Cross girls were too heavily engaged in entertaining the old goats of the command and staff at division and higher headquarters. So the club was serviced by a detail of our own people and brightened only occasionally by a visit of the division Red Cross director to replenish the supply of writing paper and ink.

Battalion clubs appeared to be the answer. Captain Bodrigo, the S-4 (supply), issued the prefabricated Butler buildings and the battalion commanders were oriented on the program.

The clubs were erected, outfitted, and well decorated due to the ingenuity of the soldiers, the industry and artistry of the Japanese, and the enthusiastic drive of our scroungers. Colored nylon parachutes were spread and draped from rafters, booths and orchestra platforms were built of salvaged lumber, broad Filipino peasant hats were hung inverted under lamps for indirect lighting, and paint was spread daringly in bright colors. The bars covered with airplane aluminum were provided with refrigerators and Coca-Cola dispensers. A talented Japanese artist using house paint on canvas or beaverboard painted voluptuous Petty and Vargas girls in seductive poses and scanty attire posted against backgrounds of Fujiyama, palm groves, or tropical beaches.[3]

The special units battalion took over the erstwhile unpopular regimental club in their area and made it their revitalized own.

These clubs were then stocked with beer, Coca-Cola, Toddy (shudder), and packaged or canned snacks. And as soon as Captain Bodrigo made the necessary contacts they also stocked whiskey. Some whiskey could be obtained from the States but we had to rely heavily on the one reliable Filipino brand, "Four Feathers." At no time did we use the native bootleg variety so popular in Manila, doubtful alcohol with color and flavor added, and aged in minutes.

The clubs were operated on a nonprofit basis, initially funded by more or less voluntary contributions from all officers, who were urged to buy shares ranging from five dollars for a second lieutenant to twenty-five dollars for a lieutenant colonel. If the officer left the regiment he could cash in his share for its face value.

The only expenses after the purchase of the stock were the pay of the voluntary bartenders and the Filipino janitors so the price of a one-and-one-half-ounce shot of whiskey starting at twenty-five cents rapidly fell to fifteen cents. Occasionally when a club was embarrassed by an accumulation of funds the price dropped to a dime a drink or a happy hour ensured full attendance and the desired poverty.

Amazing. I found that the sales of beer, Toddy, and Coca-Cola far exceeded the sale of whiskey. The tastes of the drafted men of 1945 were quite different from those of the volunteers whom I had known in World War I.[4]

These battalion clubs were a mixed blessing. They were a great success in keeping the men out of trouble but caused me a good deal of official harassment. The inspector generals of the division and higher commands recommended that they be closed since they were nonregulation, hard liquor in service clubs was forbidden, and the method of funding was unusual, suspect, or downright illegal. The chaplains took the position that making whiskey available to enlisted men was immoral. There were protesting letters written to the chief of chaplains and some to Cardinal Spellman, to the WCTU, and to the B-Bag column of the *Pacifican*. But I still do not credit the rumor that my misdeeds had been reported to the pope. Cardinal Spellman must have had more important duties to concern him.[5]

I agreed with the inspectors that some of the charges of irregularity were correct—this type of club just hadn't been done before. But I firmly denied that our program was in any way illegal or immoral; I was only breaking or bending regulations and violating custom.

I pointed out that some soldiers were going to get drunk in any case. If necessary they would go to Manila or the villages where doubtful whiskey, women, and trouble of all sorts was readily available. Due to the weakness of our State Department, the commissioner, and our generals in dealing with the Philippine government, police, and criminals, all the odds were against our men. So I intended to give my men better whiskey at a fourth of the Filipino price. Then if they got paralyzed drunk their buddies could pour them, undamaged, into their downy little bunks right next door safely to sleep it off.

I believe that the generals secretly approved of the program. At least they remained tactfully silent. So we continued our immoral activities and I survived the criticism of the do-gooders and the church.

The surgeon reported a further decline in the venereal rate, which was to be expected. The recruits who loaded up for a big evening with four fast shots of low-priced, one-hundred-proof bourbon frequently never made it to the bus. Last, our casualty rate dropped abruptly. A few men continued to be beaten up, robbed, or jailed in Manila, but only one 342d soldier was murdered between the opening of the clubs and the deactivation of the regiment in October of next year, nine months later.

This unauthorized venture into the night club business actually received a favorable reaction of a sort from the brass. Brigadier General

Gjelsteen, division artillery commander, brought the commanding generals of the Ninety-third and Ninety-sixth divisions into the 342d area on an informal inspection of our building program. When I described the operation of the unit clubs, they seemed quite interested; they inspected the four enlisted men's night spots until closing time at taps and then inspected our newly opened officers club until 0100 the next morning.

The Red Cross

During the first month of my command the Red Cross tent had remained practically unused. The writing paper, Coca-Cola, and the volunteer corporal who sometimes managed the "bar" just didn't have the required attraction for the troops. I had never been favorably impressed by the Red Cross. I retained vivid memories of World War I when a soldier coming off the front could buy a nickel pack of Spearmint at the Red Cross for a dime. This was in deep contrast to the friendly issue of free doughnuts and coffee by the Salvation Army lassies. But the location of the large circus tent was potentially too valuable to neglect so I had the dusty (or muddy) floor overlaid with cement and some bright paint laid on to improve the drab interior.

On seeing the improvements the director was influenced to send two girls from the division pool to take charge and sell coffee, cocoa, soft drinks, and snacks on a part-tine basis. Further, if I would build quarters for four properly secured just outside the regimental main gate he promised to assign four girls for permanent duty in the club.

I would.

Volunteer carpenters, electricians, and painters were plentiful. With the help of the ubiquitous Japs the prefab went up and was partitioned, water and electricity were laid on in record time, paint was spread, and a bamboo fence with topping barbed wire was erected. A two-holer Chic Sales with an ornamental crescent moon and two stars hand-carved in the door was built over a pit near the rear fence.[6]

The Red Cross director inspected the layout and pronounced it good.

The Red Cross quartet was quite an asset and I noted that the tent was becoming a popular spot for the lads to spend their spare time and money. It was also a constant source of amusement and trouble.

In due course the promised young ladies moved in and a sentry was posted at the gate to ensure their privacy.

Next morning I was visited by the outraged director.

"It's disgraceful sir, the way those girls have been treated! Humiliating!"

"What is disgraceful, Mr. Simmons? How have they been humiliated?"

It was a horrifying story and I directed Colonel Holt to investigate the matter immediately.

Holt returned in an hour with an intermittent smirk coming and going on his normally serious face and reported what he had found. "Shortly after the girls pulled in yesterday, two of them went out to the latrine. Just about the time they got well settled a deep rough masculine voice from below yelled, 'Fer gosh sakes, ladies, can't you hold it a couple o' minutes? We're paintin' down here!'

"They must have gotten a little hysterical about it, I guess—anyway they tore one of the hinges off the door getting out of there.

"I took a look at the scene of the crime and found a loudspeaker rigged in the box between the holes and a telephone wire running from it through the back fence and up to the top of that little hill two hundred yards to the west. Nothing there except six beer cans, cigarette butts, and a lot of scuffed tracks.

"I've got a list of the men who worked on the building detail and can find out who worked on the Chic Sales. Then personnel can look up which of them have had telephone experience and I can ask CID to take fingerprints off the beer cans."[7]

I duly considered the fright and humiliation caused by the prank and carefully weighed them against my admiration for the ingenuity of the pranksters and the value of the story. Holt sat waiting for further orders, his face carefully neutral, but obviously suppressing his natural urge to howl with laughter. I finally pulled my thoughts away from their hither and yonning and made a decision.

"Colonel Holt, in dealing with a crime as serious as this we must be absolutely sure that we accuse the right men. We want no chance of a mistake being made by proceeding with undue haste. So you are to proceed very slowly, thoroughly, and carefully in your investigation."

"Yes sir. I'll investigate very carefully and make sure that I do not accuse an innocent man," concurred Holt enthusiastically.

The mystery of the voice from the pit is still officially under investigation. But the story caused a lot of wholesome merriment as it went the rounds of the regiment.

One morning the director dropped in again, this time not as pugnaciously as he had when reporting the latrine atrocity. In fact he was quite pleasant as he spoke of how well the girls liked their custom-built quarters and their duties in the canteen.

"But they are a little miffed that they haven't met you," he added.

"That's right, I haven't met them I'm sorry to say."

"But I think you should."

"You're quite right, Mr. Simmons, but I'm not clear on the New Army procedure for meeting Red Cross personnel assigned to my unit. Should I lean over their coffee counter and leer at them until they ask what I want? Or ask that redheaded corporal to introduce me? Or just wolf-whistle when they walk by?

"No, I prefer the stuffy Old Army custom of having newly assigned personnel report to my headquarters and I would appreciate it very much if you would bring them in and introduce them at their convenience."

He saw the point and handled the matter very correctly. The ladies made their official call before going on duty next afternoon. Nice lot of good-looking, cheery chicks. So nobody was put out, that is, until the next crisis.

One of the girls came to my office in a flaming rage and made a tearful complaint. All of the officers of the regiment had silenced her, wouldn't even look at her anymore. The only reason she could think of was that she had been unexpectedly called on duty and had been forced to break a date with one of the lieutenants and she knew that he was spreading stories about her. Yes, she was quite sure about the lieutenant. He was doing his best to ruin her reputation.

Something very odd about this. I knew that I would look at this shapely young plaintiff, no matter what her reputation was, in fact—

"I'll certainly look into the matter at once, Miss Allen. Glad you came in."

I asked the accused officer to come in and informed him of the charge the lady had made against him and asked him for his story.

"Yes sir, what she said was correct as far as it goes. I invited her for a dinner dance at the Manila Hotel last week and she accepted. Later she said that she could come for dinner but had been put on emergency duty at eight o'clock and couldn't stay for the dancing.

"So we had dinner and I brought her back and delivered her to her quarters at 7:45 so she could change into uniform.

"About nine, I stopped by the division officers club and there she was, still party-dressed, with that new major at the general's farewell party."

The director told me that the two-timing young lady was ostensibly puzzled and hurt by her abrupt transfer back to the division pool.

Theater

The theater had been a movie screen at the lower end of a slight swale on a hillside, with a movie projector at the top of the hill. The space between was adequate for the regiment seated or sprawled on the hillside, weather permitting. Cowboys, Indians, gangsters, and vampires performed nightly after sundown and the welkin was generally kept ringing with gunfire and/or screams from 2000 to 2200 nightly.

Lieutenant Archibald, the aggressive young recreation officer, was not satisfied with having the troops sitting on their blankets for the shows, especially after or during a rain. He wanted a theater, a stage, curtains, lights, and dressing rooms. And comfortable benches for the audience. So did I.

So I approved his plan in principle, with the provisos that:

1. the benches be built with a slant at a comfortable angle;
2. each row of benches be two inches higher than the row in front;
3. an officers section be placed and marked in the halfway-back center section;
4. all benches face the stage.

The lad really made his reputation on this project. He assembled a crew of ex- or would-be carpenters and electricians, located a former architect's draftsman to draw the plans, calculated the bills of lumber, nails, paint, and cloth required for Captain Bodrigo to buy, requisition, trade for, or steal, and borrowed a bulldozer with an artistic driver from the engineers.

Footings were dug and concrete poured anchoring the upright pillars or beams so that they would withstand a hurricane. The carpenters and electricians did an excellent job, and the painters spread the white and golden-yellow paint. The engineers on the earth-moving job put the icing on the cake. They scooped the swale out in a gently curving parabolic section, front to rear, compounded with a segment of a section of a normal circle from side to side, which permitted every member of the audience to have a clear, frontal view of the stage or screen.

My only contribution to the project was performed when I was requested to test the suitability of four prototype benches and decide on their respective comfort. I found that the bench that had the seat and the back sloping ten degrees to the rear was best. The Japanese went to work on a production line basis and the parabolic swale was fully equipped with benches that would be easy on my frame during two-hour performances.

In late January 1946 we had the theater opening. Lieutenant Archibald had visited the USO manager of AFWESPAC and by well-calculated statesmanship and braggadocio persuaded this overpaid Hollywood reject to pay us a visit and inspect our theater.[8] He was properly impressed by the stage, lighting effects, and the visibility afforded the audience by our parabolic seating arrangements.

"This is the best layout in the Philippines," he exclaimed. "I'd like to try out all my shows here."

"Do you mean," I asked, "that we'd get the first performance of every show coming to the Philippines?"

"That's right. But it depends—can you guarantee an audience? We've got to have two thousand before we can put on a show."

"Yes indeed! Our strength is twenty-two hundred at present." I didn't mention that this regimental total was spread wide and thin from Manila to Mindanao. "We'll have the rest of the division filling up the standing room clear to the hilltops. We guarantee you a full audience."

"Good. We'll put on 'Panama Hattie' on the twenty-second and we'd like to run over the lines that afternoon."

I could understand the USO viewpoint. They were enduring all the hardships of travel into the tropical wilds in order to entertain "our boys" for a mere three hundred to five hundred dollars a week (plus all expenses). After making these sacrifices they naturally wanted their art appreciated. I'd seen it before in Saxony when I was told by the division commander that I had to draft and truck two thousand "volunteers" fifty hot and dusty miles because some woman (Berg-something) and some clown with a violin would not appear before an audience of less than five thousand men and CCA's quota was two thousand.[9] There was no use in fighting the requirement if I wanted to get the shows. It was up to me to get an audience of two thousand loudly applauding heroes.

After the USO honcho left I had a talk with the personnel officer. With four companies on detached service and one battalion in Mindanao we had a scant eleven hundred men in our understrength remainder to fill the required audience.

So I issued invitations to the other regiments and battalions of the division, giving them quotas and one thousand reserved seats for the show, which should take care of the two thousand bench spaces. Then in order to be very sure I mobilized a reserve.

I asked Lieutenant Maynard to furnish six hundred Japanese, specifying that they were to arrive after dark but before curtain-raising time. They were to fill up any vacant seats in rear and the standing room only area. They were to clap their hands loud and long whenever the Americans did so, and would refrain from yelling their customary "Hoi! Hoi!" of applause. Since the Japanese would be wearing salvaged American fatigue uniforms they would be seen by the USO people only as an unusually enthusiastic group of "our boys" who hadn't had time to change into khaki. At the end of the performance they were to run, hubba-hubba, for their trucks parked two hundred yards to the right flank rear. Maynard promised a well-selected, organized, and rehearsed section of the audience and said that the Japanese commander would be there himself to ensure that all went well. Mentioning the Jap colonel gave me to think—I should have him seated with me, to return his hospitality. But since a number of the gilded staff of AFWESPAC as well as the press would be present, I couldn't. Imagine what the *Pacifican* and Drew Pearson could do with "American Brass Fraternizes with Jap War Criminal—Colonel Triplet." All I could do was reserve seats for Maynard and the colonel in the last row and ask Maynard to try to explain the situation.

The theater opening was an unqualified success. I had conducted a name contest and a board of NCOs had selected "memorial theater" as the winning entry. Lieutenant Archibald had caught this ball and run with it. The name was arranged in lights. White tablets, one on each side of the stage, illuminated by lights topping two carved torches each, bore the names of members of the regiment who had been killed in action.

I loathe making speeches but Archibald insisted that I must. So I mounted the stage and with my customary modesty mentioned that the theater was the biggest and best in the Pacific area. I then passed out verbal bouquets to the architect, engineers, carpenters, electricians, and the lad who had won the name contest. Then I introduced Lieutenant Archibald as the initiator and guiding genius who was now and hereby appointed a master of ceremonies. The show was on.

Colonel Holt told me later that during my talk the AFWESPAC special services officer had remarked, "Gee, you people have wonderful discipline out here. Every time an officer tries to talk in Manila you can't hear him on account of the booing and sometimes they throw things."

I must admit that I had been somewhat concerned lest some hoodlum do exactly that and then I would be forced to pull him out from under the woodwork and nail his skin to my headquarters wall as a warning to other potential hissers and booers. General Styer and General Lear might be big enough to take booing and rock throwing—I knew I couldn't.[10]

"Panama Hattie" was a routine comedy that was apparently very entertaining for the troops. Being partially deaf and mentally too slow to understand the wisecracking and fast patter of professional comedians, it meant little to me. But the Japs, understanding even less, did their duty nobly. The USO manager assured me after the show that we'd get all of the first performances. The actors were pleased to perform before such a responsive audience.

Our good friend the USO director scheduled the operetta "Rosalinda" for February 22 at our theater. Considering our depleted strength I again issued invitations to other units of the division and requisitioned several truckloads of Japs to furnish the appreciative audience required by the USO. I also sent a note to General Mueller inviting him to my quarters to meet the regimental staff and battalion commanders and have drinks before the show.

Shortly thereafter his aide called and said that General Mueller was a teetotaler himself and questioned the advisability of serving liquor in the regimental area. That put me in a dilemma—here we go again.

Since I had already invited a dozen guests in addition to my own people I could not afford to cancel the party, so the show went on. General Mueller was as always a thorough gentleman and my guests had no inkling of his disapproval. He evidently approved of the 342d in general, however, because during an inspection by General Styer our regiment was the only divisional unit looked over in detail. But he did find my forthright statements sometimes hard to take. When General Styer was looking over our bamboo "cathedral" he commented, "This is a very nice chapel—original—well designed." Not being handicapped by false modesty I remarked, "Yes, we think so. In fact we admit that we have the finest area in the Pacific theater." General Styer chuckled in appreciation but General Mueller blushed a bright pink on hearing my braggadocio.

Again during the evening performance of "The Chocolate Soldier," General Styer commented, "It's a beautiful theater—and such comfortable seats!" I clamped my tongue for once but General Mueller goaded me, "Colonel Hinton (my ancient enemy of the 341st) says his are much better."

That did it. "See that bank of seats," I asked, "the right third of the theater? Those men are all from Hinton's outfit. They like them. The 343d are on the left. The 342d is in front of us, and division troops are in rear." In my outrage I almost mentioned the Jap PWs I was entertaining.[11]

Lemery Rest Camp

A detail of one officer and a dozen men of the second (working) battalion were operating the division rest camp on the sea at Lemery, a village near Batangas, so I dropped in for an unannounced visit. The camp layout was excellent and well run. The only criticism I could make was that it was operating at about half capacity and the lack of customers was certainly not the fault of my people.

The camp was located in a beautiful setting, a coconut grove adjoining a black sand beach on a small bay. The water was clear, the surf was reasonable, and fish were abundant. Framed tents were irregularly situated among the palms, giving the occupants a feeling of freedom and privacy. In addition to the kitchen and mess built in native fashion, a small canteen was operated in a nipa bamboo house to provide necessities and minor luxuries (beer and the ubiquitous Toddy). An adjacent nipa-roofed serving area equipped with tables and chairs was pleasantly breezy and shady. Fishing gear was available for loan from the canteen but appeared to be in small demand.

A local fisherman had been hired with his barranca to take soldiers sailing or fishing as desired. His craft was a twenty-foot dugout outrigger canoe with bamboo seat and an outsized loose-footed leg-o'-mutton sail. Being an amateur sailor, I asked the "commodore" to take me out. He was delighted to have an interested customer so we waded out hip-deep to his craft, climbed aboard, and I hoisted the stone anchor while he paddled for sea room.

The barranca was a crude craft. Propulsion and steering was by the heavy wooden paddle, unsupported by oarlock or cleat of any sort. Since both hands had to be used in steering, as soon as I hoisted the sail the commodore took a turn of the sheet around a wooden peg, one turn around his ankle, and gripped it with his prehensile toes. Then correcting our wild dash to windward with his paddle, we were off.

The commodore who had probably never worn a shoe in his life was able to cope with the varying wind strength by gripping, releasing, and taking in the sheet with the toes of one or both feet as readily as though he had a pair of extra hands. He did, however, have to cast off the turn around the peg to haul the sheet in.

The sailing was magnificent. The outriggers enabled us to stand up to a breeze that with our oversized sail would have capsized a "civilized" craft, and the low freeboard gave the impression that we were flying even faster than we actually were. We were certainly making more knots than I had ever made under sail before.

After observing the commodore's technique a few minutes I asked him to let me handle the ship. He was as pleased as a preacher with a new convert and helped me get settled. It was difficult. I could handle the paddle of course but to his amusement I had to take two turns around the peg before I could even hold the sheet with my pitifully underdeveloped toes, and hauling in was impossible. Some ten minutes later my feet developed such hellish cramps from their unaccustomed exercise that he mercifully relieved me from command and I returned to my duties as chief deckhand and bailer. The tin can I used as bailer was aside from the paddle the only piece of equipment aboard. No life preservers, no spare paddles, no water jug, no nothing.

I told General Melasky about my visit and made several recommendations. Although my men were running the show they needed some support that only division could provide. I asked that the division recreation officer continually advertise the rest camp in the division and unit publications and that all commanders be influenced to grant passes to men to visit the area. I wanted two more barrancas or larger craft and the procurement of life preservers for all hands at full capacity. The general readily agreed to the proposed publicity campaign and the use of recreation funds for the expansion of the fleet.

I provided the water cans and the requirement that life preservers be worn. I did not wholly trust the commodore's assurance that the water-logged craft would float even if capsized or filled and there would certainly be no help in time for a nonswimmer who fell overboard. The water cans were a necessary precaution against the possibility of a crippled craft being blown to sea. Oh yes, spare paddles too.

Unfortunately, due to the press of other business I never saw the camp again. It died of anemia and was closed out three months later. The palm trees, beach, swimming, and sailing could not compete with the attractions of Manila, the barrios, movies, live USO shows, and the increasing comfort of the home camp.

Three.

Settling In

Quarters and Assistants

A pair of former carpenters proposed the construction of a small nipa-roofed house for my use and consulted with me on the floor plan and location. Their ideas on the interior layout were so much better than mine that I left the architecture completely to them. Then I chose the location on the crest of a knoll overlooking the movie screen. It would be very convenient to watch a movie from a comfortable chair on my front porch. The quarters were excellent—in fact they were luxurious by military standards. The indoor flush toilet with septic tank and tile drainage was the first in the division area and a showpiece for the entertainment of distinguished visitors. The location that I had selected was disastrous, particularly after the theater was completed. Just imagine being compelled to hear a Wild West, gangster, or horror movie from 8:00 to 10:00 every night.

My far-flung duties took up my days and I found it necessary to do all administrative paperwork at night in my new quarters. The light always attracted a number of insects to beat at the insect-proof screening. A few were always able to squeeze through the thatched roof or the cracks and crannies of the door sills and then flutter around the light. Together with the humid tropic heat they made constructive concentration difficult. Then one evening there was a black flash across the desk from my left front and a large spider seized a moth that had been annoying me. "Mike" had moved in to help me.

Mike was a hairy black spider with a leg span the size of a silver dollar who had appropriated the northwest corner of my in basket as his home. He was not a web-spinning type; he was an opportunist. He would wait patiently until an exhausted or off-balanced bug fluttered down from the light to desk level, then pounce. A flurry, one bite, and he would drag the victim to his lair and perform a vivisection.

We regarded each other with mutual respect and consideration. The orderly and I were careful about shuffling the papers and the Japanese houseboy was instructed never to dust the in or out baskets. On his side, Mike never interfered with my paperwork and would scrooge up in his corner when papers were being moved.

He was a superior household pet. He was self-feeding, house-broken, didn't shed hairs or chew the furniture, very quiet, would (probably) bite only in self-defense, and by taking care of the bugs was a big help in the regimental administration.

I was quite concerned when one evening I found him missing from

28

his post. The orderly firmly denied having murdered him by carelessly depositing a fresh load of papers and the Japanese swore he had never dusted him to death, so I could only assume that he had moved into more comfortable quarters in the thatched roof.

Thievery was rampant and thieves were so deft at their trade that I had no chance of coping with them myself. I needed a dog.

There were no breeding kennels in Manila and the half-starved, cowed, ribby curs so frequently seen were not what I had in mind. In desperation I finally went to the Manila dog pound.

The Filipino keeper said that he had several dogs on hand and invited me to look them over. As we entered the large communal cage there was a four-way dog fight going on, with a half-breed chow clearly emerging as the winner. He broke clear of the fight, charged the pound keeper with bared fangs and fearsome sound effects, and chased him out of the cage. Then he jumped at me, licking my hands and pleading to be taken away from there. He was apparently half chow and half Filipino or Chinese wonk, hated Filipinos and liked me. It was a case of love at first sight for both of us. I bailed him out of jail for three dollars (Philippine) and took him to my jeep, where he proudly took possession of the back seat. From this throne he cursed Filipinos and Filipino dogs all the way to camp.

He thoroughly investigated my or rather his new quarters and evidently approved of the layout. He also thought well of American rations. But when I tried to persuade him to sleep that night on a cushion or folded blanket he rebelled.

"No thank you," he indicated. "Filipino dogs don't sleep on beds—too hot—I'll sleep on your desk if you don't mind."

I did mind, two or three times, and a hell of a lot of good it did me. I was sleepier than he was, so after three fast rounds he slept on the desk. Probably a good idea—cool, out of reach of snakes, and a good lookout post with a view over the woven nipa half-wall.

He awakened early and cursed a Filipino who was walking too near his house and almost got the Japanese orderly when he tiptoed in and slammed frantically out. I introduced them through the screen, assuring Chow that Seska was our friend, and Seska that Chow wouldn't eat him. They both accepted my statements reluctantly, and Seska got warily on with his work while Chow returned to his desk criticizing my choice of friends with throaty rumbles until I took him to the mess. He fell into the routine very readily, taking his post in the jeep on inspection trips, guarding my back while walking through camps, lying under my desk during office work, and sitting behind my chair at mess. By observing his conduct I deduced that he had belonged to a Caucasian, probably had been heavily involved in the Battle of Manila, and adopted by an American soldier. He remained quiet and aloof when an American approached but would raise hackles, rumble, and prepare for action any time a Filipino or Japanese came near. He even had difficulty at first in fully accepting my driver, T-5 Gai, in spite of Gai's assuring him that he was neither Filipino nor Jap—Chow just didn't trust Orientals, not even Chinese Americans.[1]

He remained faithfully close at all times except when near shooting. He would ride with me to the firing range, then jump out and leave for home at a gallop without even excusing himself. He had evidently had a gracious plenty of gunfire in the past and wasn't having any more. I certainly couldn't count on him for help in case we were ambushed. His only use then would be to carry the indefinite news of trouble somewhere back to headquarters; he'd be out of sight before the second shot was fired.

But he did have the most desirable quality of watchfulness, jumping from the desk and padding around with throaty growls at every nocturnal approach. Finally I had to change the route of the guard post around the headquarters area to exclude my quarters. The only alternative was being awakened at eight-minute intervals on every passage of the sentry throughout the night.

As the heat of the spring weather increased, so did Chow's discomfort. His heavy coat was a misery to him, more suited to a Siberian winter than to an equatorial summer. It was indeed strange that a chow, his parent, would ever be brought to a tropical climate in the first place. I borrowed a pair of clippers from our Chinese barbershop and with a few brisk battles gave him a close haircut, too close. He initially enjoyed the result, frisking about in the sun like a puppy until he came down with a bad case of sunburn. So we fought the Battle of the Sunburn. Salve for the next week and he remained sick in quarters until his fur grew to a length of three-eighths of an inch. I finally found that an inch of fur was the optimum protection from cold, heat, and sunburn.

Strangely enough, Chow did not know how to play. He would observe with interest when I threw a stick or a ball but would obviously be puzzled as to my motive or what he was supposed to do about it. And any attempt to rough him up or roll him over had best be done while wearing heavy gloves or preferably full armor.

He had no sense of humor. Life to him was grim and earnest. His mission was to growl at all lizards rustling in the thatch, footsteps in the night, and unidentified strangers approaching at any time, and to bite Filipinos or Japanese unless restrained. But so far as Americans were concerned he gradually became a soldier's dog. As I was talking to a contingent of men who were going home on points in April, Chow wandered about among the group, looking up a few old friends. After the men had entrucked and left for the port Chow came back and took his post in the jeep, proudly wearing a Pacific Theater Medal, a Good Conduct Ribbon, and a Purple Heart on his collar.[2]

On my first day with the 342d after the evening mess several stalwarts of headquarters and headquarters company reinforced by a troop of surgeons from the medical detachment assembled at the volleyball court for the evening game. They played with no umpires and with a minimum of rules in order to obviate delay: "T'hell with the rules, let's play volleyball." Feet under or claws well over the net were quite acceptable. Teams of four to twenty men on a side were organized informally as players became available.

I was invited to take the place of the intelligence officer who was hobbling off to his quarters with a sprained ankle. It was during this catch-as-catch-can, no-holds-barred match that I first met my jeep driver, T-5 Gai.

The rotation of the players brought me opposite a medium-sized lad of obviously Chinese ancestry with a well-developed physique, astounding agility, and perfect muscular control, a Chinese acrobat type. He immediately made quite an impression on me. At that time Kung Fu and Tai Chi were almost unknown to the Western world but he must have been expert in these martial arts to be able to remove simultaneously two strips of skin from my forehead and shin while spiking a ball that was being set up for me.

After he had slammed the ball down to stun the dentist he and another son of Han, Corporal Fong, performed a brief triumphal dance while chanting the first three bars of "The Stars and Stripes Forever."

This pair, Gai and Fong, made a terrifying team at the net. Their weird Chinese war cries were disconcerting to the opposition and after a week of bloody encounters I had to insist that they wear tennis shoes instead of combat boots and cut their fingernails shorter.

I never knew much about Gai although for five months I spent more time with him than with any other member of the regiment. He was my driver, bodyguard, scout, and backup man all over southern Luzon. I particularly liked his habit of pulling his carbine out of the dashboard boot whenever he dismounted. Reassuring.

Gai's service record showed that he was born in Canton, China, in 1921. I never learned much more than that. I tried listening to his English, almost understanding—at any time it should make sense—but the sentence would end unintelligibly or inconclusively. We both spoke Chinese but mine was Mandarin Peipingese and his was Cantonese, about as similar as Italian and Swedish.[3] He understood my Missouri pronunciation perfectly but would have to resort to sign language, sketches, or written notes to get his meaning across. He wrote quaint but understandable English with penmanship much superior to my own.

Gai was definitely not the stereotyped inscrutable Oriental; he chattered and chuckled frequently about situations or people he noted while driving through the barrios but could go into a flaming rage on the slightest excuse. Since his appearance was quite similar to many of the Manila Chinese or Tagalogs, Filipinos would frequently hail him in Tagalog. Gai, his racial and national pride insulted, would angrily shout his reply in "English." But the only part of his answers that I could understand were the "godam," "summabish," "bassad," and "muthalav" with which he salted his indignant rebuttals.

His really big days were when I went to the 342d officers club, which was initially a European-type house in Manila. Then he would go to "Wong's place." The Wong family and crew spoke Cantonese and Gai would return at the appointed hour full of Chinese food and high spirits, refreshed and ready to cope for another week.

I was delighted for Gai and sorry for myself when he was repatriated to the States in the spring of 1946 with the avowed intention to return to school. I was pleased to receive a letter from him a month later. It read in part: "If I really got too much of homesick I'm willing to reenlist the old outfit. The 342d really have a very good record of everything. I am so proud all of the officers and men."

I thought as highly of that paragraph as I would of a citation or the Legion of Merit. If a discharged soldier thought along those lines it was proof that what I'd been doing for the last seven months was worthwhile.

But now let's get back to the grim present.

Three weeks after my arrival I received thirty-nine new second lieutenants, twenty-nine fresh from OCS and ten of the West Point class of 1945 (all of the infantry of that class assigned to the Philippines).[4] Fearing the effect that our New Army might have on these young men, I gave them a talk that I hoped would brace them to cope with the current situation.

"Gentlemen, welcome to the 342d Infantry Regiment.

"From your point of view you have joined us at an unfortunate time. The excitement and glamor of the war is over and you are facing the more difficult period of demobilization. The army is returning to civilian life. This affects our attitude and dictates our missions.

"Very little military training will be done. What is required we will do well.

"Our principal objective is to return our men to civilian life as decent, orderly, and better-educated citizens, not as a mob of disgruntled hoodlums.

"The essential security, control of guerrilla units, and surrender points for Japanese troops are the military missions that we will carry out in our area. These duties have first priority.

"The educational program will have priority to the fullest extent permitted by those military requirements.

"Third priority is the entertainment of the men with athletics, competitive shooting and combat firing, movies, and USO or soldier shows.

"Last we will work toward building up our quarters and areas to improve our living conditions.

"The division commander has informed me that this regiment has the best spirit in the division. We will hold that position. It will require leadership, particularly on your part, since you will be most closely in contact with the troops. This leadership will be your most difficult task.

"With a few exceptions you have had no experience in command. That experience with troops, with line troops, is what I intend to give you. Therefore you will initially be assigned to rifle and heavy weapons companies.

"Finally I advise you to hold to the character, values, and ideals that your previous experience has developed in you. Don't permit yourself or your command to get sloppy. You are dealing with a nonprofessional army (just couldn't say civilian army) in which you cannot hope to attain the perfection to which your previous training has accustomed you.

"You will be faced by two dangers—intolerance and acceptance. Steer a firm, straight course between them.

"Again welcome to the regiment. We're glad to have you with us."

In assigning these officers to the units I used an unusual method to avoid having personnel impersonally hammer square pegs into round holes. I called a meeting of battalion commanders and had them cut a deck of cards for priority of choice.

The personnel officer then called in one of the new lieutenants, seated him before the group, and read his service record. The lad was then asked and encouraged to talk freely about his civilian and military experience, athletic record, education, ambitions, and preferences. He was then sent from the room and the commanders were asked, in the order established by the cards, if they wanted him assigned to one of their companies. Personnel made a note of the desired assignment and the process was repeated starting with number two on the priority list as having first choice of the next officer.

As a result the lieutenants were selected by commanders who liked their past records, future potentialities, bearing, and conduct under fire during the interview.

A probable improvement—I should have had the company commanders make the selections.

The West Pointers were a disappointment. Six of the ten were dispirited, disliked or were hostile to the military service, unreliable, and generally unsatisfactory. Later when the Twelfth Division of the new Philippine Scouts was being formed I was called on to furnish junior officers for transfer to the Scouts. Six times I amazed division personnel by saying, "Yes, I have a Lieutenant Ducrot, West Point 1945, that you can send to the Scouts."

Why, I wondered, were 60 percent of the West Pointers completely useless when the OCS lads were all sharp and dedicated? Finally it hit me. The class of 1945 received their appointments in 1941 when smart parents were looking for safe shelter for their darling boys—the draft was calling and war was looming. And what could be safer than four years at West Point?

I've been told that the class of 1946 was worse and that there were three resignations of the class of 1947 on V-J Day.

Thanks to the machinations of my good friend and chief of staff, Colonel Yale, I had a considerable overstrength in junior officers. In order to keep all hands happily busy I appointed several of the senior lieutenants, the old-timers, to special regimental staff positions that are not authorized on the table of organization. One ingenious lad who had studied civil engineering was appointed as regimental engineer to oversee construction projects. The labor officer was given two assistants, one to hire and distribute Filipino labor, the other to take charge of the Japanese requirements. The A&R officer was given an athletic officer and a recreation officer to specialize in their fields. The I&E officer was assigned an ex-reporter to take charge of information and a former high school teacher to inject new life into the education program. The guerrilla affairs had three assistants for personnel, supply, and finance. The busiest regimental staff areas were reinforced, such as personnel (to make a continuing study of eligibility for repatriation), intelligence (surrender points and propaganda), and supply (a persuasive young man with flexible morals was appointed as chief scrounger with two larcenous assistants).

Expedition to Mindanao

Colonel Holt and Colonel Ward returned from a week of reconnaissance on Mindanao and reported very favorably on the situation there.

The proposed campsite on the Del Monte plantation looked promising and was well situated with respect to the supply dumps that the third battalion was to secure.

The rumored Japanese holdouts (if any) were quiet. Our people were unable to find anyone with firsthand knowledge of Japanese on the island.

The Moros were angrily concerned about the prospects of a Christian

Filipino government but there was apparently no thought of open revolution. There was a good deal of talk about independence and Mindanao setting up as a separate nation. But it was believed by the local Americans that the Moros would remain generally quiet and simply maintain their ancient custom of killing any Christian Filipino who dared set foot on their Moslem island.

More guerrillas showed far less aggressiveness, banditry, and inclination to power politics than those on Luzon.

At last I received a firm date, January 8, for shipping the third battalion to Mindanao, so the program of packing and transfers of personnel went into high gear.

Immediately after issuing the warning order I received a petition signed by several NCOs of the battalion offering to resign and be reduced to privates, providing they could be transferred to other battalions and stay in the home camp. The I&E officer reported a sudden influx of applications for educational courses from men who had heretofore betrayed no interest in higher learning. I received three anonymous letters protesting the use of combat veterans for further perilous duty against Moro rebels and bandits and recommending that all such veterans be transferred from the third to the first battalion.

I turned all of these letters and petitions over to Colonel Ward for his information and action and scheduled a meeting with the NCOs of his battalion.

I promised them that I would accept the resignation of any NCO and would then ship him to serve in Mindanao as a private until he was recalled for repatriation on points—if he was still alive.

I informed them that applications for I&E courses had been closed out as of December 1, 1945.

Last, I assured them that combat veterans were exactly the type of men we needed and would use in dealing with combat situations in Mindanao.

My popularity was probably due for another sharp drop. There would be an increase in my anonymous mail, letters in the 341st scandal sheet and the *Pacifican,* and red-bordered inquiries from congressmen about my brutal treatment of their constituents.

But that fire never got started. Early on January 8, I inspected the mess and troop quarters on this production-line Landing Craft Infantry at the Manila dock, the troops started aboard at 0900, and the lines were cast off as scheduled at 1200.

I wanted to see how the third battalion was doing on Mindanao. I also wanted to take a leave. I noted that I was becoming increasingly short-tempered, particularly with the Filipino guerrillas and politicians who must be handled with Chinese suavity for the best results.

I heard rumors about a patrol through the islands by the Philippine Navy. Aha! I would combine business with pleasure. Felt a bit guilty about it because the voyage to Mindanao would take at least ten days, and I should take a plane, but t'hell with it, I like ships.

I sailed on a Filipino frigate from Manila on January 23, 1946. Her number was 223 and she was known to the crew as the *Carmelita*. The ship was small, fifteen hundred tons, and presumably fast since it was designed for convoy escort. For reasons of economy in fuel and rations (to be explained later) she seldom attained a speed of more than five knots during the voyage.

Her design was quite conventional, closely resembling one of the smallest Italian coastal freighters. From fore to aft was the forecastle, forward well deck, the bridge, after well deck, and the poop—a short, dumpy, graceless silhouette. The bridge complex contained the officers' quarters, wardroom, galley, and crew's mess, all in dollhouse sizes. The crew's quarters were in the forecastle and the poop.

The armament was modest, a pedestal-mounted 75-mm. gun on the forecastle, another on the poop, and a twin 20-mm. antiaircraft gun on each wing of the bridge. A small radar dish was mounted above the bridge but I never saw it in use. The armor on the bridge might stop a 20-mm. but I estimated that any other part of the ship could be riddled with .30 armor-piercing bullets.

The captain was a Tagalog with a strong dilution of Spanish and Chinese genes, a very courteous man with a spare frame and lean features. He explained the mission, tracing the proposed voyage on the small-scale map for my benefit.

"We sail for one month through the islands, Luzon here, through here, to Mindanao, around Mindanao, back through here, around Luzon, and back to Manila. Maybe three weeks, maybe five weeks. How long depends on trouble."

"What kind of trouble?" I asked—the Filipinos use the word trouble for anything from a thorn in the foot to World War II.

"Perhaps Japanese, bandits, Moros, pirates, smuggling ships, any kind of trouble. We look at other ships. We stop everywhere and ask."

So I spent an entertaining few days of fantasy anticipating a brisk clash with Malay or Sulu pirates in the southern seas and wishing that I'd brought my favorite M-3 instead of a pistol, but unfortunately I never would have a more peaceful voyage.

It was still a remarkable experience. I occupied a small cabin with an American lieutenant of the quartermaster corps who was being stationed on Mindanao. There were five settings in the common mess. The lieutenant and I sat in lonely splendor for the first setting. We were followed by a squad of Philippine Army soldiers who were apparently the marines. Third table was occupied by the ship's officers; the twenty-eight-man crew were served next in the fourth and fifth shifts.

The cook-steward, the hardest-working man on the ship, was a good-humored little fellow who appeared to be on duty around the clock, even though he had two very capable mates who seemed to alternate on duty. His cuisine was simple; he deep-fried everything except rice, coffee, and fruit juice, and I know he didn't change the oil in his deep-fry boiler, at least not during the first ten days. On my last day on the ship I was in his closet-sized galley admiring a newly caught fish. Glancing into his deep-fry pot I noted a couple of fragments of thoroughly deep-fried corned beef that the QM lieutenant had furnished as the pièce de résistance for our first dinner at sea. We'd had nothing but freshly caught fish ever since.

My first night was very active and unrestful. I had a deep suspicion that I was being attacked by bedbugs or worse things crawling and nipping like the French cooties of WWI. Nothing was visible by flashlight or the dim cabin light so I put it down to a belated case of psychosomatic Thirty-first Infantry guerrilla hives. Just itched and scratched until six bells sounded at dawn. But they weren't hives, they were bites, and I mentioned them to my cabin mate who was climbing groggily out of his bunk scratching vigorously.

"Hawh!" he sneered. "You want to see some bites, just get a load of these," and he bared his well-nourished frame. The poor fellow was a mass of red and itching welts over his whole body. He started looking for the enemy.

"Goddalmighty! Ants!"

On the underside of his mattress there was a moldy torn place in the cloth. In it was a seething, undulating, crawling, wimbling nest of microscopic red ants. My trouble had not been a nest of ants. I had merely been nipped by a few scouts and foragers who had gotten lost in the darkness.

We called for help. The horrified steward gingerly doubled the mattress, took it to the railing, and consigned it to the deep. He returned shortly with another, a well-worn but fairly clean one, plus a can of DDT. As he dusted the complete interior and all contents of the cabin with the insecticide he was still muttering his bafflement.

"Jesus Christ! How come? VIP cabin everything new. Bran' new—right from warehouse. Doan' know."

I did. Everything in storage deteriorated rapidly in the humid, molding, insect-infested, rusting, rotting Manila climate. My unfortunate companion had gotten a bran' new mattress that had been stored at the bottom of the stack and been homesteaded by a colony of little red pests who were looking for a cozy nest.

It was difficult for me to keep a clear idea of where we were or where we were going. The crew tried valiantly to keep me abreast of the situation but my understanding of their limited English was even more limited. Only when the captain showed me the course on the chart and wrote the prospective dates and times did I understand our progress in looking for trouble.

At our first stop at a small town on Mindoro, I told the captain that I would like to go ashore with the shore party and take a walk through the town. I asked him when I would have to be back.

"You stay een thee town as long as you prefer," he said, paternally patting my arm. "We nevair sail until you come here." I had never before been extended such a privilege on any ship, and this was a warship too.

We stopped frequently, not only at our scheduled ports of call but at many other places, for a wide variety of reasons. One overnight stop was so that the second officer could visit his family. Another time we anchored off a small village where the price of chickens was very low and the crew bought all that were available. They were brought by boat to the ship in crates, alive and squawking, and stowed on the after well deck. The chickens were not to be added to the ship's stores; they were investments made by individual crew members who would sell them for a considerable profit in Manila. In the meantime they provided an ever-present source of entertainment.

Whenever the crew became bored, and always during the dog-watch, a pair of owners would each select the most promising cock from his crate and after "introducing" the birds to the proper degree of mutual rage would release them to do battle, springing, spurring, and fluttering about the deck. Then after one featured warrior fled the field (they were apparently never really hurt) pesos would change hands, the birds would be run down by the audience and returned to their crates, and another pair of gladiators would be selected for the next chukker. It was amazing that none ever was lost overboard in spite of the wide open, wire-rope railing.

Again we anchored off a small town where no patrol went ashore and no business was transacted. Instead we had ladies day and a dozen or more of the town beauties were boated aboard. It turned out to be a rousing party that carried on until 0200, with whoops and shrieks and the padding of barefooted flight and pursuit over the decks and through the corridors. Then after a peaceful interlude I was brought wide awake and upright by a blood-curdling female scream and hearty masculine laughter twenty-two inches from my right ear through the 3/32-inch partition between my bunk and that of the chief engineer. Subsequent sounds indicated that the chief was making good progress so I staggered out to the mess for a cup of cold vintage coffee—for once the chef was not on duty.

When it became clear that no breakfast was to be expected I took the first shore-bound boat and managed for some hot and very powerful coffee at a shack that was apparently a snack shop of a sort. I declined anything further, recalling Sergeant Bueler's veteran advice in Panama, "Remember, lieutenant, any time these natives ask you to eat with 'em don't eat nothing but bananas, coconuts, and hard-boiled eggs—nothing that they can get their fingers in."

I spent the morning admiring the boats and canoes along the beach. They were all dugout types of various sizes, some having the freeboard built up by planks laced to the gunwales with thongs of vegetable fiber.

All had outriggers on one or both sides. According to construction, size, and sail plan, these craft were called bancas, barrancas, bintas, bolits, and praos. After I had learned some of the names and was trying to use them, the friendly owner of a banca was often amused by my abysmal ignorance when I admired the sea-going lines of his binta (bolit, barranca, etc.) and would delightedly set me aright.

These islanders were wonderful seamen—or boatmen. They shoved off the beach, jumped in, and paddled or sailed away in their canoes as casually as an American boy handles his bicycle. Even the small children were paddling dugouts. Of course they were perfectly safe— nothing short of a typhoon would capsize the outrigger-stabilized canoes and if they did capsize they would still float. Moreover, these sea-oriented children could all swim like ducks.

I returned to the ship about 1400, hoping that the cook was back at his post. He wasn't. My exhausted cabin mate told me that ladies day had continued until 1100 when the last of our luscious visitors were ferried ashore. The frigate was what the navy calls a happy ship, a very happy ship.

That evening as the steward served a banquet of rice, deep-fried fish, deep-fried asparagus, and deep-fried green peas, he extended an invitation from the captain to go to town with the crew. The ladies had invited us for a return engagement. Foreseeing that the night in town would doubtless resemble the preceding twenty hours on the ship, I chickened out. I declined with thanks on the grounds that I was too weary to do the party justice, and turned in to make up six hours of sleep.

On one of my shore-going expeditions I found a cuttlefish bone on the beach that measured fourteen inches in length, an exceptional size, and I brought my trophy aboard. The next morning the first officer netted a very large squid that he believed had a larger bone. It looked like a very inedible fish. The sac, of a light lead-blue color, was sixteen inches long. It dwindled in girth to the four-inch head, in which two large, cold, pale blue eyes stared malevolently. Ten-inch tentacles writhed around what the mate called the bite, the parrotlike beak that tears the fish caught and held by the tentacles. After the cook had deep-fried the squid I was presented with the bone, which was measured with great interest on the part of all present. Alas, it came out to a mere 13 5/8 inches.

But the crew had gotten the fixed idea that I was in the squid-bone-collecting business and for the rest of the voyage I was continually being presented with more cuttlefish bones than I was really interested in owning. Especially the fresh relics, which smelled like dead coral. They went out the porthole immediately after the proud donor had received my thanks and left.

When we docked in Legaspi the local volcano that towers its symmetrical cone eight thousand feet above the town was smoking briskly. With the cape of grayish white ash around the crest it looked better than a Japanese painting of Fujiyama. But I have an unreasoning fear of volcanoes.

"That volcano looks like it's going to blast loose, captain. When do you think it's going to blow?" I inquired.

He gave me a reassuring grin. "That mountain always smoke like that. She nevair blow up except every ten years. Now it is only nine years."

Throughout the voyage the sea was a glassy calm and the economical five to six knot speed was ideal for trolling. I learned that the trolling was the principal reason for this leisurely speed—so we wouldn't outrun even a tired fish. And the fishing was great. Not that I did any fishing; I spent most of my time in a deck chair abaft the 75-mm. gun mount on the poop, reading pocket books on crime and the detection thereof. The crew did the fishing.

It always started with the ship's boy, Corto (Shorty). He kept three hand lines trolling, one from each quarter railing and one dead astern. He had devised an ingenious audio-video alarm system to warn him of a strike. The end of each heavy line was firmly tied at the top of a stanchion of the railing, and paid out with the baited hook, over the rail. Six feet of line was then hauled in and tied to the railing with a light string that would break when a fish took the bait. At the bottom of the six-foot loop Corto tied a rag and a tin can.

He caught a lot of fish with this rig, enough to feed the crew, but never pulled a fish in. In the Philippine Navy rank had its privileges and the handling of every fish went right up the pecking order.

When a bonito struck, the light string broke, the tin can clanked over the railing, and Corto and I sprang full awake. There was the rag, fluttering on the taut starboard railing line, and a sizable fish was thrashing on the end of the line a hundred yards astern. Corto yelled, leaped to the line, and started hauling on it with all of his fourteen-year-old strength. The nearest seaman yelled, pushed Corto into the scuppers, grabbed the line, and hauled at the fish. The bosun burst on the scene yelling, pushed the seaman aside, and pulled in a few yards of line. The officer on the bridge yelled, pushed the engine room telegraph to "STOP," dashed down the ladder and around the chicken crates to the poop, and took the line. The captain, awakened when the engines stopped their soothing rumbling, galloped out of his cabin in his skivvies, yelling, and pushed everybody out of the action. He then landed the fish while the crew cheered, yelled, and advised. Then all hands, including a couple of oilers from the black gang who were attracted from the engine room, gathered about the expiring bonito, poking it to make it twitch, and admiring its size, vitality, color, and probable edibility.

After the fish stopped flapping and responding to pokes the steward bore it off to the galley, the captain returned to his nap, the officer of the watch rang "Slow Ahead," the ship resumed her course, and the crew returned reluctantly to their duties. This procedure never varied. The captain hauled in every fish that was caught during our eight days at sea and there were enough fish caught to provide the pièce de résistance, deep-fried, for every meal consumed by the ship's company. That way the captain could sell the rations provided on the Manila black market.

On landing in Mindanao, I was met by Colonel Ward, who had been notified of our arrival by a radio message from the *Carmelita*. I found the battalion comfortably quartered on the Del Monte plantation and the men appeared to be in good physical and mental health. Thievery was not a way of life with the Moros as it was with the more highly civilized Tagalogs so they were having no difficulty in guarding the warehouses and dumps for which they were responsible. No concrete reports on wild Japanese had been received and the Moros were definitely not going to have any part of a revolution as long as the Americans were in control and probably not even after we had gone.

My inspection was limited to one day. That evening I received a radio from division, "return soonest by air." Soonest was a DC-3 that was returning to Manila next morning, so I was aboard, holding my breath for a hairy, down-slope, short-run takeoff over a precipitous ravine some hundred feet wide and deep. The pilot gave the passengers an unusual briefing.

"Everybody stand as far forward as you can so I can get her tail off the ground or we won't make it."

The dozen passengers rose and crowded up against the crew compartment door and t'hell with all this seat belt nonsense. The pilot put his brakes full on, revved the engines up to a full-powered scream, released his brakes, and we were immediately at the point of no return or rather no abort. As we lifted over the ravine I looked into the depths and sure enough there were three tangled masses of crumpled aluminum wreckage at the bottom of the brush-covered slope—planes that hadn't made it. That field had evidently been designed for the prompt elimination of unreliable planes and indecisive pilots.

Four

Thievery

Thieves

Filipinos are in the opinion of all who have served in the islands the most persistent, ingenious, dexterous, and expert thieves in the world.

Several Filipinos have attempted to excuse their people, stating something like, "Oh yes, there are too many thieves. It is because of the war. So many people could live only by stealing from the Japanese."

That is so much nonsense. Filipinos were experienced thieves long before Magellan discovered the archipelago in 1521. According to the ladies of the Old Army, even the most trustworthy household personnel would practice what they called little stealing, presumably as opposed to outright big stealing, burglary, or robbery.

To practice little stealing the number one boy (the butler) yearns for some desirable article such as a silver cigarette box, which is normally kept on a side table by the sofa. One day it is moved to another table and is replaced by the sandalwood box. Two days later the silver box is transferred to the sideboard in the dining room. If its absence from the living room is not noticed, in due time it moves to the pantry, where it can be immediately produced if it is missed. If the lady does not ask its whereabouts in the next few days the box goes out the back door and no one can remember having seen it for the last month.

Little stealing takes time but it is time profitably spent. And what if the mistress does notice and rescue one item that is slightly misplaced? There are six more pieces being moved that she hasn't noticed. But most Filipino larceny is not so subtle.

I had first become acquainted with Filipinos in 1936 when the army transport *U.S. Grant* tied up at the dock in Manila.[1] The ship's stewards warned all passengers that portholes must be closed at night. Why? To foil the thieves operating from the small boats and dockside. These ingenious individuals used light bamboo fishing poles, around the tips of which they bound three or four fish hooks. They would then insert the hook end of the pole into any open port, sweep it around the cabin, and drag out any article that the barbs had caught provided it was small enough to be pulled through a thirteen-inch porthole. They had no luck with mattresses, suitcases, and grown people, of course, but clothing, ladies' purses, bedding, towels, and small babies went through easily.

My present troubles with thieves ranged from the extremely petty to some quite serious losses. After I had replaced my Filipino orderly with a Jap PW, the boxes of my cigarettes and cigars used for the entertainment of guerrilla chiefs went down at a far more reasonable rate.

A Filipino carpenter who was required to open his toolbox when leaving the regimental area had fifty-eight stolen articles in his box and pockets. The guard searched the next twelve and found stolen articles on eight of them.

But the serious loss was in trucks and jeeps, stolen or hijacked. Truck drivers were required to chain and padlock their steering wheels when they left their vehicles. That presented no obstacle to a Filipino equipped with a bolt cutter stolen from engineer stores. The drivers would remove the distributor rotors additionally to disable the trucks. Every truck thief of any standing carried rotors for a jeep, as well as for 1.5-, 2.2-, and 5-ton trucks, and could get a locked and rotorless vehicle under way in ninety seconds or less.

Drivers were finally required to stay with their vehicles at all times. Then the technique changed. Two or more Filipinos appearing on each side of the cab, apparently chatting with the driver, would produce pistols, order the driver out, and drive away with his truck and his carbine. The only safeguard was two or more armed men per truck.

As they grew bolder, pistols were used with increasing frequency. I lost eighty vehicles in three months and during one red-letter week I had ten stolen. None were ever recovered. The endless supply of trucks in the quartermaster stock as replacements was all that kept us in business.

I went to see the AFWESPAC provost marshal about the problem, intending to insist that he get his young men on the ball and recover some of my trucks. I had known him well as the transportation officer of a tank unit in 1931. In fifteen years he had aged thirty—grayed, haggard, distraught, and morbidly cynical. He was in a foul humor. Being provost marshal of AFWESPAC was evidently not pleasant.

He listened impatiently to my sad story, sighed, and broke into a monologue, delivered with deep feeling.

"Hmmm, so you've lost ninety-three trucks? And you want me to help you get them back? Do you know how many army vehicles have been sold in Manila as army surplus? No? Well, the figure is exactly 638. And have you any idea of how many repainted army vehicles are now registered and licensed as jeepneys, buses, and trucks in Manila? That figure was 8,164 as of last Saturday. If I had any backing I could recover 7,500 of our vehicles. If my men arrested every Filipino they saw driving an army-type vehicle they'd be right more than eleven times out of twelve. I could apologize to the twelfth and give him a pack of cigarettes and a refill of gasoline and send him happily on his way.

"But if I made a serious move to get back one lousy jeep I'd probably be cashiered. If a Filipino steals my own pistol or jeep outside of a U.S. Army post boundary, it's his and I'm forbidden to make a move to get it back.

"If your driver leaves his seat and a Filipino can slide into it he must be let strictly alone. If your driver attempts to pull him out he'll be arrested by the Manila police for assaulting a Philippine citizen and while he's being arrested the other fellow will drive away. Two days later there'll be another pink or purple jeepney in business.

"There was a navy captain two weeks ago caught a Filipino lifting his wallet. Broke the fellow's arm. Called the police. He's still in jail charged with mayhem and will probably do time unless that gutless commissioner does something about it—but that sonofabitch McNutt's never done anything yet so no charge against the pickpocket of course, he's the complainant.[2]

"There's only one answer. Any time one of your boys catches a thief in the act, kill him. But make sure he's dead. Then you can claim that he was a Huk or a bandit and you get away with it. But if he lives, a Filipino lawyer will bring the case before a Filipino court and your man won't stand a chance. He'll probably spend two years in Bilibid penitentiary making bamboo furniture unless you can court-martial him first. Don't ask me why—I just work here."

No help there. I left, even more baffled than before. Was it General Styer, U.S. Commissioner McNutt, the State Department, or President Truman who were knuckling under to the Filipinos in such an abject fashion? Like my provost marshal friend I didn't know, I just worked here.

I did have some success in prosecuting one case against one of my own men. The CID who were amazingly persistent, efficient, and loyal in their uphill fight against heavy odds produced evidence showing that Corporal Stoegl of the service company of the 342d had driven his truck for a Filipino gang that was robbing warehouses. He had made two trips a night for two nights and for this service he had received $1,500 as his share. That figures out to $375 per load, evidently a profitable business. Crime did pay in Manila.

With the approach of Filipino elections, banditry and ambush became a serious problem for the Americans, and assassinations considerably reduced the number of aspiring politicians. The road between Manila and Clark Field was closed daily from 1600 to daylight, since anyone making that trip in darkness, even though well escorted, was sure to be attacked. Bandits in that area, Bulucan country, were well armed and had a deadly technique for acquiring trucks, weapons, and other loot.

Two machine guns were usually sited to fire across the road, adjusted at the correct elevation to barely clear the hood of the vehicle that was approaching. They tried to avoid damaging the rolling stock. A jeep would be allowed to pass the first gun, then the second gun would start firing in time to catch the passengers in the stream of bullets. Any attempt to halt, turn around, or back up would be stopped by the second gun. Survivors who tried to escape on foot to the flanks were mopped up by machine-gun and rifle fire.

But there were survivors. This seems more reasonable when you consider that at the machine-gun rate of 600 rounds per minute at a muzzle velocity of 2,700 feet per second the bullets are traveling one-tenth of a second and 270 feet apart—almost a city block. A car making 30 miles an hour moves 4.4 feet in one-tenth of a second and will not be hit more than twice or three times by a steady stream of bullets. Putting it another way, an athlete (or a badly scared sedentary type) running at the common sprint rate of 100 yards in 10 seconds has an even chance of getting through the stream without being hit. He makes a yard in one-tenth of a second and is not more than 10 to 12 inches thick. Of course he'd have to pick his time just right, and I wouldn't recommend the practice as a habit, but there were survivors, until the thugs started dropping logs on the road.

Any vehicle was fair game—American, Philippine Army, military police command, constabulary, or civilian jeepney (stolen jeep converted to taxi). At first the bandits would kill a truckload to get the truck and their weapons. Later when Manila was glutted with stolen American vehicles they committed wholesale murder for the spare parts they needed for repairs.

In our area south and east of Manila the problem was initially not so serious. We did not have the wholesale organized murder by the Hukbalahaps to contend with.[3] The bandits in our area were merely freelance highwaymen. They were not so well organized, not so persistent, and frequently proved to be shockingly poor marksmen. Colonel Evans, making an inspection trip to visit his widely deployed battalion, was fired on in daylight by a probable half dozen riflemen. With two staff officers and his driver he dismounted and put down a barrage of carbine and pistol fire through the greenery that routed the thugs with no apparent casualties on either side. And six rifles against three pistols and a carbine are long odds.

Once more I got in the bad graces of the senior Red Cross girl when she asked permission to take a truckload of girls and soldiers on a picnic to Pagsanjan Falls on the south side of Laguna de Bay.

"Certainly," I agreed. "The men will have to be armed, and I'll send an escort to trail you. I'll put a combat-experienced sergeant in charge of the convoy. Can you furnish refreshments for an additional ten men?"

"But this will be just a Red Cross picnic, colonel, and I will be in charge. There's no need for the boys to bring their tools—I want them to forget all this military stuff for the day."

"Well, those are the conditions, take them or leave them. You might get held up. Armed, there's less chance of it, and with two well-armed and spaced truckloads there's no probability of trouble."

She had to agree to my terms to get the transportation, but stomped out in a redheaded flaming fury about my dictatorial attitude. I just couldn't seem to get along with that girl.

Two days later I sent her a copy of the *Pacifican* with two items broadly marked with red crayon. On the day following her picnic there had been two ambushes on the road she had taken. One American officer and his driver had been killed and a truckload of Philippine Scouts had been massacred. She still didn't like me.

At Camp Blackjack a 342d sentry heard suspicious sounds near a storehouse on his post and when he approached a man jumped up and ran. The thief would not halt so the sentry ran after him. He was led past another member of the gang who let the sentry go past and then shot him between the shoulder blades. The sentry died shortly after telling his story.

In order to prevent any more such stupid losses I put out a standing guard order: "Never chase a suspicious person at night. Halt and question him as prescribed for interior guard duty. If he does not halt or if he runs, shoot him and call the guard. Do not approach the body until you are reinforced."

It is easy to put out orders, it is often difficult to get them obeyed. Three weeks later one of my men spotted a prowler and tried to run him down because, as he told me, "I didn't want to hurt anybody." Exactly the same thing happened except that this man lived to regret his humane impulse every time he tried to shove his withered arm into a coat or shirtsleeve.

Some bad mistakes were made. An example—while hunting for Huk-balahaps (Bulucan communists), a squad of the Philippine military police command ambushed and wiped out a team of the Philippine CID who, disguised as Huks, were also looking for Huks.

Early one morning the Eighty-sixth Division MPs delivered a very naked, sunburned, mosquito-bitten, and exhausted young man, a service company jeep driver, to the 342d officer of the day, unnecessarily pointing out that he was out of uniform. Captain Stief later reported to me with the story. On the morning of the day before, the boy had picked up his favorite Filipina and taken her for a ride, naturally into the boondocks. They were held up by a party of five bandits who tied them up. The thugs then had a lively debate that went on for three hours. The girl kept up a running translation for the entertainment of her apprehensive boyfriend. The topic of discussion was, "Shall we kill him, or both, or let him, her, or both of them go?" At last the matter came to a vote. The three-to-two majority verdict was, "Let them both go." The robbers left with everything the soldier owned except his boots. Fortunately for him, his size twelves couldn't possibly be cut down to Filipino size.

Captain Brown was driving his jeep alone—very unthinking of him. He was ambushed by a pair of highwaymen, one using a submachine gun very inexpertly. A lively match between gunner and pistoleer ensued. No one was apparently hurt but the jeep had to be towed in to the park and died of its multiple wounds.

The Black Market

We initially had a great deal of trouble with Filipino peddlers who combined sharp business deals with black marketing and theft. A normal guard system could not possibly keep them out, since the entire perimeter of the camp was open, so additional guard patrols as well as the vigilance of NCOs was required to control them. Even that was difficult since a Filipino peddler with a bag or wooden box looked exactly like a Filipino carpenter with a bag or box of tools. Also, in most cases the hired carpenter was also a peddler or thief. Last, while enthusiastic about preventing thefts, the troops were not at all educated about apprehending peddler/black marketers.

One morning I saw two Filipinos enter the second tent from my office, the quarters of the headquarters commandant. Believing that the captain was out, I moved at a pussyfooting canter to arrest a couple of thieves and was taken aback to find the officer not only in his tent but handing over seven cartons of cigarettes for a pair of carved buffalo-horn figures.

This was a distressing situation. The headquarters commandant had the additional duty of drawing and distributing cigarettes and other rationed items to the troops on an equitable basis. To divert them to his own use was not only black marketing; stealing was conduct unbecoming an officer.

I confiscated the cigarettes and horn figures, placed the captain in arrest in quarters, and directed the officer of the day to turn the Filipinos over to the provost marshal. I gave Colonel Holt the situation in detail and told him to draw up charges against the officer.

"I would advise against it, colonel. Black marketing has always been condoned or ignored in this regiment. In fact your predecessor used to brag openly about the good bargains he was able to make for cigarettes or candy. So I'm afraid that court-martialing an officer for black marketing would have an adverse effect on your popularity."

Well—popularity—that was a new concept for a regimental commander. But I seriously doubted if I could win a popularity contest anyway so I adhered to my resolve to eliminate chiseling officers in the 342d.

"My popularity is not a matter of importance, Holt. The charges will be drawn up and since I am the accuser and principal witness it's your job to do it. 'Conduct unbecoming' of course, with specifications on black marketing and on diversion of rationed items to his private use."

The charges were drawn up, signed, and forwarded for trial. But I found that Colonel Holt was in closer touch with the spirit of the AFWESPAC New Army than I was. The charges were disapproved and returned with an endorsement stating, "It is not the policy of this command at this time."

So all I could do about it was to enter a derogatory statement in the captain's efficiency report and have him transferred to another regiment that didn't mind having chiseling or thieving officers.

The presidente of Marakina sent me a note requesting me to appear as a witness at the trial of the two Filipinos who had been delivered to his chief of police by our military police and charged with black marketing.

Odd court, no jury, just a benevolent-appearing, slender, white-haired mestizo judge. Lawyers for the prosecution and defense, defendants, and court clerk were all there, just as in an American court. The small courtroom was crowded.

The proceedings seemed to follow much the same sequence as those of an American court but were conducted in Tagalog, so I am sure about only two phases of the trial.

An opening statement by the prosecution accused the two men of violating the law of the Philippine Commonwealth against (just what I don't know—the interpreter was very vague in his translation).

The defense counsel stated in several emotional paragraphs that his clients pled guilty, offering only the extreme poverty of their families in extenuation. His plea was supported by a chorus of sobbing and wailing by the numerous members of the impoverished families.

I was called to take the witness stand, said "I do" to an oath read to me in Tagalog, told my story through the interpreter, and produced the evidence. The seven cartons of cigarettes and two horn figures that I produced from my war bag appeared to rest the case for the prosecution. No cross-examination, so I stood down.

After another speech by the defense I was surprised to be called to the witness stand again. This time the judge spoke to me directly—in English much better than the interpreter's.

"Colonel Treeplet, what should be the sentence for these men?"

This unusual variation of Anglo-Saxon law as adapted and warped by a Filipino court found me at a total loss.

"Your honor, I am only the complainant and a witness in this case. Also I have no idea what would be an appropriate sentence under the civilian law of the Philippine Commonwealth. So I do not think it would be right for me to say anything about the sentence."

"But eet ees your command wheech has been injured, coronel, so you should have the right to determine the sentence. In this case you can recommend confinement in the penitentiary for as long as two years and a fine of up to two thousand pesos." Sobbing from front two rows.

Good God!

I thought furiously for a few seconds. The American captain who had chiseled the cigarettes intended for the troops had been barely slapped on the wrist so it would certainly not be right to jail these poor devils. They had only provided the opportunity for his chiseling. But everyone was looking at me; a sentence was expected. Two years? One year? Six months? Ridiculous! And then I had it.

"Your honor, I believe that it would be appropriate to sentence these men to go together to every town and barrio of your district and tell their story in the marketplace to all the people. Tell them that peddlers, traders, and black market dealers are not permitted in the camp of the 342d Infantry Regiment. Tell them that if they enter my camp with goods to sell I will arrest them and confiscate their goods and any American money, clothing, cigarettes, or other American goods they have—without payment. Tell them if they enter my camp wearing American uniform clothes they will leave camp naked."

The white-haired judge listened grimly, seemed puzzled, then slowly beamed all over his wrinkled face. The prosecutor, the defense counsel, and the interpreter joined him in pleased (or amused?) grins.

The judge then composed his normally pleasant face into a stern mask, figuratively adjusted the black cap, turned to the fearful culprits, and delivered a harsh five-paragraph pronouncement in Tagalog, ending with a crash of the gavel.

A stunned silence ensued until the meaning of the sentence percolated through the courtroom. The next few minutes were confusing. I know that I shook hands with the judge, the presidente, the clerk, the interpreter, both lawyers, and the convicts. Then there were most of the impoverished relatives and a trio of policemen who caught me and made speeches in Tagalog as I worked my way to the door.

Well, my popularity was probably at an all-time low in the 342d but it looked as though I'd stand a good chance of being elected the next presidente of Marakina if I cared to run for the office.

But the lectures that my convicted black marketeers had been sentenced to give (and actually gave) throughout the district had little effect. In fact I suspect that the results of the trial were interpreted and probably advertised as typical American softness rather than clemency. At any rate the Filipino infiltration continued and I achieved a high degree of unpopularity among the natives. They didn't mind being arrested and turned over to the provost marshal but my (possibly illegal) confiscation of their goods and all items of American origin really hurt them. But I believe that the program was effective in that we got no repeaters—once was enough.

The editor of the *342d Redoubt* called on me for counsel.

"I want to publish an editorial entitled 'The Evils of the Black Market,' colonel, and I'd like to incorporate your ideas on the subject."

"I'll be delighted to help you, sergeant," and I squared away to give him a few paragraphs of wisdom. Opened my mouth to speak and after a thoughtful interval I closed it.

Why, actually, was the black market wrong under the current conditions? Take cigarettes, the principal objective of the market, for example. There was no rationing on the home front in the United States so American civilians were not deprived if our men traded their ration to the natives. The ration was ample for the troops. Cigarettes were not manufactured in the Philippines so the local economy was not hurt. The Philippines were still a commonwealth of the United States so there was no import duty and the Philippine government was not harmed. The exorbitant cost of American cigarettes in the Philippines was therefore due only to scarcity and greed.

So if an American soldier who did not smoke should take his ration at the rate of $1.50 per carton and traded it to a Filipino for a souvenir worth $3 and the Filipino sold it for $4 to a man who normally had to pay $8, all participants were benefited and happy with their bargains. The American tobacco industry was stimulated and no one was harmed except the Filipino profiteers who usually made a profit of 800 percent.

I came out of my trance; the editor was still expectantly waiting, pencil poised.

"On second thought, Kamchak, I believe that I had better write a few notes on the subject. I'll have them ready for you tomorrow noon."

I mulled over this question the rest of the day, talked to the judge advocate general and the inspector general at division. During a period of insomnia I reviewed all angles of black marketing that I could recall, and it boiled down to this:

The sale of government property (gasoline, for example) was illegal but stealing and wrongfully disposing of U.S. property was criminal in any case and never mind the black market.

Disposing of one's own personal property (watches to the Russians or cigarettes to the Filipinos) was nobody's business but one's own. When I sold my ten-year-old ten-dollar watch to a Russian at the Mulde River Bridge for three hundred dollars the transaction made both of us very happy and harmed no one.

So when the editor of the *Redoubt* entered my office next day I reluctantly backed away from the question. Honestly stated, I weaseled out.

"I've given this question a good deal of thought, sergeant, and just can't think of anything of interest to say about the black market. The AFWESPAC and division orders on the subject are quite clear and don't require interpretation or elaboration. I'm quite sure you can find a lot of more interesting subjects to write about—the recreation area at Lemere, for example."

"But colonel, next to going back to the States this black market business is the hottest subject. All the men are talking about it. I'd sure like to give them the reasons it's wrong."

I felt like the legendary colonel of the old army joke who when cornered as I was shouted, "There are no reasons for it. It's just my policy." But I restrained myself.

"Well, Kamchak, if you can think up something interesting on the subject go ahead and write it up. I must admit that I can't."

Time passed but the *Redoubt* never carried an editorial on the black market. Sergeant Kamchak couldn't think of any reasons why Filipinos shouldn't buy cigarettes from Americans either.[4]

Five.

Japanese

A Major Problem

Getting live Japs was a major problem for us. Live Japs also had a major problem getting to us. We were maintaining details of the reinforced intelligence platoon at nine surrender points, which were advertised to the holdout Japanese by leaflets and loudspeakers manned by our Nisei. A great many Japanese probably wanted to surrender and a good many probably tried it, but very few made it. They were scattered throughout the islands in small, disorganized groups, starving, half naked, largely unarmed, and burning with malaria.

The Filipinos were understandably hostile, having suffered under three years of Japanese maltreatment and atrocities. Consequently, if a Japanese refugee was now seen by a Filipino of any age or sex, the alarm was raised and he was hunted down and killed like a poisonous snake. Even the recognized guerrillas, nominally under our command, were not enthusiastic about bringing them in alive. It was easier (and much more fun) simply to kill them—and sell their looted possessions to the souvenir-hungry Americans.

Personally I cared nothing about the starvation or slaughter of Japanese. They had conducted the war with an official and individual brutality that put them beyond consideration as soldiers. I felt, with the Filipinos, that there were still too many Japs in the world. However, it was my official duty to get them in alive if possible without risking American lives. And the wild Japs, when fed, wormed, dosed with atabrine and tamed, provided us with excellent and reliable laborers.

I noted great differences between Japanese and Germans. When Germans felt that the odds were against them, they would kapitulieren in large numbers; the Japs would launch a frenzied but hopeless banzai attack or commit suicide. But if captured the tame Japs were much better to deal with than tame Germans. The Germans would start to demand their rights under the terms of the Geneva Convention; the Japs feel that a captive has no rights and are amazed by and grateful for humane treatment.

One emaciated Jap leading private succeeded in running the gauntlet on November 2 and was delighted to be captured. When questioned he said, "I just had to come in and surrender."

"Why did you have to come in—were you ordered to surrender?"

"No, I was not ordered. I ran away because I was junior."

"What did being junior have to do with it?"

"All privates had been eaten and I was junior leading private."

In early November the Japanese situation began to become pressing in the southern part of my area. The presidentes of towns and barrios reported thefts or robbing by bands of Japanese and sightings of signs of holdouts. The largest band was reported by various Filipino officials to be from fifty to five hundred men. These holdouts were located in an organized and well-controlled group in the northern mountains of the Camarines Norte peninsula and were periodically raiding the coastal villages.

On November 9, I sent C Company to Tagoawayan by LSM 131, hoping that this show of interest might entice the Japs out of the jungle or frighten them well into the interior. I was quite concerned when I received a laconic radio message next morning from the expedition commander:

SEND SEA PLANE EVACUATE SIX MEN STOP REQUEST FIVE QUARTS PLASMA END

Damn! Looked like they'd run into serious trouble with fighting Japs, so I alerted the rest of the battalion while Major Hankins got more information on the situation. We were delighted to find that the six casualties were one case of malaria, two of dysentery, and three heroes who had scraped themselves on coral while wading ashore. The plasma was required by the surgeon for some of the twenty-nine Japanese who had surrendered when they saw the landing party come ashore. We arranged for a navy plane, delivered the plasma, and got our sick and wounded back the same day.

C Company stayed in the area for a week waiting for more Japanese, and finally collected three more. A further stay appeared to be fruitless; the jungle was almost impassable in the wet season, and the men were not thriving on their ration supplement of green bananas and coconuts, so I recalled them. The captain sent a message to the Japanese commander by a Filipino runner, saying that he would return in a few days to surround him again, and inviting him in the meantime to apply to the squad of the intelligence and reconnaissance platoon, which would remain at Tagoawayan to accept his surrender.

During the last week of November a group of twenty to thirty Japanese began coyly exchanging messages with our surrender point on Tago-awayan. But it required several days of patient negotiations and propaganda by our Nisei before any results were obtained. The Japs simply could not believe that the war was over; they were suspicious of our intentions, and could not conceive of humane treatment for captives. They were also physically and spiritually tough enough to resist capture until they were at the point of death.

The commander of this group, Junior Officer Shibata Masares, belonged to the Kando Infantry Company, Manila Defense Headquarters.

He wrote quaint but understandable English, which simplified negotiations. The warm, friendly tone of his letters was not what one would expect during a parley between enemies, more like congratulating an opponent at the end of a tennis match. His last literary effort follows.

Headquarters Kando Infantry Company
Manila Defense Headquarters
Please allow me to say congratulations on your great victory of the war and deepest application for your Army and Navy, also nations who have done their best during the war time.

We read your kind advice note dated November, saying that the war was ended but first time we could not believe it because we were educated that our country is never surrendered before.

Moreover we have heard of nothing about the war news since your troops landed this island. How could we imagine of it.

But after reading of that note, we suffered certain cares and tried to collect news about the war. About two weeks ago we find some newspaper and understand that our country is really surrendered, August and the war ended. According to the order which is issued by Emperor, we noted to stop the fighting and surrender your country.

Therefore we will not resist any more and surrender to you under disarmed conditions and hereafter we like to do our best for peace and friendship of both countries.

As soon as we understand the surrender of our country we also should surrender but unfortunately at that time most of our members were very weak and some of them suffering from beriberi because of limited food and lack of vitamins. Therefore it was necessary to us to take enough foods and rest.

On the other hand we spend several nights for searching of men who still do not know surrender of our country and war ended. At last we find two navy men and we believe that there are none of Japanese Army and Navy in the island anymore.

As recently these sick and weak men getting normal conditions we came here for surrender.

We shall be very glad if you kindly accept our surrender.

Although our father country surrendered to the U.S.A. our feelings and minds are very happy because we have done our best during the war time and now the U.S.A. is victor of the war and hero of the world.

We are very glad to see the peace again between the U.S.A. and Japan.

By the surrender of our country the war ended and we are not

your enemy any more. We will promise you our sincerity and express highest respects, good friendship hereafter.
(signed) Shibata Masares
Junior Officer

The following day Lieutenant Masares marched his emaciated twenty-seven-man army out of the jungle and formally surrendered to the sergeant in charge of the I&R surrender point.

We now had a clearer picture of the Japanese situation in Camarines Norte. There were probably four hundred men in the group of holdouts, commanded by Captain Yamada, a Regular Army officer of the former 105th Imperial Infantry Regiment. He was unusually tall for a Japanese, "as tall as an American" according to the Filipino messengers.

His men were fairly well armed but were actually committing no atrocities and were causing little trouble. To be fair about the matter, Yamada was seriously avoiding trouble. Every week or ten days he would leave his jungle home and raid a village, taking one or two carabao and four to six sacks of rice to feed his starving warriors. His men never injured or molested the natives or inflicted property damage, that is, aside from taking what they required. Even then, as required by the rules of civilized warfare, Yamada gave the owners of the property his written receipts, payable in yen when presented to a Japanese Army paymaster.

The natives of the raided village would then claim that four carabao and twelve sacks of rice had been stolen. Our government, ever eager to distribute the wealth of the American citizenry, would pay the claim without question, and everyone was happy. Particularly pleased were the Filipinos, each village looking forward to the next raid like gamblers anticipating the results of a horse race. Selling rice and carabao to the Japanese in falsified numbers and at inflated prices was a most profitable business.

There was little to be done in this situation. The C Company expedition that I had already sent out had taken four days just to reach the foothills of Yamada's stronghold. Supply of this company over the jungle trails had proven practically impossible. The jeeps bogged down and couldn't make the muddy grades. Supply by parachute was considered; it was possible to deliver in the right area on smoke signal, but in the heavy rain forest the supplies would never reach the ground. Last, if we pushed the Japanese too hard there would doubtless be a fight and I certainly agreed with the idea that there should be no more casualties.

So I put out more radio-equipped posts of the reinforced I&R platoon to report the Japanese movements and accept the occasional surrender of a man or group too worn down, sick, or starved to run any more.

Finally I started a running correspondence with Captain Yamada, which was to continue for many weeks. I wrote to him in English, since he was said to be able to read English, but had our Nisei also write Japanese translations to avoid any chance of misunderstanding. The letters were then sent by courier jeep and landing craft to the nearest I&R patrol or surrender point, then by a well-paid Filipino runner who would follow the jungle trails until he was halted by one of Yamada's outposts or patrols.

Yamada would then write a reply and return it by the same runner.

My efforts to win a peaceful settlement were in vain. I informed Yamada that the war was over and invited him to come out with his men and surrender. He replied (in Japanese) that the war was not over; Japanese forces had been temporarily driven into the mountains but it was unthinkable that Japan would surrender. The United States and Japan were going to be at war for a thousand years (unless the Americans admitted defeat) and he was personally going to keep the war active for the next fifty years.

I called upon the Japanese officers in the stockade to assist in my propaganda campaign and they were most helpful in their letter writing and advice. Yamada replied that he could not rely on the statements of captives. He countered with a proposal that if America and Japan were at peace, Japanese and American planes could fly together. If we would have a Japanese and an American plane circle Mount Labo side by side he would know the war was over and would come in. That letter must have been written during a malarial delirium, because American pilots should be able to fly Japanese planes.

I was grasping at any straw, and applied to AFWESPAC for a Japanese plane and a pilot who could fly it. Unfortunately all the planes available had been so damaged by gunfire, weather, or souvenir hunters that not even a marine pilot would consider taking one of them off the ground. My proposal that a Zero fighter might be repaired by cannibalization of other wrecks by our PW mechanics, and flown by a PW pilot, was not favorably considered by General Styer's air corps liaison officer. He was quite firm in his refusal.

"Absolutely out of the question. You gotta remember that Japs just don't think like human beings. Your Jap pilot might just get patriotic and do a banzai kamikaze dive right smack in the middle of AFWESPAC headquarters as soon as he got off the ground. No way!"

The periodic raids continued but Yamada was always careful or considerate enough to avoid any village that one of our I&R patrols happened to be occupying.

On December 1, I tried sending a force into the jungle to make contact. This time we used a rifle platoon to safeguard one Nisei and two PWs who wanted to help in the operation. Again the approach was difficult and supply almost impossible. It required one day by motor truck, one day across the bay by landing craft, and approach by jungle during the late rainy season. The air corps plastered Mount Labo with leaflets composed by our Nisei and PWs. I felt sure that our platoon was in little danger if they encountered the Japanese but was quite concerned about the safety of the PWs used as scouts or emissaries. I had to admire their courage in volunteering for this mission because if captured it was quite possible that they would be immediately executed as traitors by their fanatical countrymen.

This effort continued for ten days, with the platoon being supplied by Filipino cargadores, but with no success. The Japanese faded away before their advance, and all our men ever found were their abandoned campsites.

On December 10, Yamada made a mistake, a serious mistake.

During a raid for food he kidnapped six Filipinos, three men and their wives, and took them back into the jungle. This was serious and I was forced to the opinion that this group must be eliminated.

I informed the division commander on this development of the situation, and he approved my plan to send a punitive force of guerrillas to eradicate Yamada's band, provided I was cleared by AFWESPAC. I readily received clearance by AFWESPAC, provided that one of "my guerrilla units" volunteered for the job. It seemed that, although we fed, clothed, equipped, and paid them, our command status over our irregulars ranged from vague to nil.

The Anderson and Saber Battalions

There was a guerrilla unit, the First Anderson Battalion, in camp not far from Marakina. They were a fully recognized battalion of some northern hill tribe, well armed and soldierly. It was expected that this battalion might be retained and incorporated as an organization in the Philippine Army, with practically all of its members volunteering to remain in the service. In any case they enjoyed soldiering, their morale was high, and as scouts and woodsmen they were well suited to the task at hand.

I sent for the battalion commander, Lieutenant Colonel Maras, whose tall frame and spare, saturnine features indicated a strong Spanish strain in his ancestry. He arrived at our operations tent in a torrential rainstorm with his equally drenched operations officer. They shed their ponchos, shook hands all around with my staff, took seats, and looked eagerly expectant. I briefed him on the recent developments in Camarines Norte.

"I am now going to send a force into Camarines Norte to capture or eliminate this group. Since you have a unit that is capable of doing the job I am offering you the opportunity to hunt this group down. Do you want this job?"

Maras seemed initially startled by our change in policy, and then obviously pleased—killing Japs had been off limits for so long. But then he became strictly businesslike.

"Yes sir. We would like very much to hunt these Japanese."

We furnished large-scale maps of the area on which Major Hankins had plotted the locations of the Japanese raids and former camps as well as their present reported and surmised positions on Mount Labo.

I then asked, "How many men will you take in with you?"

"I will take almost all except a guard for my camp, about six hundred."

"Good. I will furnish trucks to move your men from your camp to the Philippine coast guard station at Mauban. The coast guard will take you across the bay to Capalonga or Tagoawayan in two landing craft. They can carry 120 men per day, making two round trips. That is the bottleneck. It will take five days or six to move your men and one or two days to move your supplies. In one week you should be assembled and ready to move out. When can you start?"

"We start tomorrow morning, daylight, 0700, sir."

"About weapons, your battalion is well equipped with small arms and I'll send you three full combat loads of ammunition in the morning. But how about heavy weapons? Anything we have is at your disposal. I know that you don't want howitzers or antitank guns but do you want machine guns, light or heavy, .30 or .50 caliber? Or mortars—60- or 80-mm.?"

"No, coronel, I know this place. It is very steep, very hard. The way is very bad. The weapons would be too heavy, except could I have one 60-mm. mortar and possibly one hundred shells?"

"They will be on the ammunition truck. Now about rations. Your regular ration is all right for camp but for a hard campaign you will need better food. I can't send you fresh meat—it would spoil before it reached you. But canned meat and fish I can send."

"No, senor—coronel. These also would be too heavy. From here, where the boats land, we will have to carry our rations over the trails in the mountains. Maybe we use carabao, maybe we use cargadores. I would like only to have two times the regular amount of rice. Nothing else. That will be one thousand two hundred pounds of rice daily."

"Right, two pounds of rice per man per day, but what about fish, meat, and vegetables?"

"We will need no more. The rice is light, dry, and easy to pack. We will eat half. The other half we trade in the barrios for fish and all else we need."

"Ah yes, good. Very practical. Now about trucks—I will have nine trucks at your camp at 0600 tomorrow; six trucks for your first echelon of 120

men, two carrying eight days of rations, and one for the mortar and
ammunition. I'll follow up with one truck of rice every four days. Now
about tentage—do you need shelter tents?"

"No sir, they would also be too much. We will build shelters if we need
them."

"As I recall, you have a surgeon. How about his equipment and supply
of medicines?"

"Yes sir. He is a very good doctor and he has his kit that he has used
before the Japanese trouble. But he does not have many medicines."

"Right. My surgeon will make up a military surgical kit and a pack of
medical supplies. I'll bring him out with me in the morning and he can
talk it over with your doctor. Anything else?"

"Yes, one thing. Our radios are all discompuesto—they do not work,
and—"

"Very well. Our COMO will take in our first battalion radios and turn
them over to your communications officer tomorrow morning."[1]

"No sir. I do not wish to have so many radios. They are too heavy and
I will use messengers between the companies. I would like to have one
radio with spare batteries and parts. I will leave two men with each of
your outposts here, here, and there. Then we can talk to them through
the outpost radio—they can talk to your men and your men can talk to
you." It was a very neat and economical solution to the communications
problem.

"Anything else? No? Then good luck and good hunting."

Colonel Maras and his S-3 donned their ponchos, shook hands all
round, grinned, saluted, and disappeared into the blackness and pound-
ing rain. I must say I admired the man for his workmanlike approach, his
evident capability, his esprit, and his soldierly attitude. The way he insisted on eliminating all nonessentials showed that he knew his business.
He knew from experience that on a rough campaign in wet, mountainous
jungle there was no place for luxuries such as heavy weapons, canned
rations, or tentage.

As an afterthought I directed the surgeon to pack twenty thousand
atabrine tablets in the medical kit he was working on. Filipinos are not
as prone to contract malaria as Americans are but they sometimes do. If
they could be persuaded to take atabrine it would eliminate the danger
and decrease possible evacuation requirements.

Next morning I accompanied our little convoy to the Anderson camp
and found a hive of activity. It was raining heavily; it looked like the wet
season was going on forever this year.

Colonel Maras had prepared well. His men for the first echelon were already formed by truckloads in twenty-man groups. They were in helmets
and ponchos, with weapons slung reversed. Their meager possessions

in packs, rolls, or bags were sheltered under their ponchos, giving their normally trim carriage a dumpy, humpbacked appearance. I doubt if there was more than one blanket or shelter half per man—certainly no one had both. Few luxuries such as canteens or mess kits. They had no coffee or tea, and water was running in every mountain stream. Bamboo joints would furnish cook pots, cups, and eating utensils as needed. I would also have bet that there wasn't a razor, pair of socks, or change of clothing in the company. These people were traveling light. But every man in this echelon had a poncho, which led me to wonder.

"Colonel Maras, I see that all of your first group have ponchos. Do all of your men have them?"

"No sir. There are 187 men without them. But they will go later and perhaps it will not be raining then. The dry season must come soon."

"But it will certainly be raining before you get back. You need 187 more? I'll send two hundred over this afternoon. That will give you enough for the men on post in your camp guard."

"We shall be glad to get them. The ponchos are very good in the rain and for when we make camp."

Ammunition was being distributed—forty rounds per rifleman. A few paulin-wrapped bundles were heaved into the lightly loaded ammunition truck and the men swung aboard the personnel trucks and settled on the benches. They moved off in the heavy downpour.

Colonel Maras and I moved to a nearby tent where we found my surgeon, Captain Bergbaum, and the Anderson medico in conference over the medical supplies. The current subject was atabrine and whether the men would take it after they'd discovered its godawful taste. Maras put an end to the discussion.

"I will tell them. They will take it."

I mentioned how pleased I was with the esprit and businesslike attitude of his battalion.

"Yes, they like it," Maras replied, grinning. "They hope to get many things to sell to the American soldiers."

I hadn't thought of this mercenary aspect, but why not? Not too long ago we were hiring Tuscarora Indians for five dollars per British scalp, and the British were paying their Senecas one pound for an American hairpiece. We might get excellent results by offering ten dollars per Japanese ear—make it the right ear. But no, that wouldn't do. Not many American finance officers could distinguish between Japanese ears and Tagalog ears, and these mountain people who hated the lowlanders might not be too choosy. So we'll leave it at salable souvenirs.

As I left the camp with Captain Bergbaum, I asked him, "And how did you do with the Anderson medical service—the doctor and his prewar tools?"

"Doctor!" he said contemptuously. "I don't know how these people get a license to practice. The only treatment he knows for gangrene is amputation. Never heard of the sulfas or penicillin."

I regarded this highly educated, ignorant, intolerant, immature, self-satisfied young twerp with considerable distaste. Spared from the draft to complete his education, commissioned first lieutenant to serve his internship in the army, promoted to captain and ordered to the field after V-J Day, he was totally without medical or surgical experience. Yet he was sneering at his opposite number in the guerrilla battalion who had spent half a lifetime effecting cures and operating with inadequate medicines and tools and the last three years under impossible field conditions. This young man needed a jolt.

"Well, captain, I'm sorry to hear that. Those men are going to get shot at and I've got to send a good competent surgeon with them. I'll have to keep Lieutenant Brown with the third battalion because they'll be going to Mindanao any day now and the other battalion surgeons are just graduated medical students. So you'll have to get your gear together and go along with these people."

"But my responsibility is with the regiment, colonel. I can't—"

"Your responsibility is with any part of my command where you're most needed, captain. There's nothing going on in the regiment that a good medical corpsman can't take care of and we have a field hospital half an hour away. So you're the one to go. Report to Colonel Maras as attached for duty at 0800 tomorrow."

I let my extremely unhappy doctor sweat that out for a few hours. At noon mess I gave him a chance to do some constructive work in lieu of arduous field duty.

"Well, Bergbaum, are you all packed for your vacation in the picturesque countryside of Camarines Norte?"

"Yes sir." A very unenthusiastic, even sullen reply.

"I trust that you remembered to take your rain gear and atabrine. And you'll have a few cases of gangrene so remember to pack your sulfas and penicillin."

"I've packed everything that I will need, colonel," meaning "Mind your own business, colonel, and stay out of my field of operations."

"Here's an idea, Bergbaum. Maras is sending his doctor off with the third echelon day after tomorrow. Do you think you can bring him up to your AMA-New York standards with an intensive thirty-six-hour course on sulfa pills, sulfa powder, and penicillin injections?"

Bergbaum was brighter than I'd thought—caught on right away.

"Yes sir. I'm sure I can." His enthusiasm was touching.

"Good. Take your plunder and report to camp immediately. You live with the doctor and instruct him in the wonder drugs. I'll check with Maras and you at dawn day after tomorrow on the doctor's progress and competence in modern medicine. Then we'll see—"

Bergbaum, still slightly apprehensive but hopeful of reprieve, did a good job in the next couple of days and did not have to accompany the guerrillas in the field.

We had just dispatched the last group of the Andersons when I received a message from one of our outposts on the southwest shore of Camarines Norte. A gang of one hundred Japanese had raided a village the day before and stolen pigs, poultry, and rice. They had also taken one man with them when they retired into the jungle. They were on the opposite side of the peninsula and over the mountains from Yamada's Labo Mountain Japs but might be part of the same crew.

At any rate they also had to be captured or eradicated so I immediately sent the Saber Battalion after them. It was much simpler than the Anderson deployment. They went by truck to Calauag, thence by narrow-gauge railroad to Ragay where they set up their base camp.

There was alleged to be only one passable trail among the foothills around the southeast flank of Cerro Labo and with luck we might pinch both gangs of Japs between the two battalions on this main trail.

The Sabers, 438 strong, moved out on December 17 and were in position on the morning of December 18, eagerly anticipating the plunder they would sell to the souvenir-hungry Americans. I felt as though I were loosing two packs of hounds on a fox or, rather, on a tired, gaunt, rabid wolf.

As the Sabers were moving out from their base camp on December 19, I received a message from Tagoawayan reporting that the Filipinos who had been kidnapped on December 10 had been released unharmed and had returned to their barrios. The Japanese had used them as guides to lead them on the main trail to the other side of Cerro Labo and had taken the women along only to ensure the earnest cooperation of their husbands.

At this point I would have liked to revert to my former attitude of watchful waiting. But since both guerrilla battalions were now moving into position, and since the roundup campaign promised to be short, I decided to keep cheering them on by radio.

It was a slow, wet, miserable war. The rainy season was still holding on. The supply boats were thrown off schedule by frequent storms. The railroad supplying the Sabers was in trouble with flooded tracks and flood-weakened bridges. And these troubles of our supply people were comparatively minor. The guerrillas were packing their supplies through swollen streams, over steep and muddy trails, or through virgin jungle.

It was a lot of man-killing work for fifty dollars Filipino (twenty-five U.S.) per month.

The Japanese continued to be elusive. It was only on Christmas Eve that Colonel Maras made a firm contact. He reported three Japs killed and four captured. The rest retired up the slopes of Mount Labo where I wished them a dismal Christmas and a disastrous New Year.

The war on the peninsula was proceeding very slowly. On January 15 the Saber Battalion sighted forty Japanese but before they could close in, the Japs took off like spooked deer and made a clean getaway into the dense jungle on Mount Labo's southern slope. I was beginning to suspect that the Sabers were probably afraid that they might catch the Japs—they were a Tagalog battalion—and catching forty armed Japanese? No way. I was almost convinced that I should withdraw the guerrillas. But if I did, the raids on the coastal villages would be resumed with the larcenous claims of the Filipino peasantry emptying the pockets of the rich American taxpayers. Then we'd have to do it all over again and the difficulty of getting an expedition into that back country made me decide to maintain the status quo.

On January 23 the Anderson Battalion on the north side of the peninsula was in contact with a hundred Japanese and had them steadily on the run. Colonel Maras finally reported that he had them penned against the coastline, cut off from roads and trails, and was moving in for the kill.

A welcome surprise that I received on my return from Mindanao was a message from the I&R team with the Anderson Battalion. On February 3 they had surrounded an estimated one hundred Japanese and killed eighty-six of them. The remainder broke out of the net and escaped into the jungle. Unfortunately there were no prisoners. The guerrillas were evidently losing their patience, probably because two of their men were wounded in this skirmish.

From a diary found on the body of a Japanese lieutenant it appeared that since December 20 out of a total of 230 men they had lost forty-five captured, drowned in stream crossings, died of fever, deserted, and abandoned as hopelessly sick. That number, added to the eighty-six just killed, was a total loss of 131, so Yamada had a remnant of not more than ninety-eight men still with him. It was evident that the guerrilla campaign, although painfully slow and grueling, was paying off, and that the Japs had been badly hurt.

I therefore made a final appeal to Yamada to make an end to this stupid business and come in to talk the matter over. I would normally never have offered an enemy such generous terms but his tough stubbornness was most admirable. Also I wanted to get him out of my hair at any reasonable price. So I sent him the following letter:

Headquarters 342d Infantry
Office of the Regimental Commander
APO 450 c/o Postmaster
San Francisco Calif
25 February 1946

Captain Yamada
Japanese Army
Bicol Province, P. I.
My Dear Captain Yamada:

I have been following your activities for the past three months with considerable interest. I have made every effort to accomplish your peaceful surrender without loss of life or injury to your men.

While it was necessary for me to take strenuous measures during the period 20 December, 1945 to 3 February, 1946, I did so with regret, since the war is now over and there is peace between our nations.

Since you do not believe the war is over, I admire your heroic adherence to your avowed intention of holding out against our forces. However, I am sure that, if you were certain that the war is over, you would cease bearing arms. Continued fighting under such circumstances would be the conduct of a bandit, and from your excellent reputation I know that you are not a bandit. What was once heroic warfare is now hot-blooded murder and senseless destruction, and as a professional military man, I wish to do all I can to avoid further useless killing.

I realize that you have not surrendered because you are probably not sure that the war is over. Therefore, I am sending you copies of newspapers and magazines which cannot be classed as propaganda. Further, I am sending you some letters from Japanese officers and soldiers who are now temporarily honorable prisoners of war while waiting their turn to be shipped home to Japan. Your one-time First Sergeant Haike Yamase, who was captured in November, has already returned to Japan.

Last, I request that you visit me as a guest at my headquarters at Marakina, Luzon, for a day or two. I wish to have you see the situation with your own eyes, inspect the camp in which we are temporarily holding Japanese, see the clothing, medical care, and food with which they are provided, and talk to them on any subject you desire. I have heard that you speak English well, so an interpreter will not be necessary, but you may bring another officer with you if you wish.

After a day or two, or at your request, I will return you to your men in Bicol Province, unharmed and not humiliated in any way, and free of any promise of any sort.

After your return to Bicol, we will be delighted to receive the honorable surrender of you and your men if you desire to do so. As the last Japanese commander to surrender in the world, no shame can be attached to you, and your nation and the Emperor will receive you with honor.

If you still do not wish to surrender, we will resume the campaign as before.

Lieutenant [illegible], my liaison officer, with my attached Filipino troops, has been directed to establish contact with you by using one of your men whom we found too exhausted to defend himself. This man has consented to carry this letter. I request that he be not injured in any way.

My liaison officer will arrange a meeting with you, and escort you to my headquarters and back to your troops in the event that you refuse my invitation.

Sincerely,
W. S. Triplet
Colonel, 342d Infantry
Commanding

Again the messenger, this time the Japanese soldier, came back with a firm refusal, and the campaign was resumed.

On March 23 a detached company of the Anderson Battalion stalked a group of fifty Japanese and killed twenty-eight of them with a loss of one of their own men dead. It now appeared that Yamada would never be able to accept my hospitality. The loot recovered from a tall corpse, dressed in the rags of a captain's uniform, included a battered briefcase containing his diary, Japanese war bonds, a postal savings book in his name, and a file of my letters. Too bad, I would be delighted to have a man of his type as executive or as a battalion commander.

Holdouts

On New Year's Eve we received startling news from Corregidor. The island had been garrisoned by American forces since it was recaptured in February, and since October it had been occupied by G Company and twelve hundred prisoners working over the entire area. Guerrilla patrols had beaten the bushes and the place had been thoroughly searched during the cleanup campaign. In addition an estimated six thousand sightseers, soldiers, sailors, civilians, WACs, and nurses had combed the island for souvenirs during the past ten months.

And yet twenty wild and ragged but fully armed Japs popped out of the brush on December 31 asking permission to join our regularly fed PW labor force. The affair is best described in the following dramatic opus by a staff writer of the 342d *Redoubt*.[2]

During the midmorning of New Year's Eve, PFC Moore of G Company was prowling alone through the brush of Corregidor's topside looking for souvenirs that wouldn't explode. He suddenly had that feeling that he was not alone and looked up to see a fully armed Jap standing fifteen feet in front of him.

The Jap bowed and hissed politely—as well as he could bow with that long-barreled Ariska held at the ready. In halting but clearly understandable English he stated that he had learned that the war was over and would like to arrange for the surrender of his command.

Our hero, PFC Moore, stuttered that he was sure it could be arranged, and backed off, matching the Jap's repeated bows. Out of sight he really made time back to the company.

The captain, as soon as he was persuaded that Moore was sane and sober, took just enough time to get out of his bathing suit and into khakis before he started out with Moore and a quartet of riflemen to arrange this mysterious surrender.

As they reached the agreed spot the English-speaking Jap again stepped out of cover, this time without his rifle. He saluted, bowed, and hissed inhaling.

"I understand that you want to surrender," opened the captain.

"Yes," said the Jap, who wore the tabs of a warrant officer on the rags of his uniform shirt. "I have learned that the war is over."

"March your men to my camp. I will receive your surrender there," proposed the captain.

"Let's grab the bastard now—he ain't got his gun," whispered Corporal Koontz, raising his M-1.

"Shut up!" hissed the skipper.

"But," says the Jap, "we would like to surrender now."

"Where are your men?" asked the captain.

"Right here, sir," and the Jap waved his arm.

Well, the brush was alive and crawling with them. When they stopped coming out there were twenty ragged, barefooted, scrawnily whiskered, but fully armed and well-fed Japs lined up behind their commander. Corporal Koontz swallowed his chewing tobacco. Arms were stacked in place and soon thereafter there were 1,221 Japanese in the stockade.

How had they learned that the war was over? And where had they been hiding for the last four months?

For the first month or two they had remained hidden in a cave under the cliff down near the high water level on the northeast corner of the island, living pretty thinly on their hard rations and what fish they could catch.

During the second month they started raiding the G Company kitchen. They had no trouble getting enough food from the storeroom and leftovers from the refrigerator so, until they began sickening from malaria, they were very comfortable.

But they could find no medicine for the fever, and the crowded life in the cave became monotonous.

One night the warrant officer found a tattered copy of the *American* magazine in the kitchen and took it back to practice his English.

Next morning he read an illustrated description of the surrender aboard the battleship *Missouri* in Tokyo harbor—and other pictures of MacArthur and the Emperor Hirohito himself in apparently friendly conference.

During the pursuit of Yamada we had been picking up a few Japs here and there in a more peaceful way. In December the Philamerican Regiment had caught a Jap "spy" and turned him over to us for interrogation and execution. The spy was a very dark, long-haired, wild-looking Indonesian type, who tried to tell us all about himself but spoke a language that no Filipino linguist could understand—and a few simple words of Japanese. He had tattoo marks on his shoulders and hips that an anthropologist said identified him as a member of the obscure tribe of Mandayas. Aha. Finally located a man in the Filipino CIC who could understand Mandayan and got his story.[3] This was simply that he had been captured and held for a long time by the Japanese, a band of 190 who were starving in the mountains. He was so frightened that he could not remember where they were. He had run away when they had taken him into strange country. No, he could not lead troops there. He wanted nothing more to do with Japanese. I couldn't blame him for his attitude.

In February a small band of Japs raided Norzgoray, the former home of the Forty-fourth Hunters, and were pursued by three strong patrols of the Hunters without results. Next day in the same area three Japs popped out of the roadside brush, hailed the 342d courier, and thumbed a ride to camp. He drove up and proudly delivered them to my office.

"You were taking a hell of a chance," I remarked, eyeing the trio of bowing Nipponese, "out on that road alone in the first place, and driving all the way back here with those cutthroat characters sitting behind you."

"Oh no sir, I searched 'em and they didn't have a thing in 'em. I wouldn't a done it with Filipinos but these were Japs and they sure were glad to see me."

In March our surrender outpost at Mauban reported that two natives had been killed and large pieces of the thighs had been cut from the bodies. It was obviously a case of cannibalism by wild Japs in the area but the native police had had no success in finding them.

In March we received a report that twenty-seven Japs were operating as pirates in the small islands near Pollillo. They had started their new trade by stealing small bancas and had graduated by capture to one large banca and an interisland trading schooner. I arranged for a patrol to search the area in a navy sea plane. The patrol located them on a small, otherwise uninhabited island where they had constructed crude huts and were engaged in gardening. The schooner was missing but three large sailing bancas were drawn up on the beach. In accordance with our policy of taking them peaceably if possible the plane buzzed the area and returned to base. Odd, I thought, the suppression of piracy was formerly a navy job. But our triphibious army could admittedly do practically anything the navy could so we were stuck with it.

Further Jap raids were made on Pollillo and neighboring islands and fishermen and trading craft were halted and robbed by bancas and schooner crews reported as many as thirty to sixty men armed with a heavy machine gun, machine pistols, and rifles. The pirates did not operate in the traditional manner. No one was forced to walk the plank. In fact, since the victims always hove to at the first burst across the bow, no one had been hurt. But the natives were complaining about the lack of protection, so we planned our next move. It was a good plan.

The navy PBY carrying two squads of riflemen and eight volunteer Japanese PWs would touch down offshore in front of the beach where the bancas were drawn up. Since the Japs beached their boats there it would be suitable for a rubber boat landing and it would cut off the Jap escape by sea.

The eight PWs would then go in by rubber boats equipped with Japanese flags, picture magazines, megaphones, a safe conduct letter, leaflets, cigarettes, and sixty K-rations. The PBY and riflemen would cover the PWs during the landing.

The PWs would contact the wild Japs, feed them, and hopefully convert them. If converted, we would transport them to Manila in successive planeloads.

If they declined to be converted we would recover our tame Japs, if possible alive, and destroy the pirate shipping. I would then recommend the island to the air corps as a strafing and bombing range for immediate use. It was small, with sparse vegetation, and the running targets would lend realism to the exercise.

Yes, it was a beautiful plan, simple and workable, but it could not be used. The PBY developed persistent mechanical ailments found to be terminal. It just couldn't get off the water, and was the only one available.

I then arranged for a small landing ship to take a platoon of riflemen, a section of machine guns, a 60-mm. mortar crew, and the squad of tame Japs to the island. They made the landing, too late. The huts, vegetable gardens, and an abandoned banca were there but the Japs had been frightened away by the obvious interest shown by the first PBY reconnaissance.

The patrol landed on five other islands in the vicinity and the PWs picked up and converted a group of six starving Japs. This party firmly disclaimed any maritime ventures or knowledge of the pirates and were hotly indignant in denying the charge of their cannibalism near Mauban.

Then a motor patrol passing through Mauban met a Filipino runner who had just come from Infanta. The man said that there was a large group of Japanese there who were looking for Americans. So the patrol dashed off for Infanta and found eight Japs patiently waiting in the town hall. The presidente said that he had had no trouble with them but would be glad to get rid of them. Also, there was the cost of feeding them, which he hoped the Americans would pay (it came to an astonishing total).

These eight men readily admitted that they were the pirates we were looking for. The other nine, they said, had long since sailed, trying to reach Formosa in the schooner they had captured.

One of our sentries on the regimental perimeter, drowsing in the heat of the afternoon sun, reacted sleepily to the sound of soft footsteps behind him. He turned, rifle at "port," then came to a wide awake "on guard" at the sight of two scrawny, bewhiskered Japs who were waving a surrender leaflet in each hand and grinning tentatively. Their story was that five of them had worked their way ninety miles south, through guerrillas and bandits, to the nearest American troops they could find, and had been observing us for three days. These two had come in as a trial balloon; the other three wanted to wait to see if their scout party survived and would watch us one day more to be sure. Next day we got them, same place, same time, captured by another much more alert double sentry post.

Since there appeared to be only twenty-five to thirty Jap stragglers still at large I recalled both the Andersons and the Sabers, leaving only one company of the Sabers commanded by Captain Ortiz to patrol the area.

I thanked Colonel Maras who had carried the brunt of the expedition by giving him a letter that included a strong recommendation that his battalion be incorporated as a unit in the Philippine Army, as he and his men earnestly desired.

I hoped that the Japanese situation was settled in Bicol Province or could be easily held in check by the local police or the Philippine constabulary. But on April 14, Captain Ortiz of the Saber Battalion received information from the natives that a band of 120 Japanese was still at large and cultivating the remote vegetable farms that Yamada had described in his diary. Ortiz said he was moving into the hills to annihilate them. It was discouraging, reminded me of the mythical many-headed Hydra that gave Hercules so much trouble—every time he cut off a head, two more grew on the stump. Were it not for the I&R platoon teams that were counting the bodies and making the reports I would have been skeptical of the guerrillas' claims of how many Japs had been killed.

In any case, if the Japanese were not eliminated by the end of May, I intended to pull out all guerrillas; it was just too difficult to supply them. So since Captain Ortiz had not made a firm contact by May 31, I recalled his company to rejoin the Anderson Battalion at the depot.

In reviewing this cleanup campaign I was impressed by four aspects of such warfare: the persistence of the Japanese in holding out and evading our forces under the most impossible conditions of starvation and sickness, the difficulty of supplying the troops with the simplest necessities under such conditions of pursuit in mountainous jungle, the length of time (December 10 to March 2) required to conclude a fairly decisive campaign, and the economy of warfare as practiced by these Filipino guerrillas. Their loss of one man killed and two wounded, as compared to two hundred Japanese killed and captured, was an enviable combat record that within my experience was unequaled. It was evident that these mountain tribesmen did not believe in taking chances or offering the foe a fair fight; the object was to annihilate the enemy with little or no loss to themselves.

In early June a group of unrecognized guerrillas (bandits) encountered a band of Japanese near Norzgoray and killed three of them. I sent a platoon patrol to the area with tame Japs and the usual propaganda equipment. Eleven Japs surrendered the first day and fourteen came in the next. We were glad to get them because the division was repatriating Japs faster than we could catch them. Even after we caught them they had to be fed, wormed, cured of malaria, and rested for two weeks before they could use a pick or shovel with good effect.

Six

Guerrillas

Beginning Acquisitions

The administration of guerrilla units, principally the weekly supply of rations and basic medical supplies, was carried on by the guerrilla affairs officer, Major Hankins, and his three capable assistants.

Guerrillas were divided into two classes—recognized guerrillas who were known to have been organized and who had contributed to the defeat of the Japanese, and a horde of others whose claims ranged from doubtful to false.

The recognition of certain units was made by AFWESPAC in close coordination with the Philippine Commonwealth. The recognized guerrillas were to be paid for their services at some time in the indefinite future and some of them might receive back pay from the date of the American surrender of Corregidor. Since this would add considerably to the gross wealth of the Philippines, the Filipinos were naturally trying to have practically every adult male recognized as a guerrilla of three years of service. Claims had been made by a total of 250,000 men in the island of Luzon, which was absurd. If every Filipino who made the claim had actually been an active guerrilla, the Japanese Army could not have existed on the island.

The unrecognized guerrillas, hastily organized in so-called corps, regiments, battalions, and squadrons after the shooting stopped, did have arms, unfortunately. Even the gangs of outright bandits had American, British, or Japanese weapons, which they had stolen, bought, or looted from a battlefield. With these weapons they were settling personal and family feuds, raiding neighboring villages, killing Japs who were trying to make their way to a surrender point, and ambushing the police, the Philippine Army, and Americans for still more weapons and ammo.

There was considerable pressure by Filipino governors, would-be governors, presidentes of towns, and members of congress to have their particular organizations of guerrillas recognized, uniformed, equipped, and paid. The money as well as the weapons would greatly increase their chances in the elections scheduled to take place in April of 1946. In the meantime they were using what weapons they had to eliminate rival candidates long before the elections, easier and more certain than conducting political campaigns.

I began to get acquainted with guerrillas just five days after joining the regiment. Three base engineer soldiers had jeeped into the hills southwest of Marakina and had been ambushed. One man, badly wounded, had escaped. Since the incident occurred in the 342d sector, Major

Hankins visited the survivor in the hospital but learned little except the approximate location of the ambush. One of our recognized units, the Fandangas Battalion, was camped a few miles from the suspected area, so we paid them a visit.

On approaching the camp we were halted by a small, neatly uniformed, barefooted sentry armed with a 1903 Springfield who shouted something incomprehensible but his meaning was quite clear. He meant, "Halt! Dismount! Who is there?"

Hankins braked and we dismounted. Under the impression that Spanish was the common second language of the country I broke out with "Amigo. Donde esta el commandante?" meaning "Take me to your leader."

This brought another shout that doubtless meant "Turn out the guard!" A dozen diminutive, variously armed men boiled out of the woods around us, formed double rank, and on command of the sergeant (the only one wearing combat boots) presented arms. I noted that those armed with barangas and machetes gave the proper saber salute. The sergeant then asked, "Weeth whom do you weesh to see, sar?" and we were promptly on our way to their headquarters with a guide.

Major Fandangas was a small, aquiline-featured mestizo, perfectly uniformed and highly polished. He was quite concerned about our report of murders taking place less than five miles from his camp and immediately dispatched a captain with a combat patrol of two squads to search the area. I was impressed with their businesslike attitude and the enthusiasm with which they mounted their truck and jeep and got under way.

In the meantime we inspected the camp. The men appeared to be personally clean and their motley collection of weapons was kept in good condition. Some men were in squad tents, others in shelter tents, but all tentage was well erected and placed to the best advantage in the irregular, wooded terrain. Sanitation as required in an American camp did not exist. Latrines and garbage pits had been dug but were only for show, since they were shallow and unused, while the rest of the area was used, that is. Flies swarmed around the kitchen tent where the noon meal was being prepared.

Urged by the major, we stayed for lunch in spite of the flies. The menu was rice, boiled dried fish, yams, corned beef, and canned beer. The beef was served particularly in our honor (it is well known that Americans have very weak stomachs and just can't take fly-specked dried fish).

I have said and will say much against the Filipinos with whom I dealt during this period. But I will also maintain that Filipino courtesy and hospitality is unsurpassed. They may go hungry tomorrow but they offer the guest the best they have today.

About 1600 the patrol returned with the stripped bodies of the two engineers. The captain stated that they had found signs of a bivouac that had been occupied by ten or twelve men in the woods near where the shooting had occurred. Some of them had worn Japanese boots, some had sandals, and others had been barefooted. American rifle cartridge cases were found at the scene of the ambush. But there was no one within two miles of the area, nothing to indicate where they had gone, and nothing to show whether they had been Japanese holdouts or Filipino bandits.

Since only American weapons had been used, Major Hankins and I had no doubt about the nationality of the culprits, and I suspect that Major Fandangas had the same suspicion.

We saw the blanket-wrapped bodies of the engineers off to their base in Manila with a message stating the circumstances of their recovery.

Just before leaving, Major Hankins restated our requirements to the battalion commander:

To keep the peace in his area (difficult—see below).

To patrol and disarm bandits and unrecognized guerrillas.

To search for and arrest any suspects in the murder case.

To capture and bring in Japanese—alive.

My rapid orientation tour during the first two weeks gave me a blurred impression of Spanish names, unpronounceable Filipino names, hand-shaking, ceremonies, gleaming gold teeth, wonderfully coordinated and uniformly sized little men, eighteenth-century courtesy, clean uniforms cut down from American sizes, bare feet, polished weapons, dirty kitchens, filthy camps, all-out hospitality, requests for ammunition, and confusing conversations about Filipino politics and the anticipated or dreaded independence.

While inspecting the first two units I pointed out the unsanitary conditions of the camps and told the commanders that for the health of their men they must insist on cleanliness. They were quite agreeable but were honestly puzzled. They simply saw no connection between flies, filth, and health. To them my requirement was just an American phobia.

After thinking this matter of sanitation over at some length I came to a wiser conclusion. My mission was to support these units with bare necessities until their status of recognition was determined, then disarm them, take in equipment, pay and discharge them if recognized by AFWESPAC, and return them to their home province. I was not equipped to make soldiers of them or teach them Anglo-Saxon standards of military sanitation. They were living in their camps as they were accustomed to live in their home barrios. They were amazingly healthy and had a natural immunity to disease under conditions that would kill American troops. So why should I require them to measure up to our standards of sanitation? To do so would keep us all miserable and accomplish nothing. I stopped pushing sanitation, and we were all much happier.

When I visited the Balera Battalion, I received another lesson in Filipino politics. The Baleras were deeply concerned about their coming independence. Their reasons were principally economic—the Philippines were so poor, what would they do without American support? This was a reversal of the usual position, downtrodden colonies seeking independence from the oppression of imperialism. I began to suspect that aside from the Tagalog politicos most of the people would have preferred to have the Philippines remain secure as a commonwealth of the United States.

I found the Baleras to be unusually vague about their numbers, weapons, and equipment. This vagueness about their strength was characteristic to a degree of all of the units that I had inspected. They were positive on only one point, their length of service. They had all sprung to arms on the date of the American surrender. Another peculiarity that all guerrilla units had in common—a full complement of officers. Even though a battalion might have a total strength of only 150 men, it would have all the officers' positions filled and a full roster of senior noncommissioned officers but no privates and very few corporals. I also noted that the rank and seniority of the officers appeared to be in direct proportion to the degree of blood relationship, married relationship, or friendship with the unit commander, and had nothing to do with military ability or achievement.

There was a method in their vagueness about their equipment strength. The less they admitted having, the less they would have to turn in when they were disbanded and the more they could keep for sale, "political purposes," or future banditry.

In order to begin to get some facts on the guerrilla business I required all units to support their claims for recognition and pay by submitting complete rosters of their personnel, with names, addresses, birth dates, and length of service in each grade. I also required lists of weapons and vehicles by make and serial number.

I got the lists since I assured the unit commanders that a man without a weapon could not be considered a guerrilla, that the records on American weapons issued would be checked, and that the data on personnel would be verified at their hometowns and barrios before payment was made.

Most of my statements were false—sheer bluff. We had no records of what American units had issued them. The rosters and lists they gave us were also largely false. There was apparently no ammunition in all of Luzon. But the lists served some purpose. In order to get the maximum number of relatives and friends on the payroll, many weapons were listed and turned in that we would never otherwise have seen. In effect in many cases we were buying battle-worn rifles and pistols for nine hundred dollars or more each. That was expensive, but the lack of a weapon put a heavy burden of proof on a claimant that he had served as an active fighter.

In many cases we were able to point out that a boy born in 1928 or later was not of military age at any time during the war and required proof of his participation. Our efforts at least slowed down the looting of the U.S. Treasury. We didn't stop the swindle, we just made it more difficult.

I really had little to complain about, comparatively speaking. One evening at the division club I was mourning over some of my guerrilla difficulties in conversation with Colonel Carter of the 343d. In turn, between his alcoholic sobs, I heard his sad story.

"You think you have troubles? I was ordered to pay off and discharge a battalion up on the coast without investigation or question. Curious situation, so I went up there with the paymaster and intelligence to look them over.

"This battalion was in a fishing barrio. Camped, hell. They lived there. The lieutenant colonel in command was the barrio presidente, and his executive, the major, was his brother. All males who could pass for eighteen or more were officers or NCOs down the line to a few corporals. There were no privates, no weapons, no uniforms, and no military equipment—not even Japanese. Nothing but boats, nets, lines, and fish spears. I was curious about how these people were recognized so fast and my orders to pay them without question.

"I asked the light colonel, 'How many Japanese did your battalion kill during the war?'

"'Oh, but sar, we deed not keel any Japanese.' The fellow was very honest and seemed puzzled that I should ask such a stupid question.

"'I tried again. 'Well, how many fights did you have, how many men did you lose?'

"'We had no fights and we lose no one except two men drown een the beeg storm last year.'

"'But what did your battalion do during the war?'

"'We caught leetle feesh for the Japanese.'

"'You caught fish for the Japanese! For the Japanese? How can you claim to have been guerrillas fighting for the United States?'

"'Oh, but sar, the Japanese send us out to catch feesh for them. We catch beeg feesh and leetle feesh. We throw the beeg feesh back or hide them—we sell only the leetle feesh to the Japanese.'

"These two-faced sonsabitches had really made a good thing of it. They'd made a good living during the war by selling fish to the Jap quartermaster. Then these Filipino senators from that province get this guerrilla idea and jam the recognition through and I had to put out over three years' pay for everybody on their padded roster, plus 10 percent for overseas duty and the bastards never spent a night away from their stinking barrio.

"That added up to over nineteen thousand dollars for the presidente as a light colonel, and I imagine that after splitting with the senators he holds on to six thousand dollars—oh sure, the whole deal was rigged. 'You vote for recognizing my guerrillas and I'll vote for recognizing yours.' And then to the presidente—'You organize your barrio into a guerrilla battalion, you get paid for three years' service, and I get two-thirds of the payroll.' And then to the gullible or frightened Americans in AFWESPAC, 'We want this heroic guerrilla battalion recognized and paid for three years of perilous service without investigation or question.'

"So those people don't catch fish any more—the conniving bastards are independently wealthy."

I talked over some of these guerrilla problems with officers of the AFWESPAC staff and was told that I was fruitlessly fighting the inevitable rape of the treasury. Our liberal, left-wing, Democratic politicians had the starry-eyed view that if the notorious wealth of our American citizens were distributed among the Filipinos lavishly enough they would love us. And how to spread a few million or billion? Of course, pay all Filipinos for three years of combat as guerrillas. Then they would be sure to love us.

Stupid politicos. The Flips had never loved us, not even when we liberated them from Spain in 1898, nor in the subsequent eight-year insurrection, and they sure didn't love us now.

But it was clearly my disagreeable duty to distribute the wealth.[1]

Notable Units

The most notable units with their unforgettable characteristics were the following:

Anderson Battalion	Capable field soldiers and Jap hunters.
Second Provisional Regiment	Impressive appearance—very soldierly.
Forty-fourth Hunters Regiment	Old Army customs and hospitality.
Eighty-seventh Squadron	Jolly cutthroats.
Eleventh Regiment	Mutinous.
Bulucan Regiment	Leaders in filth, laziness, and larceny.
Thirty-first Regiment	Politicians and gangsters. Dangerous.
Regimiento Corps de Monte	Banditry, murder, assassinations.

I wish to emphasize that all of the guerrilla units possessed all of the above characteristics to a greater or lesser degree—the units cited were just the most notable.

On November 9, I was honored by a visit from Colonel Tereso de Pia of the Forty-fourth Hunters, who talked Filipino politics for an hour. The

Philippines were to have elections in April 1946 in preparation for their independence, which they would receive on July 4.

Colonel Pia distrusted the honesty of the elections and felt that there would be much trouble between the Manila politicians, the wealthy landlords, the people of the provinces, and bandits. There were too many weapons at large in the Philippines, too many bandits. This I could understand. But I could not understand his firm stand against independence. Filipinos had been wanting independence since we liberated (stole) them from the Spaniards in 1898.

"What weel become of us when the United States leaves us? There weel be mooch trouble."

Come to think of it he was probably right. The islands would be reminiscent of China under the warlords, a vicious four-cornered melee between the elected Manila government with the army, the landlords with their hired gangs, the provincial governors and their militia, a possible uprising by the armed peasantry, coups d'état by ex-guerrilla groups (such as Pia's regiment), all well seasoned with bandits, thieves, and tribal or inter-village feuds. But Filipino politics were outside of my sphere of knowledge, responsibility, or action, and I told Pia so.

"But what weel the American Army do when the trouble begins?"

"I expect that we will be neutral and do nothing. After you are independent, what you do among yourselves is your own affair, and we would have no right to interfere. Our army will probably continue to leave your country as fast as ships and planes are available."

He seemed quite disappointed and discouraged by my answer. He'd evidently hoped that I had inside information that we would take an active part—on his side. But what his side would be I still had no idea—provincial warlord?

I then disapproved his request for rifle and pistol ammunition to help him through the trouble and accepted his invitation to witness a formal guard mount in his camp on November 15 in honor of the birth of the Philippine Commonwealth. He suggested as an afterthought that I might also bring the 342d Infantry band to provide the music.

For the birth of the Philippine Commonwealth, Colonel Holt and I formed convoy with the band and drove to the village of Norzaguray where Pia's Forty-fourth Hunters were camped. Colonel Pia met and escorted us through his camp, which as guerrilla camps went was in excellent shape. Training in weapons and close order drill was being conducted throughout the area. Since this was a Commonwealth holiday the training was, of course, purely eyewash to impress us. It did.

The formal guard mount went off well. The men were clean and sharp-looking, their 1903 Springfields were in excellent condition, and their precision perfect. Holt and I complimented and thanked Colonel Pia and started to take our leave.

"Oh no, coronel. We have the Retreat parade in one hour. You must see the Retreat."

We saw the Retreat, and a well done ceremony it was. I was again impressed by the superior performance of the Filipinos in close order drill. It takes weeks for some American soldiers to learn to keep step and some never get it. But all Filipinos seem to be born with that coordination, probably the result of thousands of years of survival. Those who were not physically fit, agile, and well coordinated simply did not survive their intertribal wars and headhunting games to have descendants.

At "officers front and center" I was surprised and pleased—no, overcome—when two lieutenants came forward and presented me with a Japanese naval samurai sword and a rising sun flag, while the others grinned from ear to ear.

Pia later told me that this was the first sword captured by his unit. He pointed out that the navy used the shorter swords, due to the restricted quarters and bulkhead openings of ships. Appropriate to sea-going tradition, the sharkskin hilt was decorated with golden fish and seashell charms. When the hilt was removed to expose the tang, the name of the maker was found to be Kayuza and the date was 1800.

Army officers should never receive presents from their subordinates. But that is a custom that I was required to break repeatedly in dealing with these people. Filipinos are Orientals. In giving a present they hope to make a friend (or obtain a favor). Refuse their present and you announce yourself as not a friend. And I had enough enemies to deal with already.

After the Retreat parade once more we said adieu.

"We thank you very much, Colonel Pia. You have a fine regiment. Now we must—"

"But sir, won't you have a drink with us at our club? Our officers would be most pleased."

So we moved to the club, which was established in the Town Hall, where the officers, a few wives, and many of the local beauties were assembled. Colonel and Senora Pia headed the reception line in Old Army fashion. Holt, myself, and a trio of his staff with their wives in the line, the rest passing by with bows, curtsies, handshakes, and names. The officers then gathered in clusters on the bar side of the hall, drank Scotch, and talked power politics; the ladies formed groups on the opposite side, sipped Coca-Cola, tittered, twittered, and waved fans.

The women were all in the mestiza costume, bodices of stiff gauze with high-shouldered sleeves, long flowing skirts in bright colors, with gold or mother-of-pearl ornamentation here and there, all topped by typically Spanish combs. They were uniformly doll-sized, pretty as pictures, shy as a harem suddenly exposed to a guided tour, and colorful as a swarm of butterflies. All seemed to speak elementary English but burst into rapid-fire Tagalog when they really had anything to say. Several of the ladies made commendable attempts to talk to me but I simply could not register their soft voices. I could barely understand the men—it was impossible to understand the women. So Colonel Holt had to carry on the conversation with the girls for the American side and carried out his duties with his customary efficiency and unusual enthusiasm.

Mrs. Francisco, an accomplished pianist, played for an hour, sometimes accompanying an equally gifted quartet who sang in English, Tagalog, and Spanish. When the concert ended we again tried to leave but once more we had underestimated Filipino hospitality.

"But coronel, we will be very unhappy if you do not stay for dinner. We have already made the preparations for you."

By that time we didn't want to make anyone unhappy so we stayed. We dined in such state as was never seen in the U.S. Army, the White House, or Buckingham Palace—served by a staff of lieutenants who were directed by a finger-snapping and hissing major.

The menu was magnificent. The bouillon was followed by fish that Colonel Pia said were trapped, kept in small pens, and fattened for two weeks. Next came a leisurely succession of courses, tamales stuffed with vegetables and meat, chicken chow mein, roast chicken, and roast suckling pig. The dinner was topped off with papaya and brandy, and a memorable dinner it was.

The ladies withdrew in consonance with Victorian custom, leaving the men to their cigars, cigarillos, cigarettes, and more brandy. After an hour of brandy, Jap-killing yarns, and Filipino political aspirations, we sought once more to take our leave.

"But coronel, now we have the dance, and the ladies would be—"

So we stayed, of course.

The party moved to a large barnlike building that was illuminated by a Coleman gasoline lantern, a carbide lantern, and dozens of small Tiki torches improvised from beer cans filled with kerosene and fitted with cloth wicks. Walls and rafters were draped with colored paper ribbons in a carefree way that would horrify an American fire marshal. Pia led us to our places on the balcony at the end (aha, it was the theater, not a barn) where tables were set up for his guests and staff. The hoi polloi stood or sat around the sides of the theater where the chairs had been moved from the floor. The orchestra, a piano and several stringed instruments, occupied the low stage.

The dancing alternated between American-style and schottisches, minuets, and many-coupled figure dances that I had never seen before. One formal figure dance, with ten couples on each side of the square, lasted twenty-five minutes. It occurred to me that these dances had probably not changed since they were imported from Spain in the sixteenth century. Dignified, courtly, with precise sweeping movements, they were a magnificent show.

I excused myself from dancing because I doubted if my limping 220-pound performance in combat boots would be any pleasure for my hostesses who in high heels stood about as tall as my shirt pocket. But while I made the rounds trying to talk to the ladies, my capable executive gracefully represented the American Army on the ballroom floor.

At midnight, slightly apprehensive about what he would suggest next, we took leave of Colonel Pia and our hostess. Both of our drivers appeared to be very well fed but fairly sober, so we checked our guns, formed convoy, and returned to our camp as though to another world.

In late November, I received several complaints from the presidente of Norzagaray that troops of the Forty-fourth were stealing, annoying the local women, and beating or terrorizing the men of the town and surrounding barrios when they attempted to defend their women or property.

Colonel Pia's story was quite different. He claimed that Norzagaray was a hotbed of thieves and bandits. His sentries and anti-Jap patrols were frequently ambushed or sniped by bandits or wild guerrillas who must be from the town or barrios. Pia believed that the presence of the Forty-fourth curbed the potential violence and banditry in the area, but for the safety and happiness of his men he would like to move to another location.

There was probably a good deal of truth in both stories; at least both sides were having people hurt and sometimes killed. Something had to be done.

The Batute Battalion was camped in a thinly populated area and was on excellent terms with the civilians in the neighborhood. Since both the Hunters and Batutes were Tagalog and the Batutes would probably act as a catalyst between the Hunters and the Tagalog civilians, moving the Hunters to this area seemed a good idea. Pia approved and the move was made.

The S-2 reports immediately indicated an increased level of skulduggery in the Norzagaray area, so Colonel Pia's story was evidently the right one after all.[2] Pia presented me with two boxes of Alhambra cigars with his thanks for moving his regiment from the dangerous neighborhood. And he would like to have fifty thousand rounds of .30 caliber.

Yes, I took the bribe and placed the cigars in the guest drawer of my desk, along with the gift cigarettes and bottles of "Four Feathers" that I used for the entertainment of visiting guerrillas.

"Sorry, Colonel Pia—no ammunition."

Major Cabo Chan who commanded the second battalion of the Eighty-seventh Squadron (note the weird nomenclature) invited me to dinner at their camp on January 4. I shuddered at the thought, since it had taken ten days and the best efforts of the surgeon and his wonder drugs to get me over the effects of the Forty-fourth Hunters party. Again, however, I sacrificed my stomach on the altar of my country and accepted.

It was a wonderful party but to say so is a redundance. All Filipino parties are wonderful. The guests included General Peralta, Colonel Anderson (who formed and fought the Eighty-seventh), my old friend Colonel Pia of the Forty-fourth, and the Honorable Nolasco, the mayor of Manila.

One of Chan's young captains entertained me with a story of how they had captured a patrol of four Japanese in the early days of their organization.

Having four Japanese prisoners on hand presented quite a problem. They couldn't keep them, and they couldn't kill and bury them because the area was alive with Japanese search parties and any recently excavated area would be investigated. Release them? Unthinkable. Incinerate them? No—bones, teeth, and buttons won't burn.

Then a former employee of the Rizal cement plant proposed the ultimate solution.

The plant was working three shifts, turning out cement for the construction of Japanese blockhouses. The ovens were burning limestone around the clock; the immense cylinders, loaded with stone and fifty-pound iron balls, rotated, rattled and clanked about their horizontal axes, crushing and grinding the roasted limestone into powdered cement.

"We jus' put thee Japs een thee next load of limestone—shoes, clothes, everytheeng—and turn eet four-five hours. No blood—no color—no notheeng. One load veree fine cement for Japanese blockhouse." And the small captain grinned reminiscently, a gold-toothed ivory smiling Buddha. Damned savages.

After the first shock of visualizing four Japs scrambling in the tumbling total blackness, trying to stay on top of ten or twelve tons of sliding stone and smashing iron balls, I had to admit that it was a morbidly amusing, very effective, efficient, and final means of disposing of embarrassing bodies, bones, teeth, and brass buttons and belt buckles.

Following the dinner Major Chan presented me with a Japanese sword that his battalion had captured in Bulucan and a letter that the adjutant read describing the skirmish.

The Thirty-first Infantry Regiment, organized and commanded by the self-commissioned Colonel Capobre, was not recognized by the Philippine government and occupied a position at the bottom of my list with other bandit units.

On January 2, 1946, however, Colonel Capobre and a dozen of his senior officers called on me with a long and impassioned plea for my assistance in achieving their recognition. Capobre, an Al Capone type in physique, morals, and actions, had jumped on the guerrilla bandwagon immediately after the Japanese surrender in the Philippines and had organized a goodly number of the Manila underworld into a regiment.

Due to unusual stupidity, naiveté, or venality on the part of some American supply personnel he had been well supplied with arms, uniforms, and other equipment, including thirty-four trucks. He was now demanding full recognition by the Philippine and American governments with full back pay for three years plus 10 percent for overseas duty.

He also requested quantities of ammunition of all types and gasoline for his outsized motor pool in order that the Thirty-first Infantry could be a stabilizing influence during the "troubles" of the elections to be held in April. I agreed that his regiment could well be a stabilizing force in Manila and that I would see what I could do in the matter.

It's very corrosive to the character, dealing with Orientals. I was learning to be silent, suave, sympathetic, evasive, courteous, and noncommittal—and remain as unpinnable as a drop of mercury. So I sent him on his way with hope, enough hope so I could entice him into a position where I could disarm his thugs en masse.

A very mild, unobtrusive, and unsoldierly young lieutenant called on me very early the next morning while I was convalescing from the effects of the Eighty-seventh Squadron's orgy. He identified himself as a member of the CID and presented me with some disturbing news.

He stated that a black market ring of American ordnance corps men had delivered 64,000 rounds of .30 caliber rifle machine-gun ammunition to the Thirty-first Infantry Regiment at 0100 this morning and that Colonel Capobre had personally paid them 12,000 pesos for it. The CID, warned of the transaction by their undercover man in the ring, had let the deal, delivery, and payment go through as planned in order to have a firm case before arresting the gang. But the guerrillas could not be allowed to keep the loot. Obviously not. The shy young officer, having dumped this can of worms on my plate, oozed unobtrusively out of the picture and left me to cope with it.

I thought of several methods of approach. They ranged from bad to worse. If I or the guerrilla affairs officer went to Capobre and requested the ammunition we would get a derisive denial that he had it, or worse, a defiant "No! You can't take it." If I brought a force to search the camp Capobre would probably resist and a lot of people might get hurt.

Aha. A better idea, a combination of Oriental duplicity and overwhelming force. Like attracting a fly (or rather a hornet) with sugar and hitting him with a sledgehammer.

I had some telephone conversations with Colonel Ward of the third battalion and the CO of our attached tank battalion.

Then I sent a radio message to Colonel Capobre directing him, his executive, and his battalion commanders to report to my office at 1100 to discuss the latest development about the recognition of his unit.

Capobre arrived on time, in an unusually arrogant mood, which was reflected in the attitude of his accompanying officers. After the mutually insincere felicitations I provided coffee and some of Colonel Pia's excellent cigars and regretfully informed the group that in spite of my most diligent efforts I was making no progress in achieving their recognition as a guerrilla unit.

That statement was like currying the fetlocks of a hock-shy mule. I need say no more—Capobre and Company took up the conversation from that point on. After forty minutes of Filipino and American politics, and pleas and demands for assistance for these postwar warriors, my communications officer interrupted by delivering a radio message he had just received. I read the message and closed the discussion on guerrilla recognition.

"All right, Colonel Capobre, I shall continue to give your requests every appropriate (and that's a weasel word) consideration. And now I'd like to take up another matter.

"Last night a criminal gang in the American ordnance depot delivered 64,000 rounds of .30 caliber ammunition to a dissident group of your regiment. Your supply officer, a Major Alvares, who is said to be the leader of the gang, received it. Some of the Americans heard talk that Alvares is going to be the next regimental commander after he has gotten rid of you and your senior commanders. That is the real reason I asked you over here, for your own protection while my people recovered the ammunition, and—"

Capobre burst out of his chair, arms waving.

"That ees eempossible! Who told you thees? We have no ammunition—not one cartridge." He was displaying an interesting mixture of anger and apprehension, turning plum-colored and sweating at the same time. He'd make a losing poker player.

"Take it easy colonel. I realize that you know nothing about this matter—neither you nor your loyal commanders. But I assure you that the Americans who delivered it have all been arrested and have confessed. The delivery was made at your camp at 0100 this morning and 12,000 pesos were paid—"

"But I was een thee camp last night. I heard nothing of eet. I do not believe eet."

Capobre and his four compatriots were all standing, uniformly purple with rage, and obviously contemplating murder—mine.

"Of course you knew nothing of it but it's quite true, I assure you. But there's nothing to worry about now—this message from Colonel Ward states that he has recovered the ammunition.

"So now I suggest that you can return safely to your command. I'm sure that you can deal with the mutineers without further protection. Good-bye gentlemen, please call on me if I can be of any further assistance in this matter."

That six-thousand-dollar loss must have hurt them badly. The combined glares as they left would have raised blisters on a coconut.

Colonel Ward dropped in an hour later to report on the results of the raid. With the light tank company as advance guard the third battalion had rolled past the Thirty-first outpost and into the center of camp at twenty miles an hour and were looting the storage tents and magazine hut before the stunned guerrillas got their gaping mouths closed.

They found the 64,000 rounds in question neatly stacked exactly where the undercover man had helped unload the cargo. In the confusion of reloading it into our trucks a good many additional cases of ammunition, crates of mortar bombs, and a goodly number of rifles, pistols, machine guns, and mortars were taken. In fact a clean sweep of Capobre's war chest had been made by the licentious, looting American soldiery.

While driving to the area of the Second Provisionals, I saw three men on the road ahead who appeared to be armed. Corporal Gai speeded up, braked to a skidding halt, and manned his carbine. One of the men was armed with a 1903 Springfield; his companions carried bolos and fish spears. I asked the man with the rifle who they were.

"We are soldiers of the Regimiento Corps de Monte." This was an unrecognized unit that I had not visited yet but had a reputation of banditry.

"Why are you carrying a rifle outside of your camp?"

"We go to fish. I carry the rifle against the Japanese."

There were no fish to be speared within a long day's walk so I was skeptical. These characters were more likely looking for a chance to get more rifles and we were certainly lucky to have spotted them at a point that was bare of cover.

"There are no Japanese around here and you do not need the rifle. I will take your rifle." Gai and his carbine persuaded the fellow that I was right. "And your bandoleer. Now tell your captain that the American commander of this area has taken your rifle because you had it outside of your camp. I will tell your colonel also when I visit him."

Bolos and fish spears are tools rather than weapons, so I let his buddies keep them, but I had to have that rifle. Too many people were getting killed in that neighborhood.[3]

Seven

Twenty-first Replacement Depot

At last I received orders to take over the Twenty-first Replacement Depot as a processing area where I could assemble, disarm, pay off, and discharge my nine thousand guerrilla wards of Uncle Sam. F Company under the command of the very capable and reliable Lieutenant Buergin was the logical unit to run the depot and I moved the guerrilla affairs staff in with them to take care of the pay and discharges.

The depot was large enough to accommodate an understrength division, with framed and floored tents, prefabricated offices, battalion-sized kitchens and mess halls, showers, and latrines. Canvas cots and kitchen equipment including gasoline ranges were in store, ready for issue. The camp was surrounded by rolls of concertina barbed wire in a deep ditch barrier to discourage the infiltration of thieves and the illegal exit of motor vehicles.

A week was spent to make the move, check the property, become oriented to the job, and prepare to receive the customers. When Buergin reported that he was ready I ordered three units in to the depot and quartered them in adjoining areas near the administrative offices.

That was a gross mistake, a mistake of exactly the same type and degree as assigning units of Arabs and Israelis, Irish and Ulstermen, or Germans and Russians to adjacent camp areas. The Tagalog, Igorot, and Illocano units not only were from different provinces but also were of different races, spoke different languages, and their fathers had been mortal enemies for ages past.

The first order of business had been taking in all weapons for as many as they would admit having, then searching for weapons they had concealed in their personal plunder, personal caches when indicated, and a constant search for weapons that were buried or hidden anywhere in the unoccupied portions of the depot. And a cached or buried pistol or hand grenade is hard to find. So the peace of the tropic nights was broken occasionally by the bark of pistol, the blast of grenade, or the rattle of an M-3 submachine gun.

The casualty rate was never high and there were no mass or unit confrontations due to the efficiency of Lieutenant Buergin and the cooperation of the unit commanders, but it was constant. A dozen men were killed in the two weeks required to clear these units and a dozen more hospitalized with serious wounds.

General Anderson offered us a battalion of Philippine Scouts to assist in preserving order at the depot and I was delighted to accept their services. Major Dulnuan, the battalion commander, was a dark, muscular, grim-countenanced Old Scout who proved to be a very competent officer. I gave him a briefing on the situation and made him responsible for preserving order in the camp—in brief he became the provost marshal of the depot while Buergin concentrated his efforts on the administrative aspects of the job. I assumed the overall command since I did not want to reduce Buergin's status and Major Dulnuan could not be subordinated to Buergin.

The effect was excellent. The Scouts were absolutely loyal, well trained, and strictly controlled by Major Dulnuan's iron hand. They looked on all guerrilla units with a cold, nonpartisan, impartial contempt. I used them not only for interior guard duty between the various guerrilla camps but also to patrol the night spots and markets in the nearby villages where trouble often started.

The Scouts were particularly appreciated when two guerrilla units, the Eleventh and Forty-first, showed signs of mutiny for more pay. The commanders were regretful and tactful about it; they merely stated that unless pay was granted for a longer period they could not control their men and there would be much trouble and destruction of property.

I called the tank battalion commander immediately and asked him to loan us a platoon for a few days to help keep our mutinous friends in line. I directed the S-3 to report to Major Dulnuan, brief him on the situation, and request him to have a company of Scouts prepared to take part in infantry-tank training in the vicinity of the Eleventh and Forty-first camps to quiet their potential unrest.[1]

When the tanks arrived Major Dulnuan reported to me with a Scout company and I introduced the tanker lieutenant who was to operate under his command. The major then asked what the operation was to be. Since I knew that he had gotten all details from the operations officer I made a serious mistake. I gave him a poker-faced wink.

"I'm attaching the tank platoon to your battalion so that you can give them and your men some very interesting combined infantry-tank training. Use the central parade ground and the areas around the Eleventh and Forty-first camps. I'm sure it will be of benefit to both the tankers and the Scouts and very instructive to the guerrilla regiments."

"But colonel," he said, with his eyes filling up and about to overflow, "please do not treat me as a child, I am weeth you een thees theeng." He had evidently been looking forward to a battle or massacre.

"Of course you are, Major Dulnuan," I rejoined hastily. "You are responsible for keeping order in the depot. The operations officer has given you the situation and this so-called training is to show your men and the guerrillas that the tankers are with you in this thing. You will have a platoon of tanks under your command, or a company if necessary, until the Eleventh and Forty-first are discharged. I believe that with you in charge there will be no trouble. If there is trouble I am sure that you can take care of it. When I spoke of infantry-tank training I was merely indicating what you can tell your men."

That speech evidently repaired all the damage I had inadvertently done to his pride. He swelled up five feet five inches tall, grinned, and replied brightly, "Oh yis sar, but my men, I tell them notheeng."

This was my first experience with the extreme sensitivity and absolute loyalty that was so characteristic of the Philippine Scouts. During the next two years I made frequent mistakes in dealing with these men of alien cultures but tried to make no mistake more than once. At the end of my tour I began to feel that I knew a little—a very little—about the Scouts.

The Eleventh and Forty-first had apparently given up their idea of mutiny for more pay. But one day a north wind was blowing from the Forty-first camp toward the Bulucans. It was too strong a temptation for the fun-loving, high-spirited arsonists of the Forty-first. The grass was tall and dry. A few matches, and a solid wall of flame moved steadily toward their old foes. They would not only scorch a few Bulucans; they would burn a hell of a lot of American property.

The Scout sentries were on the job. They turned out the guard and prompt backfiring soon reduced the threat of vast property damage to a mere smoke nuisance. The dust churned up in and around and through the Forty-first camp by the subsequent realistic infantry-tank training by Major Dulnuan's heroes more than compensated for the smoke and the Forty-first settled down again for a little while.

The Scout battalion proved useful on another occasion, when the CID reported that a gang of bandits had framed a plot to raid the finance building in Manila about February 16 and make off with the contents of the Philippine Treasury. It was an ambitious but quite feasible plan, provided enough force was used.

E Company of the 342d was, of course, already on guard there and even though they were at half strength they were probably capable of holding the place. But since the raid was reported to be planned as a full-scale military attack in probably a light battalion strength I did not want to take any chances.

I moved one company of Scouts into the area by night, doubled all guard posts, and provided supports at the vital points to counter the raiders' reported plan. Major Dulnuan held another company alerted to entruck and move rapidly to the scene as soon as the action started.

In spite of our precautions our trap was detected, probably by an inside man among the treasury employees. At any rate the CID member of the gang reported that they had dropped the idea. That was unfortunate. Had the raid been made, there would have been a hundred or more bandits less to terrorize Manila.

Aside from the hot-blooded murder and mayhem there were numerous aspects to this irregular warfare, most of which appeared to be intended merely as good clean fun. They booby-trapped the seats in their neighbors' latrines until no one had the courage to venture there after dark. Even in broad daylight it became customary to raise the lid of a seat c-a-u-t-i-o-u-s-l-y, looking for the concealed trigger string and listening for the "pop" of the grenade igniter. During this careful investigation all those who had previously checked their own seats and were comfortably at work would lean forward in a strained, apprehensive silence like runners on the starting mark. And if a door was slammed or a truck backfired at that critical moment, a stampede of panicked, partially clad heroes would jam the exits.

Even after they had been satisfactorily disarmed, our guerrilla friends continued to engage in an amusing sport called "making Moros." To play this game a dozen Bontocs, for example, would lie in wait by a road or path at night until two or three men approached speaking Tagalog or Illocano. These unfortunates would be overpowered and then circumcised, slowly, with a dull mess kit knife. The big joke was, of course, that the Mohammedan religion of the Moros required circumcision and performing this operation on a Christian Filipino "made him a Moro." The dull knife was preferred to ensure that the full-throated whoops and screams of the victims were turned up to full blood-chilling volume during their conversion.

After this experience we quartered all units with as much space as possible between them, placing them in the extreme corners of the depot. We also required that each unit maintain a club-armed perimeter guard to discourage intruders, but this precaution was naturally completely ineffective. The guards had to operate in pairs or patrols, and forced conversion to Islam remained an occupational hazard of guard duty at night.

The concentration of guerrillas at the depot continued to provide a never-ending source of entertainment. One night about midnight my phone buzzed.

"Sergeant Martin, F Company, colonel. The lieutenant would like to get some help here, sir. A gang of Gooks is stealing our mess hall. There's a lot of 'em and we don't have enough to run 'em off. We'd like to have another platoon—"

"Wait a minute, sergeant, I don't want to get anybody killed over a few groceries—" I could hear the distant tapping and rattling of small-arms fire in the background.

"Few groceries, hell!" exploded the fiery sergeant. "There's at least three truckloads of 'em and they're stealing our mess hall and kitchen."

Then I got the picture. Salvaged corrugated iron roofing was going like hot cakes for five dollars (Philippines) a sheet in the Manila markets. Having stolen all the sheet iron that could be looted from other locations this gang, well equipped with small arms, trucks, and crowbars, had bridged the barrier trench. They had then driven off the guard and put out a defensive perimeter while the rest of the gang was prying loose sheet iron and loading it on the trucks.

The battle didn't last long. It apparently ended about the time the regimental officer of the guard and his two off-duty reliefs roared off to the rescue. By the time the reinforcements got there Lieutenant Buergin had already gathered in the fruits of victory, a 2½-ton U.S. Army truck half loaded with sheet iron, four M-1 rifles, and one dead and two crippled gangsters who were identified as being former members of Colonel Capobre's Thirty-first Infantry Regiment.

The Bulucans

As long as the guerrillas had been camped in the countryside I had never insisted on American standards of camp sanitation. When they were brought into the Twenty-first Depot, however, I insisted that they use the latrines and garbage pits properly and keep their camps well drained and clear of rubbish. They had done reasonably well, initially, although they were obviously obeying the orders merely to humor these superstitious Americans. Who could be so stupid as to believe that flies and mosquitoes would make them sick?

There had been increasing dissatisfaction over the pay scale for guerrillas. Officers were paid at the American rate, why should the lower ranks be paid on the 50 percent scale of the Scouts and Philippine Army? Also there was the matter of time credit for service. Some men in some units were given back pay to the date of the American surrender, three and a half years. Then the whole unit should get the same credit for service. There had been no fighting to mention until the Americans had landed in 1944. After all, a man who had enlisted in October 1944 had seen just as much combat as a guerrilla who had been merely running and hiding from the Japs since 1942.

But what could they do about these obvious injustices? Of course the Tagalogs had the answer. They would strike. And how would a strike bring the Americans to reason? We will hit the Americans at their most sensitive point. We will refuse to keep the camp clean; we will live as we do at home. That will do it.

I noted quite a change in the depot during my next inspection. Paper and rags littered the area. Garbage had been dumped indiscriminately around the kitchens and the company streets. Piles of filth around the tents indicated that the latrines were no longer in use. Clouds of delighted, high-living flies buzzed about the debris.

I called a meeting of the half dozen commanders. They one and all were distressed by the attitude of the men they were supposed to command.

"Yis sar, we have forgot to have our men police this morning."

"You must have forgotten to have them police for at least three days. I can tell by counting the piles of dung outside your tent doors."

"Yis sar, we will tell them."

"I don't care what you tell them or whether you tell them anything. I want this depot fit to live in. And you are responsible to me to see that it is. Either you get your men to do it—I don't care how—or you and your officers had better pick up your shovels and start doing some useful work."

I had to soften my tone because four of my "regimental commanders" were showing signs of breaking into tears.

"So you say you forgot. OK, I will believe you. Now I am going to forget and you had better believe me. I will forget to deliver rations to the dirtiest unit in the depot. I will forget and I will not remember until I can walk through your camps with clean boots and breathe without smelling your stink."

"But sar," Colonel Guzman protested, "eef we are too hard on the men I fear that there weel be trouble and many properties weel be destroyed."

"That's quite all right. If trouble is started we will end it quickly and you or your men will have money deducted from your pay for all the property that is destroyed. That is all, gentlemen."

Next morning I inspected Colonel Villanueva's Rizal Regiment, which had been the filthiest the day before. I found him voluble with promises, most of his men asleep, the piles of excrement more widely distributed, and nothing done. I made no comment; none was necessary. I simply left him and telephoned Lieutenant Maynard.

An hour later two trucks filled with Japanese and their guards rolled up to the Rizal storeroom and emptied it of all rations. They also took everything from the battalion kitchens. It was just like stirring an ant nest. The cooks yelled, the officers protested, the sleeping camp awoke and ganged around, howling and threatening. The Japs worked on with calm disregard of the resulting hysteria and I suspect enjoying it. By an arranged coincidence the tank platoon howled into the vicinity, tanks loaded with Scouts, and Major Dulnuan following up with two companies of Scouts deployed.

Lieutenant Buergin mounted a truck and made a speech, which was given a running translation by one of the Rizal officers. It was short and pointed.

"We have taken your food. There are four things you can do.

1. You can go back to sleep. Then you will need no food.
2. You can leave camp. Then you will be dropped from the rolls for desertion.
3. You can make trouble. If your officers cannot control you, we will.
4. You can work. After you have finished, you can eat."

Then the trucks, guards, Japs, and rations rolled away. Major Dulnuan took his Scouts and tanks off for more training, and I left Colonel Villanueva and his hoodlums with it.

At some time in the afternoon, work must have been started on an unprecedented scale, but too late. Colonel Villanueva called on me at my quarters at 2200 but since I had other problems that were pressing I told him that I could give him no time then—I would call on him in the morning.

Next morning I visited Buergin and found him grimly delighted.

"The ration squeeze did the trick, colonel. These bastards were shoveling dung and digging new garbage pits by lantern light."

We went over to see Villanueva, whom we found to be in an anxious and Christianized state of mind. His area was, indeed, groomed, and his men were still hard at it. I noticed that while they didn't look happy about it they certainly appeared to be bright-eyed and alert. Missing a couple of meals had evidently done them a lot of good. I was delighted to be able to order the ration truck to make a delivery before noon.

After my tour of the Rizal camp I ordered another meeting of unit commanders.

"Good morning, gentlemen. I will make another inspection of your commands tomorrow, starting at 1300. Beginning with supper, the dirtiest unit in the depot will start missing meals until they are in satisfactory condition. If you are in doubt about what I mean by satisfactory I suggest you call in Colonel Villanueva and ask permission to look over his area. The Rizal Regiment has done a magnificent job and I am sure that Colonel Villanueva will be happy to help you with his advice."

Villanueva blushed a rich purple with uncertain pride while the others merely looked uncertain.

As I left the depot an hour later I noted that men were turning out unhappily in several of the camps, armed with picks, shovels, and machetes.

Next day I found the Folsoms to be improved but still a pigsty. The Eleventh was worse. But the Bulucans won the contest by a full length. They were worthless, unlikable, untrustworthy, and filthy. They stole from the neighboring villages, other units, their own supply rooms, and each other. Today, two days before the weekly ration issue, Colonel

Guzman complained that his storerooms had been robbed and that they were out of food.

"I've no doubt you are out of food, Colonel Guzman. Your men steal or bribe food from your storerooms. Your guards probably get the most of it. Then they trade the stuff to the civilians for women or liquor."

"But colonel, my men are starving."

"Quite possibly, but you were issued your full ration and I can't help you further."

As we walked through his camp I noticed a very plump, smooth, well-filled sack under a cot. I went in, picked it up, and took it to the entrance.

"Why, colonel," I said as I untied the sack, "this might be some of the food you say was stolen." I emptied it on the dung-covered ground at the entrance. "Amazing. It's flour—U.S. issue flour. And how does it happen to be under a cot in this tent? Have it swept up at once and put in your garbage pit. Who took it from your stores? Investigate and take action against the thief."

This little play was repeated several times during our walk-through, with hoarded cakes of rice, beans, flour, coffee, and bacon being uncovered and dumped on the filthy ground for inspection. Guzman was silently glum and his thugs glared purple murder.

I commented caustically when I found that a kitchen crew had been using one end of their battalion mess hall as a latrine. But I found that the cooks of the next battalion had a better solution; they used their walk-in refrigerator. This use of the refrigerator had several obvious advantages: it was close to their work, it was out of sight, flies couldn't get to it, the smell was locked in, and the excrement could be walked on by bare feet with impunity after it had frozen. I had suddenly had enough.

"Good, Colonel Guzman. I notice that there has been a little improvement in your housekeeping, but your regiment unfortunately is still the dirtiest in the depot. Please let me know when you have your camp ready for inspection." Since his storerooms were already empty there was no need for a detail of Japs to take up his supplies.

On driving through the first village after leaving the depot I noted an open-air market in a side street and drove by to look it over. It was conducted by a number of Filipinos in partial uniform who looked suspiciously like some of my heroic guerrillas. They were doing a thriving business in dry rations, canned goods, cigarettes, cots, and blankets with the local civilians.

I returned to camp and asked Major Dulnuan to bring a squad of his Scouts. He readily identified the proprietors of the market stalls as Bulucans and his men cheerily confiscated their goods. There was no point in arresting the men—they were acting by the direction or with the tacit consent of their commanders. The Filipino police would do nothing except confiscate the goods or demand a cut of the profits. And I was certainly not interested in putting them up for trial when the charges would certainly be disapproved for political reasons. But I was, by confiscating their loot, rapidly winning the title of Best Hated Bastard in Luzon.

Colonel Guzman visited me again next morning.

"My men earnestly wish to work on the camp but they are so weak from hunger that they cannot lift themselves from their beds. So I must ask you to deliver rations to us so that we can work."

"That is all right, Colonel Guzman. Don't worry about the camp. Your men can go on using the refrigerators and mess halls for latrines, since they won't be eating there. And in a few days without food they won't need to go to the refrigerators or mess halls at all. After your regiment is gone I'll have a company of Japs clean it up for you. Don't worry about it." And I smiled (although it hurt my face to do it) and patted his shoulder in a most friendly fashion as I firmly escorted him to the door.

I had anticipated a complete victory in not more than three days and looked forward to concentrating my efforts on the next unit. But I was completely baffled by the toughness and passive determination of the Bulucans.

On my next visit to the depot Guzman's heroes had had no rations for a week. Most of them were apparently sleeping all day and probably stealing all night. Or they might have been buying back some of the food they had previously sold to the civilians. At any rate cooking was going on in all of the kitchens.

Each kitchen was equipped with a battery of gasoline-fired field ranges. The white gasoline fuel was fed through a paper filter in order to prevent clogging the burners. These filters had to be changed daily for efficient operations. The F Company cooks had demonstrated the filter-changing and use of the ranges to every guerrilla unit on arrival and supervised their cooking until they thoroughly understood the operation.

But the Bulucans had discovered a much simpler method of using these sophisticated cooking fires. They removed the burner unit and threw it in the garbage pit. They piled wood in the bottom of the range, poured the gasoline over the wood, balled up a piece of paper, lit it, and threw it into the pyre. After the initial explosion they had a rousing fire for boiling their rice. Since firewood was not available they were chopping up the wooden frames of their cots for fuel. Losing the cots was no hardship for people who had slept on bamboo floors all their lives. The cots were not entirely wasted, however—the heavy canvas had been removed and cut up to make sandals and slippers.

These people were ingenious and in a way economical. They found that sections of canvas cut from a tent were good substitutes for the wool blankets they had sold, and much more comfortable in hot weather. And ten-inch slits cut in the middle converted them into very acceptable rain gear to replace the ponchos they had traded. Then, since the tent was gone, the poles, frame, and flooring were used to fire the kitchen ranges. Nothing was wasted.

It was now evident that the last two or three empty tents at the end of each row were being used as latrines. Apparently some of the more refined Bulucans were not squatting just outside their tent door to relieve themselves, they were using the empty tents next door.

I pointed this out to Colonel Guzman who did not seem to be shocked and told him that these tent floors must be cleaned up and scrubbed as well.

"Yis sar. I have told them. I weel tell them again."

Two days later Lieutenant Buergin called me.

"Colonel Guzman asks that you inspect the camp, sir. He says that everything will be completed by 1600 and he wants to draw rations for supper."

"What has his outfit done?"

"As far as I can see, not a damned thing outside of trying to steal from us and the Ifuagos. Two of 'em were shot by Dulnuan's Scouts last night."

"All right, I'll be there at 1600. Have a ration truck standing by for delivery."

I was eager to have the impasse settled, and intended to deliver the groceries at once if there was the slightest sign of an honest effort being made. In fact I arrived at the depot half an hour early, hoping to get the trouble resolved as soon as possible—acting the part of Simon Legree becomes wearing. Colonel Guzman was not at his headquarters but hurried up from his troop area to meet me. He appeared somewhat nervous.

Clouds of smoke indicated a broad series of fires at the far ends of the company streets, and I assumed that they were burning debris. At last we were making progress and I could order the ration truck up to unload. Maybe I wouldn't get court-martialed for cruel and unusual treatment after all.

We passed a battalion kitchen where the cooks were still hacking cot frames into usable stovewood lengths with their machetes. Turning into a company street I noted that the piles of dung about the tents were considerably thicker and the normal number of men were making slippers and ponchos out of U.S. government canvas. As we moved farther I became aware of the source of the fires—the two or three tent floors and frames at the end of each company street were burning briskly. The tents had been pulled off the frames and were being hacked up into poncho-sized strips. The Bulucan cleanup campaign was on in earnest.

I said nothing—the situation was beyond words. But as I turned back to Buergin's headquarters I was doing some progressive thinking.

With the units that had been processed earlier I had made attempts to charge the responsible individuals for the cost of arms, equipment, and vehicles that they claimed had been stolen—*after* they had established their status as guerrillas by their possession of the equipment. Letting them get away with hiding these sinews of war but for future use or sale was both costly and dangerous. But in every case I had found that "it is not the policy of this command at this time." Nothing must be done to irritate the Filipinos or they would not love us.

But this case of outright defiance and senseless destruction was so extreme that it required action. Physical action would not do. We couldn't have the Filipino politicians screaming about martyrs.

Then the situation became clear. The war was over. The U.S. Army was going to have hundreds of square miles of surplus tentage and tons of cots on hand, which would only rot in our warehouses for decades until it was destroyed as unserviceable. I was forbidden to charge the guerrillas for their own "lost or stolen" arms and equipment that had been issued to them, but nothing had been said about the depot equipment that was charged against me. So I would sell the Bulucans as much of the camp as they wanted to buy and I certainly wouldn't ask higher headquarters anything about it. And in the meantime I would continue saving the American taxpayers six hundred dollars a day in rations for the regiment.

So gathering my guerrilla administration staff in conference with Lieutenant Buergin, Major Dulnuan, and Colonel Guzman, I laid out the program.

"The payment and discharge of the Bulucan Regiment will be expedited and completed by noon Saturday. This is Thursday. That will probably call for some night work on your part. The regiment will be moved out of camp and formed on the parade ground by companies at 0700 Saturday to receive their pay and discharges.

"At 0700, Lieutenant Buergin, your supply officer and his crew will check tents, frames, cots, kitchen gear, and all other equipment that Colonel Guzman holds from you on memorandum receipts. You will consolidate a list of destroyed, damaged, and missing equipment. You will evaluate this equipment at the cost price and inform your finance officer of the total.

"The finance officer will calculate the percentage of the total regimental payroll that must be deducted to pay for the equipment. Each officer and man then be paid in full, less his pro rata share of the damage to depot equipment. The balance will be returned to finance with the payroll.

"Major Dulnuan will perform his normal duties as provost marshal, see that the camp area remains clear after 0700, maintain security of the payroll, preserve order as the men are paid, and escort them by truck convoys to their dispersal areas as they are paid off.

"Last, Colonel Guzman, please let me know when your regiment is ready for inspection so that I can start delivering rations again.

"Are there any questions?"

There were none. Lieutenant Buergin was his usual stern and non-committal self. The guerrilla administration staff was pale but resolute. Major Dulnuan appeared to be looking forward to Saturday morning with grim humor. Guzman was simply stunned. I had heard a couple of interesting rumors about him and his crew. First, he was planning to run for governor in Bulucan, using his gangsters with their cached arsenal to eliminate political opponents and otherwise favorably influence the election. Second, the regiment was going to join the Hukbalahap en masse. My planned curtailment of their pay would be very unsatisfactory to his mutinous heroes and his popularity and chances for election would probably be seriously jeopardized thereby. As for the regiment joining the Huks, no change there. They'd been Huks long before I had met them.

I left the meeting contemplating the early retirement that I would doubtless be urged to take as soon as the politicians, Filipino and American, got the news about this unhappy situation and my drastic solution.

Actually it went off very well. When the last truckload of lean, hungry, bright-eyed, vituperous heroes was escorted from the camp under Scout guard I found that we were turning forty-three thousand dollars back to the U.S. Treasury, undoubtedly the most profitable deal in surplus property ever made in the history of our army.

Bontocs, Philippine Army, Illocanos, Capobre Again

One regiment from the Bontoc hills caused me a good deal of concern with their perpetual bathing. They bathed morning, afternoon, and night. All showers were running twenty-four hours a day whether anyone was bathing or not, and the furnaces roared continuously, trying to keep up with the demand for hot water. During my first inspection after the arrival of the Bontocs, I mentioned it to the commander.

"Colonel Tabayan, I am delighted to see how clean your men are. But they should turn off the showers and laundry taps when they leave. We cannot afford to waste water and fuel like this."

"Oh yis sar. I tell them."

And the showers continued to run, full on, day and night.

I learned that these men were from a mountain province where the cool streams ran full the year around, a bountiful wealth of water without end. They simply could not comprehend that water had to be conserved or paid for. Alas, these were the first shower baths that they had ever seen, and such wonderful baths too. Simply by turning little wheels a man could be cooled, warmed, or scalded at will.

"Colonel Tabayan, I see that your men are still forgetting to turn off the water when they are through bathing. I suggest that you place a guard on every bathhouse to remind them."

"That ees a good idea, sar. I do that."

He did. Some of the sentries slept; others just wandered away. Most of them shed their clothes and bathed. And the water continued to run, day and night.

A very polite man from the City of Manila Water Works appeared at my office and regretfully but firmly stated that, due to the water going down in the reservoir so fast during the dry season, he would have to cut off the water for the depot unless we drastically reduced our abnormal rate of consumption. My thousand wild men from the Bontoc waterfall country were using almost as much water as Quezon City.

All else having failed, I called on Captain Stief and his motor maintenance crew. They firmly closed all water controls in the area except one faucet per battalion kitchen, one laundry tap, and one shower head per company, and firmly welded them in that position.

In early March three Philippine Army units, one regiment and two separate battalions, were ordered to the depot and assigned to me for training. They were to review some of their previously unsatisfactory basic training, to include firing weapons on the Eighty-sixth Division firing ranges. It was probable that my main problem would be safeguarding depot property and supplies.

The regimental commander was in arrest in quarters pending investigation of his stolen truck ring, and the supply officer of one of the battalions was in prison for his wholesale disposition of equipment that should have been issued to his unit. But such things were, of course, to be expected. I had previously borrowed a Philippine Army finance officer to help expedite the payment of guerrillas, and he was presently in prison for personally collecting "income taxes" from the pay of the enlisted men.

Shortly after these PA units had arrived we paid off and issued discharges to the Eleventh and Forty-first regiments, but they refused to leave the depot. It was a genuine sit-down strike. I had stopped the issue of rations but now they had money to buy food and were apparently determined to stay until they received what they considered to be full payment, three years' back pay for everyone down to the last recruit.

I had enough force to deal with the situation—Major Dulnuan's Scouts could make them frantic to leave in a very few minutes. But then we'd have a good many martyrs in the Manila hospital and the morgue. Unfortunately, it seemed the only solution.

I informed General Anderson of Philippine ground forces of the situation and pointed out that he should be prepared for unfavorable reaction from the politicians and press when I moved the mutineers bodily out of the depot.

Anderson countered neatly. "If your regiment or our Philippine Scouts move them out there's bound to be a hell of a stink. But what about those Philippine Army outfits you have for training? I'll make 'em available to you for tactical use as well. Why not have them clear the depot? Then any casualties will just be the result of a family brawl."

I was delighted to be shown such a practical way out of this unpleasant chore so I ordered the attached PA regiment to do the job. It was just like ordering a regiment of chickens to chase a brigade of rabbits out of a barnyard. They fixed bayonets fearfully, moved in timidly, and stopped uncertainly. Then they all milled around, both the PA and the guerrillas, in groups of various sizes, urging, defying, ordering, arguing, pleading, making speeches, and yelling at each other. In the meantime many of the more level-headed guerrillas were stealing everything that could be lifted and were loading the loot into the trucks that were standing by to take them away.

Finally, since the PA had made no progress from 0800 to 1400, I sent in a large gang of Japs who under heavy Scout guard unloaded the trucks of all material of American origin. The mutineers gave up, climbed aboard their trucks, and were driven off to their dispersal points under Scout escort. Major Dulnuan remarked that most of their shouting as they left was not fond farewells—it was threats that they were going to join the Huks and bury us. But after all, what were two thousand more bandits in the Philippines? There are one thousand islands. That's only two bandits per island, and there were already hundreds of bandits per island.

After a peaceful three weeks the Twenty-first Replacement Depot, now renamed Camp Blackjack, exploded with more violence.[2] The main gate guard, since most of the guerrillas had been discharged, had been reduced to two men, one American and one Philippine Army sentry. One night a truck with a number of Filipinos aboard drove up to the entrance and the PA sentry stepped out to check it. The men in the truck shot him eight times before he hit the ground. The American covering him with the machine gun dived for cover and shuddered behind his sandbags while the gangsters riddled his partner and drove away. Not one shot was fired from the machine gun. It was the most shameful exhibition of cowardice of my knowledge and drastically lowered American prestige in that part of the world. An attempt to court-martial the man on the charge of abandoning his post failed for the usual political reasons, and all that could be done was to transfer him to duty where his gutless behavior would not jeopardize his buddies.

The Philippine Army regiment was made up of Tagalogs, one of the separate battalions was composed of Illocanos, and the other was totally Igorot. Trouble started between the Tagalogs and Igorots, with the usual nightly ambushes and beatings, until the Tagalogs were afraid to leave their tents at night in less than squad strength. A Tagalog military policeman patrolling alone was literally butchered.

Then the Illocanos got into the act, jumped a squad of Tagalogs, and two dead and three injured went to the hospital. The Tagalogs were thoroughly disliked by their countrymen and as I saw it deservedly so. They had been the tribe most closely associated with the Spaniards for more than three hundred years and with the Americans for forty-eight years. In these three and a half centuries they had acquired all of the undesirable attributes of both of the ruling civilizations and none of the better qualities. This combination, added to their natural propensity toward theft and murder, made them particularly unsuited to be the controlling race in the Philippines. Yet having the advantages of numbers, education, comparative wealth, and geographical position they were and unfortunately always will be the dominant faction.

The election date was rapidly approaching and the rate of assassinations and kidnappings accelerated on the political front. Too many weapons were available, the present governors of provinces were maintaining private armies of ex-guerrillas, and would-be governors were organizing armed bands of thugs to ensure their own election. The Philippine constabulary and the military police command were influencing the prospective vote in some areas and afraid to venture into others. During the two days before the election there were seventeen allegedly political murders in my sector, and I was very happy that it was none of my business.

The election proper went off much more quietly than anyone expected, with Roxas winning at a walk. It is possible that the reason there was very little shooting on election day was directly due to the shootings that had taken place in the preceding weeks. The people voted for the winners and the priests said Masses for the losers.

The country was far from being united, however. The Hukbalahap, the community "army against the Japanese," was holding a large portion of Bulucan province, with their strength centered on Mount Ayarat north of Manila. The timid advances made against them by the Philippine government forces were totally ineffectual.

Capobre had finally made it; the Thirty-first Infantry was recognized by the hitherto reluctant Philippine government. He had apparently converted enough politicos to his cause by putting on a magnificent

16,000-peso party for members of the legislature. Since we had robbed him of 12,000 pesos' worth of ammunition I was not (thank God) invited. I'd have rather attended a dinner with the medieval Borgia family.

This eight-thousand-dollar brawl, plus wads of pesos placed in the itching palms of influential senators, swung the vote in Capobre's favor, and AFWESPAC immediately stamped the favorable recommendation "approved." That was something like our Congress contracting with the Mafia to furnish the Secret Service, but it was none of my business and the ball was in my court, so I ordered the Thirty-first in to the depot.

Each guerrilla unit depending on its site had been issued one to four two-and-a-half-ton trucks and one to four jeeps for the service of the units while camping in the field. As soon as the units came into the depot these vehicles were taken in by F Company and placed in the motor pool. They were then serviced by our maintenance detachment and dispatched with American drivers as required for depot or guerrilla business.

The Thirty-first Infantry, however, due to Colonel Capobre's capable machinations with American supply personnel as well as Filipino politicos, had gained control of thirty-four vehicles. He had turned in five trucks and two jeeps as required on entering the depot, but refused to bring the other twenty-seven vehicles into camp. Lieutenant Buergin further reported that Capobre had then forced his way into the F Company motor pool with an armed squad and recovered the jeep that he had just turned in. He had then refused to halt for inspection of his trip ticket at the gate on leaving the camp for Manila. On his return he had told Lieutenant Buergin that he, Colonel Capobre, would never halt for an American sentry and would run over him if he got in the way.

Again I invited Colonel Capobre over for a visit, this time to discuss payment of his troops. When he arrived I was talking to Lieutenant Buergin and asked Capobre's indulgence for a moment. Then I went on.

"As I was saying, lieutenant, I'm not satisfied with the way you're controlling the main gate of your depot. The sentries on duty there are not positive enough. They let me in and out of there twice yesterday without checking my trip ticket. They didn't even halt me."

"Well, they know you, sir, and they—"

"The orders are that the sentry halts everyone. Me, General Styer, you, or the Angel Gabriel, we all halt and have our trip tickets inspected. And another thing, the sentries are completely unprotected in case anyone tries to force their way in or out of the depot. I want a bullet-proof sandbag emplacement built there at the entrance, with a light machine gun swivel-mounted for all-round fire, a slow-down barrier, and a swinging bar that will stop a tank. There'll be fifty Japs and four thousand sandbags out there by 1400 so you can have the job done by Retreat.

"Then you man the gate with a Cossack post—one man to halt the vehicles, inspect papers, and swing the barrier, one gunner and leader to cover him, and one NCO to see that they do the job right.

"If anyone does not halt on demand the gunner is to open fire. Don't shoot at the tires—the vehicle is valuable U.S. property that I'm responsible for. Shoot the men.

"Then you deliver the bodies to the U.S. or Philippine Army hospital for the death certificates. Return the vehicle to your service detachment.

"Last, you send me the gunner, all witnesses, and court-martial charges for murder. I'll have him tried and acquitted within twenty-four hours. And then I'll pin a Commendation Ribbon on him at Retreat the next day. Get the idea?"

"Yes sir." Buergin rose to his feet. "I'll have the gun in right away and the emplacement and barriers will be finished by Retreat."

"I'd like to have you wait a few minutes, and escort Colonel Capobre back to the depot. And thank you for coming in, Buergin."

The lieutenant left, putting on a very good act as a slightly chewed-out company commander. I turned to the colonel, whose plump face showed a sheen of perspiration.

"My apologies for this delay, Colonel Capobre. I asked you over to discuss the matter of pay and U.S. property, particularly trucks that you hold. I understand that you are having difficulty in controlling some of your people who are not obeying your orders to bring in the trucks that the United States has loaned you. You have my sympathy. Of course, until the trucks are turned in at the depot and your property lists are cleared by Lieutenant Buergin your regiment cannot be paid. But you can count on me to do all I can to help you."

Three days later all of the Thirty-first Infantry trucks were under Buergin's control and I relaxed. That was very stupid of me. Colonel Capobre had not relaxed—he was quietly making the rounds of American officialdom and Filipino wheelers and dealers, getting his former trucks declared "surplus to the needs of the service" and arranging a very quiet auction with four bidders (his relatives and friends).

Fortunately, Lieutenant Buergin got wind of these shenanigans through a friend in AFWESPAC G-4 where the deal was being pushed through in the lower levels as a very minor matter.[3] With his usual presence of mind and aggressive action Buergin wrote up a credit memorandum receipt, relieving the commanding officer of the Thirty-first Infantry Regiment of all responsibility for all of their trucks, and sent it to him by message center for the late-afternoon delivery. He then moved the vehicles in convoy to the 342d Infantry motor pool in Marakina and arranged for the papers to credit him and to debit the commanding officer of my service company as the sole owner of the trucks.

That afternoon, as scheduled in the discreetly advertised sale notice, a number of Filipino lawyers, money men, and gangsters arrived with a quintet of officers and NCOs from AFWESPAC to conduct and bid in the auction. Capobre was not present; the participants already had their instructions.

Lieutenant Buergin led the party to his motor pool as requested and then produced the papers that conclusively proved that the vehicles with the stated serial numbers were not assigned to the Thirty-first Infantry and were not in the possession of the depot pool; they belonged to the commanding officer of the service company, 342d Infantry. Buergin later told me that the reactions of the group were quite varied. One Filipino banker had a slight stroke, two lawyers promised legal action, one American sergeant broke into hysterical laughter, and the two American officers (who had no doubt lost their bribe money through Buergin's underhanded action) glumly talked about an investigation.

Knowing Capobre as I did, I am sure that by this time he occupies a high and powerful position in the government and is the wealthy crime king of Manila or has come to a bloody end in the attempt to achieve one or both of those exalted positions.

Eight.

The New Army and the Old

Diversity

One night in early December while making a spot inspection of the guard I found one sentry sitting down and another lying down on post, both sound asleep. I drew up the standard charges of loitering on post against both men and sent them to the division general court for trial.

Two days later General Melasky entered my office and handed me the papers.

"I want you to drop these charges, colonel. I want the boys to get as much rest as possible."

This New Army concept of interior guard duty was so amazing that I literally had no words.

On his next visit the general told me, "You don't have the spirit of the civilian army or the Black Hawk Division, Triplet."

"How is that, sir?"

"Well, you ought to go around and talk to the men, find out what they want, and ask for complaints."

"Do you mean that I should walk around and ask them what they want to complain about without their commander's knowledge, sir?"

"Certainly, I do it all the time."

"Well, general, I can't. I've held practically every grade from recruit to colonel and even as a buck sergeant I never asked privates how the platoon should be run. I'll hear any man's complaint, providing he's passed on to me by his commander. Even then I'll hear the commander too so I get the full story."

"I tell you, Triplet, you'll never stand a chance if the newspapers or congressmen get started on you. You'd better get in touch."

By this time I realized that he'd been driven around the bend, mildly insane, by unthinking, unscrupulous, or treasonable newspaper columnists and politicians. So I humored him by a weasel-worded, ambiguous answer, just to close a profitless conversation.

"Yes sir, I probably should."

But I would never go snooping around like Harun al-Rashid asking for complaints—these people complained plenty without my encouragement. All the complaints I'd heard of were about going home and ships, and not even MacArthur could do much about increasing the number of ships on the Pacific ferryboat run.[1]

Found a newspaper in my in basket, a mimeographed job put out by the neighboring 341st Regiment. The large, hand-worked headline, "342d Throttled by Brass!" caught my attention. The article below stated that I had "strangled the 342d *Redoubt* with censorship" and gave partially true and largely imaginary details about my interference with the freedom of the press that is guaranteed by the Constitution.

The true part was that I had directed the information officer to review all items before they were mimeographed and to delete or modify those that were untrue or unfit to print. I required the deletion of filth, obscenity, profanity, fruitless complaints, and the half-truths and rumors that were presented in the style made notorious by Pearson, Winchell, and similar garbage dispensers.[2] And I had as alleged deleted the scurrilous article that charged that the post exchange officer was making personal profit on the sale of PX goods.

So I got the *Redoubt* staff together and held forth with a quarter-hour monologue on the responsibility of the free press, censorship, regimental esprit, columnists, the *Pacifican* B Bag column, anonymous letters, decent language, and the depths reached by the Soviet-slanted *Pacifican* in catering to the lowest 10 percent of the troops.

I further promised that I would continue to strangle this portion of the free press and if any article that violated my policy was printed those responsible (reporter, writer, editor, and mimeograph operator) would hastily leave with their chevrons removed and their shirttails afire for the most unpleasant assignment and duty that I could find for them.

Last, I cautioned them to use discretion in talking to their fellow newsmen in other units because if any more of our dirty laundry was washed in the columns of another unit paper I was prepared to make immediate changes, ranging from a new editor to stopping publication of the *Daily Redoubt*.

They took it badly, of course, but were all attention, and I hoped that my discourse had gotten them on the right road. No, that would be too much to expect. There would certainly be a leak and this, coupled with my other reactionary sins, would result in my immediate relief and transfer or retirement.

Getting out of this rabble in any way looked quite attractive.

But General Melasky beat me to it and left for a disability (psychiatric?) retirement on December 12.

Shortly after the general left, Colonel Yale mentioned my interference with the prerogatives of the soldier newsmen.

"By the way, Triplet, remember when the 341st paper came out with that headline, '342d Throttled by Brass!'?"

"I certainly do—after that I really tightened the garrote and squeezed. What brought that to mind?"

"Right after it came out General Melasky told me to go down to the 342d and get you in line with the division policy of the New Army."

"Well, Yale, if you had done that you'd have come back to the general carrying my application for a transfer to a soldiering outfit."

"Yes, that's what I thought. That's why I just happened to forget about it until just now."

So ended the first battle of the hardest campaign I'd ever fought.

Nice fellow, Colonel Yale.

The morale of the troops in AFWESPAC, particularly that of the service troops in Manila, was low. Mass meetings and demonstrations that were organized by professional agitators were being frequently held in the city. It appeared that we were reaching the same stage of dissolution as the Russian Army in 1917 and that the agitation was coming from precisely the same source.

General Styer on January 8, 1946, had consented to address a mob of fifty thousand demonstrators who demanded his presence. He was hissed and booed off the platform. Again, General Lear, commander of army ground forces, got the same outrageous reception. In the Old Army such conduct would have been considered mutiny—in the civilian army it was evidently accepted as normal.

In order to ensure that my people did not engage in such mutinous and futile conduct I used a rather voluminous memorandum on the situation and required that it be read and discussed by all ranks in company school periods.

The memorandum may have been unnecessary. Actually, my men were just too busy with their construction work, Japs, and guerrillas to be interested in demonstrating about anything. Every week or two port calls would come as a pleasant surprise for groups of high-point men, sending fifty to sixty back for discharge.

In every case I addressed the group just before they left, discussing their imminent return to civil life as outstanding citizens, their influence on the government by their wise use of the vote, and the wide difference between statesmen and politicians.

In every case I noted the probable effect of my memorandum—they listened with interest. But I never became accustomed to soldiers clapping at the end of the talk like an audience applauding a vaudeville act. The Old Army would never do that.

New Brooms

In mid-March, I received a real windfall among the replacement officers. Lieutenant Colonel Stangle, fresh from running an infantry training center in the States, was assigned for duty with the 342d. Six feet by 220 pounds, with the build and face of a retired wrestler, very competent, decisive, and conscientious, he was a veritable tower of strength—just what was needed.

We were short of senior officers, long on junior officers, had no experienced noncommissioned officers, and as many privates as second lieutenants in the 342d. No enlisted man had more than two years of service, with one notable exception. I was maintaining the detached third battalion in Mindanao at a reasonable strength of six hundred but the rest of the regiment on Luzon was in sad shape with a total of 580 men. A reorganization was indicated.

I closed out two rifle companies in the first battalion, one in the third battalion in Mindanao, and E Company in the second battalion. The service company was kept at full strength, but headquarters, cannon, and antitank companies were reduced to cadres. All headquarters, regimental and battalion, were reduced to skeleton strength.

Colonel Stangle was placed in overall command of the Twenty-first Depot, guerrilla processing, and Philippine Army training with F Company and the Scout battalion as his working force. Colonel Holt remained in charge of the skeletonized regiment in Marakina. Lieutenant Colonel Evans, another replacement, was placed in command of the second battalion, responsible for Corregidor and the Philippine Treasury. Colonel Ward remained in charge of the third battalion in Mindanao. It was a good working organization, which left me free to make extended visits or reconnaissance trips without neglecting any of our responsibilities.

Colonel Stangle did a magnificent job with his heterogeneous command, clearing the last of the guerrillas from the depot by April 1 and pushing the Philippine Army units through a heavy training program with the help of the Scouts and our overstrength of second lieutenants. He did have to modify his style in one respect. His deep voice normally registered a startling volume of decibels and within his normal conversational range of one hundred yards American lieutenants would spring to attention, guerrillas plotting murder would turn pale, and Filipino officers would burst into tears when he spoke. He complained that frequently he would tell a Filipino officer to do something and the lad would take off, full speed, in the wrong direction. When recalled and questioned it usually developed that the officer had little or no idea of what he had been ordered to do—he was simply stunned by the volume and was leaving at a gallop to do almost anything useful. When the colonel finally learned to control his voice to a whisper he got really superior results.

A week after Stangle took over the depot Colonel Miraflores of the Philamerican Regiment, just discharged, invited him to a guerrilla party at the Manila Hotel. I wasn't invited, presumably because I'd cut off their rations for two days during my cleanup campaign. But after seeing Stangle next morning I was very happy to have missed the show. If they'd done that to Stangle, whom they'd genuinely liked, what would they have done to me?

It had been a real wing-ding in the 6,000-peso bracket, laid on with the usual lavish Filipino hospitality. After a rousing evening of roast pig and all the exotic trimmings washed down with a great variety of drinks, Colonel Stangle was thanking his host before leaving. Colonel Miraflores had then proposed a nightcap or stirrup cup. Since "Coronel Stangel ees a beeg man, he gets a beeg dreenk," he received a highball glass of rum diluted with what looked like water. It wasn't water, it was gin.

Captain Richardson, the 342d intelligence officer, was also suffering. Colonel Miraflores had requested that his guests, many of them from other guerrilla units, either leave their sidearms with their drivers or check them with the hotel desk clerk. During a lively political discussion on independence, one of the guests had risen and leaned well forward to hammer a weighty political point down his opponent's throat.

"Pardon me, Colonel Ramos," said Captain Richardson in an intentionally carrying whisper. "Don't look now, but your revolver is showing."

Colonel Ramos blushed, and removed the .45-caliber Smith & Wesson sidewheeler, which he had "forgotten," from the holster at the small of his back under his coat. He weighed the weapon and fingered at the hammer a few moments while he regarded young Richardson with a look that Al Capp would later make known as "the double whammy." But his better judgment finally prevailed and he sent his artillery out to the desk clerk by his adjutant. As the party broke up Colonel Ramos also mixed a special drink for his "good friend, Kepten Reechardson"—two ounces of whiskey diluted by eight ounces of vodka.

Both of my heroes had been betrayed by their patriotic pride. Even when they'd realized that they'd been slugged they just wouldn't admit that any drink was too strong for an American.

Major General Paul Mueller had taken over command of the division while I was relaxing with the Philippine Navy. I had known him as a fellow student at the Command and General Staff College. During our first conversation it was evident that there would be a beneficial change in command policy. I was delighted to know that in the future I could count on the support of the division commander in my efforts to maintain a good regiment.

Among other matters that we discussed was his desire to see Corregidor the next day with a party of eight. I jumped to an understandable but totally false conclusion. I arranged for the launch for 0800 and radioed the CO of G Company to "Stand by for working inspection by commanding general and party of nine arriving 1000."

Next morning I was at the dock at 0800 to meet and guide the inspectors. You can imagine my horror to find that the inspecting party consisted of General Mueller, four sightseeing staff officers, and four cute little cupcakes from the Red Cross. And I was fifteen miles from my radio.

I couldn't quite look the garrison commander in the eye when he and his stiffly starched cohorts met the inspectors at the dock. But all hands including the battalion of neatly washed sons of heaven seemed to find the inspection quite enjoyable.

In early April, General Mueller was ordered to General MacArthur's staff in Tokyo, and Major General Kramer assumed command of the division. Kramer was a short, blond, stocky officer with Old Army ideas worthy of Von Steuben. He had an unusual habit, most striking: he ate cigars. He joined the division one evening and Colonel Yale phoned me that I was to take him and General Styer to inspect our battalion on Mindanao next morning.

I joined the general in the cool gray dawn before breakfast and noted that he had a cigar clamped in the corner of his mouth. I couldn't fathom how a man could smoke a cigar before breakfast, but noting that it was unlit I offered a light. Kramer shuddered and said, "No, thank you," and his aide looked shocked. During the day I was continually fascinated by the progress the cigar made. Still virgin-tipped, millimeter by millimeter it slowly shortened until just before lunch it completely disappeared.

We flew to Mindanao in General Styer's luxuriously upholstered converted B-17, and found Ward and his third battalion in good shape, well dug in, and having no troubles. The Moros were remaining quiet and thievery was well under control.

On our return we stopped at the base on Leyte where they had been having a great deal of difficulty with thieves. There were not enough men in the local service units to mount an effective guard on the extensive supply dumps, so the commanding colonel had found an unusual solution to the problem.

He had formed a guard of his Japanese PWs commanded by American NCOs, equipping them with clubs, flashlights, and whistles. The modus operandi was simple and quite effective. The Japs would place a load of enticing "bait" in an exposed and apparently vulnerable and unguarded area of the depot, just inside the perimeter wire where all the passing natives would see it. After nightfall two or more Japs would take their post in ambush. At sight or sound of intruders the Japs would dash in, use their clubs, turn on flashlights to see what they had caught this time, blow whistle for American NCO to bring jeep for the bodies, and repeat the performance throughout the tropic night.

It seemed to be a good idea—conserved American manpower, protected property, influenced the natives to be honest, put those who couldn't in the hospital or cemetery, and alleviated the boredom of the Japs. I mulled over the idea of filling out my own depleted squads with a few well-selected sons of heaven.

General Kramer proved to be a very tough commander, just what the

Eighty-sixth Division had needed for the past three years. He asked for decent haircuts, and the troops weren't impressed. He announced that hair more than two and one-half inches long would be considered effeminate, and company commanders still had to direct soldiers individually to get their waving locks shorn. Finally he equipped the military police at the gate with a ruler and required them to measure the hair of every man leaving the post. Anyone having an effeminate haircut was returned to his unit under arrest. He was then required to be marched by his company commander to and from division headquarters for two hours of school per night, six days a week, for one month.

One burnsided replacement in the medical detachment and three curly-locked recruits in three of my line companies were caught and delivered by Kramer's Gestapo. Imagine, if you can, the feelings of both commander and culprit as the officer marched his single sinner more than a mile to division headquarters and observed him take part in two hours of close order drill and calisthenics under the cold and relentless supervision of a sergeant of the military police. Then at 2100 came the march back to the company, punctuated by remarks from the company commander. "Kalunkavitch, if you ever do anything like this again I'll (various gruesome promises)."

Another healthy innovation made by Kramer was a reasonable pass system, with a midnight curfew for men on pass, in order to reduce the Manila casualty rate. As in the case of haircuts, a week went by with men returning at all hours of the morning, and some (AWOL, hospitalized, dead) not returning at all. Then came the blow—if a man did not make the midnight deadline he would be arrested at the gate and his regimental (or separate battalion) commander would be called to come and pick him up. I supplemented this order with a postscript: if I was called to pick up one of my heroes his battalion and company commanders would accompany me.

I chortled merrily at the wails of my colleagues of the 341st and 343d until at 0300 one black, rainy morning I was called to the division main gate. My extreme unhappiness was compounded by deep chagrin—the military police had apparently made a mistake in reporting the unit of my delinquent and I had roused the wrong battalion and company commanders from their warm beds. The MPs were not at fault. The man had said he was from C Company. "Why?" I asked the culprit from the service company. "Well sir, I sure as hell didn't want Captain Stief coming down here to get me out."

In my next officers school I urged the company commanders to be more diligent in warning their wayward flocks about returning to the fold before midnight. I further suggested that any black sheep that was stupid enough to wander right into the arms of the MP at the main gate after curfew should get the book thrown at him. Filipinos were able to evade the guard at any time, day or night; why couldn't our young men do it too? If necessary an extended review of scouting and patrolling would be beneficial.

I had never credited Kramer with a sense of humor—I had never seen him in other than a deadly earnest mood. Six weeks after he had started kicking the division out of its postwar inertia, however, he declared a holiday "in appreciation of the considerable improvement in the division, the intense cooperation of all members of the division, and their unswerving concentration in performance of duty."

Ha! The words intense cooperation and unswerving concentration were particularly amusing. After a yardbird had done fifty hours of night drill and calisthenics in "Kramer's College" for failing to get a haircut he was going to be pretty intense about getting the barber's cooperation on the next one.

Kramer probably aroused resentment among the troops by his cruel and unusual methods but he won a high degree of alertness in attention to orders as well. The editor of the *Redoubt,* a sergeant of sixteen months' service, asked me, "Is General Kramer trying to make a Regular Army outfit out of this division?"

"No, sergeant," I replied, "your word 'trying' implies possible failure. General Kramer never tries to do anything. Give him six months and the Eighty-sixth will be the equal of a Regular Army division."

Many of us regretted his return to the States for retirement in late May.

The Pacifican

The eighth of June was a momentous day in the history of AFWES-PAC. Brigadier General Shea, the Eighty-sixth Division commander since Kramer's retirement, called me to his quarters at Reveille.

"I've just realized that right now I'm the senior officer in the Philippines," he said, offering me a cup of stout, black, vintage coffee. "General Styer is in Japan with most of AFWESPAC. I've looked over the dates of rank for the rest of the list, and I'm it."

I couldn't fathom what his standing on the seniority list had to do with any known situation so I remained silent and sipped cautiously at the coffee that had apparently simmered on the back burner all night.

"Can you—," he hesitated, and revised his question. "Is your regiment solid enough to withstand the impact of nineteen card-carrying communist replacements?"

"Indeed we are. I'm short of men, we're spread thin on several fronts, and I'll take anything including Japs, communists, Republicans, Democrats, or chimpanzees as fillers."

"Good. In that case you're about to get the complete staff of the

Pacifican including the editor—a second lieutenant. Understand that he used to be assistant editor of the *Daily Worker* before Joe Stalin ordered all commies in the U.S. to get into the army information and education programs. In exchange for these nineteen Red Star heroes I want your best officer that's capable of running the *Pacifican,* your best NCO to back him up, and any man you have that can do newspaper work. Have them report to headquarters in an hour—no, at 0800, with a jeep and two trucks. I'll deliver your replacements at noon or shortly after."

To save time I phoned Colonel Stangle. At 0745 my very capable information and education officer and the equally capable regimental sergeant major reported to General Shea with the complete *Redoubt* staff in tow. A small convoy then left for Manila with all of the literary talent of the 342d aboard, escorted by a military police patrol and led by the doughty General Shea.

Arriving at the *Pacifican* printing plant, Shea ordered the utterly stunned staff to pack up their personal plunder immediately and mount the trucks for transfer to the 342d Infantry Regiment. There ensued a good deal of wailing about their MOS ratings, specialties, and constitutional rights, but the general assured them that their records would be changed to give them appropriate infantry MOS ratings as riflemen and that the commander of the 342d would ensure that they were fully qualified in those specialties in the very near future.[3]

Shea had told me to expect my replacements by noon, so by that time I had assembled my unit commanders and personnel officer and briefed them on what he had told me, then continued with my own instructions.

"S-1 will assign the eighteen enlisted men at the rate of one per line company and battalion headquarters detachment. Service, antitank, and cannon companies, two apiece. Headquarters company and medics one each. Give the surgeon the biggest one—he needs a litter bearer. Assign the officer to the staff as assistant adjutant until I find out what he can do.

"Now these men will be treated exactly as any other replacements, no hazing and no favoritism, exactly the same. You'll add them at the foot of your guard, duty, fatigue, and pass rosters. General Shea warned me that there would be a lot of complaints. If so, and you can't handle them, I'll be available."

Actually it was approaching Retreat when an exasperated military policeman entered my office.

"Sergeant Watson, reporting with one officer and eighteen EM replacements, sir."[4]

"Thank you, sergeant, I expected you five hours ago. What was the delay?"

"Hell of a job, sir. Sent 'em to their quarters to get their gear and report back, and they took off in all directions. Some complained to the inspector general, some cried to the chaplains, and some just went plain AWOL. Had to run 'em down all over. Just like trying to carry a goddamn shovelful of mice. But we got 'em all."

"Nice going, sergeant. Ask the lieutenant to bring them in, please, and thank you very much."

Lieutenant Wesen, a fairly tall, well built, very well nourished, soft-looking young man entered, followed by his crew, and on my prompting reported the detail present. They were typical of the service troops stationed in Manila—personally dirty, unshaven, long-haired, and side-burned, glowering with suspicion, outrage, defiance, anger, and fear. I was reminded of the letter that the Duke of Wellington wrote to the prime minister when the latter emptied England's jails to furnish replacements for the British Army in France: "My Lord, I know not what effect the men you have sent me will have upon the French, but by God they terrify me."

I noted that most of them wore sergeant's, corporal's, or technician's chevrons. Two of them I recognized as having accompanied General Eisenhower on his disastrous inspection tour.[5]

"Take seats, please."

They slumped on the benches lining the walls of the tent, a few continued glaring at me, the majority morosely studied their shoes. I gave them the usual "Welcome to the 342d Infantry Regiment, the best line regiment in the Philippines and probably in the Far Eastern theater," then added a paragraph to the usual script.

"Some of you are unshaven. Most of you are wearing weird and filthy costumes. All of you need haircuts. Your boots are not dubbined. Normally appearance like that would call for immediate reduction to the grade of basic private in this regiment. Since it is apparent, however, that you have been taught very little about soldiering, I will give you until Reveille to get yourselves in shape."

By this time I at least had their full attention—their eyes were on me instead of their toes, variously registering alert interest, apprehension, dislike, and pure one-hundred-proof hatred.

Lieutenant Wesen spoke up.

"Sir, we want to make a complaint."

"So? And what is your complaint?"

"We protest our summary arrest, conviction, and punishment without a fair trial."

"What crime have you committed that you should be tried for, lieutenant? Haven't heard of it—and haven't heard of your arrest. If I do I'll order charges and you'll get your trial, rest assured of that. In the meantime report your detail to the personnel officer next door. He'll give you your assignments. That will be all, thank you for coming in." My replacements had evidently changed a bit for the better during our chat.

They stood up and raggedly followed the lieutenant's lead in saluting, probably for the first time since they had been in the Pacific theater, and filed out.

Ten minutes later the lieutenant was back with a request for leave and a jeep.

"I had planned on staying in Manila for the weekend, sir, and left everything in my quarters."

"Didn't you get General Shea's order to pack up and bring your gear with you?"

"Yes sir but I thought I would go on pass over the weekend and report back on Monday."

"It seems that you may get that trial you want after all, lieutenant, for disobedience of orders. You'll get no jeep. I'll give you until midnight to get your plunder out here. Report to the motor pool. They may have a freight truck going to Camp Blackjack this evening. If they do you can go with it to Manila and return. Or you may be able to get a civilian bus at Marakina. Curfew is at midnight. Make it. If you can't get to Manila, the post exchange officer can probably sell you a toothbrush and razor and perhaps you can borrow a clean uniform."

I was agreeably surprised next morning to learn that he had made it. Shea came by on a short visit to ask how the recruits were doing.

"Very well, sir. No trouble at all."

"Restez tranquil, mon ami—there will be, I'll be surprised if I don't get a congressional investigation out of it but I'm looking forward to it."

I had a great deal of admiration for the lad. It required a high degree of moral courage to buck the current trend toward softness and communistic ideas in the military as well as in our body politic. He had not only ruined his chance of getting a second star; he was probably on his way to losing the one he had. There are very few men of his caliber.

I looked over the Sunday issue of the *Pacifican* with the interest of partial ownership. It had changed. There was no editorial on "Democracy in the Soviet Army," no slurs against the "power-mad brass," and the "B-Bag" contained only reasonable requests for information. News items were factually reported. The *Pacifican* had become a newspaper rather than a poorly disguised front for the Kremlin's propaganda.

But I had spoken too soon when I told General Shea that all was well. Captain Adams of headquarters company reported that his Sergeant Dubinsky, the erstwhile assistant editor of the *Pacifican,* had been AWOL at Reveille. The Sunday edition of the *Manila Bulletin,* a radical English-language paper, came out with a column headlined "*Pacifican* Staff Sentenced Without Trial." This article, allegedly based on a personal interview with my missing warrior, stated that the *Pacifican* personnel had been arrested without reason in a mass razzia, condemned by General

Shea without trial, and sentenced to hard labor in the 342d Infantry Regiment. There they had immediately been forced to cut grass in the hot afternoon sun while Jap PWs stood by and laughed at them. A congressional investigation and punishment of the responsible officers was being demanded.

Monday morning Captain Adams brought in the missing scribe as I had requested.

"Oh yes, captain, I must admit to having made a mistake. I asked personnel to assign the man with the highest educational qualifications to your company. I am now quite sure that he would be of more service to the United States as a basic rifleman. With your concurrence I'll transfer him to F Company."

"Yes indeed sir, I sure can't use a man like him as a sergeant."

I handed the delinquent sergeant a pen knife.

"Cut them off," I directed, indicating his chevrons.

"But I haven't had a trial," he objected.

"No trial is necessary. I require that my noncommissioned officers be reliable. You were absent without leave and while AWOL told several lies that were damaging to the prestige of the United States and that were then published in the *Manila Bulletin*. You are not reliable. Therefore you are no longer a noncommissioned officer in this regiment and if you are wise you will cut off those chevrons. If you continue your psychotic yearning for a trial you will get one. Then you will not only lose your chevrons, you will also lose pay and spend some time in the stockade at hard labor. It's your choice."

Dubinsky cut the chevrons off.

"Now, captain, please send Private Dubinsky to F Company under guard. I've notified Maynard. The paperwork will be completed this afternoon."

That afternoon I had all of my unwilling replacements in for a talk on items of mutual interest. They were much cleaner looking than they had been on their first appearance. After discussing point by point the obvious lies that Dubinsky had furnished the *Manila Bulletin,* I continued.

"It is a serious offense to speak, write, or print anything against the president, the secretary of war, Congress, or the governor (or commissioner) of any state or territory in which you are stationed. While on the *Pacifican* staff you were guilty of offending all of these, and should have been court-martialed.

"The mass meetings in Manila, called for and advertised by you in the *Pacifican,* would have been mutiny, and the call to hold the meetings as well as what was said there would have been sedition, if not tacitly condoned or ignored by AFWESPAC. Again, you would have been court-martialed.

"In the future you will not say, write, or print anything in public to damage the reputation of this regiment until after you've gone through command channels, giving all commanders concerned a chance to right your alleged wrongs. If I can't do justice to the problem I'll make an appointment for you with the inspector general or General Shea.

"General Shea informs me that you are all trying to get your congressmen to call for a congressional investigation. That's good. We both welcome the idea and perhaps I can get sent back to Europe to do some real soldiering.

"Last, the CIC informs me that there are probably Soviet agents among you. I'd like to have them remain—I've met the Red Army but I've never knowingly seen their snoopers.

"That is all—thank you."

They all rose and saluted, together this time. They seemed thoughtful—too dazed to see free speech, the free press, the rights of the common man, organized sedition, and the party line kicked to pieces right before their glazed eyes. No Soviet agents remained behind, not even Dubinsky.

All remained quiet on the front for a month. Then Shea asked me to meet him at headquarters. He handed me a paper.

"The AFWESPAC inspector general has been wearing a path in here lately and I've been answering a hell of a lot of questions. Take a look at numbers 7 and 8 in that questionnaire. Can you give me the answers for them?"

The questions read:

7. Why did an officer of the Eighty-sixth Division threaten the ex-staff of the *Pacifican* with a court-martial if they took up their case with the War Department?

8. Why did an officer of the Eighty-sixth Division order the ex-staff of the *Pacifican* not to write to their congressmen?

"Yes, general, I can give you the answers. It just happens that I wrote out and filed both talks that I had with your ex-Pacificans and I'll have both manuscripts here with my answers at once."

The answers were in some detail, with the conclusion that: "The inferences in the above questions are the result of some member or members of the ex-staff of the *Pacifican* assembling excerpts from unrelated sentences in my two talks to these replacements (copies attached) in such a manner as to form vicious lies."

The *Pacifican* campaign then ended in a deep quiet. I was delighted to see that the lads turned out quite well after they got their feet on the ground and were put to work. In fact, two of them were later promoted for their superior service in training Philippine Scouts. They evidently weren't a bad lot—they just hadn't been brought up right.

Lieutenant Wesen as editor of the *Pacifican* had acquired some notoriety for a series of scathing articles on the injustices of the army court-martial system as compared to the benign justice of civilian courts. With my mordant sense of humor I appointed him as trial judge advocate to investigate and prosecute the cases coming before the special court. The joke backfired. He tried three cases and won three convictions with sentences that were so harsh that I had to reduce all of them to more reasonable terms and to suspend confinement on condition of good behavior.

Nine.

Philippine Scouts

A New Assignment

On June 20 I was directed to report to Major General Anderson, commander of Philippine ground forces. I entered his office assuming that my troubles with the Bulucans had caught up with me. Would it be a transfer, retirement, or court-martial? It proved to be much worse than I had anticipated. With no preliminaries to soften the blow, Anderson let me have it.

"Triplet, I'd like to have you prepare to turn your Twenty-first Depot and the rest of the guerrillas over to the Philippine Army, and take over the training of ten thousand new Philippine Scouts to be used in the occupation of Japan and the Marianas."

"Will do, general—but I think you ought to know that you have selected the one man in this theater who is most psychologically unsuited for dealing with Filipinos."

"We don't think so. I've discussed the matter with General Styer, Shea, and others, and it's my opinion that you're the one who can best do the job. The Scout division is presently assembling recruits and will be ready to start shipping them to you on Monday. G-3 has been working on some of the details and I suggest that you check over them with him."

Somewhat stunned, I looked up his G-3, my classmate, in his plush-lined, fan-cooled office, and asked him about the details he'd been working on. He was just as languid now as he had been as a cadet twenty years ago. Aside from the date the Scouts were to be ready for shipment to their occupation stations he had nothing constructive to offer.

"What training area do I get for the job?"

"We really don't have a suitable area; they're all occupied or turned over to the Philippine Army. You can't stay at the Twenty-first Depot, of course, that's going to the Philippine Army too. All I can suggest is that you go out and look for a place. Here's a list of the areas we have or can get for you. Let us know when you find one you want and we'll assign it to you."

G-4 was much more interesting but just as ineffectual.

G-1 was a ball of fire—said he could start delivering recruits at any time, starting at 1000 Monday.

The interview gave me a startling view of the operations of the general staff of the higher echelons. It also presented quite a problem. It was very well to look for a training area. That was easy. But to find an area capable of housing and training ten thousand men, with essential water laid on, plus the luxury of electricity if possible, that was difficult, particularly since I was to start receiving recruits within the week.

I looked over an abandoned recuperation center, a Japanese concentration camp, a PW camp, and an MP stockade, which were on the list of areas available. All were ridiculously small, all had been practically destroyed by looters, none had room for training, and all except the recuperation center were surrounded by fences and rusty rolls of massed barbed wire. I would never willingly start training recruits in such a depressing environment.

As a last resort I dropped in on Colonel Jenkins, the hard-bitten, leathery, realistic, and most hospitable commander of the Fifth Replacement Depot near Paranaque. Since his depot was operating at 40 percent capacity he granted me half of his area, sufficient to house eight thousand Scouts. He regretted not being able to give me more room but felt that he had to hold 10 percent capacity available for emergency use. In desperation I accepted his offer with great relief and sincere gratitude. I could at least house and feed the first increments there and start basic training until such time as a larger, more suitable area was located or prepared.

Tent floors and kitchen-mess halls were already in place, with water and electricity. The latrines, however, ditch type and tent-covered, had been filled in. I badly needed forty latrines inside of three days. Forty ditches, thirty feet long, eight feet deep and two feet wide, with seats—impossible. I just didn't have that much digging power, even counting Maynard's Japs.

So I visited a nearby engineer battalion and presented the problem to the alert young major who commanded it.

"That's easy, colonel, I'll lend you a ditch digger. If you'll just show him where you want the latrines—of course, the ditch'll only be a foot wide."

"Quite all right, that way they can straddle and squat, like they've been doing all their lives, and I won't have to build seats. The only reason for a two-foot latrine ditch is that a man can't dig a narrower one. Can't fall into a twelve-inch ditch either."

An hour later a capable young corporal appeared in my area, driving a rattling, full-tracked, mechanical monstrosity, carrying a twelve-foot beam-derrick that supported a dredgelike chain of small toothed buckets. I showed him where the line of latrines was to go.

He cranked up his machine, clanked slowly into position, and let the beam carrying the chain of buckets down to ground level. A couple of minor shifts to get his line correct, and he pulled another lever. The bucket chain started to rotate, the head of the beam sank into the ground, and the rising buckets each discharged a shovelful of earth to the side. I was fascinated—what will they think of next? The head rapidly nosed down to the required eight-foot level, whereupon the lad started urging his contraption forward, at ten feet a minute. I left him with it, marveling over these wonders of modern technology. In a day the young man dug half a mile of latrines, including the 100 percent reserve ditches, probably a record.

Successive rapid changes in orders from Philippine ground forces the next day reduced the requirement from ten thousand to eight thousand to sixty-six hundred Scouts to be trained for shipment by November 1. This reduction in numbers made the job possible, barely possible, considering the restrictions of the training area.

There were five mess halls of a normal four-hundred-man capacity, with sixty-six hundred Scouts and five hundred Americans to feed. The Americans, due to the difference in rations, would use one mess in two servings. By using standing trestles instead of tables and chairs we planned to feed 1,650 Scouts per mess in one continuous serving for each meal.

There were 430 tents of twenty-man capacity. We would quarter the Scouts at twenty per tent, the American cadre at the rate of twelve men per tent, junior officers eight per tent, and still have tentage left for offices and orderly, supply, and cadre school-rooms. Captains and field officers would bring their own wall tents.

During my next visit to Colonel Jenkins he gave a monologue on local thievery.

"We aren't far from the penitentiary, and a good many 'graduates' have settled in the neighboring barrios over the years. We've had a good deal of trouble with 'em.

"They're pretty clever. They strip completely or to their drawers and oil themselves, so that even if they're caught, a man can't hold 'em. They walk on all fours to distribute their weight so the floorboards won't creak.

"They know that a man will generally hide his valuables and pistol under his pillow. Well, they lift his mosquito bar and tickle him on the cheek with a feather. He slaps at the mosquito and tosses and turns. When he moves the thief's other hand goes under the pillow. Another tickle and the hand comes out with the loot. Then they gather up his clothes and B Bag and ease out.

"They used to be a curse. But we haven't had so much of that lately. There's a wooded arroyo that runs up just inside the southern depot boundary. It used to be that late every afternoon a lot of natives would infiltrate into that area, just like infantry moving up to the jump-off line before the big attack. After dark they'd jump off and after Taps we'd start losing a lot of stuff.

"Then one evening just before dusk I sent a squad of MPs up that draw with tommy-guns and had another squad posted with rifles on a little knoll overlooking the upper end of the area. The MPs pushed ahead, firing through the brush, and the riflemen took care of them as they broke out of cover. It's worked pretty well, we've gotten twenty-three killed and crippled so far, and the last couple of drives we saw none at all. Also the thieving isn't near so bad as it used to be. A lot of people say that capital punishment is no deterrent to criminals but I claim that a .30-caliber bullet sure deters the man it hits in the right place."

Colonel Stangle prepared to turn the Twenty-first Depot (Camp Blackjack) and the remaining guerrillas over to the Philippine Army. This project, however, did not get off the ground for months, and the best he could do was to strip F Company of a few men for the training cadre. By turning over the Philippine Treasury to the Philippine Army we formed a cadre of 526 men and 32 officers, leaving only the band and a caretaking detachment at Marakina.

On June 23 the lads boiled out to the Fifth Replacement Depot, and the First Replacement Depot (PS) became a going concern. Supply trucks were rolling in to be unloaded. Kitchen storerooms and refrigerators were filled. A uniform and equipment processing section was set up and clothing laid out by sizes. Tents were unrolled and raised over the floors sufficient to take care of the first increments of recruits.

This feverish activity of organized confusion continued until well after dark. From then until midnight we organized. We spread the thin strength of the cadre to take care of four prospective battalions of 1,650 men each. Each battalion had four companies of 418 men, divided into four platoons of 103 men each. Each platoon had four 26-man sections, each containing three squads of 8–9 men each. Certainly not a tactical organization but it would serve quite well for basic training.

We had enough officers to command the battalions but after the essential staff officers were appointed we were short of company commanders. Several companies were commanded by master sergeants and technical sergeants of less than two years' service. Sergeants who had largely been given promotions to fill vacancies for morale purposes were to lead hundred-man platoons. Sergeants, corporals, and first-class privates who had literally never commanded anything or anyone before were to be responsible for the twenty-six-man sections. We would have to select the most promising former Scouts, ex-Philippine Army recruits, or former guerrillas of experience to lead the 768 squads.

It was an organization the like of which had never been seen since the invention of the Roman legion, but it left us enough strength for administration and planning staffs as well as training specialists.

For greater training efficiency we used the specialist system. Each specialist was to study one lesson to teach daily, and his delivery was to be checked the night before. Then beginning next morning he would repeat the instruction, like a phonograph record, once an hour throughout one or two training days, until all units had attended his session. Due to the language problem, time had to be given between sentences and the wording had to be held to the simplest basic English so that all instruction could be translated by the English-speaking recruits, and most instruction was conducted on the "monkey see, monkey do" basis.

The training areas were limited to the fringes of the depot area bordering our camp, the company streets, and five baseball diamonds. Some instruction could, of course, be carried on in the squad tents, and would have to be in the tents during rainy weather. "Inclement weather instruction" programs formed an important part of our training schedules.

There was absolutely no room in the depot for headquarters or service company personnel, a motor pool, or billets for the regimental staff. This was an impossible situation, since we could not run the depot from the Marakina camp at a distance of thirty-five miles.

But just across the road from the depot I noticed a large stucco, tiled-roofed house, with several smaller houses and outbuildings, standing vacant on a two-acre plot. I investigated the situation and woke up the caretaker from his siesta in one of the small shacks. The buildings were all in bad condition but habitable. There was no electricity but our generators could supply that. Water was available and there was enough room for a motor pool and maintenance shop. By use of auxiliary tentage and by building sheds for maintenance shops it would do quite well. From the caretaker I learned that this complex belonged to a Filipino lawyer in Manila and got the address of his office. It was a long shot, but I was desperate and took it.

I called on Mr. Luis Quito, the lawyer landlord, a pleasant, plump little man, very elegant in tropical white linen. He modestly mentioned his service in the Philippine Army under General MacArthur at Bataan with a touch of nostalgia.

I told him that I wanted to occupy his property until October 31 in order to properly train Philippine Scouts in the depot. I admitted that I was not authorized any funds for rental and could not pay him one centavo for the use of the place. He seemed quite interested in exactly what we intended to do there and I sketched where I planned to build my maintenance sheds from salvaged lumber and corrugated iron. Then he made the proposal that after we were through with the place we leave all construction in place as payment in full. I readily agreed to this most generous and unlawful proposition, we shook hands on the bargain, and I left with his most courteous permission to occupy the place at once. No papers were necessary—a gentleman's agreement would do.

The complete success of my mission was most puzzling. The thrice-used corrugated iron and lumber that we would leave, even at five dollars

(Filipino) per sheet, would not come near the rental of the estate for one month, to say nothing of a third of a year. Did he plan on putting in a whopping claim for damages later? I'd have to take a chance on that. Or had I found a genuine patriot? I had always been skeptical about patriotism: I'd only known one real patriot in my twenty-eight years of service to date. But Mr. Quito never submitted a bill or claim for damages of any sort, so I can only conclude that as an ex-member of the Philippine Army he had made this generous gesture for sentimental reasons, or patriotism.

On June 24, four days after receiving the initial order, I reported to General Anderson that the 342d Infantry Regiment was ready to receive recruits at the First Replacement Depot (PS). That afternoon we got our first five hundred; the next day we received one thousand, and after that they poured in. These men had been assembled, medically examined, and partially uniformed by the Philippine Scout division. This permitted us to start our training cycle without delay. I regretted that almost half of them were Tagalogs but was delighted to find that many of them had had previous military service, a few in the Scouts, and more in the Philippine Army. Most of them claimed guerrilla service and the remainder had doubtless had practical experience as bandits.

I counted heavily on developing these ex-servicemen as a cadre of noncommissioned officers as early as possible, in order to relieve the strain on our rapidly shrinking American contingent. I planned to use them initially as leaders of the 768 squads; after two weeks we would select 256 of the best to command the sections; another two weeks and we would choose 64 of the most aggressive and responsible of these men as platoon sergeants.

It would be an impossible task for me, the personnel officer, and the battalion commanders to make the selections efficiently, and it would be difficult for the company commanders. The burden of selection must fall on the enlisted cadre of the 342d, who were now commanding the platoons and sections and who were in a position to observe their charges from Reveille to Taps and frequently after Taps. All that the officers could do in this situation was to counsel the cadre men on what types of men to look for—intelligent, aggressive, and responsible veterans. But of course they knew that already.

Again I was amazed at the natural aptitude of Filipinos for coordinated precision of movement and rhythm. Add to that the salting of ex-servicemen and guerrillas and it is understandable that they could take part in a formal parade within a week of their enlistments. On the other hand the sight of 1,650 men being taught close-order drill on a baseball field was discouraging. I went to Philippine ground forces to see my ineffectual classmate, the G-3, and told him that the best available training area and facilities were totally inadequate for the job. He was properly sympathetic but could apparently do nothing about it and fobbed me off on the chief of staff. He also listened to my tale with sympathetic appreciation of my difficulties.

"Well, you ought to go see Colonel Stoeger, headquarters, AFWESPAC," he advised.

"No," I replied. "After all, getting the facilities for a Philippine ground force job is your baby. I just train the troops and I'm telling you about the conditions under which I have to train them. You'd better look it over, and you go see Colonel Stoeger. I don't know him and you do. In the meantime I'd like to see the general."

I saw General Anderson, who shortly called in the chief of staff, G-3, and G-4. After telling my story for the fourth time that day I left all four considerably concerned and the staff members very unhappy.

Next day I received quite a delegation from PGF and AFWESPAC headed by General Anderson and including the doughty Colonel Stoeger. It was evident that they too were quite unsatisfied with the ridiculous training conditions and the undesirably crowded living area. I soon learned that the principal cause of their concern was not the difficulty of training and the discomfort of the troops—MacArthur was going to visit the Philippines on July 4.

The visitors were most favorably impressed by the appearance of the new Scouts in basic drill and the manual of arms. General Anderson was particularly interested in their performance.

"Triplet, how many of these men do you think could be in shape to take part in the Independence Day parade—that's three days from now?"

"All of them that have combat boots, general—about one thousand as it stands now. No trouble with uniforms and we have the equipment. They were born knowing how to keep step, and can put on a parade tomorrow if they had boots."

"What boots do you need?"

"About six thousand pair, size 4 to 6½ in E to triple widths."

"Telephone your requisition in to G-4 and we'll see what he can dig up. In the meantime I'd like to have you prepare to take part in the parade. It's to be a straight procession up Rizal Avenue. The Philippine government has asked for American representation and it would be most appropriate to have the new Scouts take our part. G-3 will give you the details."

Three days was not much time to get our recruits in shape for a public appearance at the birth of a nation, but for two days we stopped all other training and concentrated on it. I pulled the 342d band out of Marakina and distributed the bass and snare drummers around the training areas. They beat the 120 per minute cadence constantly while the Scouts practiced forming and marching in mass formation. The

American instructors darted about like sheep dogs, correcting the cant of the rifles and the snap of the heads on "eyes—right!"

About fourteen hundred additional pair of small, wide boots arrived, and I began to feel more confident about our showing on Independence Day. But I was not at all confident about the reception we would get. For the past year Filipinos had been assuming an ever-increasingly inimical attitude toward Americans, and when G-3 informed me that we would head the procession I felt like the lead scout of a patrol in enemy country. After all the Scouts were U.S. troops and on Philippine Independence Day they would actually be foreign mercenaries instead of Filipino citizens.

So it was with mixed emotions that I led off the Independence parade on the morning of July 4, 1946. I was quite proud of my recruits of ten days' service—they were swinging along splendidly. The 342d cadre men acting as company and platoon leaders were performing far beyond my expectations (or theirs). The twelve-piece 342d band was thumping out "The Stars and Stripes Forever" as though they had a full complement.

But my American color bearers were carrying the U.S. flag and the colors of the 342d and I fully expected that these symbols of colonial oppression would draw a barrage of decayed eggs, fruit, and small deceased animals. There might be a great deal of trouble between the Scouts and civilians because while I could rely on Scout loyalty I could not count on the discipline of a ten-day-old organization. I could only hope that the cadre could keep them under control.

So as we swung into Rizal Avenue, I was amazed when we were greeted by a continuous roar of applause from the dense crowds of Filipino observers. A constant ripple of cheering and hand clapping accompanied the appearance of the Scouts. I had never imagined that U.S. troops would ever again be welcomed in Manila, but there it was. The salutes that we received in return from President Roxas and General MacArthur were anticlimax; we had been saluted by the population of Manila throughout the approach march. It was a good day.

Filipino Recruits

I was beginning to learn something about Filipinos, aside from thieves. Spending little or no time in the office during daylight hours, I was able to observe and become better acquainted with our recruits and their peculiarities. They were all in excellent physical condition. More important, they were deeply interested, took pride in their work, and were enthusiastic about the military service. We worked them to exhaustion, fed them to repletion, and pushed them through the training schedule with improbable speed.

One major difficulty in teaching a military bearing was the initial tendency of many recruits who had had no previous service to jerk off their caps and bow to officers and NCOs. This was the conditioned reflex that had been built into the Filipino peon for centuries by the Spanish, to pull off the hat and bow to the landlord, the priest, the doctor, the mayor, or any other member of the educated professions or privileged castes. We could teach military courtesy and have our pupils react perfectly for company grade officers of normal size, but when a field grade officer or even an outsized sergeant came suddenly into the view of the recruit the cap-off-bow routine would be instinctive. It took a full week to convince them that they did not take the cap off for priests, only before ladies and God.

While making the rounds of the training areas one morning I stopped where a company was being given a lecture and demonstration on first aid. The ground was soggy from the last rain. There were no seats, of course, so the recruits were squatting comfortably on their heels. A lad immediately in front of me with his bare toes spread and gripping the mud like a chimpanzee was taking notes with diagrams on the lecture. Observing the group more closely, I saw several notebooks and pencils in diligent use. Never before in my service had I seen such a sight.

Again, I observed a company that was going through some particularly joint-wrenching calisthenics. Squatting at the edge of the field were three young men weeping bitterly, with sobs, muted howls, and big tears rolling unashamedly down their cheeks.

"What is the matter?" I asked. "Where are you hurt?"

They remained squatting, their pain evidently put them beyond responding to the basic requirements of courtesy. But one replied.

"Sar (sob), I cannot take eet any more."

Another, wiping his eyes, was a little more explicit.

"The sssergeant essay to us (sniffle), 'You cannot etake eet any more.' He essay 'Fall out.'"

I took a firm grip on myself, came very close to squatting alongside and howling with them, and then to my horror found myself saying, "That ees OK. You eat beeg supper and sleep good tonight. Tomorrow you can etake eet all right."

In spite of my past unfortunate experiences with these people I felt that if they had enough pride to weep with rage when they couldn't keep up, I could make soldiers out of them. The spirit was there. All we had to do was build the body around it, and infantry basic training taught by sadistic platoon sergeants does build bodies fast and well.

These lads apparently enjoyed their work and entered into serious situations with the esprit of small boys playing cowboys and Indians.

There was a major difficulty with the ration. The American supply service was simply not set up to provide fish, rice, and fresh vegetables. Meat was substituted for fish, and canned beans for rice, while vegetables also came out of cans from California. My recruits started to suffer. Certainly they liked meat, but giving them meat twice a day was like feeding children from a candy store. The human stomach just isn't capable of taking care of a continual feast.

With our overworked surgeon in tow, I visited the PGF G-4 and explained that I had five thousand upset stomachs that needed more rice and a hell of a lot less meat. He got on the phone to AFWESPAC G-4 and learned that there was a general shortage of rice. We had to support Japan, Chiang Kai-shek, the populations of all the islands we had taken from the Japs, as well as the Philippine Army and the Scouts, and the rice-growers of Texas and Louisiana were having difficulties in keeping up with the demand. There was a general worldwide shortage of rice.

So in conference with the G-4, quartermaster, and surgeon of Philippine ground forces my surgeon reached a fairly satisfactory compromise—fresh fish would be substituted for half the meat, canned fish would be furnished when available, and bread and potatoes would be issued in lieu of all the rice we were short on the Scout ration. PGF was firm in stating that they would not provide canyaos and balutes for the Scouts. I could not understand this decision since the materials were readily available and the recipes quite simple. For example:

Canyaos: Tie up dog. Give plenty water but do not feed for four-five days.

On fifth day give dog all the rice he can eat.

Beat dog to death all over with light clubs—makes meat tender.

Wrap dog in banana leaves.

Bake dog in pit with coals or hot stones 3–4 hours.

Stomach and intestines with rice stuffing especially tasty.

Balutes: Let hen set on eggs ten days.

Knock small hole in top of egg.

Insert straw and stir contents.

Suck contents through straw.

Note: Thirteen- to fourteen-day balute very hard to suck through straw. Maybe have to open shell, pour chicken out, and eat with fingers.

Inspecting the mess at mealtimes was fascinating, particularly at breakfast. A Scout would have his mess kit heaped with rice at the first kettle. On top of the rice would be placed a spoonful of scrambled eggs. Across that, a sardine or a piece of fried fish. The potables would be last in line, fruit juice and coffee. I had anticipated that they would take their fruit juice first with their only canteen cup, and come back later for coffee. But the Scouts had a simpler solution: have the cup filled with orange juice, pour it over the fish, eggs, and rice, and then present the empty cup for the coffee.

Knives, forks, and spoons remained in the pocket. Fingers served best to break up the fish and eggs, ball the pieces into a sticky clump of sweetened rice, and then pop the delicious combination into the mouth. I resented the hour that Major Simms, S-3, slipped into the training schedule on the subject, "Use of knife, fork, and spoon." These people had been doing very well using their own methods of eating for the last ten thousand years. Why not let them continue for the next thirty years? The mess tools were three minor pieces of equipment that we could eliminate.

Of course, the wasted hour at best had only a superficial effect. I noticed that as an officer passed through the mess hall, the use of knife, fork, and spoon increased directly in ratio to his proximity, and decreased directly with his distance after he had passed. The cooks and kitchen police also continued their evening custom of assembling a large common platter of leftovers (and holdouts) for an after-work snack, placing it on the floor in the kitchen, squatting around it on their heels, and happily ingesting the goodies without benefit of artificial aids.

As we approached the individual marksmanship season for our new Scouts, I became most apprehensive about the results. The Twelfth Division (PS) on their initial firing for record had qualified 8 percent of their men, which is I suspect the all-time low since the invention of gunpowder. They of course had been ordered to retrain and fire a second course but I hoped that we could avoid such humiliation. With the Twelfth Division's outstanding failure in mind, we concentrated on preliminary marksmanship for the depot Scouts. Firing positions, sighting exercises, trigger squeeze, procedure, and dry firing were repeated ad nauseam under the tutelage of cadre specialists whose service records showed that they could shoot well.

As soon as the first company was ready for live firing we trucked them to the Eighty-sixth Division range. The first exercise, sighting-in with single shots at two hundred yards, prone position, was carefully explained in English, which was interpreted for the "country boys" in Tagalog, Illocano, Longot, Visayan, Bontoc, Pampangan, Panganisanian, and Moro.

Each man was to fire one well-aimed shot at his target, which was marked with the same numbers as the stake at his firing position. The target would then be pulled down, the man in the pit would place a black spotter in the bullet hole, the target would then be shoved up again, and the value of the hit signaled by a marker on a pole. The firer would then mark the location of the spotter on the miniature target printed in his score book and calculate the correction he must make in elevation and windage to put the next bullet in the center of the bull's-eye. He would then correct his sight setting and fire again.

The first order of fifty recruits took their prone positions on the line, with their recruit coaches lying beside them. The cadre men, each in charge of five firing points, distributed one eight-round clip to each firer. The first sergeant who was commanding the company gave his orders.

"Lock and load! Ready on the right? Ready on the left? Ready on the firing line? C-o-m-m-e-n-c-e f-i-r-i-n-g."

I insisted on this method of giving the command to fire. Drawling the "commence firing" with a falling inflection will usually have a soothing effect on a nervous recruit and influence him to take his aim, perfect his aim, and squeeze the trigger for a good shot. This precaution was, however, totally in vain. There was the crash of a solid volley as forty-nine recruits jerked their triggers, followed by a stunned silence, but not for long. One lone belated shot, fired by an old Scout who had taken marksmanship long before, rang out on the left of the line. "Aha," thought each recruit. "We do it some more." And a rattling ripple of irregular rapid fire built up all along the line.

Cadre men were dashing from man to man shouting "cease firing," depressing muzzles, or slapping the firers on the shoulders. This would have a momentary effect, while the bewildered Scout was trying to understand what was wanted. Then he would evidently think "Aha! He mean shoot faster," and he would proceed to empty his clip. Targets were moving uncertainly down and up, bearing widespread spotters, but the momentary absence of a Scout's target never slowed his fire. If his own target was down, no matter, "I weel heelp my companion Binwac," and he would put a couple of rounds into the target next door until his own reappeared.

It was quite confusing, sounded like a brisk brawl on the Meuse in 1918. Rifles were cracking, ricochets howling, cadre instructors yelling, gravel jumping, targets bobbing, dust boiling, whistles blowing, and target frames and numbers dissolving in flying splinters, but the mad minute came to an end only after the last bullet had left the bore.

As the dust cleared away and the targets finally came up with widely scattered spotters inserted in the few bullet holes, I began to realize how the Twelfth Division (PS) had qualified only 8 percent of their men as marksmen. I could not understand, however, how three of my ambushed parties had fought their way clear without a scratch. Observing the plowed ground, the splintered target frames, and the virgin bull's-eyes, it would appear that a man being shot at could not move anywhere without getting killed—his only chance would be to stand perfectly still. As long as he was being shot at he would be comparatively safe.

The chagrined first sergeant who was commanding the company reassembled its four hundred heroes, conscientiously gave the detailed instructions again, with pauses for the ripple of translation, and deployed the second echelon on the firing line.

"Lock and load! Ready on the right? Ready on the left? Ready on the firing line? C-o-m-m-e-n-c-e f-i-r-i-n-g!"

Crrraassh! Rattle! Klattery! Bang!

When the rifles had all run dry for the second time I asked the first sergeant if he thought that issuing the cartridges one at a time might be an idea worth trying. He did, and in time the wild men absorbed the idea of slow fire, putting each precious bullet in or near that black spot in the center of the target.

The first company turned in a score of 78 percent qualification as marksmen or sharpshooters, considerably better than the 50 percent I had alternately feared and hoped for. As the same cadre men remained as specialists on the marksmanship training and range detail they became increasingly expert in their instructional methods and in surmounting the language barrier. Anticipating the idiosyncrasies of their wards, their qualification records crept up through the eighties. Finally one conscientious young technical sergeant proudly turned in the seldom-achieved record of 100 percent qualification and received a well-deserved battlefield promotion to the grade of master sergeant.

One evening we received a typhoon warning and I felt that I should jeep back to Camp Blackjack and the regimental area to check on the preparations being made to withstand the storm. It was dusk and there was danger of ambush during the hour's ride. I asked Major Wyrak to give me six reliable Scouts from his battalion, two to "ride shotgun" in my jeep, and four in the following escort jeep. The lads reported and I briefed them on the trip, "enemy capabilities," and their duties. I might well have been inviting them to a picnic. They clicked their safeties on, slipped clips into their carbines, and snapped their belts to shove the first cartridge "up the spout." They climbed aboard the jeeps, took positions facing the right and left fronts in a most professional manner, and seemed to look forward to the venture with grim but pleased anticipation. Major Wyrak had sent me experienced ex-servicemen, ex-guerrillas, or ex-bandits who undoubtedly knew all about ambushes—probably from both sides. Very comforting to have them along, even if we might encounter their brothers and cousins en route. They would probably even know the password if we ran into a Hukbalahap war party.

A hurricane in the Pacific is called a typhoon. Others say taifun, Chinese who started the name say Tai Feng, literally translated as too much wind. It is. We were threatened by three typhoons that summer but fortunately they all wheeled away toward China or Japan without too much damage to us. The fourth one, although it never got beyond the tropical storm stage, almost flattened us.

Our anti-typhoon drill was simple and well rehearsed. All clothing that could be gotten on was to be worn, topped off by fatigues, poncho, and helmet. It seemed ridiculous to wear all those clothes in the tropics but we faced the probability of spending a day or two in flooded ditches in cold, heavy rain, and the insulation was important. All other personal gear was stowed in B Bags. Cots were folded and tied in bundles. All lumber and corrugated iron was tied in large bundles, since planks and iron roofing sheets flying at 70–150 miles an hour would be as deadly as artillery fire. Official papers were stowed in company safes that would presumably not fly. Personal equipment was full canteens, two days' hard rations, full pack, and weapons.

When it became certain that we would be struck by high winds, the order would be given to strike tents. This was done by loosening the ropes on the tent stakes; then all hands who could get a grip lifted both tent poles off the floor and walked with them toward one side of the tent. The tent and ridge pole, of course, came down flat, falling to the opposite side with a crash. Upright poles were laid parallel to the ridge pole. The tent was then folded up to, and tied fast to, the pole with guy ropes, making a long, slim, and heavy cylinder that we hoped would stay with us.

On July 16 the wind was strong before Reveille, coming in fifty-mile gusts, and tents were beginning to rip at the seams. A message from Philippine ground forces stated that that typhoon would miss us, but it was evident that, typhoon or not, our tentage had to come down. I reluctantly gave the order to make everything fast, strike tents, and assemble in the mess halls that would shelter us through anything short of a typhoon.

In case the wind reached typhoon strength we would retire to the sides of the arroyo bordering the camp, dig in, and shudder in our icy water-filled fox holes for a day or two.

It was a dark, wet morning, with the heavy rain driving horizontally and the black clouds scudding low overhead. The slatting canvas, rippling and billowing in the gusts, was hard to handle. Work under these conditions was far more confusing than were the rehearsals we had previously carried out on a calm and sunny afternoon. A tent bellied out to the shape of a blimp, tore out all the stakes on one side and rose, carrying a dozen Scouts who were desperately clinging to the guy ropes, eight to ten feet off the ground before it collapsed again in a momentary calm.

A corporal was urging his section on in collapsing their tent.

"Now, you saddle-colored, lily-fingered, weak-backed bastards, everyone up! Goddamn you, put your backs into it, One, two, three—up. This way, you sonofabitch! Now down! Flatten her! Hey, jughead, gimme that line!"

When the tent was secured I called the hard-working young NCO aside.

"You don't talk like that to your men, corporal. You can see that they're doing their level best for you and doing pretty well too. Never insult them, just tell them what to do like they were American soldiers."

"Yes sir. But I was just talking to 'em the same way I got talked to in my recruit training. I thought that was the thing to do." Which is a hell of a commentary on the methods used at some training centers—probably commanded by a disciple of General Patton.

It was a miserable day and night. The heavy, cold rain drove through screens, shutters, and crevices, and the Scouts suffered severely from the unusual chill. My dog Chow was badly frightened and followed me closely, wet, scared, and shivering with the cold. He sniffed me frequently to find out how badly I was frightened. Most unusual, he consented to be wrapped in a raincoat and shivered, steamed, and whined all night. We set up our headquarters in a kitchen so we could promptly order the evacuation as soon as the roof started to go.

As far as room was concerned we were quite cozy, each battalion of 1,650 men eating and sleeping while wedged into a mess hall normally large enough for 400 men to eat at benched tables. The Scouts, however, uncomplainingly dozed and slept, some on the trestle-tables, others sitting or squatting underneath, the rest huddled in the aisles or against the walls. Those on the trestles were lucky—the water was five inches deep on the floor at times during the night.

At Reveille it was still raining hard but the wind had dropped. Our camp looked like a lost battlefield but collapsing and rolling the tents had saved them. The Fifth Replacement Depot area seemed to be badly battered with some tents gone, others tattered, and everything drooping. On receiving a message from PGF that the typhoon was veering away to the northwest I ordered the tents up.

While the men were struggling with their sodden, flapping canvas monstrosities, I received a call from G-4 of PGF.

"We've got a company of Philippine Scouts for you to take in; their camp was destroyed last night."

"OK, but you ought to see my camp. It looks like a lost cause."

"Well, whatever you've got it's better than what they've got; their camp is gone."

So with our overstrained facilities we all edged over a little and played host to a most miserable and bedraggled band who literally had nothing except the sodden khaki they were shivering in.

On July 24 in order to relieve overcrowding and to win larger training areas I organized a second camp for the fourth battalion at the abandoned PW camp at Lupow. We had had to furnish several junior officers for transfer to the Philippine Scout division and were down now to six officers per battalion rather than the normal complement of thirty-five.

That meant that the enlisted men of the cadre took on even more duties normally performed by officers of long service.

I at first had seriously doubted our ability to do the job with the means at hand. It was not reasonable to expect a second lieutenant after a short tour as a recruit and three months of officers candidate school to do a satisfactory job of commanding a four-hundred-man company—that's larger than most peacetime battalions. It was equally unreasonable to expect a corporal of less than a year's service to do well in the command of a platoon of a hundred men. Many an officer in the Old Army had ten years of service before he was given command of a skeleton company of seventy-five men and many never had a larger command. But the cadre men did their jobs, three to five ranks over their heads, and did them magnificently.

I watched Private Duncan, a former disciplinary problem, fussing over his three squads of recruits, checking the fitting of boots, teaching the use of mess gear, insisting on the correct angle for the cap, and going into a fit of apoplectic rage at the sight of a speck of rust or an unbuttoned pocket. What a change—just a short time ago he was wearing his own shirt not only unbuttoned but with the tails out as well.

In observing these lads at work I rediscovered some great truths. An American soldier given responsibility will live up to it. Given a constructive job that by all normal standards is impossible, he will probably do it. The greater the responsibility and the more constructive the job, the greater the chance that he will do it well. Last, he will be far happier filling a difficult requirement than he will be with nothing constructive to do.

I had only one serious difficulty with the 342d cadre men—they were too rough in their language and sometimes brutal in their requirements. I recalled what the corporal had told me on the morning of the tropical storm, "I thought that was the thing to do." They just hadn't been brought up right; that was the way they'd been treated themselves.

So I gave the assembled cadre a short talk about their dealings with their recruits, forbidding the use of profanity, obscenity, or insulting terms, a harsh or brutal tone of voice, and the use of pushups or double-timing around the field as punishment for minor mistakes. The Filipinos were too eager and willing to deserve such treatment and too proud and sensitive to take it well.

We were extremely fortunate in having Staff Sergeant Severino Pulido in the 342d band. He was a tall, well-built American citizen of Spanish-Filipino ancestry, and a professional soldier of many years' service. He was an accomplished musician, could play any of the normal band instruments, and had a gift for command. His ability to speak Tagalog gave me an idea—we needed a depot band. When I asked him for his opinion he was sure that given the instruments and twelve to sixteen men of his own selection he could shape up a satisfactory Scout band.

For the instruments I misappropriated some of those furnished by the athletic and recreation fund and borrowed more from our own attenuated band. Pulido unearthed an unused glockenspiel from somewhere in Manila, I didn't inquire how. S-1 Personnel delved through his records and turned up three Old Scout bandsmen and three dozen recruits who claimed to have played some sort of instrument or who wanted to be musicians.

Pulido eliminated a third of the aspirants in the first tryout. With the remaining material he started to work, and work is the correct word. His men put in a long eight-hour day of tooting, tweedling, thumping, and clanging, now and then united in a few bars of recognizable music.

I noted that in all his dealings with his recruits he required that they stand at attention, report smartly, address him as "Sir," and obey briskly. He was a stern disciplinarian and a demanding taskmaster.

The printed music for the various parts was in short supply and impossible to obtain for an unauthorized band. Pulido borrowed the tattered sheets of music from the 342d band and spent several nights copying the parts by hand on ruled typing paper, designating them as march number one, march number two, etc., for simplicity.

We had had three parades, with the American enlisted cadre acting as officers and senior NCOs. Except for the first parade for General Anderson, when I used the 342d band, we had been limited to the rattle and thump of one bass and one snare drum to keep time. Ten days after he had started training his men Sergeant Pulido reported that his band was ready for the scheduled Retreat parade with "The Star-Spangled Banner" and two marches.

His young men did very well indeed, playing march number one to bring the battalions on the field and march number two for officers front and center, but the national anthem was unrecognizable until "the twilight's last gleaming," and got really straightened out only on "the perilous fight." March number one was then played again for the review.

Sergeant Pulido stamped into my office that night looking like a destroying angel who has just accomplished his mission.

"Sir, I apologize for the national anthem at the Retreat review. It was—"

"Think nothing of it, Sergeant Pulido. After all, you've had the band only ten days and the marches went off perfectly."

"They can play 'Star-Spangled Banner' perfectly too, sir, the trouble was five of the recruits misunderstood and started on march number one again. But they will never do it again." (Dear God! Had he shot them?) "After this they will always remember." (No, he has probably just staked them out on anthills for the night. I was afraid to ask.)

"Thank you, Pulido, I'm sure they will." And he stamped out again.

In comparing Sergeant Pulido with some of my most outstanding officers I would rate him as being number five in making a success of our training the Scouts at the depot. With his help the recruits began to feel that they were really a part of the United States Army. Now they had the music and the banners of which they had heard so much in tales told by the envied and admired Old Scouts in the barrios before the Japanese trouble.

Two weeks later we received a visit by General Anderson and some of the inspecting staff from PGF and AFWESPAC. I invited them to take the Retreat review and the first and second battalions with four and five weeks training respectively put on the ceremony. By that time I had become accustomed to the amazing aptitude of Filipinos for close-order drill and merely felt proudly complacent when they swung on the field in columns and formed masses with the precision of veterans. But I was dumbfounded when Pulido produced his concealed ace while passing in review. As the band approached the reviewing stand he signaled with his baton and swung it to the salute. The music stopped and the drums and trumpets sounded the two ruffles and fanfare due a major general. Pulido swung the baton to end the salute and the band resumed the march music without missing a beat. I was completely surprised and so were my visitors. Although this courtesy has spread widely and has now become common practice, Severino Pulido was the first to develop and produce it before his startled commanding general (and his dumbfounded colonel).

Ten.

The FFFFFT

Organization

I was informed in mid-August that I would shortly be required to organize and train a new, separate Scout unit, the Forty-fourth Infantry Regiment (PS). After the minimum of necessary training I would take the regiment to Okinawa for occupation duty. There we would relieve the Twenty-fourth Infantry Regiment, which had a well-earned reputation for mutiny, murder, and rape, and was still making the main island a quivering hell on earth.

The skeleton 342d would be used initially as the cadre and the Forty-fourth would have a complement of fifty Americans and sixty Filipino officers. At such time as the American enlisted cadre could be released the 342d Infantry Regiment would be deactivated, the officers transferred to the Forty-fourth, and the enlisted men would be transferred to other units in the Eighty-sixth Division.

The twenty-second of August was a very large day. The name of the First Replacement Depot was changed to the Twenty-fifth Replacement Depot (PS) for no logical reason, causing considerable confusion in correspondence and records. All Scout units were authorized and required immediately to sew on the shoulder patches of the Twelfth Infantry Division (PS). This patch was a disaster in heraldry; it consisted of a frontal view of a mustard-yellow carabao skull on a red field and was neither inspiring nor beautiful. Yet the feeling at PGF was that this unappetizing symbol should be required for all Scout units in the future, rather than worn as a distinctive symbol of the Twelfth Division only.

I also received the order activating the new Scout separate regiment, the Forty-fourth, that was to be attached to the Eighty-sixth Division.

We had encountered a great deal of inertia and administrative delay in our effort to turn Camp Blackjack and the PA units being trained there back to the PA. The Philippine Army just wasn't up to the job of carrying its own weight and realized it. So for a short time I found myself carrying a rather wide field of responsibilities. These were:

342d Infantry Regiment
Twenty-fifth Replacement Depot (PS)
Twenty-first Replacement Depot (PA)
Forty-fourth Infantry Regiment (PS)
Corregidor

The 342d of course was spread over all of the other elements like a very thin coat of icing on a very thick cake.

Of course the Forty-fourth Fighting Filipino Foot (already referred to in light conversation as the FFFFFT) consisted of one major in command, two lieutenants for personnel and supply, one sergeant-major, and one clerk for the paperwork. But immediate preparations had to be made for the reception of recruits, and the varied array of responsibilities looked imposing when I presented the impossible situation to General Anderson, PGF.

I requested that a determined effort be made to jerk the Philippine Army out of its habitual coma and require it to take over Corregidor, Camp Blackjack, and the training of the PA units stationed there. I committed perjury by swearing that Lieutenant Colonel Gomez and his Scout officers were now perfectly capable of running the Twenty-fifth Replacement Depot (PS) and requested that Colonel Gomez be directed to relieve me of that command immediately. These changes would permit me to concentrate my very attenuated 342d troops on the formation of the FFFFFT.

General Anderson took a sympathetic view of the matter, the telephones started to buzz, the gilded staff took their feet off their desks, the mimeograph machines started to turn, the Philippine Army shuddered and burst into tears, and Gomez wrote his own recommendation for promotion.

Little else happened until mid-September when the 342d was united in their coconut-palm-decorated regimental area and we could concentrate on midwifing the birth of the new regiment.

At that point although I was still commanding the 342d my principal employer was the Philippine ground forces and the new Forty-fourth Foot would be attached to the Eighty-sixth Division for administrative purposes only. So for all practical purposes my connection with the Black Hawk Division was ended at this point.

By the end of August we started receiving a few officers for the Forty-fourth Infantry Regiment (PS) in the camp at Marakina. I had succeeded in turning over Corregidor to the PA but was able to obtain nothing better than a firm date, September 15, for my relief from the Philippine Army training center at Camp Blackjack and the Scout training at the Twenty-fifth Depot. I ruthlessly stripped most of the Americans from both of these areas, however, in order to start with a reasonable cadre for the Forty-fourth. After all, Camp Blackjack, the Twenty-fifth Depot, and Lupow were all going concerns—the Forty-fourth had to start from scratch. It would also do the Philippine Army and Colonel Gomez a great deal of good to start fending for themselves.

We now had the initial advantage of a well-experienced American cadre of enlisted men who had been dealing intimately and very successfully with Filipinos for two months. There were less than three hundred men in the 342d now but there were only half as many men to train, so I was confident that they would do well. We had also received a fairly complete complement of company grade officers during the last week of August, half being Filipinos, the rest Americans direct from the United States.

I had worked out a plan to have both the 342d and the Forty-fourth regiments work, play, and live together in the same area, intermeshed at all points to promote education and understanding by observation and imitation. Each American section leader and platoon sergeant was to live with his unit, with his Filipino understudy readily at hand. One officer of each company was to remain assigned to the 342d in order to have direct command over the cadremen; the others were all assigned to the Forty-fourth. Every American acting as a noncommissioned officer, technician, or specialist was to select a Filipino understudy and push his education until he could take over the job.

In only one respect were the units separated: due to the differences between the Filipino and American digestive systems an American mess had to be maintained by each battalion and by the regimental head-quarters company. Filipino officers were messed with their American counterparts (except when checking the Scout messes) but were kept happy by the high proportion of rice that was made available.

PGF informed me, a week in advance of their arrival, that I would receive recruits from a wide spread of provinces, mostly from rural, island, and mountain districts. Very few would be from Manila and the lowland plains—recruits from these areas had all volunteered at an early date and were in the Twelfth Division (PS) or the Twenty-fifth Depot. I feared that such a far-flung recruiting net would bring in men from a wide variety of tribes, which would not be conducive to mutual understanding or a peaceful existence within the regiment. I had had considerable unfortunate experience with intertribal warfare on a minor scale while dealing with the guerrillas, the Philippine Army, and to a lesser degree with the Twenty-fifth Depot Scouts. How to prevent this apparently chronic Filipino trouble was one of my greatest concerns. I now knew a little about Filipinos but not nearly enough.

So I talked the matter over with American officers of experience in the Philippine ground forces or Scouts, and when my first Filipino officers reported for duty I asked their advice on how to assign the recruits from the various provinces. The opinions of the Americans and the advice of the Filipinos were identical. Since the men were coming from different areas, spoke different dialects, and had different customs, they should be formed in companies according to their tribal origin. We should have each company consist wholly of Moros, Ifugaos, Bennguets, Bontocs, Illocanos, Visayans, Panganisanians, or Tagalogs, for example. Then they would be among friends, could talk to each other, and we would have no interracial trouble within the companies.

I thought this matter over through many an hour of insomnia for a week, and had recurring nightmares about racial wars between the companies. Then I dropped in on my harried S-1 and his Filipino understudy, Lieutenant Dayot.[1]

"Good evening, captain, lieutenant. Glad you're here, Dayot, I wanted to catch both of you to discuss troop assignments.

"Our first five hundred recruits will arrive tomorrow at 1000. You will, of course, take note of each man's alleged or possible MOS. I'd also like to have you pay particular attention to his race or tribe. Of course you can generally guess that by his province, but that doesn't always hold true. Lieutenant Dayot, I'd like to have you as our expert on Filipino personnel affairs talk to every man until you are sure of his background.

"Now it is of primary importance to send electricians to communications, drivers and mechanics to the service company, druggists to the medics, and big men to the cannon company, trying to put the round pegs into the round holes.

"A second and very important requirement for you, Lieutenant Dayot, I want you to see that the men of the tribes are so dispersed that there is not more than one man of any tribe in any squad. I want to break up old group friendships too, and smash the cliques before they start. Of your first twenty Tagalogs you assign one to each company and separate detachment in the regiment. Scatter your first twenty Ilongots the same way. You assign 'em to the companies and I'll take it from there. Got it?"

"Yes sir, we are to make an even distribution of men from different tribes and provinces among the companies." The Filipino seemed uncomfortable and very disapproving even as he repeated my instructions.

"What do you think of that method, Dayot?"

"Yes sir. It is no doubt a very good idea. But as you intend to organize the squads the men will frequently not be able to talk to each other and they will have no friends in the company."

"Well, Dayot, I have heard that all Filipino children have been taught some English in school, perhaps not well, but they do have some basic English. And that's a much better start than most recruits get in the French Foreign Legion. They will learn more English now and much faster than they ever did in school.

"As for their friends, I'm having you separate them on purpose. If a man lines up before you with four friends, you assign him to A Company, a friend to B, one to C, the next to D, and the last to battalion headquarters detachment. Each man will then have his old friends in the neighboring companies, he'll have men that talk his dialect in the next squad or platoon, and he'll have to use English to talk to anyone in his own squad.

That way we may prevent this damned senseless intertribal, inter-unit bickering that we've been cursed with in the past and all the recruits will be speaking fluent basic military English in six months."

Lieutenant Dayot, who was a most intelligent young man and a walking encyclopedia on all things Filipino, tactfully but reluctantly agreed. None of my senior American friends were so kind; with one doleful accord they prophesied trouble. What or how much trouble they couldn't say—such a weird idea had never been tried before in the forty-five-year history of the Philippine Scouts. Just like carrying high explosives and detonators in the same box over a rough road.

So on September 1, 1946, the Forty-fourth Foot came into being as a fully integrated unit, long before integration became a headline word in the United States. And in spite of gloomy forebodings the radical idea was most successful; all of the violent difficulties that the Forty-fourth ever had were with other units and Okinawans.

Granted that for the first few days the recruits looked askance at their "foreign" squad mates, they were completely overawed by the size, coloring, actions, strange smell, and the volume of the incomprehensible sounds emitted by the even more foreign cadreman—and he actually lived in the end of their tent and supervised practically every move they made throughout each long and entertaining day. Dogs don't fight in the presence of a grizzly bear.

By the end of the first week the Moro regarded the Visayan as his "companion"—a strange one, Allah knows, and a Christian infidel, but still a companion. As the weeks passed, the lone Illocano would speak of "my companions," meaning his polygamist assembly of squad mates rather than his old friends or tribesmen.

I have tried to trace the origin of this term companion, which seems to mean friend, "the man I am walking with" or "the fellow who was caught with me at the scene of the crime." Was it a direct translation from the Spanish *compañero?* Or was it derived from the stilted style of the outdated primary school textbooks furnished in Filipino schools since 1902? All Americans of Philippine experience are sure that it comes from the Spanish; the Filipinos are equally certain that it is English as the language should be spoken.

The 342d cadre strength was being continually depleted by returning men to the United States who would not be replaced. It was therefore necessary to expedite the selection of Scout understudies for all NCO grades and technicians.

There were, of course, many mistakes made in the initial selection, since the positions were naturally filled first with men who had the best knowledge of spoken and printed English. Education, however, does not necessarily go with command ability or desirable character and many adjustments would doubtless be necessary. A backwoods hunter would probably develop into a better squad leader or platoon sergeant than the initially selected Laoag schoolboy.

I wished to enable the company commanders to make such changes in personnel as might be required and yet avoid humiliating their erstwhile acting NCOs by reduction in rank. Therefore for the first month no chevrons were worn by understudies and no promotions were made.

On October 1 chevrons designating permanent rank were worn on the sleeves and painted on the helmets and helmet liners. Promotion to permanent rank would be painfully slow, according to the following table:

			Permanent Rank			
Acting Rank	1 Oct.	1 Nov.	1 Dec.	1 Jan.	1 Feb.	1 Mar.
Master Sergeant	Pfc.	Corp.	Sgt.	St. Sgt.	Tech. Sgt.	Mr. Sgt.
Technical Sergeant		Pfc.	Corp.	Sgt.	St. Sgt.	Tech. Sgt.
Staff Sergeant			Pfc.	Corp.	Sgt.	St. Sgt.
Sergeant				Pfc.	Corp.	Sgt.
Corporal					Pfc.	Corp.
Private First Class						Pfc.

By following this schedule an acting master sergeant who was found by January 1 to be more suited to the duties of a staff sergeant could be transferred to his new duties without too much loss of pride or prestige. With the lower ranks the shaking of the big chunks to the top and the little ones to the bottom would go on for some time, but in six months we should have achieved a state of equilibrium.

At long last the Philippine Army units at Camp Blackjack had completed their review of basic training under Colonel Stangle's stern supervision and iron fist and I was ordered to turn them and the camp over to the PA. This released Lieutenant Buergin and his handful of heroes to join our skeleton regiment at Marakina.

Colonel Stangle took over the job of regimental executive and I was able to give Colonel Holt command experience by assigning him to the first battalion. At the same time we received thirteen second lieutenants newly graduated from officers candidate school. I was amused to note that we now had forty-four lieutenants, exactly the same number as our strength in privates.

Unfortunately we didn't have that many for long. Two nights later five of the lads took a jeep and started for the Manila fleshpots. They dropped through the center section of a bridge from which the planking had been removed. Two were killed and the others so badly injured that they were never returned to duty. It was an odd occurrence in that there was no ambush or looting of the bodies. The investigating CID people could only theorize that the trap had been laid to eliminate a little-loved Filipino politico and that the trappers had been frightened and ran away when they found they had caught the wrong man.

Filipino Assistants

Lieutenant Dayot, the assistant S-1, was the first Filipino officer to report for duty with the Forty-fourth. He was a most capable, alert, and intelligent young man who had a thorough knowledge of his country and countrymen. In addition he had a most pleasing personality; he gave one the impression of Maurice Chevalier. Given any reasonable opportunity I was sure that he would be a future president of the Philippines. He'd get my vote.

In addition to his other duties I gave him the task of giving an orientation talk to each contingent of incoming recruits. He was magnificent in the job and it was a pleasure to observe his handling of a most difficult lingual situation. His talk in the most basic English covered the wearing of the uniform, decent behavior, and the customs of the military service. The new Scouts would give intense but largely uncomprehending attention. Now and then he would elaborate or relate an anecdote in one of the major dialects and fifty faces in one section of the audience would brighten with understanding. A wisecrack in another language and another group would chuckle in appreciation. He knew four of the principal dialects of the country and used them to play on his audience like a master on his violin.

I had asked him to emphasize the prohibition of theft and gang fights and he rammed those points home like Moses imposing the Ten Commandments on the wayward Children of Israel. He must have reached all of them. In my twenty months of association with the men of the Forty-fourth we had no thefts and only one murder within the regiment, and they won a wide reputation for reliability and soldierly conduct in all respects.

My dealings with guerrillas had given me a great antipathy for Filipinos. I knew everything about Filipinos and was positive that in spite of their expressed friendship and overwhelming hospitality they were all self-serving, treacherous, ineffective, thieving rascals. I knew that given American officers I could control any number of them as enlisted men—but Filipino officers? Never!

Which merely shows my abysmal ignorance on the subject.

Some sixty small, neat young men from the Twelfth Division (PS) reported as the framework of the new Forty-fourth Infantry (PS) separate regiment, and were assigned to the Caucasian-commanded cadres. There were two majors, four captains, and a horde of first and second lieutenants to become acquainted with. And I began to learn something about Filipino officers. A very general description of their characteristics follows:

1. Absolute loyalty to their unit, duty, and commander—loyalty to a degree unknown among American troops.
2. Fear of responsibility.
3. Pleasing personalities.
4. Lack of initiative. A few had initiative—most didn't.
5. Excellent instructors of their men.
6. Regulation-bound.
7. Superior physique and coordination.
8. Low alcoholic tolerance and no drunkenness. I was astounded by their preference for a beer in one hand and a Coca-Cola in the other, sipped alternately, and the effect thereof.
9. Emotional. Strong feelings that they didn't mind showing, quite different from the Anglo-Saxon reserve.

I was particularly struck by the fear of responsibility. Like any unit commander, when I approach a group or activity I expect the senior officer or NCO to report, or come to meet and tell me what is going on. These people would merely look apprehensive, gave the impression of huddling for mutual protection. I would ask, "Who is in charge?" Each officer would look right and left, hoping that someone in the group was senior to him, and if an American of any rank was reasonably near they would lay the onus of command on him—an American corporal would do.

On thinking it over I suppose that fear of responsibility, lack of initiative, and a slavish adherence to regulations are the result of three hundred years of peonage under their Spanish masters, when aggressive peons were eliminated as possible troublemakers or rebels.

These officers were almost all former Scouts, Philippine Army, Philippine constabulary, and/or guerrillas, and most of them had had some combat experience. Most of them were Tagalog, since these lowlanders had the greatest educational advantages. Several of them deserve special mention.

I have already described Lieutenant Dayot as most useful in the initial formation of the Forty-fourth. Any time I needed information about tribes, customs, or Filipino psychology I called on him.

Lieutenant Bonilla was a Moro, a most unusual type. Moros are usually short, skinny, religious fanatics, mean as cobras, and look it. Bonilla was short but plump, tolerant, good-humored, a Filipino Billikin who, Fiona told me, did a wonderful rumba, while Lee recommended him for the cha-cha.[2] His religion forbade alcoholic beverages but he risked the displeasure of Allah and Mohammed at every regimental party. I still cherish one of the family Kris that his father sent me.

Captain Amor, his name appropriately translated as "love," was another outstanding dancer and entertainer of the ladies in spite of his diminutive size. He had a pleasing personality, could con the torch from the Statue of Liberty, and had a gift for scrounging, so he went to S-4 as chief scrounger. Had a beautiful little wife whom he had to leave in Manila when we embarked for Okinawa. She saw the ship off, presenting the ladies of my family with leis of pungently sweet flowers. Before the hills of Luzon had faded in the distance Captain Amor was making good time with a receptive Red Cross Filipino.

First Lieutenant Apeles was tall—a lot of Spaniards in his ancestry— with a slightly pockmarked visage, a degree in civil engineering, the intelligence to adapt his education to our use in the field, and the initiative to use it. His ambition was to install water and sewage lines, flush toilets, and bathtubs throughout Manila. He was also placed in the S-4 staff with the unauthorized title of regimental engineer. He worked wonders with little or unsuitable material and inadequate tools.

Lieutenant Tabuka was a Bontoc, dark, reserved, and unobtrusive. He was the lad who returned from home leave and presented me with his uncle's head axe and hardwood, bamboo-bound shield that bore the marks of hard service. He quoted his uncle as saying that the constabulary were so thick in his area that he saw little chance of using them any more. Besides, he said, he had already made his reputation and was now too old to make war.

Captain Ileto was a graduate of the U.S. Military Academy in the class of 1943. He was small, pleasant, and the best chess player I've been beaten by. I spotted him as a good man and the Philippine Army agreed with my opinion. He was on their general staff in 1950, commanding general of their staff college in 1955, their national intelligence coordinating agency 1958–1964, commanding general Philippine constabulary 1966– 1972, vice chief of staff Philippine armed forces 1972–1975. Retired as a three-star general in 1975 and was appointed ambassador to Iran and Turkey.[3]

Captain Suatengeo was also a graduate of West Point in 1943. He was a tall, well-built man with a Spanish reserve. He had gone into the United States Army in 1944 and was a member of the First Parachute Infantry Regiment in 1944–1945. I was entirely mistaken in Suatengeo—I judged his cool, noncommittal, reserved attitude to be anti-Americanism, probably caused by his treatment at West Point and in the army by ignorant Caucasians to whom all Orientals are gooks. But in retrospect he was cold in dealing with his fellow Filipinos, came to regimental parties but never played with the hoi polloi, never drank, just observed. So I now believe that he lived as the reincarnation of some ancient Spanish Don Suatengeo, just couldn't unbend. Further, when I was leaving Okinawa after a year of duty as Ryukyus D/C-C/S, and in no way connected with the Forty-fourth, Captain Suatengeo attended the farewell party given by the officers of the regiment for my family. Some of the officers, with an eye to army politics, had other engagements.

Captain Zialcita was a surgeon, a tall, slim, capable officer of excellent physique and pleasing personality. He was in the Philippine Army, captured at Bataan, and a veteran of the death march. Wore his hair in a short crew cut and after two beers and a Coca-Cola was the life of the party. His imitation of a Japanese PW camp commander would lay the audience in the aisles. When I was stationed at West Point in 1949, Fiona was startled to hear the characteristic Filipino "sssssst" behind her, turned, and there was Zialcita, grinning from ear to ear. After the embrazo—

"Captain Zialcita! What are you doing here?"

"Oh, about a year ago I became interested in playing tennis. I am touring the United States with the Philippine tennis team."

I was quite well satisfied with the Filipino officers we had received. They seemed to be satisfactory, excellent to superior. An exception, Major Gomez, M.C. As the senior medico of the regiment he had to be regimental surgeon and I hoped for the best.

During the next few days I observed and talked with the lad now and then, put my observations together, and wished I had someone else in his place.

Major Gomez was a well-built officer of good appearance, obviously a Spanish-Tagalog mestizo, educated, very stupid, morose and withdrawn. He envied and hated Americans and had a great dislike and contempt for his fellow Filipinos except other equally well-educated Tagalogs. I think he even disliked himself.

He was afraid of making mistakes. Mistakes are most often made by men who assume responsibilities and do things, therefore in order to avoid making mistakes it is obvious that one should avoid responsibility and do nothing. He did.

He was unobtrusive to an extreme, the invisible man, never seen or heard unless one looked him up or sent for him. Normally one forgot his very existence.

He was very unhappy. He was unhappy about being transferred from a cushy job with no responsibility in the Twelfth Scout Division, he was unhappy about not being promoted, and was really desolated about the prospect of foreign service in Okinawa. Remembering Lieutenant Colonel Gomez, my successor in the Scout replacement depot, I wondered if all of these undesirable qualities ran true in the Gomez family. So much for practical psychology.

I first learned something about his professional competence when he and I arrived neck and neck at the side of an American cadreman who had taken a caliber .45 bullet just above his belly button. Major Gomez very properly pulled out a morphine syrette and jabbed it at the lad's upper arm, then at the thigh, hard, seemed to be requiring an unusual amount of force to get the hypodermic in. My wounded warrior who until then had apparently been suffering little pain and was in mild shock tried to sit up and protested vigorously.

"For Chrissakes, Doc, take it easy! You're s'posed to pull the plastic cap off the needle first, then it goes in real slick."

He did, and it did. He then pasted a .75-inch band aid over the .45-inch hole and eased away to call an ambulance, passing the buck to more competent hands. I resolved then that if I ever needed surgery and Gomez was in the vicinity I would take a hefty slug of bourbon and do the job myself with mirrors and a pocket knife.

Major Lopez was the chaplain, a solidly built Tagalog of good appearance in uniform. In his priestly robes he was magnificent and put on an excellent Mass. He was normally sullen, American-hating, and treacherous.

Captain Stief, the capable commander of the service company, selected and introduced my driver, Acting T-5 De Leon. The lad was tall for a Filipino, slender, well built, with a bold, open look. He was an Igorote from one of the mountain tribes and had the dark complexion of his Indonesian ancestry, but a rather aquiline cast of countenance indicated that a Spaniard had climbed his family tree. His family had moved to Manila before the Japanese trouble and he had attended the schools of the city.

I first learned that he was a "wild man" during our own USO show that featured the native dances of the various tribes. I was astounded to recognize my supposedly civilized driver, armed with spear, shield, and head axe, as the star performer in the Igorote cast, stabbing with bloodthirsty enthusiasm at my second driver, Moteo, who I knew was a Kalinga.

The Spanish name was unusual among the mountain people and I wondered how he got it. Was it from a Spanish ancestor of long ago? Or did his family merely adopt the name as protective coloring when they moved into the lowlands? I don't know. He didn't say and I didn't think it would be tactful to ask.

De Leon was quite a linguist, speaking Tagalog, Japanese, English, and the dialects of the Igorote tribes. He had enjoyed school and, being intelligent, had benefited from his twelfth-grade education.

I asked him what he would do if he decided to leave the Scouts at the end of his enlistment.

"I am going to be a detective or a lawyer, sir. I would rather be a detective, but a lawyer has better pay."

I noted the words "I am going to be," which he used rather than "I would like to be." The difference in phraseology made me take a second look. A lad with that attitude—he deserves a little help.

"I can't give you a start in police work. The Scouts on Okinawa don't have MPs. But the Twelfth Division Scouts in Luzon have everything— MPs, counterintelligence, and a criminal investigation detachment. Would you like to transfer to the Twelfth Division?"

"Oh no sir, I want to stay in this regiment."

"Well, a detective or a lawyer should know something about law. I have some law books. Would you like to read them?"

"Oh yis sir."

So when we reached my quarters I presented him with three weighty volumes on common law, criminal law, and military law, which I'd been carting around unopened since my first-class year at West Point.

He took them as though they were the stone tablets of the Ten Commandants.

"I will return them in good condition, sir."

"No, do not return them. They are all yours."

I know that he put them to good use. There was always one of them in the compartment where most soldiers carry paperbacks or comic books to while away the waiting time of long conferences. So if I'm ever thrown into the slammer in Manila, I shall certainly call for Chief Detective, Police Inspector, Counsellor, or Judge De Leon to come to my rescue.

Oh yes, among his other virtues De Leon was an excellent driver, his machines never ran out of gas or broke down, and he always dismounted with carbine or M-3 in hand, scanning the surrounding terrain.

Eleven

Cultural Differences

Order

The newly formed Forty-fourth was composed of excellent but most unsophisticated recruits from rural, mountain, and island provinces of the Philippines. Few of these men had any previous knowledge of modern devices such as, for example, the telephone.

Therefore as part of the training program I required that all non-commissioned officers learn the use of the telephone installed in each company and battalion headquarters.

In practice this training in telephone communication went through several unsatisfactory phases:

Phase 1. The telephone rings. The NCO in charge of quarters jerks awake and regards the devilish instrument with frozen horror until it stops ringing.

Phase 2. The telephone rings. The NCOCQ cautiously lifts the receiver and when a plaintive voice asks who the blue blazes is there he drops the phone.

Phase 3. The telephone rings. The NCOCQ lifts the receiver, cautiously states, "B Company Orly Room, Corpral Bantoc speak." Then when the calling party identifies himself the NCOCQ firmly hangs up.

We finally got to the stage where I felt that I could get my messages through. I called headquarters of the third battalion and was delighted to get a quick response.

"Third battalion headquarters, Sergeant Mahmud speak."

"This is Colonel Triplet, do not hang up, don't put this phone down."

"Yiss sar. But the Coronel Treeplet he ees not here."

"But this is Colonel Triplet speaking."

"Yiss Sar, I go look for heem."

"Wait—" But it was too late, and five minutes passed while the blood pressure zoomed. At long last, "Sar, the Coronel Treeplet he ees not here."

"But this is Colonel Triplet. Let me speak to the battalion com—"

"Yiss sar, I go look for heem again."

So I hang up and jeep over to the third battalion. As I draw up in front of the headquarters I am met by a proudly saluting Scout sergeant who reports, "Sergeant Mahmud, sar. Someone want speak weeth you on telephone, sar."

We had lessons on "How to Make Beds," a strange requirement to most of our pupils, who had always slept on pallets laid on the bamboo floor. This was followed by an hour on "The Use, Care, and Cleaning of Mess Equipment" with detailed explanation, demonstration, and class execution of the proper handling of knife and fork. They were already familiar with the use of the spoon to cope with anything too sloppy or sticky to handle with the fingers. They did fairly well at it as long as they were watched, so I felt that we could now concentrate on military subjects. But I had not anticipated the toilet paper crisis.

Our initial issue of toilet paper had been delayed for a week as were so many other vital supplies. We had filled the gap with bundles of outdated *Pacificans,* old files of bulletins, and extra copies of orders. It was not really an emergency; toilet paper was not even missed by the Scouts recruited from the distant hills, islands, and jungles.

Finally the great day arrived and a truckload of toilet paper was distributed to the companies in the late afternoon.

Next morning at Reveille the camp had a most festive air. One truck-load of toilet paper had been innately festooned from tent to tent and from pole to bush all over the area—looked like a Manila fiesta.

I reluctantly agreed with Major Simms, the S-3, that we would have to squeeze an additional hour of instruction into our crowded training schedule, entitled "The Proper Handling and Use of Toilet Paper," to be supervised by the American section leaders.

Filipinos are a most courteous people. One aspect of their courtesy is the lowered voice. There is some logic in this custom: it is discourteous to shout, therefore the soft voice is the polite form of address, and the softer the politer.

Although they were capable of clacking away at each other with a volume perfectly understood within pistol range, our Scout recruits would drop several decibels in questioning their American section leaders, use a softer tone when speaking to their company or battalion commanders, and lower their voices to inaudible whispers when reporting to me. With my blast-damaged eardrums I found this recognition of my rank to be most annoying; I could see the lips move but couldn't read what they were saying. They weren't paralyzed by fright—they were just being extremely courteous to a man of my age and rank, exactly as they would speak softly to a patriarch of their family or barrio.

Finally I held a meeting of all of the Filipino officers and asked them to help me.

"Please assure your Scouts that I appreciate the thought behind the soft voice, that it is Filipino custom. That is very well for Filipinos because your people have such acute hearing. But in the service of the United States your men will be continually encountering American officers who cannot hear as well as Filipinos, and the older or more senior these officers are the less they can generally hear. Therefore in the American Army the customs of courtesy are reversed and a man reporting to or talk-ing with an American colonel or general should do so loudly and firmly.

"So please convince your men that when one of them reports to an American field officer or general he should stand up as though he were nine feet tall and personally owned that part of the world. He should salute, never bow. Then he should report loudly for example:

" 'Corporal Tangat, commanding third squad, first platoon, A Company, sir.' "

The Scouts got the word. I was frequently amused thereafter when some unsuspecting motherly inspector general received his first blast from a Scout NCO—one ancient colonel jerked right out from under his pince-nez, and some of them perceptibly jumped. Mostly they simply winced a bit. But no one received a repeat, and none asked the reporting soldier any of the usual idiotic questions, presumably for fear that they'd get blown off their feet again.

My new cadre men who had rejoined the regiment from Corregidor and Camp Blackjack also had to be oriented on the use of the voice. I overheard one of my veteran sergeants giving one of his newly arrived friends a discourse on this matter.

"You gotta talk easy to 'em. It's like this—you're over six feet tall, you weigh 195, you got three stripes and a rocker, and you're the first redheaded, green-eyed, freckle-faced monster this little recruit has ever seen. He's five-feet-two and weighs maybe 98 pounds. Now how'd you like to have some purple-skinned, green-haired, red-eyed, 300-pound, seven-foot general bellow at you in Martian all of a sudden? It'd scare the livin' be-Jesus outa you. You gotta talk easy, and keep it simple."

Couldn't have said it better myself.

By mid-November the Forty-fourth had a full complement of thirty-eight hundred men and was well on the way to basic training. We had had great difficulty with the supply of uniforms and boots since the depots had been drained of small sizes by the requirements of the Twelfth Division (PS) and the First Replacement Depot (PS). But Major Schneider, now our very capable S-4, had not been stopped by the empty warehouse shelves. He had raided the salvage dumps and warehouses and obtained fifteen thousand American-sized Class X (unserviceable) uniforms and several thousand small Class X boots in fair condition. He then contracted with a Filipino tailoring firm to repair and cut down the oversized uniforms to fit our men. The boots were put through the quartermaster repair service.

The avidity of the rural recruits for combat boots was pitiful. A man who had probably never owned a pair of shoes in his life, when told that there were none on hand to fit him, would frantically start jamming his widespread, perfectly formed feet into a boot two inches too long and two sizes too narrow. Constant alertness and firmness on the part of the cadre men was required to prevent the escape of recruits hobbling out in boots that would immediately put them in the hospital. I felt that it was stupidly wrong to try to put boots on men who had such capable feet; barefooted, they could outwalk any American in these hills any day. Our Fiji Scouts had never been hampered by boots and the Askaris of the British African colonies did quite well barefooted. But boots were required by our high command and desired by the Scouts, so we put boots on them.

I was quite dissatisfied with the prospect of wearing the carabao skull shoulder patch as prescribed for all Philippine Scout units. For this corporate regiment I wanted a distinctive insignia. It would be worse than useless to appeal to PGF or to the heraldry division of the adjutant general's office. It had been my experience that requesting permission to do anything unusual was generally futile. So it was up to me to devise insignia for the Forty-fourth. After getting them sewn on 11,400 shirts, the chances of staying there would be fairly good I hoped.

But what insignia? A Moro kris, rampant, would antagonize all of the Christians and pagans. An Illocano shield would be a serious affront to the Igorots, and a Bontoc head ax would offend the Luzon lowlanders. No one group could be favored over another or we'd have trouble.

Finally my doodlings jelled on a plain shield, shaped like the plan view of a canoe, three inches high and half as wide. This would be easy to cut uniformly, had never been used by the heraldry division, and bore no resemblance to any Filipino shield. The color—red of course.

So I asked Major Schneider to find, draw, beg, or trade for a quantity of red cloth. It took some doing and several days. At the next officers school the cloth was distributed to the unit commanders with instructions for its use. Three mornings later the Forty-fourth stood Reveille as the Red Shield Regiment.

They were simple but very eye-catching insignia, certainly distinctive, and had exactly the effect on the troops that I had hoped for. The men stood up all of their five and one-fourth feet tall, flaunted their shoulder patches at their carabao-skull-branded brothers in arms, and swaggered a little.

Several inspecting officers from PGF and AFWESPAC were startled into derogatory comments about unauthorized insignia in their reports. These I disregarded. General Hazlett, who was now the division commander, was quite pleased with the innovation and as I had hoped stoutly defended the wearing of the illegal red shield by his attached Scouts. Our pride ran high until the first shirts returned from the laundry. Major Schneider had only been able to pick up a small amount of cloth here, another type there, and a third batch of the required color somewhere else. In the laundering process the flannel patches had shrunk and puckered and the cotton shields had run in varying degrees, so that the sleeve and shoulder patch were both colored the same general shade of pink. An irreverent lieutenant suggested that the regiment be renamed the Mangas Coloradas, in honor of the red-sleeved Apache chief of that name.[1]

After that disaster the officers club fund came to the rescue and Schneider was able to buy a quantity of uniform, well tested, color-fast red cotton for future use, and with repeated launderings our left shirt sleeves faded to the standard khaki again.

We had been able to draw a full complement of helmets and plastic helmet liners, both somewhat marred and beaten by hard use. Captain Stief of the service company put his paint guns to work on a production line basis and repainted the helmets in the standard olive-drab. Work came to a screeching halt at that point. I asked him to proceed to paint the helmet liners and stencil the red shield on each side, since I intended to use the light plastic liners for all purposes short of a shooting war.

"Yes, colonel, we'll have 'em painted and stenciled in two days' time, just as soon as we can get the paint."

We checked with Major Schneider. Stief was right; olive-drab was simply not to be had anywhere in the Pacific until shipments arrived from the States, and at this time no one in AFWESPAC would dare prophesy when that would be.

"All right, Stief, we have lots of paint, everything except OD. Take what you have, mix it until it looks good, and spray it on. We'll repaint in OD when the stuff gets here."

Five hours later Captain Stief arrived at my office with a brilliantly lacquered black helmet liner with a very faint tinge of green glinting in the sunlight. The freshly enameled red shield, still damp, pointed it up in scarlet on each side.

"That's the best I can do with the paint on hand, colonel. We have a hell of a lot of black enamel and not enough of any other kind."

It didn't take long to sell me on the unusual color—it was a splendid-looking headgear and this time I had a good excuse for stepping out of line.

"It's perfect, Stief, now copy it 3,899 times." The headgear problem was solved.

Our Class X combat boots with the rough side of the skin outside were never intended to be polished; they were supposed to be greased with dubbin to make them waterproof. Like all suede they absorbed water like a sponge unless dubbined. But since the end of the war, dubbin was in short supply. In order to waterproof the boots as well as to smarten the appearance of the troops I had directed that the boots be scrubbed and polish used heavily to fill the rough leather. But we found that the war-worn, weathered, and repaired boots that we had been able to get were in such poor condition that a decently uniform brown could never be obtained—the polishes available gave us a variety of all shades of tan, brown, cordovan, and oxblood. So in order to follow out the color scheme started by the headgear I notified the company commanders that all leather would be scrubbed, dyed, waxed, and polished black. All dyes and polishes except black were removed from the branch post exchange and the FFFFFT soon had the best polished, blackest headgear, footgear, and rifle slings in the Pacific theater.

One of the penalties to developing a good unit of men with high esprit is their invariable compulsion to convince neighboring units of their superiority. In this case, in the far corner of the Eighty-sixth Division area, we were fairly well isolated from encounters with other Scout units except one, a separate Scout tank battalion that was being trained practically on our doorstep. After a series of nightly ambushes and brawls resulting in three stabbings and a broken arm, I called on Lieutenant Dayot again for help. He put on a lecture, the substance of which was the military Golden Rule, "Thou shalt not kill or cripple thy neighbor except as thy duly appointed officers command thee." Again Dayot's uncanny ability to sway his audience in four languages prevailed and we had no more serious violence until some time after occupying Okinawa.

We had continuing difficulty in one respect. We tried but were unable to convince our men that they should be unarmed when they left the post on pass. The pass trucks were escorted and protected by armed guards and theoretically it was not necessary or desirable for the men to carry weapons of any sort on social occasions. That was the American viewpoint. The Filipinos knew better. They would rather go to Manila naked than to be caught there unarmed. We found it necessary to require a shakedown search of every man prior to his leaving on pass.

At first we confiscated pistols, perfected pistol racks, checks, and safeguards, and reduced a few acting supply sergeants who had keys in the pistol racks and passed out pistols to their friends. Then we found a number of mess kit knives that had been lovingly ground to a razor edge on both sides. Finally after we thought they were fully civilized, a first sergeant of the 342d cadre made a discovery.

"This man reported to the orderly room for his pass. Couldn't find my pen to sign it, nowhere. But then I saw the cap of a fountain pen sticking out of his shirt pocket. So I just reached over and pulled it out. It wasn't no pen, it was just camouflage for the hilt of a ten-inch stiletto."

So we started inspecting fountain pens as well.

Recreation

In October we were joined by the Filipino Red Cross, a quartet of pretty young Filipinas who worked for a month of orientation with our original

American Red Cross crew. I was delighted when they reported to find a former guerrilla acquaintance among them.

During the previous week I had been invited to a guerrilla reunion in the Manila Hotel. The celebration was sponsored by several of their organizations and the food and drink was laid on with typical Filipino lavishness. Colonel Alvares introduced me to my dinner partner.

"Mees Domeengo, these ees Coronel Treeplet. Mees Domeengo was magneefescent weeth the guerrillas een Panay."

Miss Domingo certainly didn't look like any guerrilla I'd ever dealt with before. She was a cupcake, an Oriental Petty Girl in a mestiza costume that would evoke cheers from a jaded audience in the Folies Bergères. She laid her cards on the table at once.

"Oh, Coronel Treeplet, I am so threeled! Yesterday I was een Panay and tonight I am at a deener een the Maneela Hotel!" and she swept the dining hall, to include the tarpaulin covering the hole in the shell-battered ceiling, with the awe-struck wonder of a small orphan seeing its first Christmas tree. She dismissed her guerrilla career briefly.

"Oh, I onlee carried the messages and theengs."

I tried to get her a drink, but without success until she was assured by me and two witnesses who vouched for me that Coca-Cola definitely did not contain alcohol. But she was fascinated by the sight of her compatriots drinking their horrendous mixtures of rum and gin that they called highballs. So was I.

When I started on my second modest bourbon and water she remarked, "I have always heard that Americans always dreenk only wheeskey. How many bottles of wheeskey do you have to dreenk each day?"

"Oh, about one bottle a day is usually enough, two or three at parties or on Sundays."

I naturally considered making a serious pass at the young lady and started formulating my approach while listening to her enthusiastic chatter about the "DC-3 Ayeeroplane" that flew the Panay delegation to AFWESPAC, the wonders of civilization in "Maneela," and riding in "Jeepneys."

In the meantime various old friends and enemies were coming over to "have a dreenk weeth the coronel." I would introduce the lad to Miss Domingo, and all hands would exchange mutual felicitations. He would then dilute my bourbon and water with a dollop from his bottle of Four Feathers, Old Mildew, gin, champagne, rum or medicinal alcohol. I would add a splash of my bourbon to his glass, and we would then sip hellish concoctions cautiously.

During a lucid moment I realized that Miss Domingo was introducing some of these characters to me. I noticed that these neatly uniformed men smiled and were very pleasant from the cheekbones down; above that line they were coldly suspicious. A rapid-fire exchange would then take place in the Panay dialect. My ESP was working well by that time and I could clearly follow the content of the conversation. These people weren't coming over to have a drink with me; they were brothers, cousins, uncles, fathers, and probably sweethearts coming over to check on the condition, conduct, and treatment of the Daughter of the Regiment. And she was scornfully firm in her assurances that this old goat wasn't going to be any trouble, and she could damned well take care of herself.

So I radically revised my plans. I would probably have just as much luck and would certainly live longer if I propositioned a member of the British royal family, so I decided that continuing my present fatherly role would be the most profitable course. Faint heart never won fair lady, but faint hearts also don't get cut out so often by vengeful relatives. Too bad—she was the only guerrilla I had ever really liked.

So being acquainted with Miss Domingo's total unsophistication I was somewhat doubtful, on seeing her in the uniform of the Red Cross, about her survival among the licentious soldiery. But my concern was for nought; Mees Domeengo remained the permanent shining light of the Forty-fourth Infantry Red Cross club in Marakina and Okinawa until the deactivation of the Philippine Scouts throughout the United States Army three years later.

Tech Sergeant Severino Pulido had had his usual success with forming a band for the Forty-fourth, and with a mere adequate supply of legally acquired instruments he had an eighteen-piece band and an excellent orchestra in operation. Now as a separate regiment I felt that we needed our own distinctive march.

The officers club board concurred with the idea, and granted $150 to put up for a prize for a march contest. The contest was advertised with the suggestion that the march should appropriately be a medley, including a few bars each of several Filipino songs. We thought that as many provinces or peoples as possible should be represented, with the typical music of flutes, beat of bamboos, and clanging gongs. Even the clack of coconut shells should be included if feasible. Sergeant Pulido then grabbed the ball and ran with it.

It was a busy month for the band. They didn't appear quite as often for parades or concerts but they worked overtime tootling, whistling, and thumping bars of music in strange cadences, most of it obviously unsuitable for march music unless it were modified. At long last Sergeant Pulido reported that the contestants were ready and suggested that the winner be selected at an evening concert at the Memorial Theater.

He had worked steadily for the past month. He had composed the theme of his own march, arranged the parts, and written the scores for the various instruments. In addition he had done full and impartial justice to his two competitors by arranging and writing their music for them.

At the theater the following evening there was a standing-room attendance. The terms of the contest were stated, the three marches would be played consecutively, and the one receiving the most applause would be selected as the regimental march.

Pulido raised his baton.

The first offering was a typical Teutonic brass band march after the school of Sousa, quite appropriate for a parade of the Schuetzstaffel down Unter den Linden, but certainly not Filipino. I was disappointed and a bit alarmed when it received a rousing general applause. "Well, after all, it will be their march and if they want it, OK."

The second entry had a weird, repetitive melody, with muted drumbeats and relying heavily on the cymbal and glockenspiel. It was definitely Oriental and I thought much more suitable. The applause, however, was light and from small clumps of the audience. The author had evidently used only the music of his own people and it had no appeal for the mass of the regiment.

The third march played had a catchy lilt and swing, with four distinct themes, and sounded Filipino. As the last drumbeat died away, twothirds of the Scouts were on their feet and howling their approval. This was it. The Forty-fourth Filipino Foot had selected their own regimental march.

The winning composer was, of course, Sergeant Pulido, and at the next parade he marched front and center to receive his well-earned prize. I asked him to remain to take the parade, while the Forty-fourth passed in review, with his band playing his opus.

But Pulido was not through with work on his march. He revised it to fox-trot time and wrote the music for the piano and the stringed instruments of the orchestra. In this form it became popular in the officers club and at the dances conducted by the Red Cross.[2]

Until the organization of the Forty-fourth every USO performance arriving on the Philippine circuit had played at the Memorial Theater. We had been shunned since the Scouts came in. Of course we had movies—Class B cowboy, gangster, and horror films—but I felt that we were entitled to live shows at least as much as the malcontents and mutineers in Manila. But discussion with the USO manager revealed that he was authorized to put on the shows only before American audiences "for our boys." Evidently the Filipino Scouts were with but not a part of the American Army, not our boys.

I was angered by this unthinking attitude and discrimination and butted my brains out against the walls of special services, PGF, and

AFWESPAC, which only increased the headache. So I determined that we would have our own shows. As a starter I interviewed my ubiquitous Lieutenant Dayot.

"Dayot, I have heard that each province in the Philippines has certain folk dances typical of that area."

"That is so, colonel. There are many such dances."

"Excellent. Do you think that you could find some of the Scouts who would be willing to take part in a show? I'd like to have them put on one dance from each people represented in the regiment. Where women are required I imagine the Red Cross girls will work with you."

"Yes sir. I think it can be arranged. We can find material for costumes—"

"The recreation fund or the clubs can probably stand a donation for costumes and props—let me know how much you'll need. You are now assistant recreation officer in addition to your other duties."

There followed a busy three weeks with Dayot recruiting talent, the Red Cross lassies sewing costumes, bush carpenters building props, and rehearsals of actors and orchestras.

Opening night played to a full audience, including fifteen hundred late arrivals in standing room only. Lieutenant Dayot had put on his usual superior performance, and acted as master of ceremonies, explaining and introducing each set.

The Red Cross reinforced by ladies from Manila performed the Tagalog candle dance in mestiza costumes, with lighted candles in each hand and balanced on the head. Two of the girls took the female parts in the potentially ankle-shattering bamboo dance, which was an exacting exercise in timing and coordination. Two muscular heroes squatted in the center of the stage facing each other eight feet apart. Across the front of each man lay a small log six inches thick and three feet long. Between the two men lay two thick bamboo poles, ends resting on the legs. A marimba and drum furnished the music. Each man grasped the ends of the bamboo poles and accompanied the beat, two beats on the logs, one beat slamming the poles together, *clack-clack-crash! clack-clack-crash!*

A man and a woman, barefooted, approached the clashing bamboos in minuet time, joined hands, and stopped between the poles during the clack-clack and stepped out just before the crash. Another couple followed them through the bamboo barrage untouched. All four continued the performances, gracefully weaving in, out, and around, together and singly, staying almost too long but always drawing clear as the bamboo grazed their feet. It was a study in timing and perfect coordination.

There were dances of all sorts, Spanish figure dances that were probably the vogue in Spain when Magellan discovered the islands, the harvest dance, moon dance, and coconut dance. Accompanying music ran the gamut of all types, from the 342d orchestra through drums, gongs, flutes, and bamboo marimba, to the rhythmic clacking of half-coconut shells. These terpsichorean offerings had all been greeted by vociferous applause of the Scouts and the delighted comments of General Hazlett and our other guests from division headquarters.

The last set of the evening was the Igorot head-buster's dance. The curtain rose on a dimly lighted stage. A thatched nipa hut occupied the right rear; in front of the hut a small fire glowed. Three men and a woman squatted at the fire, warmed their hands, chatted in low tones, and contemplated what looked suspiciously like a human head resting upright on the severed neck on the opposite side of the fire. I had the fleeting thought that I should check on the recent Reveille reports of missing persons in our neighboring Scout tank battalion. I heard a low muttering from the Scout audience.

I am still confused about the meaning of the following events. They have been variously alleged to be:

1. The story of how the head was taken as told by the taker at the campfire. (Tagalog version.)
2. A raid to avenge the taking of the head. (The Illocano story.)
3. A duel between two men of the tribe. (Visayan belief.)
4. Just a folk dance with no particular meaning. (What the Igorot said.)

A loud metallic clang sounded from left stage followed by the regular beat of a brass gong accompanied by the rhythmic thump of bare feet. A single file of six men, dressed in long colorful loincloths, carrying spears and hardwood shields, stamped their feet in time with the leader who crouched, stomped, and beat the time on his gong—two beats on the center, one on the rim. The file circled the stage twice, and the unvarying beat, two low notes, one high note, became hypnotically monotonous.

I noted that some of the Scouts were leaving, and couldn't understand why. Personally I was fascinated.

The file of warriors, at a last loud clang of the gong, halted in the shadows of the back stage and faced the front.

Two men armed with spears and the end-scalloped Igorot wooden shields sprang from opposite wings of the stage and began a darting, stabbing, shield-clattering duel, conducted with such realism and spirit that I feared we might have some very real casualties. To my surprise I recognized De Leon, my very quiet and efficient jeep driver, as one of these swashbuckling heroes. At that moment he attacked with a stabbing flurry of spear play. His opponent dropped his spear, staggered, and fell. De Leon shifted his spear to his shield hand, drew the tomahawk-like head arc from his loincloth, and sprang at his fallen foe with arc poised. All lights went out, there sounded a dull thud like a cleaver chopping out a tenderloin, then a howling screech of triumph from several Igorot throats that curled Tagalog hair halfway to Manila.

Leaving the theater was easy—practically all the audience was gone. I wondered why. The last set was the best of the lot. Then I recalled some of Lieutenant Dayot's discussions on the Philippines.

The Kalingas, Bontocs, Ifugaos, and similar tribes known as Igorots were aboriginally of an Indonesian stock akin to the notorious head-hunters of Borneo. Prior to the coming of the Spaniards they had waged perpetual warfare with the lowlanders of Malayan ancestry. Until comparatively recent times when the practice was discouraged by the American Army and the American-led constabulary an Igorot was not considered a man and could not marry until he had taken the head of an enemy, preferably a lowlander, but in a pinch any head from another tribe, clan, or village would do.

No wonder the theater had emptied early—it was remarkable that there hadn't been a riot. A reenactment of the Battle of the Little Big Horn by Sioux Indians staged before the widows and orphans of the Seventh Cavalry Regiment would have been a similar situation.

We had the Igorot dances performed twice more but only in the officers club, and these shows were never as convincing or blood-curdling as the first performance. The boys became too sophisticated. Embarrassed at appearing only in the perfectly adequate ceremonial loin cloths, they wore GI shorts under them, and the underwear sticking out at the sides robbed the sense of considerable realism. On the last session I gave up. In order to emphasize that they were completely civilized they wore not only the underwear but combat boots.

Twelve.

Gardner, Mertel, and MacLaughlin

Supporting Fire

Among the first draft of officers for the Forty-fourth I had received two remarkably capable young men, Captain Gardner and Second Lieutenant Mertel. Since he was the only officer of any experience with the 105-mm. howitzer and since he had a superior record, Captain Gardner was a natural to command the cannon company. Lieutenant Mertel had had little experience at anything. Drafted into the infantry, he had evidently been an outstanding recruit and had been sent to an officers candidate school from which he had just graduated. His records all spoke highly of his abilities and potential. I assigned him initially to a heavy weapons company where his company commander reported that he was doing a superior job. So when the veteran captain of the antitank company was due to return to the States, I called for Mertel.

"Mertel, have you had any previous duty with a heavy weapons company before you joined us?"

"No sir."

"I noticed that you were doing well with the cadre mortar class yesterday. You seemed to be quite familiar with the 81-mm. How come?"

"I just studied the manual, sir. The firing procedures and tables are all laid out there."

"Have you had anything to do with antitank weapons?"

"No sir."

"All right. Report to the antitank company for duty. You'll be executive officer for a week. When the captain leaves you'll take temporary command until I can get an experienced antitanker assigned. The 50-mm. gun will be new to you but, as you say, the procedures are all laid out in the manual."

I had of course some doubts about the wisdom of this assignment and made it only because we were very short of experienced officers at this time. By the time experienced senior officers became available, however, young Mertel and his three newly commissioned Filipino lieutenants were doing such an outstanding job that I confirmed him in his command. I never regretted this radical step in any way. The antitank company became and remained one of the best three companies of the regiment until we parted company eighteen months later.[1]

Gardner and Mertel had taken their manuals in one hand and their recruit Scouts in the other and had made two superior companies. They had put their men through theory and practice, limbering and unlimbering the guns, digging firing emplacements, camouflage, gun drill, and

160

observation of fire using homemade rubber and powered models, and realistically constructed miniature sandtable landscapes.

In mid-December the time had come for live firing. A small mountain or large hill that extended one thousand to four thousand yards distant in the southeast corner of the division reservation was selected as the general target area. The Huks and the Philippine Army had been fighting a desultory war in the area beyond the mountain for the past three days so I was cautioned to see that we did not drop any shells over the hill or outside the division boundary. Any such accident might have unfortunate political implications if we happened to endanger either of the embattled forces. So on December 14 the cannon and antitank companies had an early breakfast and rolled their guns into position in the dark. As soon as the targets became barely visible in the dawn light, fire orders were given and the first rounds were on the way. Visibility was poor, but the bursts could be seen as firing continued. The howitzers from their positions in defilade arched their shells high into the cloud cover, to fall on selected target areas in the two thousand to four thousand yard zone. The 50-mm. guns darted their flat trajectory tracer shells at point targets in the one thousand to two thousand yard zone. Trees buckled and fell, columns of dirt jumped, plumed, and dissipated, abandoned nipa huts flamed, smoke and dust drifted in thinning clouds.

It was a very successful day. The firing appeared to be directed effectively and delivered. Just how effectively I did not learn until a week later.

My family was to arrive in Manila on December 20 aboard the USAT *Brewster*. The ship was scheduled to enter Manila Bay at dawn. I was invited to accompany the boarding party in the pilot launch, which would leave the pier at 0500 and board the transport off Corregidor. So naturally I was impatiently pacing the pier at 0400. A Philippine Army brigadier general joined me.

"My name is Castedena, colonel."

"Triplet, general. Glad to see you."

"You are Colonel *Triplet*? Of the Forty-fourth Scouts?"

"That's right, sir. I'm with the Forty-fourth."

"Well, colonel, I am now doubly pleased to meet you. I wish to extend my heartfelt thanks for the very timely support you gave us in the fighting last week."

"Support? We have never supported anyone, general. You must be mistaken in the unit."

"Oh no, I am not mistaken. Do you remember the early morning of the fourteenth of December? We were fighting the Hukbalahap just east of Cerro Cabra. They had been pushing us up from the south. I left my right flank weak because I was protected by your reservation boundary and I thought the Huks would never dare to enter your area. But in the early morning they sent a column around Cabra and started to envelope my right flank. Just then your guns opened fire in a devastating concentration and drove back all of them except their leading company, which we were able to destroy. Your fire was very effective and came just at the critical moment. Again I thank you."

"I'm surprised to hear that we were of some help, general, but for God's sake don't mention it to anyone else, or some of our Red-loving politicians will peg my skin up to dry on the main entrance of the State Department in Washington."

"I understand. Rest assured that I will cause you no embarrassment, colonel."

And there the matter has rested until this day.

Major Mac

Our replacement officers were usually those who had had no overseas service during the war. A notable exception was Major MacLaughlin. In view of his qualifications and unusual experience I assigned him to guerrilla affairs in the 342d since we were dealing with guerrillas. When the Forty-fourth FFFFFT was formed I assigned him to command the first battalion. In addition to the cold facts shown on his service record and admitted by him when sober, he had a most interesting background.

His odyssey was heard piecemeal, in several chapters. He was normally noncommittal and usually talked most reluctantly. Fortunately for those of us who were interested in guerrilla warfare, he had a very low tolerance for alcohol. The first bourbon and water would turn him on and he would start a most entertaining yarn. Unfortunately, the fourth beaker of Old Tanglefoot would render him incoherent or speechless, leaving his enthralled audience cliff-hanging, just like the old Pearl White adventure movie serials. Next evening, with the first drink, someone would prompt him.

"Oh yes, major, you were telling about that submarine that delivered some machine guns and those three mysterious crates." And the serial would be resumed for another hour.

On December 7, 1941, Mac had been an infantry corporal, and was battling the Japanese hordes in Mindanao when General "Skinny" Wainwright ordered all American forces in the Philippines to surrender in May 1942.[2]

Corporal Mac had surrendered as ordered, but a few hours later he decided that he didn't care for the life of a PW—there seemed to be no future in it. He oozed through the Jap perimeter guard, stole a Springfield, belt, bayonet, and all the bandoleers of ammunition that he could stand up under. He then scouted through the country to visit some of his Moro friends. His pleasing personality and his understanding, acceptance, and compliance with the native customs and religion had made Corporal Mac well liked by the local Mohammedans in spite of his being white and presumably a Christian.

He proposed to his friends that they all take to the jungle and fight the Japanese, t'hell with this surrender idea. The Moros thought his proposal over and regretfully declined. Their fathers had been enthusiastic about war and had held the Spaniards to a standstill for three hundred years. They had fought the Americans for eight years but had been soundly whipped. Now the Americans had been totally defeated by the Japanese. Therefore it was obvious that trying to fight the Japanese would be the height of folly. No thanks, they didn't want any part of fighting the Japs.

But they offered a constructive suggestion. If Corporal Mac wanted to fight he ought to go back in the hills and join up with the pagans who had resisted conversion for five hundred years (Allah send their godless souls to burn in Gehenna). They liked to fight; they even fought each other.

Corporal Mac was disgusted with the gutless, pusillanimous attitude of his former friends and in desperation took their advice. He toiled over the trails and pushed his way up through the trackless jungle with his tools and overload of ammunition, dodging Jap posts and patrols. On the first slope of the central mountain mass he was suddenly confronted by a pair of the wild, dark, long-haired, spear-armed pagans who had defied Mohammed and his zealots for four hundred years.

Probably due to his winning personality and amusing attempts at sign language they took him to their village, where he was welcomed, tentatively, by the chief. Fires were built in pits and a feast laid on for the evening. After dinner there was dancing by the Indonesian-type young men, flourishing spears to the beat of two drums, coconut hulls, and short lengths of bamboo. As a rousing conclusion to a well executed and very realistic mock battle the dancers all charged at Corporal Mac with blood-chilling yells and stabbed their spears at his shuddering carcass, stopping just short of drawing blood.

Mac was frozen with fear—fortunately. He later learned that his horror-struck paralysis was what saved him. The pagan custom with strangers was to find 'em, feast 'em, frighten 'em, and if they fled finish 'em. They wanted no truck with Nervous Nellies.

Having passed his initiation test with laurels, Corporal Mac was then invited to dance. The only dancing he knew was the ballroom type with a female partner, but the bare-breasted ladies available just weren't able to partner him so he was at a total loss. He couldn't even tap dance.

But hold—an inspiration. He fixed the bayonet on his beat-up Springfield, stepped out in the middle of the fire-lit circle, and went through the manual of arms at his own commands. His encore was a demonstration of bayonet drill—high port, on guard, butt stroke, right and left parry, high parry, long thrust, short thrust, jab, and on guard.

His act was heartily applauded by the audience except for one dour character who was evidently claiming that his spear was superior to the bayonet in every way. And Mac was considerably shaken to find that he was expected to prove the comparative worth of his own weapon on the field of honor, right now.

So he and his challenger were squared off, Mac with his bayoneted rifle and the pagan with his spear and oblong, hardwood, rattan-laced shield. Mac was worried about three things: he wanted to stay alive, he didn't want to kill or even hurt the pagan, and he sure didn't want to get his bayonet stuck in that wood shield. The spearman after hopping about making two or three feints dashed in and stabbed at Mac's belt line. Mac was badly scared—don't stab the shield and don't kill the fellow. So he just parried left and circled right. The man bore in again, trying for the brisket. Mac parried hard right, stepped in as the parried spear interfered with the shield work, and slammed the butt into the fellow's solar plexus. The pagan collapsed and spent the next five minutes writhing and trying to breathe. That really laid the audience in the aisles.

The rest of the evening was spent by Corporal Mac in teaching the young warriors the handling of the spear in bayonet-fashion, with the guard, thrusts, parries and, above all, the butt stroke. It was hairy work. Since it was training for battle, the bastards couldn't get the idea of pulling their punches, and a six-foot stabbing spear just isn't designed for a butt stroke. Mac spent a lively evening trying to stay alive.

Next day Mac, the chief, and several of the older men spent hours with sign language, sketches in the dirt, and a few words of Moro, discussing the Japanese situation and Mac's proposal that they join him in fighting the Japanese. By evening they had arrived at a compromise. If the Japs stayed in the lowlands where they and the Moros belonged, the pagans would leave them alone. But if the Japs stepped out of bounds and came up in the hill country, the pagans would join Mac in the war effort.

After a month of peaceful, primitive, and most uncomfortable existence with his newfound friends and neighbors, Mac heard rumors of another American who was hiding out in a distant mountain vastness. With considerable effort he tracked him down and found a major who was engaged in the same tentative guerrilla activities with the Moros. By a circuitous series of radio relays the major had made contact with the American headquarters in Australia and had been directed by General MacArthur to take charge of the guerrilla movement in Mindanao.

Mac was made a second lieutenant on his first meeting with his new commander and attained the rank of major two years later. He had an unusual collection of commissions. One was handwritten on brown

wrapping paper, one typewritten, one printed, and one was approved—
the last one.

"Mighty peculiar people, took some getting used to. I was messing
around with one of the girls and trying to be extra polite. We were going
over to see one of her friends and I stepped aside and waved her in like
she was Queen Elizabeth and I was Sir Walter O'Reilly. Put her off me
completely. 'You afraid to go in first?' And you don't walk with a girl,
you take off and she follows you. One night I was sleeping next to one of
the chief's daughters and woke up as she was making a real serious pass
at me. Well, she was ugly as a mud fence and I'd never had a thought
like that about her, but naturally tried to oblige. We were going pretty
good when all of a sudden she pushed me off and started scratching like
a wildcat. Asked her what was wrong and she said, 'I thought you were
my brother.' Sure took some getting used to."

Weapons and radios were at last delivered by submarine but active
hostilities were discouraged. They were ordered to organize, train, evade
the enemy, and plan for the day when in cooperation with Allied troops
they would be of maximum assistance.

So Mac and his godless cohorts remained in their hills except when
they were required to keep a rendezvous with a submarine or other
guerrillas. They outposted their forest stronghold and trained for the
day when the destruction of the Japanese would be ordered by the high
command.

A great deal of Mac's leadership was required in persuading his fighting
men that their new and powerful weapons were not to be used on each
other or their neighbors. Above all they could never understand why
they should not try out their marksmanship on the Japs. Mac was largely
successful in his efforts to keep it cool, but a few undisciplined hellions
would occasionally slip down to the lowlands and ambush a Jap truck
or foot patrol with mediocre success. Then would follow the unpleasant
requirement to abandon the barrios and move the families, while the
men ambushed or delayed the reconnaissance or punitive patrols that
the Japs dispatched to locate or eliminate their elusive foes.

In 1943, Mac kept a date with a submarine to receive a shipment
of arms, ammunition, and radios. His party sweated the cargo up the
mountain trails and virgin jungle in two days and nights. Then they
opened the crates to see what goodies Uncle Sam had sent them this
time. Captain Mac pried open one crate.

"I was really put out to see this little cannon—they'd forgotten the
damned breech block. I'd never seen or heard tell of anything like it
before. A young cannon, four feet long, mighty thin-walled, a 2.5-inch
smoothbore. It had a stock, hand-grip, trigger, and sights, but a man would
have to be crazy to shoot that thing from the shoulder.

"Had four shells and some parts in the same crate but nothing that looked like a breech block. Sure couldn't shoot a gun without a breech block.

"Two other crates had nothing but shells in 'em. Funny-looking shells too, kinda like a long, slim mortar shell, tail fins and a couple of short wires hanging out of the base. I was looking over everything, trying to find the technical manual or a training manual, but the incompetent bastards that did the packing had forgot them too. Then I noticed a package of small batteries. It took hours, hell, it took a couple of days, but I found the place these batteries fitted and how the shell went in the open back end. Maybe it didn't need a breech block. There wasn't any way to lock on if I had one—no hinge, no screw threads, no bolts, no nothing. I radioed the colonel but he wasn't any help. He'd never heard of anything like that before either.

"So finally I screwed my nerve up, cleared everybody away for fifty yards, slipped a shell into the breech, aimed at a big tree across the clearing, and yanked the trigger. Thought it was likely to be my last living act. God, was I sweating. But nothing happened. I sat down and quivered and sweat a few minutes while my friends came back and made sneering remarks about this newfangled nonsense the Great White Father had sent us.

"After I got through shaking I began studying the thing again. There were the two short wires at the tail of the shell and right here were two empty terminals. Maybe if I loaded the shell and twisted the two wires around the terminals—I twisted one wire on and barely touched the other to the other terminal. Nothing happened so I twisted it on too.

"I yelled at the boys to clear out again and they backed up but not as far as before. Couple of these knotheads were standing right at my elbow. I aimed again at the trees, knew damned well nothing was going to happen, and squeezed the trigger.

"There was one hell of a crack and I felt like I'd been hit in the face with a handful of hot sand—the bastard had exploded and I was dead. Then there was a boom right across the clearing and a hunk of metal screeched by overhead. I looked around to see how many besides me had got killed and there wasn't a soul in sight. Took me two days to get 'em together again after I'd finally figured out how to shoot that damned bazooka."

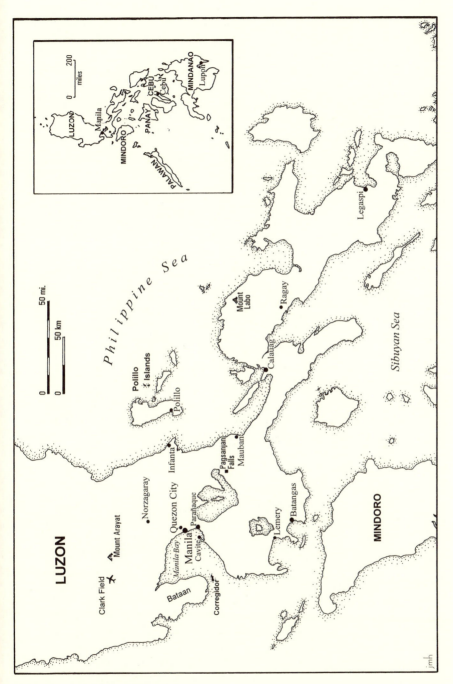

▲ Luzon and the Philippines.

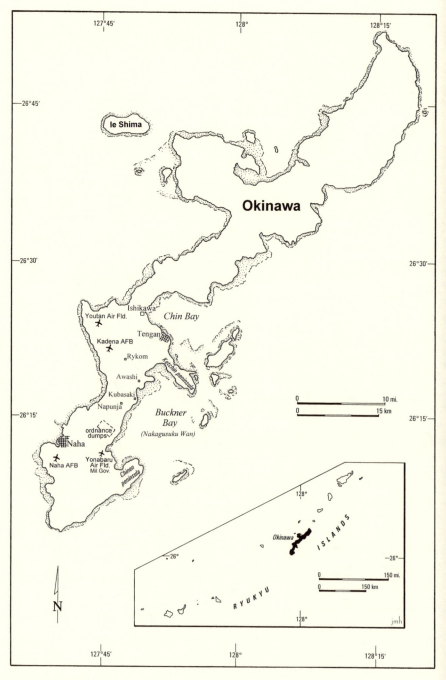

▲ Okinawa.

▲ Triplet (center foreground) with Generals Styer (left foreground) and Kramer (right).

▲ The letter of Captain Yamada, refusing to surrender.

Mariano L. Kalaw (handwritten)

HEADQUARTERS

2nd Battalion, 87th Squadron, Anderson's
(Attached to 342nd Inf. Reg., 86th Div.)

*

Subject: *Invitation*

To : *Col. Wm. S. Triplet* (handwritten)

1. *The Officers of the 2nd Anderson Bn, 87th Squadron request your presence at a*

Dinner and Dance

at Club "El Cairo," Sta. Mesa

Blvd, New Manila, on Sunday, 6th January 46
at 5:00 p. m.

V. Cabo Chan (signature)

VICENTE CABO CHAN
Maj., Inf., 2nd An Bn
Commanding Officer

Juan Nolasco (signature)

Dinner Dance

The 2nd Anderson Bn. Phil. Army, under Major Vicente Cabo Chan gave a dinner and dance at the El Cairo night club on Jan. 6.

Among those present were Brig. Gen. Macario Peralta, Col. Triplet, C. O. of the 342nd Inf. Regt. 86th Division, Col. Bernard L. Anderson, Col. Pia of the Hunters 44th Regt. the Commanding Officer of the Batute Regt. and many others, including Mayor Nolasco of Manila.

Some Manila socialites were also present, among whom are: Misses Violeta Gallego, Belen Sumulong, Fely de Leon, Luzlhati Tanchoco, Gloria Lamson, Lolita Halili, and Magdalena Jorge.

P450.00 !! Wow! (handwritten)

▲ The invitation of Major Cabo Chan.

▲ A fast sailor.

▲ A native dance.

▲ Colonel Triplet (left) with Lieutenant Colonels Holt and Stangle.

▲ Boarding the transport for Okinawa.

▲ Meeting General Hayden.

▲ The Forty-fourth Scouts.

▲ Colonel and Mrs. Triplet in a receiving line.

▲ The Triplet family: Catherine, Fiona, the colonel, Lee, and Elizabeth.

▲ The farewell.

Thirteen.

Housekeeping

Reconnaissance

Brigadier General Hayden, the commander of the Ryukyu Islands, visited the Philippines on October 13 and came out to visit his new regiment that would join him about the end of January 1947. Hayden was of medium height, plump, a graying blond, and had a very pleasant personality. I decided without hesitation that I would like working for him. I took him for a walk through the Forty-fourth area where he was most interested in our housekeeping and the basic training that was going on. Later we had lunch with General Hazlett at the division mess.

During the conversation Hayden mentioned the red shield insignia that we flaunted on shoulders and headgear. "It's new for Philippine Scouts, isn't it? The carabao skull is the only Scout patch I've ever seen before."

"Look, Fred," answered Hazlett, "I'm sending you my best regiment. Their patch is absolutely illegal but don't you make them take it off."

"I won't," promised Hayden. "Not under any circumstances."

I was much relieved by his firm decision, and thoroughly approved of his defiance of future War Department inspectors general and dictums of higher authority.

Hayden was flying back to Okinawa on the night of the thirteenth and invited me to go along for a reconnaissance of the island and the future home of the Forty-fourth. His invitation anticipated my request by about ten seconds. At 2200 we boarded the four-engine transport plane, which had been converted to passenger use with paint and plush seats, and roared off into the night. Each of the two dozen passengers had a parachute and a life jacket in the seat beside him; military air transport people are always more pessimistic, realistic, or careful than the professionally optimistic characters who run civilian air lines.

An hour after takeoff I was half asleep, staring out the left window, when I noted with interest that a sheet of flame was streaking back across the wing from the inboard engine. A moment later the forward cabin door burst open and a white-faced air corps sergeant yelled, "Put on your Mae Wests and parachutes."

The two dozen dozing passengers came to full alert and started struggling with straps and buckles while the plane winged down, circled hard left, and straightened out for a return to Manila.

I got the Mae West on in four familiar motions and started on the parachute. Difficult—impossible. It had previously been worn and adjusted by a midget and for me to get into it every strap and buckle would have to be readjusted. To hell with it. I looked out the window. The sheet of flame was longer and brighter.

Then I arrived at a more reasonable state of mind. We would continue toward Manila on three engines as long as the wing held. If the damned wing weakened or melted through, or if the blasted fuel tank in the wing exploded, we'd pinwheel down like a maple seed with every man pinned against the wall by centrifugal force and unable even to make a move toward the exit. And even if he did make the exit, what kind of a future would that offer, bobbing around in the Pacific? I decided I'd much rather ride her down than worry about my favorite phobia, sharks, for the rest of my short life. So, much to the horror and disgust of the parachuted and life-jacketed sergeant, I put my parachute back on the seat, sat down, and tried to enjoy our last few moments as much as I could under the circumstances.

Before I could get my cigarette lit (in spite of the "no smoking and fasten seat belts" sign) the fire was quenched and a few minutes later we wheeled again and resumed our way to Okinawa with three engines.

We landed at Kadena Air Base about 0130; the party was met by sedans and General Hayden drove me to his headquarters area where I put up at the guest house. I asked the Okinawa desk clerk to wake me at 0600 so I could leisurely breakfast before the general's staff conference at 0800. It was then 0200 and I enjoyed three hours and fifty minutes of technicolor nightmares about burning planes, parachutes, and sharks.

I was awakened by a jackass-like braying in the corridor outside my cubicle accompanied by an adenoidal gobbling in undoubtedly British accents. I can endure the British when they're quiet and keep a low profile but not when they review their pornographic adventures in Tokyo at full volume before breakfast. My hackles rose.

I donned a bath towel, took my toilet kit in hand, and stepped into the corridor. Facing me was a short, fat, red-faced British brigadier, flanked by two fawning lesser ranks wearing the red-banded caps of the British general staff.

"Why don't you just knock on the door?" I asked him in my pre-dawn ungargled gravely voice.

"What, what?" he gobbled.

"Aren't you the boy that's supposed to wake me up at 0600?"

"Why no, no, I'm not."

"Well, in that case, remember that these are officers quarters and keep your noise down," I reminded him, and stalked off to the bathroom in what might be described as an outraged silence on the part of all parties.

During the next three days that our British cousins remained on the island our relations were perfect. They sat at a table on one side of the mess, I sat at one on the other side. Several times I intercepted a puzzled stare, which obviously indicated what they were wondering—"What kind of an American is that? Damned colonial, insulting an Englishman first." And on meeting the brigadier and his consorts one morning on the rather inadequate walk they discreetly single-filed and made way, evidently taking me for a maniac who might prove to be violent if crossed. Must be, to have the audacity to reprimand a British brigadier.

When I reported to General Hayden's office he and his staff gave me a briefing and map study on the general situation, the occupation, and the areas available to the Forty-fourth. The main camp for the regiment would be Napunja on the east central coast of the island. A smaller area three miles north of Napunja called Kubasaki would probably hold one battalion. A small camp called the MG (military government) area might be suitable for officers with dependents. Immediately after the briefing I left with the engineer to make a personal reconnaissance of these areas.

The island was beautiful and the climate perfect. Before the war it had been a favorite summer resort for wealthy Japanese. The crushed coral roads laid by Seabees led through mildly rolling or hilly country cut by frequent arroyos.[1] The low stone walls and mounds of rubble were rampant with flowers. Collections of small thatched huts, some fourteen feet square, were frequently seen in the wider arroyos and small valleys.

I asked the engineer, "I notice that all the villages are built on the low ground, never on the hilltops. Why?"

"Well, everything on Okinawa was almost 100 percent destroyed. The Okies have a phrase for the American invasion. They call it the iron typhoon. So these are all new construction—wood, thatch, and salvage canvas. They wouldn't stand up against a typhoon and the natives know it. So they build on the low ground and hope. Then there's the water problem too; they don't have to dig their wells so deep in the bottom of a valley. These piles of rubble and broken walls you see on the high ground were their old villages, but with stone walls and tile roofs they could take the wind."

"I haven't seen any rice paddies."

"No, they grow camotes mostly, a kind of sweet potato. There's a little rice in the north but most of it has to be imported. They get Louisiana and Texas rice nowadays."

We turned into Napunja, the abandoned camp that had been built near the ruins of the Okinawan village, Arakachi. It was very abandoned, a quonset hut camp with doors swinging ajar on single hinges, rags flapping, and rubbish in the streets and piled in the corners of the huts. It was just as the Twenty-fourth Infantry had left it when they had been exiled to Iwo Jima. Their complete lack of soldierly or even human qualities was evident in the total wreckage they had left behind. We looked over the condition of the water tower and pumping plant.

"Can you put this plant in operation?" I asked the engineer.

"Yes, we should have it in shape for you by the end of the year."

"And what about repairs to the huts—windows, doors, floors, and leaks?"

"I'm afraid we can't help you on these, it's taking everything we have to keep the island pasted together. You'll just have to rely on your troop labor for minor repair and maintenance."

"What about Okinawan labor?"

"We aren't authorized to hire the natives for anything except cooks, maids, and house servants. A political matter—labor unions—hire American. Have to import American civilian labor."

"Pretty costly, isn't it?"

"Sure it's costly. We get the stateside unemployables in the first place, they're incompetent on the job, and they're as expensive as gold teeth. It takes two thousand dollars to get a man here with guaranteed return ticket, and then they get twice stateside pay. Fifteen hundred dollars a month for a bulldozer operator, twelve hundred for a truck driver, and a water boy makes a hell of a lot more than I do. And a contract doesn't mean a damned thing to the contractors. We had an appropriation to build quarters on the west side of the island and contracted with Atkinson-Jones to build 'em. You ought to go over there and take a look some time. The funds are gone, we have a nice set of concrete streets and miles of sewer lines with nothing on either end of 'em, no quarters and no sewage disposal. For the same money I could have hired Okinawans and built. But you can't fight city hall. We've asked for more money to get the quarters built."

We left Napunja for the old military government area near the ruins of Ukuma a half mile to the south. This small camp consisted of a dozen quonsets ascending a clay ridge and was basically in much better condition than Napunja. There was a wooden, pagoda-roofed structure suitable for a club and in a shallow ravine below it was a quonset mess with kitchen capable of operation on short notice. At the foot of the ridge on which the quonset barracks stood was a small two-room stone house. The crowning jewels in this structure were a shower bath and a flush toilet. The military government people as usual had done themselves very well indeed. In the same spirit I marked this spot as my very own, hoping that my family could join me to enjoy the luxuries.

Camp Kubasaki three miles north of Napunja was perched on the hillside on the opposite side of the road from a salt marsh facing the ocean. It was also in the sad condition typical of the Twenty-fourth Regiment, an abandoned military slum. There was no evidence of theft or looting, just a sabotaged and abandoned ruin.

I asked the engineer about native thieves; anything abandoned or left unguarded in the Philippines was usually gone next day.

"The Okies are pretty honest. We've never had any trouble with thieves so far."

"Sounds impossible in the Orient but I'll admit I'm prejudiced. Why not?"

"Sometimes, not often but now and then, you'll see an Okinawan with the right hand off at the wrist. Maybe he lost it in an accident. Most probably he was a thief who got caught. I say he was a thief because the chances are he's honest now. They watch the one-handed people pretty close. If he gets caught again the other hand comes off. So far I've never seen a no-handed Okie. I guess losing one hand is enough to keep anybody honest after that."

I spent a busy week on Okinawa. I reconnoitered routes and inspected campsites in detail. I counted quonsets and planned the disposition of troop units. I checked water sources, tanks, pumping plants, and plumbing fixtures. I watched the engineer electricians working over the generators and power lines. I looked over Ishikawa beach, the summer resort of the island garrison. This beach was backed by the fishing village of Ishikawa, which I feared might lead to trouble with the natives.

Alas, it was used by all the occupation troops, air corps and service troops, transportation corps troops, and Filipino service units. I would not expose my Scouts to the potential trouble threatened by this interracial situation. So I located another beach two miles north which although smaller in extent was an equally beautiful spot and would serve very well for the Forty-fourth.

I looked over Kadena Air Base, the home of the First Air Division with its bomber wing, and Naha Air Base where the fighter wing was stationed. In both areas the airplanes and the service and operational buildings appeared to be well maintained. The people, both troops and dependents, were apparently living under grim conditions of bare quonset housing, mud, duckboards, and misery.

Naha harbor where the transport carrying the regiment would dock was quite inadequate for modern shipping. There was a normal depth of twenty-five feet of water at low tide and a passage of that depth had been blasted through the reef surrounding the harbor area. Naturally a ship of troop transport tonnage would attempt entering the harbor only at or near high tide. It was alleged that when a transport approached the passage all passengers were requested to take a deep breath to reduce their weight and to hold it until the ship was tied up at the dock. Since the mile-long approach was made at two knots, that made a strenuous half hour for the oxygen-starved passengers.

The outstanding impression I had of Okinawa was wreckage, deterioration, and poverty. Naha, the former capital, was a sea of rubble. The erstwhile towns and villages were waist-high stone walls and rubble partially covered with flowering vines and weeds. The three hundred thousand survivors mourned one hundred thousand dead. We hadn't done half as well in Germany. Here we had converted the entire population into sweet potato farmers, fishermen, and objects of charity depending on American handouts.

On the tenth day of my visit, with my briefcase stuffed to bulging with notes, maps, air photos, and blueprints, I returned on an uneventful flight to Manila in a slow and very comfortable PBY. Wonderful planes—they can land on the water if an engine bursts into flame.

Quarters

Prior to leaving for Okinawa, I had applied for quarters for my family, and had been assigned one of the nipa-walled houses that were being erected for dependents in the neighborhood of the Eighty-sixth Division club. They were quite suitably constructed for the hot climate, with an air space between the corrugated iron roof and the woven reed ceiling. All walls ended six feet from the floor, giving a two-foot air space between the wall and ceiling. In all except the bedrooms and bathrooms there was also an eight-inch air space between the floor and wall. This permitted the circulation of any available breezes to the fullest extent.

I noted the bare expanse of the rather long side walls of the living room, and knowing that we would have very little furniture thought that they might be improved by murals. I called on Brownie Schneider, the wife of our S-4 who had just moved in next door, and asked her advice.

She suggested that we should have a beach with rolling waves and palm trees on one wall, and the other should be covered with typical Japanese mountain scenes. Her ideas sounded good to me and I asked her to supervise the Jap painter whom I'd asked Lieutenant Maynard to send over to do the job next Monday.

After my return from the Okinawan reconnaissance I stopped in to see the wall paintings and found them perfect—beautiful, even better than I had anticipated. Then I went over next door and found the Schneiders at home.

"I've just seen the murals, Brownie. They turned out wonderfully and I certainly thank you for your help on them. That Jap is a pretty good painter, isn't he? All you have to do is wave a hand and he's got the theme."

"Well," she hesitated, "it wasn't quite that simple. In fact—"

"Why? Any trouble?"

"No, no trouble, but it did take perseverance. Lieutenant Maynard dropped him off here Monday morning early. I took him over to your quarters and made motions for the beach, palm trees, mountains, and everything that we'd talked about. The little man was just as bright as a button and kept nodding and smiling and saying, "Oh yis sir," and I thought certainly that he had it. Then I went off for a day in the Old City market.

"Next morning I went over to see how he was getting along. I was positively horrified. He'd done the beach and the mountains all right but you couldn't see very much of them. He'd painted an eight-foot blonde undulating all over the beach, and an eight-foot brunette was sprawling all over the foothills of Fujiyama. Of course they were wearing bikinis and they were very well done but I didn't think they were quite suitable as wall decorations for your children. And there was this little man, hissing and grinning, pleased as punch.

"So I told him 'No! No! Take off! Take off!'

"But he finally got the idea, and said 'OK, sir, take off,' and started mixing his paints again.

"I couldn't get over again till late afternoon, but when I did you'll never guess—"

"No, I never could—what?"

"Well, he'd taken off the bikinis. And he was so pleased with his masterpieces. I didn't say a word, I couldn't. I just went home and called Lieutenant Maynard and he came over with an interpreter and they really went on. They were both awfully polite to the artist but seemed to have a hard time getting the idea across to him. The little man seemed to be a bit put out. Finally he said that he'd been painting for Americans ever since he'd surrendered, and this was the first time that an American had not wanted two women this tall (hand at full stretch overhead) in bikinis in the middle of the picture. But if this American already had women of his own, real ones, OK, he would paint bare scenery. And he did."

Chow and I turned our cozy custom-made house in the regimental area over to Colonel Stangle and moved into our new quarters that were actually more inconvenient and not so well built.

The labor officer turned up a young Moro, Jorge, as cook and house-boy, and had his eye on a Tagalog maid whom he could install when the family arrived.

Chow took it hard. It took a couple of days of restraint and reprimand before Chow accepted Jorge on the same terms as he had endured the Japanese orderly in our old quarters.

Jorge was an excellent houseboy but as a cook he was a disaster. He could boil coffee and serve drinks gracefully but after our first deep-fried meal offered by him, Chow and I continued to take our meals in the Forty-fourth headquarters mess.

And I asked the labor officer to look for a Tagalog girl who could cook something more than rice and fish.

Transferring the regiment to Okinawa presented no great problem. It would require considerable work to put the camps in livable condition, but the quonsets and facilities were basically sound and only needed a cleanup and such repairs as were within the capabilities of our "bush carpenters."

Dependents, however, would have a very rough time. The Rykom housing area at Awasi was just being started and, using American labor, was progressing at a snail's pace. Although General Hayden had said that quarters would be available for all dependents early in 1949, I did not have his childlike faith in the prophecies or performance of the American civilian contractors whom I had observed in action on the project. As our engineer had stated, it was forbidden for political reasons to hire the natives for any construction work. Our politicians had their eyes on American unemployment and the next election year, and American civilian labor had to be imported. The Atkinson-Jones Company did the importing at a round-trip guaranteed cost averaging two thousand dollars per man. An American water boy earned fifteen dollars per day, and the operator of a bulldozer or earth-moving machine drew more take-home pay than did the island commander.

Putting up a twenty-by-twenty quonset with partitions for a family took two thousand dollars in American labor costs, and time beyond belief. An early experiment with Okinawans produced the same set of quarters in half the time for $250 in Okinawan occupation yen, damp off the printing press, and the Okinawans were eager to work. But it was the law that Okinawans must live on free Texas rice and American unemployables be employed, so I would let the American taxpayers and Hayden worry about that.

I had no intention of relying on Rykom to supply housing for our families. I would first install them in the old military government area at Irubi where bare quonsets, a mess, and a small clubhouse were available. As soon as the troop quarters were livable I would start putting up dependents' housing adjoining the Napunja regimental camp using troop labor.

In the meantime it would be a very rough life for the ladies. I assembled the Filipino officers, five Americans with wives who already had joined us, three whose families were expected, and one who was to be married shortly, and laid the grim facts on the line.

"Ladies and gentlemen, I have asked you here to tell you about the dependents' housing situation in Rykom. It is bad, grim, much worse than it is here. Rykom officers of long overseas service are still waiting for quarters to be constructed before they can send for their families and they will continue to wait for a long time.

"No Filipino officers will bring their families initially, since they have not suffered the long separation that has been forced on the Americans. The families of Filipino officers will be brought to Okinawa when quarters are available and their overseas time is built up to compare to that of the Americans who are applying for them. Quarters will then be issued on the basis of the length of separation due to overseas service.

"General Hayden has authorized me to bring the American families with the troops, provided they understand and agree to the following conditions.

"Family quarters will be bare quonset huts with makeshift plywood or canvas partitions. Dependents of officers stationed in Napunja will live at Irubi where twelve huts are available. Those of second battalion living in Kubasaki will have four huts available in the officers quarters area.

"There is running water in a few of the huts for primitive washing facilities. All baths are the community type, screened and outdoors. Toilets are open latrines. Furniture is limited to GI cots, bedding, mosquito bars, and folding chairs and tables, so bring everything you have.

"There are no kitchen facilities; you will eat in the separate mess in Irubi or in a corner of the headquarters troop mess if you live in Kubasaki.

"There is no electricity in Irubi so Coleman gasoline lanterns and flashlights will be issued.

"These conditions will obtain until we can remodel or build quarters ourselves; we can expect no help from Rykom even though anything they have or can help us with is freely offered.

"That is the situation, rougher than anything you have ever encountered before. You'll be back in the frontier days of 1870, less Indians.

"If you prefer not to expose your families to these hardships, please let me know and I will arrange your transfer to another unit in this area with no hard feelings. If you feel an urge to pioneer with your families and if they are able to take it in the spirit of a long, hard camping trip, General Hayden and I will be glad to have you with us. Think it over and talk it over with your wives for a month before you decide. Then give me your decision on November 30."

I was delighted when in spite of my purposefully gloomy presentation seven of the nine officers reported that their wives had elected to accompany the regiment. One officer admitted that his wife couldn't take it and I was relieved when the lad who was to marry a Filipino asked permission to remain in Luzon.

Of the ladies who pioneered with us, three of them honeymooning brides, I must boast that they met the very real hardships of Okinawa in every respect as well as did their great-grandmothers during the Winning of the West.

Arrival

The pilot launch, with pilot, quarantine inspectors, and other bureau-cracy, putted away from the dock. She also carried a dozen hyped-up "sponsors" of the arriving dependents. Once more "forsaking all others" (Red Cross, ANC, USO, and Filipinos) the sponsors were joyfully or apprehensively anticipating their approaching reunion with the women of their first choice.[2]

We met the *Brewster* off Corregidor and hooked up to the stage at the foot of the starboard ladder. I climbed aboard to meet my family, which I had left in Carmel fourteen months before. With the exception of my wife, Fiona, it was practically a meeting of strangers. My oldest daughter Lee whom I had last seen as a teenager was now a very adult and handsome young lady. Betty and Catharine, at twelve and ten years, were now obviously too grown up to be interested in the playhouse I had carpentered during my home leave. And I, somewhat underweight and wearing a bright lemon-colored "atabrine tan," was almost unrecognizable to all of them.

They had had a hard trip. For twenty-seven days out of San Fran-cisco the *Brewster* had frequently sailed off course, dodging a series of typhoons, tropical disturbances, and plain gale-force storms. They had been hammered by mountainous seas and high winds until the ship's officers admitted that it was consistently the roughest voyage of their experience.

The morale of the passengers had not been helped by the comments of a number of Australian seamen who were being repatriated. These experienced mariners had the unsettling habit of looking closely at the welds and critically observing the twisting and working of the hull in the roughest weather. They would then shake their heads dolefully and remark, "Pasted together, just pasted together." Another held forth praising the production-like method of shipbuilding that was largely responsible for our victory at sea on both fronts. "Great shipbuilders, the Yanks. Build ships by the mile, cut off every hundred fifty yards, sew up the ends, drop an engine in 'em, and send 'em to sea. And they don't break up very often except in storms."

Fiona and the girls had occupied a dining saloon table with half a dozen of these characters who kept them alternately terrified, amused, horrified, and always entertained with their yarns of adventures and perils of the deep. I found the girls to be quite expert in the use of nautical terms and knowledgeable in their prophecies about the weather.

We had breakfast with the Aussie mariners during the slow approach through the wrecks of the many sunken ships littering Manila Bay, and I had to agree with my family that they were a most decent and entertaining lot of table companions. Mr. MacOmber mentioned an incident that had occurred during one of the brief calm periods of the voyage.

"This Mrs. Whitehead, you know, the wife of that air corps general, really gave us a hard time the other night. We were having a little bridge game in the cabin just across and down the passage from her cabin, and maybe we were a little too loud. Anyway all of a sudden there she stood in the doorway in a kimono, looking like a destroying angel, really gave us a going over for keeping everybody awake. Then she swept around, haughty as a dowager duchess, opened the door behind her, and walked right into the broom closet."

A dour middle-aged man with beetling eyebrows and hairy hands who sat at the foot of the table was glumly silent during the meal. I learned that he was an engineer who had been warned into silence by his companions because his language was unfit to be heard by ladies and children. His crime? During a particularly rough period of the voyage, peach fritters with a tough, rubberized crust were served as dessert. After trying to cope with it normally with a fork, he stabbed at it with a knife and the fritter skidded away under the next table. Loudly and with deep feeling the engineer remarked, "Goddamned peach fritter."

As we tied up at the pier I saw that Colonel Stangle had prepared well, as usual. The escort platoon was in formation, the cars, baggage, and escort trucks were parked in rear, and Sergeant Pulido and his Forty-fourth band were playing the ship in.

When the gangplank was secured a lieutenant led a quartet of Scouts up the steps. I introduced the lad, whom I shall call Lieutenant Ortiz, and the four Scouts each presented an orchid corsage to a member of my family, with "Welcome to the Forty-fourth Infantry Regiment, Philippine Scouts," murmured in the "courteous" tone. These floral tributes were apparently most gratifying to the ladies. Damn, why couldn't I have thought of flowers? Stangle did.

Second Lieutenant Ortiz had probably been selected to head the welcoming committee because he was undoubtedly the handsomest officer in the regiment. Tall, slender, and with the dark complexion of his Spanish ancestors, he had been of considerable interest to the army nurse corps, the American Red Cross, and the local Filipino belles ever since he had joined the regiment a month before.

As he and Lee started talking I feared that my daughter had suffered a partial paralysis of her tongue or vocal cords. Her speech was so slow and distinct, her words were so carefully selected, her perfect enunciation of the simplest words was painfully clear. It was not at all like the ripple of conversation that I had heard her carry on with Mr. MacTavish an hour earlier. I wondered what the hell had happened to her, sounded like the victim of a stroke taking speech therapy, and he was just as bad.

"Manila-is-a-very-beautiful-city,-is-it-not?" she remarked carefully.

"Why-yes,-it-is-or-was-before-the-Japs-blew-it-up,-I-suppose," Lieutenant Ortiz replied, clearly and cautiously.

"And-the-palm-trees-are-so-nice."

But it was time to debark. We were played down the gangway to the medley of the red shield march and took place in the sedans, Fiona and I in the lead, Betty and Catharine in the second, and Lee and Ortiz in the last. An alert Scout rode shotgun with his carbine beside each driver. One escort truck led the convoy, and the baggage truck with the second half of the escort brought up the rear. One vehicle on this road might be attacked, two were much less vulnerable, five in column were sure to be safe, so I settled down to enjoy the reunion.

Fiona was quickly oriented on current life in the Philippines when she discovered my "grease gun" occupying the rear seat with us.

"What is that thing?"

"Oh, that's a submachine gun, automatic, three hundred rounds a minute—"

"But what do you have it in here for?"

"Well, I'm not wearing sidearms and it's a lot more effective than a pistol in case of trouble."

"Oh, I see," and she scanned the hills and wooded areas on each side of the road with a more lively interest.

As we drove past the barrios on the way to Marakina, I pointed out the bamboo-palm-leaf houses on their six-foot stilts. In order to put Fiona in the proper frame of mind about quarters I called her attention to their good points.

"Very neat, these rural houses, did you notice?"

"Oh yes, they're very quaint and picturesque."

"They're very practical, too. They pull up the ladders at night so they're burglar proof. The floors are split bamboo with the smooth side up so one doesn't get splinters in bare feet. The strips are laid about a quarter to a half-inch apart, so there is plenty of ventilation on hot nights. And all the dirt, debris, and garbage falls through the cracks, so housekeeping is reduced to the minimum."

"But the garbage, it must smell."

"Oh no. The garbage disposal units—those pigs, dogs, and chickens—take care of it right away. They eat anything that can be swallowed and pound the rest into the accumulated mound you see under every house. I was fortunate enough to have two pigs assigned, one for us and one next door for the kids. Dogs and chickens are in short supply so I won't be able to get our complete garbage disposal set until some time next month."

"But where's the bathroom?" she asked.

"Hole in the back corner, that's what the pigs are under the house for."

"Oh." And the poor girl began observing the household arrangements of the rural barrio with the essential interest of the army homemaker.

My introductions paid off well. When I escorted Fiona through the door of her three-bedroom, living-dining room, kitchen, and bathroom wooden-floored nipa shack, she was delighted with its comparative magnificence. And the work of Mrs. Schneider and the Jap artist was highly praised.

My daughter and Lieutenant Ortiz were still at it.

"There-will-be-at-least-five-in-the-party," ended Ortiz.

"Thank-you-so-much-Lieutenant-Ortiz. I-will-be-delighted-to-go. At-seven-thirty."

"Good.-I-will-be-here-at-seven-thirty—that-is-half-past-seven-tonight."

When the young man left I asked my oldest, "Lee, what the hell, may I ask, has come over your ability to talk? Your diction, I've never heard it so sharp, clear and slow before."

"Why Dad, I just wanted to make sure he could understand me."

"And why the blue blazes shouldn't he understand you?"

"Well, he's a Filipino and I thought—"

"A Filipino? Where did you get that weird idea?"

"I asked him where he came from before he joined the regiment and he said 'Batangas,' so I supposed he was a Batangan."

"A Batangan? He's a Californian."

"Oh dear."

"I see. His lot landed at the Batangas replacement depot. He's from Las Palmas or Los Angeles, some place in California. Anyway his family has been completely American since 1848 at least."

"Oh. Oh my. What shall I do?"

"I suggest you learn to talk naturally, but gradually. No, that's not good, better come right out with it and confess—it's a hell of a good story."

Chow accepted the family with reluctant reserve. He was able to endure them in the living room but when Fiona entered the master bedroom he strenuously objected to this invasion of my sacred sleeping area. The din was heard from afar.

"Nice doggie—"

"Guurrrr."

"BiiLLL!"

"Haaarrrr!"

"BIIIIILLL . . ."

I dashed to the rescue, found Chow on the middle of the bed, fangs bared, making threatening lunges at Fiona who was backed up flat against the wall. Even after he was assured that it was all right he took up his post outside the door and rumbled his discontent with such unusual goings-on throughout the tropic night.

An unusually vicious burst of canine cursing brought me to red alert about 0530—from the verandah. He sounded in earnest when he distinctly said, "You just touch that door and I'll bust out and tear your arm off," his customary warning to all Orientals and strange Caucasians.

I staggered out to give him my usual approving support and there was Lee sitting on the steps, wan with fatigue, while Chow with upstanding ruff and throaty rumbles promised death and destruction to invaders.

"What the devil, it's OK, Chow, what are you—"

"He won't let me in," Lee complained. "I've been sitting out here all night."

"All night?" At that early hour I wasn't at my comprehending best. Restrained Chow and opened the door so my drooping daughter could enter.

"You've been sitting out there all night?"

"Well, for the last two or three hours anyway."

"Why in the world didn't you—"

"I didn't want to disturb, well, actually, I was afraid you and mother would probably kill me for staying out so late. And that dog."

Fiona wobbled out of the bedroom and joined the inquisition.

"What in the world, why Lee, you're—"

"She got back hours ago and Chow wouldn't let her in," I explained.

"Oh you poor thing. I know how you feel, that dog. Have a good time?"

"Wonderful. We went everywhere."

"Everywhere? Where?"

"I haven't the slightest idea but it was a full evening."

"Lee, your dress is ruined. How in the world did you get all that oil on your skirt?"

"Oh, that? Well, I had to hold the machine gun."

I should have raked Ortiz and his compañeros over the coals for dragging my darling daughter through the hot spots of Manila and the banditry of Luzon until 0400, but according to orders, there had been five men and two jeeps in the party.

So I didn't.

Chow finally got the idea, he had five people to guard against the yellow peril. He became a very busy dog.

Activities

Major MacLaughlin was the only American on record who could manage carabao, the water buffalo. Hence the legend that he had been in the Philippines long enough to smell like a Filipino. At least he had the carabao fooled. These dour, vicious-looking animals are the workhorses of the Philippines, apparently quite docile when associating with the natives, except when overheated. They have no sweat glands and must be granted frequent baths or "mud breaks" when working or they go mad with the heat. They are intolerant of Caucasians and otherwise lovable carabao have been known to try to murder any white man close enough for them to scent. In common with a quarter of a million other Americans in the Philippines, I was terrified of the beasts.

So imagine my horror when the day after my family arrived I saw Major Mac leading half a ton of carabao across my lawn in the one-hundred-degree heat in the blazing afternoon sun, with my two youngest daughters giggling, chortling, and kicking on his broad rump. It was a couple of miles to the nearest mud wallow or water hole and the little cherubs just didn't realize their mortal danger. I charged to the rescue but was reassured by the major.

"He's perfectly safe, sir, gentle as a kitten. Carabao are badly misunderstood animals. Why, Filipino babies can handle 'em—that's the children's job, drivin' 'em to the wallow."

The beast eyed me, evidently decided that I wasn't a Filipino baby, snorted, and lowered his head. Major Mac continued.

"By the way, colonel, do you have a bucket or hose so I can get some water on this fellow? He's starting to look fretful."

"They've got a lawn sprinkler over at the club. You kids get off that thing and get in the house. Take your pet over to the club and get him cooled off, Mac, and don't bring him back."

Yes, maybe I'd better have the major transferred to the Twelfth Division.

I'd think about it.

Sea transport was entirely engaged in the shipment of high-point men back to the States, Japanese PWs to Japan, replacements and some families to the Pacific islands, and food to our friends and former foes. There was no space available for the shipment of private cars.

"What did you do with the Zephyr, my pretty pet?" I inquired. "Could you get anyone to haul it away or did you just leave it?"

"Oh, I sold it."

"Sold it? That antique? Who—"

"Yes, a nice young man gave me four hundred dollars for it. Of course I kept my fingers crossed until he got it up the hill and hoped that he'd be able to make the left turn onto the highway. But he did."

Four hundred dollars! She had done it again. I mentally reviewed her automotive transactions of the last few years.

We had returned from China with the Fifteenth Infantry in 1938 when the Chinese-Japanese War had become too hot for neutrals, and were stationed in Fort Lewis, Washington. No private cars had been used in

Tientsin—they weren't needed, and we hoped that we wouldn't need one in Lewis. We soon found that a car was essential. There were no rickshas in the States, no post bus service, and taxis were too expensive for a captain.

I took a bus to Seattle, our available one hundred dollars in hand, and bought the best 1926 Buick sedan in the city for ninety-five dollars. The remaining five dollars was squandered for license plates.

The roomy, heavy, square-built, twelve-year-old Buick served us well, with a few eccentricities and emergencies that kept me alert. But by employing the methods and lessons learned about antique machinery in the tank school I was able to keep her in shape to take us and bring us back. Initially a dusty-rust color, she was soon enameled a poisonous "apple green" that Fiona selected, but I found that the color on the car in no way resembled the color on the chart. That lasted a week, then I brushed on a layer of glossy black.

A couple of years later while tinkering in the Twenty-eighth Infantry service company shop I overheard a mechanic outside the window remark, "No wonder Colonel Dowell gave the Skipper the service company. The way he keeps that fourteen-year-old wreck on the road—" Yes, she was a good car, Buicks of those days always were durable, so in spite of the scurrilous comments of the mechanics I intended to keep her.

But one day in early 1940 our six-year-old Elizabeth Ann on her return from school plaintively asked Fiona, "Mama, all the kids make fun of our old square car. Can't we get a rounded one?"

So Fiona went into the automobile market. She posted a for sale sign in the rear window. The first and only prospect she got was Chief Twenty-Canoes of the Tuscarora Reservation. As he peddled his load of vegetables about the post he noted the sign and began serious inquiries about the price. The negotiations were broken off when his young assistant untactfully horned in, "Aw, chief, you know your wife wouldn't ride in anything like that."

She gave up on the advertising and contacted the nearby dealer in Youngstown, delicately hinting that she might be interested in a trade. Probably just looked wistfully at some of the later-model used cars. Her car-trading went on for a week and was concluded when the nice young man parked a 1935 Lincoln Zephyr in front of our quarters and announced the price as five hundred dollars. He would give us two hundred dollars for the Buick. The salesman and I were both disappointed when she firmly refused.

"No, I will give you two hundred fifty dollars and our car for the Zephyr, and not a cent more."

I felt sorry for the young man. I'd seen her bargain with Tientsin merchants on Chinese New Year's Eve. He was out of his class in this deal.

"OK, and there goes most of my commission."

And now she'd gotten four hundred dollars for the eleven-year-old Zephyr.

Since 1938 the basic cost of the Triplets' transportation had been $95 plus $250—$345. She'd sold for $400, a net profit of $55 over the past eight years.

"Fiona, I've been thinking about the automobile business. I'm wasting time in the army. I ought to retire and let you support me in the manner to which I would like to become accustomed. You could buy cars three to ten years old. I could tinker, paint, and polish them. Then you could sell them for huge profits. We could make a mint."

"Do you mean work for a living? No way. I like the army."

"OK, just an idea."

Since the formation of the Forty-fourth, I had conducted a weekly officers school on subjects relating not only to current training but also to inform my young men on the customs of the Old Army, the small Regular Army as it had been before it was diluted by the draft and ruined by World War II.

One evening I discussed the custom of calling on fellow officers and their families on small posts, particularly mentioning the visits to welcome new arrivals. I described some of the rules—all officers call on every other officer, families call on other families, newly arriving officers call on the commander at his quarters and are called on by other officers.

I told the lads about the use of visiting cards to introduce themselves and to provide the person called upon with a record of the visit; how they could be engraved, printed, or handwritten; how one card should be left for each adult member of the family; and how, if the family was not home, cards should be left in the mailbox or slid under the door to show that the visit had been made. Since time was running out for this session of the school I postponed the rest of my talk on the customs of the Old Army at that point.

Such instruction in customs of the service for members of the New Army would have been inappropriate; in the New or civilian army no one called on anyone. But the Forty-fourth was a separate regiment of professional Filipino mercenaries. Therefore I considered it best to use this long-proven custom in order to get all hands thoroughly acquainted and thinking of the regiment as a closely related family.

That week Fiona and the family arrived. And that Sunday afternoon we were lounging in the comparative coolness of the well-ventilated nipa-walled living room, exchanging descriptions of our separate experiences of the past year.

A knock on the verandah screen door. I beat Jorge to it, hadn't quite gotten used to a houseboy yet.

An amazing sight. There stood Major MacLaughlin at the head of a column of twenty-six well-polished young men, every bachelor officer of the first battalion behind him.

"Well, MacLaughlin, come in, delighted; Fiona, this is Major MacLaughlin, first battalion."

Mac shook hands, beaming, and handed me, Fiona, and Lee each a bit of pasteboard, a 1½ by 2-inch card with the following legend neatly hand-printed in black ink:

MAJOR BRIAN C. MACLAUGHLIN
44th INFANTRY REGIMENT (PS)

His cohorts followed, each solemnly presenting his painfully printed visiting cards like a line of customers turning in their tickets at the theater entrance.

Thirty adults, two children, a confused houseboy, and a viciously snarling dog, all gathered in an eighteen- by twenty-four-foot room add up to quite a crowd. I flung Chow in our bedroom to obviate bloodshed and slammed the door.

Our facilities for entertainment were seven chairs, six water tumblers, five bottles of Coca-Cola, and one sadly depleted bottle of bourbon.

We eased some of the crush by sending B'ann and Catharine to their room (where they stayed very temporarily), and Lee was requested to lure the younger set out on the verandah while Fiona held court in the living room. Jorge was directed to dash over to the division club for bourbon, Scotch, beer, Coca-Cola, ice, glasses, and a couple of the underemployed waiters to help him.

I have since read that the average adult puts out body heat at the level of a one-hundred-watt light bulb. I believe it. There were three thousand closely-packed watts burning brightly in the one-hundred-degree Luzon heat on that memorable afternoon.

But Jorge shortly appeared with a pair of compañeros, trundling a couple of wheelbarrows full of goodies, the dining table became a bar, merriment reigned, and we no longer noticed the heat.

As the shades of night were falling, Major Mac made his devoirs and left, closely followed by the column of his colleagues.

The Triplet ménage strolled over to the club for dinner. Betty Ann and Catharine were going on about Major Mac—he not only tamed water buffalo, he could tell stories too. Lee was comparing the points of two new acquaintances with those of Lieutenant Ortiz. Fiona was going over the events of the afternoon and remarked, "Such nice boys. They seemed to be having a good time. And they certainly do have staying power, don't they?"

That was my fault; breaking my talk off where I did I didn't tell them how to leave. The next session I'd planned to go into timing of visits, mass calls at receptions, and how to get up, say good-bye, and leave. Don't know how I can do it now. So I didn't.

In early January 1947 I was invited with Fiona, Lee, and her current date to a guerrilla reunion in the Manila Hotel. My own reliable sedan, well maintained by Captain Stief's mechanics, was in the shop being prepared for the trip to Okinawa, so I borrowed a car from the division pool. Lieutenant Boyd who was escorting my daughter drove his jeep and we formed convoy for the trip. Lee was carrying Boyd's submachine gun since he was driving, and seemed to be little concerned about the effect the well-oiled weapon might have on her best ball gown.

The party was the usual magnificent affair, laid on in the banquet room. The same tarpaulin covered the large shell hole in the ceiling (if they weren't going to repair the hole they should at least paint the tarp). The same fiery cocktails preceded and accompanied the dinner. Fiona and I were placed between Major Cabo Chan and Colonel Hernandez, both friends of long standing.

General Romulo, the "boy general" and hero of the Philippine Army, occupied the head of the U-shaped table with General Castedena and a Filipino dressed in a white civilian suit whom I had never seen before. I asked Chan, "Who is the civilian between Romulo and Castedena?"

"The civilian, he is the Hukbalahap leader, Mr. Taruc—Luis Taruc."

So I couldn't believe it.

"But that's impossible, there's a war on."

"Oh yes, but he was a very good guerrilla and has a right to come to the reunion. We gave him a safe conduct pass so he could join the party."

Never in my experience or reading of military history had I ever heard of such a situation. Evidently the age of chivalry is not over in the Philippines—but chivalry even in the Renaissance was never like this.

It was quite a lively evening. I had started with my usual emaciated bourbon and water but as the evening went on my guerrilla friends, foes, and acquaintances came around with their favorite bottles. They would add a generous dollop of gin, rum, champagne, beer, or embalming fluid to my glass, utterly regardless of its current content, and we would clink glasses to the USA, the Philippine Republic, the guerrillas, and the Samar Irregulars or whatever mob my friend had been with.

The Huk chief left the party at a reasonable hour to continue the war and our group followed soon thereafter. Much to my disgust the borrowed sedan would not start in spite of every effort by the driver, so after arranging for its safety and towing by a military police patrol we all loaded into Lieutenant Boyd's jeep. We were lucky enough to tail on to an Eighty-sixth Division pass truck for the trip back and reached Marakina without incident. Or maybe it was Luis Taruc's truce that got us by.

Fourteen.

To Okinawa

We boarded the transport and sailed for our new home in Okinawa on January 14, 1947. Ever since New Year's we had been feverishly busy, packing and crating everything that was to go with us as well as many things that probably shouldn't have gone. In addition to our jeeps, howitzers, antitank guns, and other tools of our trade we had to ship the household goods of families, extra hand tools for repair and rebuilding, kegs of nails, barrels of paint, battalion and officers club property, unit washing machines, public address systems, chapel equipment, athletic equipment, library books, theater curtains and light systems, and movie projectors. It was like moving a village of four thousand inhabitants, less houses and barns. This mountain of crates and boxes was delivered to the pier on January 12 and 13 and God help the first mate who had to figure out how to load it.

Short furloughs had been granted during the past month to all men with good records, and the outfit was in good mental health. The seventy-seven men who had been absent without leave at any time during the four-month life of the Forty-fourth were excluded from this privilege. I received a few requests from Scouts who wanted to transfer to units stationed in and near Manila. They were usually from Old Scouts who cited everything from previous service and families near Manila to their hardships suffered as PWs or guerrillas as excuses to shirk their present duty. I directed the company commanders that I would consider nothing but discharges—discharges for hardship of families, unsuitability for the military service, immorality, or dishonorable conduct. Gangplank fever would not be a valid reason for transfer.

I had sent Colonel Stangle with an advance party of six officers and two hundred Scouts on the *Brewster* on December 18 and we could rely on them to make the essential preparations for the reception of the main body.

On the day before sailing, all of our plunder except my own jeep had been delivered at the pier and was being swung aboard. The division motor pool was scheduled to furnish transportation for the troops, families, personal equipment, and cabin luggage, starting at 0600 the next morning. Preparations had progressed to such an extent that I could now concern myself with a major personal worry, Chow.

Chow had proven to be such a valuable and faithful companion that I could not consider leaving him behind. On the other hand army transport regulations were unequivocally dead set against bringing any animals aboard and the captain of the USAT *Collins* was said to be a martinet who ran his ship by the book. Application to him would be worse than useless.

I sent for Major Gomez, the regimental surgeon.

"Good morning, major. I have a serious problem and need medical assistance. I want to carry Chow aboard the transport in a foot locker and stow him in my cabin. I'd like to get something that will put him to sleep for two or three hours and some pills to follow up that will keep him drowsy for three days without danger. He weighs sixty-three pounds and is in superb health. Please see what you can do."

"Ah, yes sir."

During the early afternoon Major Gomez reappeared.

"Sir, I wish to report on the sleeping tablets for the dog."

"Yes, how many and how often?"

"Sir, I have searched the regulations thoroughly concerning the transportation of troops at sea and find that the transportation of animals except horses, mules, and dogs of the K-9 Corps in the military service is expressly forbidden. Here, this paragraph—," and he opened his well-thumbed volume of army regulations at a bookmark.

"Thank you, Major Gomez, I appreciate your concern about my official safety but I have long since looked up the regulations myself. Now to return to the subject, what I want from you is sleeping tablets, tranquilizers, or shots that will enable me to break this regulation with a fair chance of success, and make the dosage suitable for a sixty-three pound dog."

I received the tablets shortly after. I had already prepared the foot locker with air holes and had gobbets of meat split to contain the pills. Chow had not been fed at all on the thirteenth so he would be sure to gulp down a pill-loaded piece of raw meat for breakfast on the fourteenth.

But I had not foreseen Chow's suspicious nature nor his physical and psychic resistance to the effects of the drug. I gave him his sleep-laden breakfast at 0300 and at 0500 picked up his flaccid form to fold it into his locker. He came suddenly to life and declined to be put in any locker, vigorously. After three fast rounds and three bone-scarring bites he disappeared into the mists of early dawn and would not return. So I applied several large band-aids, woke up Colonel Murphy, the division inspector general across the street, and told him that when the dog returned after sleeping it off Chow was to be all his. Murphy, who had greatly admired my bodyguard, agreed heartily, and I left with the assurance that Chow would have a good home.

At 0700 as I was leaving camp at the tail of the last troop column, the Huk-Philippine Army War that was still going on just east of the Eighty-sixth Division reservation started to warm up with the thump of mortars and the rattle of small-arms fire. Both sides, however, remained meticulous about not shooting over the division boundary so I had no concern over our families. They were to follow by sedan and military buses at 1000 and load in plenty of time for the sailing of the *Collins* at 1200.

As our convoy passed over a highway bridge on the way to Manila, I noted that there had been a brisk skirmish at that point quite recently. Squads of the Philippine Army were deployed about the area looking unusually alert and businesslike and a dozen bodies in Huk or bandit nonuniform littered the scene.

On arriving at the ship I found the loading going on with the Scouts capably shouldering their B Bags (which were almost as big as their owners), slinging arms, and steadily trudging up the gangplank as their names were called. De Leon delivered my jeep to the tender care of the mate who had left one hatch open for it instead of the deckload spot that I had expected. Much to my horror I saw it swung aboard and deposited on supporting planks on the top of a stack of six jeeps. The bottom jeep was apparently supporting a load of more than four tons. I visualized a series of very long, wide, and flat jeeps coming out of that hold three days later but they were already stacked so protests and recriminations by that time would have been useless.

After observing the loading and stowage of the troops I looked up the transportation officer on the pier and discussed the manifests for some time. Then I suddenly noted that it was 1130 and the convoy of dependents was half an hour overdue. I asked the military police lieutenant on the pier to take a patrol to look them up and being totally without transportation for myself and Scouts was reduced simply to worrying about them. And I had a lot of king-sized worry material to work on. Had the transportation arrived to pick them up on time? Had the Eighty-sixth buses broken down?—they did, frequently. Had they been ambushed by freelance bandits? Had the Huk war cut off the highway? And now the *Collins.*

At 1150 the loading had long since been completed, the lines had been singled, and the transport's whistle boomed the "all aboard."

"Hold on," I said to the transportation major. "This ship can't sail at noon. Our dependents aren't here yet. And if they cut loose one more of these strings I'm going aboard to take charge."

"No sweat, colonel. The ship can't sail until the captain has his sailing orders and I've got them right here."

"Good, let me hold them, I wouldn't want to be court-martialed for piracy."

At 1200 on the nose the convoy of two buses, escort, and MPs arrived on the pier and the families disembarked. My family group was among them, but where was the sedan that General Hazlett had loaned me?

"Dreadful, simply dreadful!" remarked Fiona cryptically as I led her up the gangway.

"What, those bodies around the bridge?"

"Oh, that too, of course, but what I meant was that car. It broke down twice and if the buses hadn't been behind us I don't know what we could have done. And the crush in Manila. We were late and everybody and everything was on the streets. We only made it through due to that nice dark-haired MP hanging out the door and blowing his whistle and yelling. I thought we'd never get there and the ship would sail without us."

"Never, my pretty pet, I had the captain's sailing orders in my little hand."

Captain Brady of B Company was a large, cheery, capable Irishman, built like a prototype of the Georgia state police, which he had been. During the voyage to Okinawa, B Company was not seasick, much. I happened to be in earshot at the compartment door when Brady gave his braves a briefing just after boarding the transport. His men had been led below and were stowing their gear in the bunks of the tightly packed troop compartment.

"B Company, give me your attention."

The clattering sound of primary school English and fourteen dialects dwindled to an expectant hush.

"At ease. There will be some men get seasick when we go to Okinawa—headache, dizzy, throw up. Not B Company. B Company men will not get sick. I will tell you what to do.

"Stay on top all day. Stand up and walk around all day. Do not look at the water, look out where the water and sky come together.

"Eat all the rice you can every mess call.

"Go down to bunk only at night when sailors say go below.

"I have seasick pills here (holding up a large bottle). Every man take one seasick pill now. Any time you feel bad, go to the first sergeant. He will give you one more pill.

"I have just enough pills for you, do not tell other men.

"If any B Company man is sick I will know that you have not obeyed my orders.

"First sergeant, post two guards at this door. Relieve every half hour. No one can come in that door in the daytime except you, a B Company officer, inspecting officers, or ship's officers.

"Now give every man one of these pills," and he handed the sergeant the king-sized bottle that was labeled with marking crayon in outsized letters, "seasick pills." He publicly took and swallowed the first one himself.

Major Gomez had been totally unable to obtain motion-sickness tablets of any sort for the voyage, so I went in to ask Brady how he had gotten such a supply.

"Have one, colonel," he invited, evading the question, and the first sergeant doled out one of the precious pills. I inspected it closely.

"There's something out here I'd like to show you," hastily interrupted Brady, and led the way out the compartment door. In the passageway he halted and whispered, "Yes, it's aspirin, colonel, but I wouldn't want the news to get around to the men, or to the battalion surgeon."

I was impressed as usual with Brady's initiative and ingenuity, and was quite curious about the effectiveness of psychosomatic medicine as practiced by a layman. I assured him that I would take his pill if I felt seasickness coming on, and that his secret formula was safe with me.

The pills worked wonders. Some of Brady's Scouts who were unfortunate to be detailed for a tour of kitchen police became slightly gray or green at times. But fortified by another dose of this magic medicine they would manfully stagger back to work in the torrid, food-smelling atmosphere of the galley, and crack merry jokes at the expense of their suffering but less fortunate comrades of the other companies.

At long last we passed Corregidor and were truly under way. I took what I hoped would be my last look at Manila, Cavite, Bataan, and the Rock. The ship began to heave a bit under the influence of the Pacific swells. So did a few of the Scouts. This was surprising to me. I had assumed that an island people with seagoing forebears of Malay, Indonesian, Indian, Arabian, and Chinese stock would be congenitally immune to seasickness. With many of them, however, their ancestors had evidently lived in the hills and inland plains too long and they had lost their immunity.

But when I toured the deck in the late afternoon I was struck by the remarkable change in the appearance of the Scouts. Oranges had been issued with the noon meal immediately after sailing. After eating their oranges some of the lads had cut nostril-sized pieces and shoved them into their noses to enjoy the odor. They then observed or believed, and announced, that orange peels in the nose prevented seasickness. The news spread like wildfire and for the rest of the voyage most of the Scouts except B Company and ex-fishermen wore slices of orange peel in their noses. One style, thin slices drooping over the upper lips like yellowed fangs, gave the wearers a weird, ferocious look that would do well as the frontispiece of a science fiction pocketbook. But like Brady's aspirin it certainly helped.

The voyage was most pleasant—sunny skies, gentle swells, a few whitecaps, a well-run ship, and several stimulating conversations with Captain Nordholm, a descendant of Viking ancestors who bore no resemblance to the sea-going martinet described to me by the AFWESPAC transportation people. Of course he had probably found that in dealing with AFWESPAC he got better results with a mean, nasty, disagreeable approach. But when he was "carousing with the passengers" his Old World courtesy and his pleasant personality charmed the ladies and impressed the men.

The *Collins* inched into the miniature harbor at Naja and tied up about 0900 on a miserable morning. The temperature was down in the forties and a constant rain driven by a thirty-mile breeze chilled even the Americans to the marrow. What the weather did to the Filipinos accustomed to cold waves of seventy degrees can only be imagined.

I was very pleased when I took my leave of the captain and he told me, "This is the best unit of troops that I have transported during or since the war."

General Hayden welcomed us on the pier, observing the debarkation, and seemed genuinely pleased to see us. The Scouts having discarded their orange peels looked good as they filed down the gangplank in their lacquered helmet liners. Due to the weather they were wearing more clothes than they had ever experienced before—field jackets, full uniforms, and long johns.

Colonel Stangle and a number of his advance party were on hand with convoys of Rykom sedans, jeeps, and trucks laid on to carry us to our destinations. The troops and families were rapidly loaded and dispatched to their new homes where Stangle with his usual efficiency had cots laid out in the roughly repaired quonsets, water and electricity available, and the cooks ready to serve the noon meal. He had selected good men and officers for his party and they had all done well.

When Brady's company was unloaded at their quarters in Napunja he glanced inside the bare quonsets and roared to the supply sergeant, "Sergeant Ludorico, get me six hundred coat hangers."

That was an impossible order. There were no coat hangers on Okinawa. There had never been any coat hangers on Okinawa. But Brady had indoctrinated his men with his own aggressive initiative and Sergeant Ludorico had become accustomed to accomplishing the impossible. He assembled a ten-man detail, gave his instructions, and dispersed his heroes in all directions.

I saw the sergeant's coat hanger production line in full operation three hours later. A large coil of stiff, galvanized, heavy-gauge wire, "managed" from the Rykom engineer dump, was being unrolled and extended on a trestle-mounted 2 x 12 plank. One man measured the wire against marks on the wood and cut it into four-foot lengths. He passed the wire to the next technician who rough-shaped it around three nails set in the plank. The resulting triangle went to a pair of artists who with pliers gave it four twists and a curl and behold, a reliable coat hanger.

After Brady's braves had all their uniforms neatly hung Major Schneider appropriated the coat hanger factory and continued production for the rest of the regiment. And he as S-4 was able to get the wire legally.

Captain Brady was a martinet who insisted on perfection in housekeeping as well as in the field. The cots had to be made up with blankets perfectly taut and with a hospital fold at the foot. In the hot climate of the Marakina plain coverings at night were unbearable, so his men had normally slept on top of their cots and on really hot nights on the floor. Only a moment of tightening the blanket was then required at Reveille to make the bed to suit the captain.

The Okinawan climate was another matter. The cold rain continued blowing in at an acute angle from the northwest and the thermometer dropped to thirty-eight degrees, an Arctic temperature by Filipino experience. After tucking his family into their quonset for the night, Brady went back to his company area to see that all was well with his Scouts.

He opened the door to his first platoon quonset, turned on his flashlight, and saw fifty shivering bodies lying on their beds that were made up with three blankets in neat hospital folds. The poor devils were wearing everything they owned—long johns, wool uniforms, overcoats, field jackets with hoods up, wool gloves, and in some cases combat boots. They thought, of course, that beds were to be slept on, and no one had bothered to tell them that beds should be slept in.

So B Company was routed out, assembled, and at 2300 on a frigid night had a course of hitherto unscheduled instruction on "How to go to bed in Okinawa."

Fifteen.

Acquaintance

History

The primordial race occupying the Ryukyu Island chain is believed to be akin to the Indochinese; possibly it was Polynesian. Since it left no artifacts and there are only vague legends about its existence we can only guess at its origin.

At some indefinite period in the misty past the islands were overrun by Malays who enslaved and miscegenated with the original inhabitants and bred a race of pirates whose major source of income was the Chinese junk traffic of the Yellow Sea. The Lu Chu (or Loo Choo) pirates maintained a high standard of living and enjoyed a fearful reputation for several centuries.

An unusually active Chinese emperor of the fourteenth century, objecting to this interruption of Chinese trade, assembled and dispatched a fleet of war junks and transports that eliminated the pirate fleet and landed an army. The invaders captured the two Okinawan kings who jointly ruled the islands and boiled them together in the same pot of oil; they impregnated all of the Okinawan wives and daughters, thus laying the firm foundation of the Okinawan race. Chinese merchants and missionaries who followed the conquest continued to build on that foundation.

In 1853–1854, Commodore Perry, USN, forced the introverted Japanese to open up and look at the outside world. OK, they did. And right across the sea they saw China. In 1894 they found that fighting the Chinese was even more fun than fighting each other.

The peace treaty of 1895 gave Japan control of the Loo Choo Islands, but since the Japs could not pronounce Loo Choo they became the Ryukyu Islands.[1]

For the next fifty years the Indochinese (or Polynesian)– Malay– Chinese mélange rapidly took on a Japanese tinge, with Japanese government officials, businessmen, tourists, and the military arriving in ever-increasing numbers. They kept the Okinawans firmly in a subordinate position as hewers of wood and drawers of water, since it was common knowledge that Okinawans were too stupid to handle anything more complicated than a mattock. The only Okinawan export was Okinawans, the men as strong-backed labor and the women as entertainers. During World War II, when Japanese manpower was strained to defend the far-flung perimeter of their empire, the Japanese employed their Okinawan manpower purely as labor troops.

Okinawa was the costliest battle of World War II for the Americans, and probably the roughest in American history. Some 183,000 men swarmed ashore on the beaches after a pulverizing naval bombardment and were amazed to find no resistance, very unlike the score of landings made on the long road back from Guadalcanal.

But General Ushijima was an excellent tactician. He had pulled his 120,000 men back in order to avoid futile losses on the beaches and had organized his defense in the hills of the interior, principally in the southern part of the island. Eighty-two hard-fought days later the fighting came to an end with the suicide of Ushijima and his chief of staff.

The Americans had taken 49,151 casualties, of whom 12,500 were killed. The Japanese had lost 112,000 dead and 7,440 as prisoners. Practically every man-built structure on the island was burned or pulverized. Of the island's 400,000 civilians, 100,000 were killed or died of wounds or hardship.

The first casualties in the battle were an Okinawan farmer and a marine. The patriotic farmer, finding the barbarian round eyes crossing his sweet potato patch, attacked the nearest marine with his mattock. The marine's buddy killed the farmer with a bullet that after passing through the Okinawan then laid his friend low.

Almost the last casualties of the battle were the people of the Makabe area who committed mass suicide by jumping into a deep hole where the roof of a monstrous cave had fallen in. The hole, fifty feet across the top, sloped back on all sides from a mound in the center to a depth of a hundred feet. The whole bottom of the cave was littered with the skeletons of the five thousand suicides, most of them piled on top of the mound formed by the fallen roof. Those who had not been killed by the fall had evidently crawled away to die, since the cavern was strewn with whitened bones as far as one could see in the increasing darkness.

Near Makabe were the ruins of Mabuni and the heights of Hill 89 where the last stand of the Japanese was made. The south side of the hill is a precipice now known as Suicide Cliff where the bulk of the Japanese defenders jumped to their deaths after the suicide of their commander.

During the night of June 21–22, General Ushijima and his chief of staff, General Cho, at a midnight meal, drank farewell toasts with their staff, and dressed for the ceremony. At 0400, Ushijima in full uniform and Cho in a white kimono appeared in the mouth of the headquarters cave. General Cho said, "Well, general, since the path may be dark I will lead the way." General Ushijima replied, "Please do so. And since it is getting warm I will take my fan."

A white quilt was spread fifteen feet from the mouth of the cave, the two generals knelt on the quilt, and aides presented the knives. Each man was backed up by a friend with a sword and when the ritual cuts had been made the sword swept down and the officer was immediately beheaded.

A more dramatic but equally credible report of Ushijima's end was made by Commander Ross's maid, Chioko. She stated that she was hiding in some bushes within sight of the ceremony. She swears that after General Ushijima had made the disemboweling cut he threw or made the motion of throwing his entrails toward the American lines. Her comments as translated from the Japanese were, "It was magnificent. The supreme insult."

The Okinawan religion appeared to be a thin layer of Shintoism or Buddhism overlaying heavy strata of Taoism, devil worship, and other superstitions that they inherited from their diverse ancestry. The devils have by far the strongest hold on Okinawan beliefs and the term "devil worship" is misleading; "fear of devils" is closer to the truth.

To cope with the ever-present devils an Okinawan house is guarded by a Shi-Shi placed on the roof over the doorway. The Shi-Shi is a ceramic, metal, or wooden figure that looks like a cross between a snarling Pekinese and a roaring lion, enough to scare any devil.

For protection against devils who don't scare easily the homeowner erects a "spirit wall" across the front of the door, leaving just enough space between door and spirit wall for human passage. It is well known that devils cannot go around right-angled corners—they can move only in straight lines or long curves—so they are baffled by the two sharp changes in direction. The spirit wall is incidentally an excellent shield against observation by prying neighbors.

But when an Okinawan leaves the shelter of his house he (or she) is no longer protected by the Shi-Shi and spirit wall. That is when the lurking devil strikes, following closely and controlling his victim's thoughts, words, and deeds throughout the dreadful day. The devil must be shaken off. How can one escape?

Actually, a devil is stupid and can be evaded by the faster-thinking human. The victim can move quickly around a corner and the poor devil who is not as intelligent or maneuverable charges off on his straight line, looking in vain for his vanished prey.

A second method of escape is the transfer. The devil-haunted man directly approaches another person, preferably an enemy, and steps briskly around him. His pursuing devil will then collide with, fasten on, and haunt the other person.

A third and most popular way to deal with a devil is to get him killed. By dodging quickly across a road, close in front of a horse or even an ox cart, a man leaves his devil to be trampled to death by the animals. Killing devils became easy after the iron typhoon blew over. The surviving natives crept from their ruins and found hordes of Americans driving hundreds of jeeps, trucks, and tanks hither and yon. These strange vehicles, moving at high speeds, were found to be much more effective in disposing of devils than were the slower-moving animal-drawn carts. Unfortunately, the unsophisticated natives were unable to gauge the speed of an oncoming truck. It was quite all right with the devil when the wheels crushed the haunted Okinawan; he transferred his attentions to the driver of the vehicle who suddenly became extremely unhappy and remained haunted at least until the investigation of the accident was completed.

Family tombs rather than individual graves are used by Okinawans to bury their dead. In ancient times natural caves were used to store the bodies and bones of the family. But since the number of suitable caves was limited and the supply of bodies in the overcrowded islands increased, the families were forced to build artificial caves to house the dead.

These caves or tombs are usually built on a sloping hillside by the cut and cover method. They are wide, low, ovoid, concrete structures, with a small crawl way opening at the lower end. The shape is supposed to represent the human womb—a person comes from the womb into life and returns to the womb in death.

The body is dressed and placed in the tomb unembalmed for temporary burial. As soon as decomposition has run its full course, a year or so, the remains are removed from the tomb. The youngest nubile daughter, or, lacking a daughter, the youngest woman in the family, then separates the bones, cleans them of remaining flesh, and washes them. The bones are then placed in a large, suitably inscribed jar, and returned to the tomb as their final resting place.

A side effect of this custom is the joy with which a daughter welcomes the birth of a younger sister and the sincere welcome that a wife extends to a younger wife or concubine.

Adjusting

The first field duty that General Hayden assigned to the Forty-fourth was the elimination of Japanese stragglers. There were alleged to be at least three hundred Japs holding out in the forested hills of the thinly populated north end of the island.

I dispatched the second battalion to do the job. For a week they pushed patrols and skirmish lines over the hills and through the woods. They combed out ravines, explored caves, and even prodded around in the cavelike Okinawan family tombs. They interviewed the native police and questioned civilians, but no trace of a single Jap came to light.

Shortly after the battalion was recalled I attended a staff meeting at Rykom where Lieutenant Colonel Patton, G-2, stated that his counterintelligence detachment had located the missing Japs.

A few, dreading to go home in disgrace, had married and settled down with their Okinawan wives as sweet potato farmers. Most of them, 200 to 250, had been found among the natives working as semiskilled labor, sweepers, kitchen police, and houseboys on the Kadena and Naha air corps bases. The ex-Zero and Kamikaze pilots in particular were proving to be superior as grease monkeys and mechanics—seemed to have an uncanny understanding of what was required to keep airplanes in shape to fly.

No further action required.

As soon as the essential housekeeping and repair work was completed, the Forty-fourth resumed training in weapons and small unit field problems. The latter were carried on in the largely deserted countryside around the two posts of Napunja and Kubasaki.

One evening I received a report that a man in one of the rifle companies had gone absent without leave in the field. Where he could go I couldn't imagine, since the only way to get off the island would be by ship or military plane. But there it was, Private Tanglat had left A Company barracks that morning with his platoon, with arms and combat pack. The platoon had spent the morning working in skirmish lines through the woods, brush, and ruins west of Napunja. As they assembled to march back to camp at noon Private Tanglat was missing. A search of the maneuver area revealed no trace of him.

Five days later Tanglat was dropped as a deserter, our first. On the same morning C Company was skirmishing through the area of his mysterious disappearance. One of the Scouts was surprised to hear a faint yell, apparently coming from the clump of bushes and tall grass at his elbow. Private Tanglat was found at the bottom of a twenty-five-foot abandoned empty well.

"Sar, please some water."

A partially filled canteen was carefully dropped and encouragement shouted down the shaft, while two runners raced off for a rope. Tanglat's company commander and the rope arrived at a gallop fifteen minutes later, and the deserter was noosed and hauled out of the pit.

He then painfully stood and balanced himself on one leg—the other was badly swollen, and saluted his captain with a muddy grin.

"Sar, Private Tanglat report to thee company commander."

Medical examination revealed that the lad had a broken ankle, a dislocated wrist, a case of pneumonia, an unusually compacted digestive system, and one hell of a thirst. One of his remarks explained the acute constipation to the surgeon. "No water, I eat thee mud in thee hole."

Shortly after our first payday on Okinawa, I became aware of a king-sized problem. A good many of the men had enlisted in order that their pay might help support their families. Also, practically all of the Filipino officers had families in the Philippines who were totally dependent on them for support. How could they transmit their pay, when U.S. government checks were not negotiable outside of Manila? No private bank existed in Okinawa for the transfer of funds. And U.S. money orders were not valid in the Philippine post offices.

I took this matter up with General Hayden, who arranged to have a Philippine postal official flown to Okinawa every payday, and our problem was solved.

The official arrived on January 30 and next day he wrote two thousand money orders that the Scouts mailed to their villages and barrios throughout the length and breadth of the islands. But in my optimism I had not given the congenitally larcenous nature of Filipino officialdom due credit.

From three weeks to a month later, the news came in. The recipients of the money orders sent by our Scouts could cash them readily, at a discount of 10 to 50 percent. The rate apparently depended on the venality of the postmaster and the distance from Manila. And in many cases both were considerable.

I took this matter up with the Filipino postal official when he arrived to make the February collection. He was most agreeable and quite distressed. He admitted that the rural postmasters probably took a substantial cut, but their pay was so small and what could he do? I also found that Generals Hayden, Anderson, Styer, and MacArthur were powerless. It was a matter between our State Department and President Roxas, and there it rested until the Scouts were finally demobilized.

In the meantime some Scouts took a big chance that letters would not be "lost" or looted and sent currency camouflaged in thicknesses of writing paper. Others passed up the pay table, hoarding their money until they could take it home with them on their first leave. And the money order business fell off considerably.

Contrary to the usual military practice, I had directed and pushed the early discharge of men who proved to be unfit or undesirable in any way. There were too many good men available to waste time or effort in trying to rehabilitate unsatisfactory soldiers. I believed that every peacetime soldier should be capable of satisfactorily performing the duties of officers or NCOs up to four grades above his peacetime rank. When the army is expanded in an emergency a private should be able to command a squad section and a first sergeant could certainly command a company or a battalion.

Therefore in addition to discharge for hardship of family or other compassionate reasons (generally due to chronic homesickness) I stressed discharges under the provisions of Army Regulation 615–368 and 369 for the undesirable or unsuitable.

Men who had been court-martialed were considered for discharge after their sentences were served. Those who had company punishment records for repeated infractions, those who failed to qualify with weapons, and the frequently sick were called before a board and discharged. Since atabrine and prophylaxis kits were available and prescribed, the contraction of malaria or a venereal disease was considered prima facie evidence of willful disobedience of standing orders and lack of discipline. Timidity, shyness, fear of seniors, inability to learn a workable degree of English, improper carriage, failure to bathe, and objectionable habits were all considered as possibly valid reasons for returning the man to civil life. Consequently, in six months the Forty-fourth was reduced to a strength of three thousand first-rate soldiers who could be relied upon to become real assets to the army.

But in April we received the alarming news that a shipment of 750 replacements was on the way in the next transport. As I feared, these recruits were principally city boys, mostly Tagalogs from Manila, and of a caliber about that of the Filipino service troops who were a thorn in the side of Rykom; we started the long, hard process of training and indoctrinating these hoodlums. The training was comparatively easy; reindoctrinating such human trash after a lifetime of sophisticated thuggery was difficult.

The recruits were broadcast throughout the command with a view to breaking up cliques and separating old companions as far as possible and the veterans, particularly the now confirmed permanent NCOs, then did a very good job in squelching undesirable tendencies and forcing a fair degree of conformation on the replacements. As a small example, one morning Fiona went to the Rykom commissary in the jeep, driven by the Igorot driver De Leon. On returning to camp they passed a company of the Forty-fourth, which had fallen out alongside the road to "take ten." As the jeep passed, there sounded a piercing "wolf whistle," something that would never have occurred to the country boys and wild men of the original regiment.

As Fiona later described the incident, "I cut my eyes at De Leon and I give you my word; he had turned black. He drove into the camp, zoomed up to the house, and slammed on the brakes till we slid. He unloaded the groceries on the road—didn't even carry them in—then he jumped back into the jeep without a word and took off like a jet. Ten minutes later he came back and said, "Eet's all right, Mum, he was just a recruit, and the sergeant already chewed heem out. The rest of the men weel take care of heem."

Perhaps the job of civilizing these hoodlums might be feasible after all. Looked like we might have three thousand solid citizens helping us.

About May of 1947 an epidemic of serious sickness and death apparently swept through the Philippines, principally affecting the mothers of Forty-fourth Infantry Scouts. Requests for leave to attend the dying became so frequent that prior to asking the Red Cross to investigate and report on the validity of the emergency I required the applicant to see me between the hours of Recall and Retreat.

One evening a PFC Scout was ushered in to present his request for leave—his mother was mortally ill. He had the letter to prove it and the tentative approval of his company commander. The adjutant went out and closed the door.

"Yes, Poblete, I am told that you have a letter about an illness in your family."

"Yis sir, but I wrote it myself. I am CIC. I only weesh to see you alone. About trouble." He was practically whispering. Of course as a CIC agent under deep cover—

"OK, what trouble? Come closer, sit here." And I indicated the VIP chair at the side of the desk. A CIC agent. Damned good cover.

"Sir, Chaplain Lopez makes much trouble among the men. He talks about how they do the same work for pesos as the Americans do for dollars. He says you get fish and rice while the Americans eat bread and steak. He says American officers have their families with them while Filipino families must stay in the Philippines at home. I think you should know."

"Yes, I certainly should. I'll take care of it and it won't be necessary for you to report it to your headquarters. And the next time you have something to tell me, have a letter saying that your mother has died and your father is very sick. I'll tell your captain that you are not given leave until I get a report from the Red Cross. Thank you very much."

He rose, grinning, saluted, and left, the very picture of a grieving son whose compassionate leave has been indefinitely postponed. And left me with the problem.

Someone had been writing anonymous letters that were published in the *Okinawan,* the *Pacifican,* and Manila newspapers, about discrimination against Filipinos and the Scouts. One in particular had caught my attention just the day before. It was about a Filipino officer traveling by plane who was not served a cup of coffee by the air force flight attendant, while he did serve junior American officers. He had had to get his own.

A check of the passenger lists for the First Air Division for the last three weeks showed only one Filipino officer, Major Lopez. The *Okinawan* brought out the letter they had published. It was typed and unsigned. I could have done some typewriter-chasing but felt it unnecessary. I knew it was Lopez, writing inflammatory letters and using his position in the pulpit for political purposes.

The division between church and state applies even in the army and as long as he kept his shoes shined and his uniform buttoned I couldn't do much about him. I certainly couldn't reprimand him about his complaints concerning half pay and discrimination. He would turn my words against me in a sermon that would ruin me with the Scouts and ruin their attitude and performance.

But I'd sure have to do something about it.

I called a meeting of all Filipino officers, put on my mask of sincere, heart-to-heart concern, and tuned my vocal chords to an emotion-choked tremolo.

"Gentlemen, I have a most serious problem to put before you this morning.

"When a man builds a house he must be careful about the material he uses. He must be sure that there are no worms in the wood. If he uses a piece of worm-ridden wood the worms will multiply and the house will collapse."

Puzzled interest on the faces of the group.

"We have spent all our efforts for months in trying to organize and train the best Scout regiment in the United States Army. You have sweat blood in doing the job. You have succeeded.

"I heard General Hazlett tell General Hayden, 'I am sending you my best regiment.' You are recognized as the best disciplined, the most soldierly, loyal, and effective force in the Ryukyus command. General Hayden is proud to call upon you to pass in review before visiting generals and congressmen. He compliments the Forty-fourth as being 'just like the Old Army.'"

They were pleased, beaming with pride, a very slight sneer on the part of the padre.

"You have built well but there is a worm in the foundation timber. I have heard a rumor that there is someone among you who is working against you, someone who is spreading discontent among the men about payment in pesos, about rations, and about their treatment by Americans."

All hands were startled, especial Lopez.

"I also feel the injustice of half pay for your professionals while drafted Americans receive twice as much. I resent the attitude of some of the lower-class Americans toward Filipino troops. I am constantly doing everything in my power to remedy the situation. I cannot do as much or as well as General MacArthur but I will try."

Everyone dead serious—Lopez had turned from his usual cordovan to the color of a grocery bag and was sweating freely.

"I do what I can by maintaining the best regiment in this part of the world, by showing it off, by boasting about the Scouts to generals, congressmen, and newsmen at every opportunity.

"But we must get this worm out of the foundation timber of our regiment before he brings us down. I don't know who it is; you do."

Thorough embarrassment, glances to each other, especially at the padre, then eyes on toes.

"I am not going to investigate the rumor. If I, an American, were to take action in this case against one of you, he would write it up in the newspapers as another case of discrimination and persecution."

Yes, the major was really sweating it out.

"There are thirty-three good, solid officers among the thirty-four of you present. I will rely on the thirty-three to see that the thirty-fourth does no more harm. I am sure you will."

They were quite alert, including the chaplain. What did I mean?

"That is all, thank you."

The ranking officer, Major (Padre) Lopez, led the group from the room, looking like Judas Iscariot the morning after.

Lieutenant Bonilla waited for a word.

"Coronel, that was spoken from thee heart."

I should have felt complimented to have my performance so sincerely appreciated, but I didn't.

Felt like a damned two-faced politician.

Which I was.[2]

Sixteen.

Accommodations

Housing

My first order in Okinawa concerned sanitation. The dependents housing area at the old military government site had quonset shelters, a minimum of field furniture, and a mess, but the him and her community latrines were naturally at a distance from the living quarters. I considered the plight of families with small children, the very real danger of the night-hunting vipers, and the lack of lights.

I then asked Major Schneider to rush the delivery of twelve GI pails, each to be fitted with a plywood lid with the center suitably cut out. One of these utensils, with two inches of water covered with a thin layer of crankcase oil, was to be delivered to each quonset for night sanitary purposes.

Next morning the half dozen children were seen to be having a jolly time parading down to the mess at breakfast, each beaming little face framed in a plywood potty lid.

After the barracks, the Red Cross club, and the officers club were in good repair and operation I turned to the problem of officers family quarters. Something had to be done about getting the families out of the primitive accommodations of the old military government camp. My own two-room stone house with a quonset attached for the children was comparative luxury but still hardly adequate, and a steady stream of women and children were patronizing my bath, which had the only hot water available. Fiona had granted bathing privileges to our dependents and I reluctantly agreed with her—the only alternative, considering the temperature, was seven hot and dirty women and six grubby toddlers.

The Rykom housing area at Awase was becoming slowly, very slowly, available, and three or four quonset houses would shortly become available to us. I talked this matter over with the heads of the seven other families, pointing out that they could bid for the Awase housing or we could build our own on the west side of the Napunja area. Major Schneider (S-4), Major Simms (S-3), Lieutenant Colonel Ledbetter (second battalion), and Captain Dexter (C Company) wished to build in the regimental area. The three lieutenants preferred the housing offered in Awase now to waiting for our construction. I certainly couldn't blame them for wanting to move out. Ever since one of these child brides had been awakened from a sound sleep by a rat biting her on the lip, they had shown signs of cracking a bit.

So the young people moved to the comparative luxury of hot water and flush toilets and we oldsters drew house plans.

I selected the site of a former Okinawan house, a lot seventy feet square, enclosed on both sides and rear by a dense hedge of bamboo thirty feet tall. I noted that many of the wrecked houses had been located in similar bamboo groves and was told that the hedges were planted as windbreaks. Even in a typhoon the bamboo would not break, and in bending would divert the wind upward from the house. The house was a mass of debris and even the spirit wall was a pile of rubble.

I asked Lieutenant Apeles to build a house with a large combined living-dining room, three bedrooms, two baths, a kitchenette, and a laundry room. These requirements for a quonset were quite imposing. Looked at from the end a quonset was a half circle with a radius of ten feet. The huts came in ten-foot sections, and one could build a quonset a mile long with 528 sections, but it would still be only twenty feet wide.

Apeles shortly came up with his plea for a house that proved to be the most functional quarters I have ever occupied. He planned to cut the quonset sections down the middle of the roof line, move them apart, and weld an eight-foot section of roof between them. He proposed a sixty-foot length, which would fit within the building plot. In this twenty-eight by sixty foot floor plan he had drawn a living room and dining room eighteen by thirty-six and ten by twelve feet respectively, giving 768 square feet of floor space for entertainment. There were no halls, no dead corners, no waste space. The other family quonsets were as well planned but without the extra width that I needed for entertaining groups of the regiment.

Apeles had assembled and trained a capable crew while he had been working on the major repairs and alterations of the regimental buildings. This talent was now concentrated on putting up the five family quarters. Borrowing heavy machinery from the Rykom engineer, he was able to level the building sites, dig sewage and water lines in, and excavate large pits for the "septic tanks." The distance from the quarters to the main sewage lines was a major problem, so Apeles had procured several "navy cubes" six by six by six feet in size, hollow, which had had the primary mission of being bolted together to form floating docks during the loading operations. Long abandoned, they were now to be connected to our individual sewer lines for a final useful life as septic tanks.

All of the houses with inset dormer-type windows, plywood partitions, and plywood floors were finished within the month and the five families moved in. The work continued. A small pool, a ten- by fifteen-foot oval, was dug and cemented in the middle of the yard, and bricks from a wrecked native house paved the patio. As a sentimentalist, Fiona asked our bush masons to sign their work, so the cement topping of the rim of the pool was decorated with ten very capable hand prints.

Our quarters were now comfortable and even luxurious by the general housing standards in Okinawa, but the outside was still raw, with the red clay showing everywhere that was not bricked or cemented. I had asked the labor officer to obtain a gardener and he presented a powerfully built, genial farmer named Tosnyo and his feeble-minded but muscular helper, Matsumora. It was several days before Fiona learned why the house maids, Mitziko and Chioko, always went into hysterics every time she called or sent one of them for Tosnyo. Tosnyo would only blush and look sheepish. Finally Fiona demanded an answer of Mitziko, the more adult and stable of the maids.

"Why you laugh when I talk to Tosnyo?"

"Oh mees (giggle) you always say Tosnyo (titter) like Mees Tosnyo (uncontrollable merriment). You say Tosnyo-san—that like Meester Tosnyo."

After that primary loss in Okinawan courtesy everybody was "san"—Takuda-san in the kitchen, Mitziko-san and Chioko-san about the house, and Tosnyo-san and Matsumora-san in the field.

Fiona took full charge of the landscaping and beautification of our cobbled-up nest. In blue jeans, with her .32 Colt automatic holstered as a precaution, she would set out daily on explorations of the flower- and wood-covered ruins in the vicinity of Napunja. Tosnyo, the brainy member of the gardening staff, would follow, and sometimes serve as guide. Matsumora, the muscles, would bring up the rear with wheelbarrow, spade, and mattock. Fiona and Tosnyo had a total of two words in common, but accomplished wonders with them. Seeing a flowering shrub she would point and inquire, "Okay?" meaning "Can you transplant that bush successfully?"

Tosnyo would measure the shrub or sapling with a knowing eye, calculate its root system, consider the time of year, and estimate chances of survival. If it was not a feasible project he would say "Oki" with a rising inflection, meaning "That bush is too old or too big to be replanted at this time of year."

"Okay," my spouse would say, meaning "come on," and they would look for a more promising specimen.

"Oki?" meaning, "Is that one too big?"

"Okay," he would announce, giving his one American word a very American accent.

"Okay (dig)," Fiona would command, and Matsumora would fall to work. An hour later a new exotic shrub or tree would be blooming in its new home.

Our place began to look like a botanical garden with flowering trees, shrubs, and vines setting off the very pleasant location and breaking the strictly functional lines of the outsized quonset. Fiona's crowning triumph was a moon vine, which her crew brought in apparently without the loss of a tendril, and which continued growing at an accelerated rate after it was draped on the trellis over the front door.

The bamboo hedge surrounded the house on three sides and Fiona wanted something to enclose the front. She happened to mention this to Lieutenant Bonilla one evening. Next afternoon two truckloads of cut stone, the debris from two spirit walls, were delivered, and two masons started to reassemble them. In three days our own spirit wall was solidly in position.

It was a nice home, a beautiful place, and while it might not be up to the standard of colonel's quarters in Leavenworth or Benning it was well worth the quarters allowance I was paying for it.

When the families first moved into their new lodgings in Napunja they had their meals in the officers mess. This was a quonset near the family quarters where all officers of the Napunja garrison took their meals. The club was necessarily a completely separate institution where drinks, relaxation, dancing, and carousing were in order.

I was quite satisfied with this arrangement of having all meals at the mess. So were the other married officers—convenient, no strain on the women, meals on time, served by cute Okies in costume, and no one except the mess officer knew what was going to be on the menu. The women, however, led by Fiona, rebelled at some of the strange concoctions turned out by the very good Filipino-Okinawan crews supervised by the excellent Filipino mess sergeant. They also suspected the cleanliness of the superior kitchen that was operated by these worthies.

The heads of families put up a determined defense of the status quo but after a strong but futile rearguard action we capitulated. An arrangement was made whereby each family drew its rations in the raw state and I shortly found myself with a Japanese cook, Takuda.

The result was very odd. We were drawing the American Class A rations from the officers mess where they had been served as American, Filipino, or Okinawan dishes, commonplace, unusual, and exotic, but all good. Now with Takuda in our kitchen everything except the coffee and orange juice came on the table as some form of sukiyaki. But I had to admit that having to choose any one type of food for a steady diet, Takuda's crunchy, underdone vegetables and bite-sized meat or fish would be it. Our meals looked very much the same, day after day, but the ingredients were always surprisingly different and tasty. Every dinner was an adventure of exploration, analysis, and gastronomic delight.

During one of my flights from the office I called on the Rykom transportation officer. He showed me over his empire including the docks at Naja. Adjacent to the docking area was a junk yard, officially known as the salvage park. Anchors, chains, boilers, landing vehicles, boats, and all types of marine and amphibious material cluttered the area in groups and mounds of rusting metal. There was such a profusion of supplies on the island that an attempt would never be made to repair and use this material. The masses of wrecked and damaged boats going to waste gave me an idea.

I asked the TO if there was a boat in the yard that might be made serviceable enough for use.

"A boat? Sure, lots of 'em. Here's a thirty-two-foot launch and over there's a captain's barge. Just slap a patch over that hole, engine's in fine shape.

"No, not a motor boat, thank you. I'm a sailor and don't trust engines on the high seas. Do you have a small boat with sails that I could sign for?"

"Should have. Over here, how about this one? She's a bit dented here and there but she's sound. No need to sign for her, all this stuff will just be cut up for scrap."

"She" was a twenty-five-foot steel double-ended whaleboat, with a seven-foot beam, a four-foot depth, and a listed capacity of twenty-eight persons. The TO told the harbor master about our deal and left me with it. I hauled out the gear and looked it over. She was equipped with a lug sail and jib, both of the red canvas used in lifeboats. The mast, gaff, and boom were sound, rudder and tiller were in good shape, and a serviceable pair of oars were found to complete the inventory.

I made arrangements with the harbor master to deliver the craft to Ishikawa Beach on a tank transporter. On the appointed day I had a platoon of Scouts on hand for the unloading, figuring that a ton of boat for forty men is fifty pounds per man, a reasonable load. But I had not foreseen the efficiency of the transportation corps. The motorized crane, which the harbor master had sent with the tank transporter, plucked the ton of boat from the transporter bed like a match box, swung it over, and set it down in four feet of water with scarcely a ripple.

The Scouts promptly named her the *Wea Wei*—Tagalog for Red Dawn. The name the Americans gave her was less poetic but more proper, the *Snafu Maru*. She sailed well before the wind or with the breeze on the quarter, but made a lot of leeway with a beam wind, and pointed up like a bucket. I could get out of Chimu Bay against a head wind but it took half a day to do it. And I naturally would not sail out of the bay with a favorable wind; it would take me all night to get back. So only with a reliable beam wind from the north or south could I get out on the high seas and expect to get back the same day.

In spite of any inability to point up, the *Snafu Maru* had some very good features. Her built-in air tanks and water-tight lockers rendered her unsinkable even if one filled or was broken up. Her beam was such that capsizing her would require a typhoon or tidal wave. If capsized the handholds at the water line would enable the crew to right her with dispatch. And in general she gave me the feeling that given a compass, twenty-five cases of beer, and three hundred K-rations, I could make a landfall somewhere on the North American continent if life on Okinawa became too strenuous.[1]

I had intended the *Snafu Maru* to be for the recreation of the regiment, but found that Filipinos in their several categories did not care for sailing. The logical experts who had been reared in fishing or pearling areas apparently considered that anyone who went to sea for pleasure was insane. The people from the interior knew that anyone who willingly went to sea under any circumstances was insane. The Americans naturally had a deep distrust of any means of transport that did not have a motor and were sure that anyone who depended on sails was insane. So aside from a few lads who were courteous enough to come along, once, I sailed with my family or alone.

The one- to four-knot speed of the craft was ideal for trolling, and Catherine, our ten-year-old, proved to be the fisherman of the family. There are some people who are naturally simpatico with fish and who can attract and catch with anything better than a bare bent pin. Catherine was one of these gifted persons and quite regularly lifted sea trout into the boat with her hand line.

With a full crew Lee was the steersman, Fiona managed the main sheet, Betty stood by on the jib, Catherine fished, and I was the anchor-lifter, fish-taker-offer, occasional oarsman, and general deck hand.

After a few weeks of boating to and from across Chimu Bay, I took the boat around to a small navy repair section base known as the Ketchin peninsula where I could tie up to a dock and have better sailing in Buckner Bay with the prevailing east winds.[2]

My first voyage from the base was a disaster. The children were in school, Lee was working as secretary for Rykom, S-3, and Fiona had a wives' Kaffeeklatsch–Mah Jong party going, so I was about to cast off alone. An Okinawan who was presumably a base employee was helping me and apparently took such interest in the craft that I invited him to come along. He scrambled aboard and really got his teeth into the job. He shoved off with an oar, hauled up the main and jib, and trimmed the sheets to the northeast breeze so we could work out of the narrow canal passage into the bay.

On clearing the mouth of the passage I steered toward Tsugenshima, a small island seven miles distant. The breeze was fresh and steady on the north quarter and the *Snafu Maru* was rumbling along at her best four knots—should reach Tsugenshima in a couple of hours. Then for a split second the breeze died and before I could turn my head we were struck by a strong puff of wind from starboard. Not a squall, not a gale, just a gust of wind from the wrong direction. The boom swung over like an ax , the starboard stay let go like a pistol shot, the mast broke off at the thwart, and the whole confused mass of canvas, splinters, and strings went into the brink over the bow.

I was lucky to have brought the Okie along; he was evidently accustomed to disaster and remained cool and cheerful under adversity. We hauled the wreckage aboard, stowed it so it wouldn't interfere, lashed the rudder, and manned the oars.

My Okie friend was small, five feet four, and probably weighed 120 pounds. I wondered whether we could handle the standard navy oar. Fifteen minutes later I wanted to rest but couldn't—the little fellow was still pulling regularly, so I had to. Pulling that ton of boat quartering against the chop and breeze we gained by inches and really couldn't afford to rest. After half an hour I was totally exhausted and kept pulling only to save my racial pride. In another ten minutes my pride of race was gone; the Okies were obviously better men than we were—this one was evidently made of leather, spring steel, and rubber bands. He was just sweating and crooning a little song to himself; I was dead and doomed to swing that beam through eternity. But just as I was about to let go and to hell with it we gained the shelter of the entrance canal where the high freeboard of the boat was protected from the breeze.

Another hundred strokes and I was able to unstick my bloody palms from the oar and toss lines to my crew who had scrambled up the pier, nimble as a monkey. After wobbling my way up the ladder, muscles weak and cramping, I thanked the lad and gave him a package of cigarettes (three days' pay at local black market rates) for his part in our pleasure cruise. Odd, though, the boy often helped me cast off after that but he never again accepted my invitation to come along—too busy.

The wreck was actually a stroke of fortune. The section base chief whose mission was the repair of small craft took a great deal of interest in my mishap and offered to repair and re-rig the craft. I asked him also to convert her from a lugger to a gaff-rigged sloop and to weld a fifteen-foot, one-inch plate, one foot deep, to her keel in order to reduce her leeway on a tack. A much deeper and shorter keel would have been better for maneuverability but the area abounded in sunken wrecks, reefs, and coral heads, and I wanted the keel to clear anything that I couldn't see.

When my ship was relaunched the chief was supervising the operation of the launching crane and pointed out the new mast, wire-wound against cracking, additional stays that could prevent dismasting in anything less than a typhoon, and the improvements in keel and gaff. It occurred to me that since he was familiar with such matters he might enjoy sailing her.

"Certainly is a good job you've done, chief. How'd you like to come along on her shakedown cruise?"

"Well, colonel, of course I'd like to, but we're pretty busy here just now. Thanks a lot, some other time maybe."

I looked at the total absence of boats in his shop and the dozen idle mechanics and Okinawans who lined the pier, making caustic remarks about sailboats.

"OK, some other time. Thanks for everything, chief."

The sloop rig proved to be much easier to handle, of course, and the leeway dropped from outrageous to very acceptable. With the long keel, however, one was still slow in answering the helm to come about. Unless the jib was held hard over until the bow swung well into the wind, she simply refused to come over on the new tack. Then it was "out oar" or reverse rudder, which was a nuisance, but still better than getting a deep keel snagged on a sunken landing craft. I was usually sailing with a half crew, since Lee was working or dating and Fiona had an irrational but deep-seated fear of small craft, especially sailboats. But Betty became adept at handling the sheets while Catherine quickly developed a full understanding of wind, weather, and steering. I was as proud as they were the first time they "drove into the garage." This involves sailing the boat into the entrance, along the two hundred yards of dredged canal, dropping the jib and trimming the main to a starboard fifty-degree breeze, and dropping the main to less headway as *Snafu Maru* gently kissed the pier. This was their graduation exercise, which they passed at the "A" level on their first attempt.

Colonel Saylor of the staff moved his family into the Tengan area on Ishikawa Bay late during our Okinawan tour, and Saylor and his two boys showed enthusiastic interest in being, as he punned, sailors, so we sailed frequently thereafter with a full crew.

On my transfer to West Point in 1948, I turned the *Snafu Maru* over to the Saylor family, knowing that she was in loving hands. Six months later a typhoon tore her from her anchorage in Ishikawa Bay, flung her on the beach, pounded her to a loosely compacted ball of crumpled metal, and rolled her through the main street of Ishikawa.

Entertaining

Fiona invited General and Mrs. Hayden to attend one of our Saturday night stomps in our recently completed officers club. Realizing the inclination of the general to drive right by a guard post with a casual salute, and knowing the propensity of our own sentries to obey orders, I met them at the guardhouse at the entrance. Didn't want to see anyone shot when the driver failed to halt and show his "treep teeket."

They were a bit late, so when I escorted them into our club the festivities were in full swing. As we entered we had to step briskly aside to avoid being run down by a quartet of cordovan-colored maniacs who were galloping out with Captain Baxter on a stretcher, he loudly protesting and fighting to get off.

The general was amazed.

Mrs. Hayden was dismayed.

I was flabbergasted.

When we joined Fiona I found her not at all disturbed by the apparent lèse majesté, mutiny, or riot, and the rest of the party appeared to be going well. But after the Haydens were settled in I asked her what was going on.

"Fiona, what the hell is going on? Just now I saw—"

"It's all right, dear, it's a game they've dreamed up. Just watch."

Captain Baxter, slightly rumpled and laughing merrily, reappeared in the entrance. He was followed by five of the Filipino lieutenants, two carrying the stretcher, and all observing the dancing couples with the predatory interest of a pack of wolves stalking a herd of buffalo.

Aha. A whispered conference. They eased forward behind Captain Bammer who was whispering sweet nothings in Mees Cariaga's ear. The stretcher was shoved into the captain's hocks while Bonilla grabbed his shoulders and pulled. Mees Cariaga squealed and fled. Bammer was rushed out the door, vainly striving to sit up, restrained in the helpless flat of the back position by Bonilla's firm grip on the back of his shirt collar.

Looked like fun for all hands and since it wasn't criminal, dangerous, or "conduct unbecoming," I chortled with the crowd. Slightly reassured, the Haydens seemed to be enjoying the show.

But my dear spouse betrayed me. I later learned that Lieutenant Torak had asked her, "Ma'am, do you theenk eet would be OK eef we carry out thee coronel?"

And she had treacherously said, "Eet weel be OK."

So while Ruth Brady and I were milling about the floor she suddenly looked over my shoulder with apprehension—with horror. But then she giggled and shoved, let go, and there I was, flat on my back, on my way out into the moonlight.

I took the opportunity to caution the lads, "Don't carry the general out, I don't know if he could take it."

When we returned to the hall we found a "planting rice" circle had started.

"Planting rice" was originally a Tagalog song, usually sung by an older or incapacitated member of the village during the communal rice planting, while the others planted in tempo. The singing was used to coordinate and lighten the work like the sailors used a chantey. The American Army adopted it as a dance, couples abreast, stooping, touching the floor, rising, taking an imaginary rice shoot from the left hand, advancing a step, and stopping to plant it.

Saw the Haydens right in there with the younger set, planting rice and chanting the anglicized version with an enthusiasm seldom seen in a rice paddy:

> Planting Rice is never fun
> Work from dawn till set of sun
> Cannot stop—cannot sit
> Cannot rest a little bit.

Yes—the Haydens were all right.

And it was a very nice party.

They said so.

Colonel Stangle had organized a separate mess for the officers and families at Napunja, and the labor officer had recruited a staff of a dozen waitresses. These were selected primarily for their pulchritude and sunny dispositions; they could learn their jobs. In their colorful kimonos and obis they were quite cute, right out of the "Tea House of the August Moon."

Orders again. Fraternization with the enemy still applied and at last I was forced to take official notice of the squeals, giggles, slaps, and crash of crockery that went on as the young ladies carried their trays among the tables. So at the next officers meeting I put out the word.

"I am informed that some officers are becoming familiar with servant girls, kidding with them, making ocular, oral, or physical passes at them, and receiving passes in kind in return.

"Fraternization with the enemy is still forbidden. More important, such familiarity will ruin servant discipline and the service provided by Okinawan labor to the point where the hiring of this labor might be discontinued. Most important, making passes at waitresses in the mess is not appropriate conduct for an officer.

"The girls will not stray out of bounds unless they are encouraged to stray. When a girl tickles an officer under the chin while serving his bacon and eggs it is prima facie evidence to me that he has tickled her before—no proof will be required.

"So I earnestly suggest to any of you who must pinch Okinawan haunches to put in your application for transfer to a place where you can fraternize on equal terms. If the Okies affect you that way in February, what will you be like in the spring?"

Shortly after this meeting Captain Bammer, a talented young man with a sense of humor, a lyric pen, and an electric guitar, entertained us at the club by singing a bawdy ballad that he had composed, "Okinawan

Haunches in the Spring." It was damned well done, it was very topical, and best of all it gave me to think.

It was about time to put an end to this stupid nonfraternization business. After all, we hadn't been fighting the women. I couldn't in any way visualize Chioko, Matsumora, Takeda, Mitziko, or even Tesnyo as the enemy and I knew that there was a hell of a lot of fraternization going on in Japan where the order came from. So why shouldn't I organize a Scout-Okinawan dance at the Red Cross club?

Filipinos had a well-deserved bad reputation on Okinawa, almost as bad as that of the Twenty-fourth Infantry and service troops. The Filipino service troops had committed three murders with firearms during March and, even unarmed, terrorized the people with rape, beatings, and murder. Most of this violence appeared to be senseless, with no apparent motive and nothing to be gained. One of the Filipino officers gave me an answer that began to make sense.

"The Japanese committed many atrocities in the Philippines but they were disciplined. When they massacred whole barrios or destroyed Manila they did it under orders as a matter of policy. Their Okinawan and Korean labor troops, however, had weapons but no discipline. They committed individual atrocities simply for their own pleasure. So the Filipinos all hate the Okinawans and Koreans even more than they hate the Japanese.

"I have heard that when the first Filipino labor troops came here they would go walking. When they met an Okinawan they would ask him in Japanese, "Were you in the Philippines?" If he said yes, he was a dead man. And maybe even if he said no, he was dead."

Apparently it had been a major mistake to include Filipinos among the occupation forces. I didn't know whether I could overcome this well-earned legacy of hatred but I intended to try.

I approached General Hayden with my idea of a Red Cross–sponsored affair, including the Okies, and he called the military governor, Colonel Craig, into conference. Craig had a psychopathic hatred of Filipinos and was firmly against any relaxation of the nonfraternization order.

I outlined my plan to have a dance at the Forty-fourth Infantry Red Cross club under the supervision of the American wives and Filipino hostesses. Each girl would be chaperoned by one or both parents or other older relative or friend and could not be permitted to leave the club during the festivities. Trucks escorted by armed guards under Filipino officers would pick up the girls and their chaperones from the villages at 1900 and deliver them to their homes at 2400. Soft drinks would be served and no beer or liquor would be available on the post on the date the dance was held. Commanders of battalions and companies would be present to ensure that the conduct of their Scouts was acceptable.

Craig put up a determined fight, citing orders of higher headquarters, and fearing that the passions of the Filipinos would be aroused and the time is not yet ripe and you know what those Filipinos are like, and asserting that the party would end in a general rape of the Sabines.

I riposted by pointing out that at present we had rape, mayhem, and murder. That this was an acquaintance-making proposal, and that it was hoped that after the Scouts and Okies got to know each other better there would be more normal seduction, friendly rape, and mere pursuit and battery of protesting relatives. As for the nonfraternizing order I pointed out that the Okinawans were not the enemy—they were friends whom we had liberated from forty years of Japanese slavery.

General Hayden gave my proposal a tentative approval; the continuance of the program was to depend on how the first affair turned out. Craig left the meeting thoroughly disgruntled, stating that he was going to discuss the matter with the village elders. He and the elders did their best to sabotage our efforts and lost. The Okinawan old folks apparently had no more parental control than the permissive American parents of today and the young folks were reported to be coming if they had to resort to open revolution.

The precedent-setting dance was scheduled for April 12. Invitations were distributed efficiently and properly through the village elders who, disturbed by Craig's propaganda, were reluctant. More important, the labor officer passed the word to the maids, laundresses, and waitresses, who enthusiastically declared their intention of attending, and spread counter-propaganda most successfully.

Fiona found our maids, Mitziko and Chioko, quite unhappy because like most women "they didn't have a thing to wear." She immediately broke out her well-worn sewing machine and ran up two very fetching American-style evening gowns out of some flower-patterned stuff, which the girls then modeled with inordinate pride. I thought that they looked better in their native kimonos but decided to say nothing to delay progress.

My daughters undertook to teach the maids ballroom dancing, since that pleasant indoor sport was totally unknown in Okinawa where the men dance together, never with the women. But that evening Lee reported complete failure.

"Okinawan girls just can't dance backward—their 'getas' come off." The Japanese-type slipper or geta consisted only of a sole, a lateral strap across the foot, and a thong from the sole to the lateral strap between the first and second toes. There was no heel strap or support of any kind. It was a major problem of international scope. Dance in getas? Impossible. Give them shoes? Impossible. Dance barefooted? Hazardous and indecent.

Fiona delved into her sewing chest and came out with four yards of bright red ribbon. The girls cornered Chioko and after ten minutes of giggling and experimentation arrived at the solution. The center of a yard of ribbon was knotted at the junction of the cross-strap and the thong. Both ends were brought back around the heel, two or three turns were taken around the ankle, and a decorative bow was tied in front. A test run proved that Chioko could now dance forward, backward, sidewise, or jitterbug, and her getas would go right along with her.

Next afternoon Fiona assembled the tittering beauties of the maids' quarters and mess at the Red Cross club, passed out strips of cloth and ribbons, and conducted a class in the tying of the geta. After the usual explanation, demonstration, and execution, the girls were asked to spread the word among their friends in the villages. The Misses Domingo, Abad, Paoblete, Careaga, and Tan then cranked up a record player and put the class through a course in modern dancing.

The first Okinawan–Filipino Scout dance was a mixed success. The guarded trucks rolled in from the countryside and unloaded solemn mayors, girls' fathers, apprehensive uncles, giggling old ladies, and tittering youth and beauty. The latter were mostly, as were the elders, in kimonos. A few wore Western-style street dresses and Mitziko and Chioko were resplendent in their genuine American-style evening gowns. All had gotten the word—the getas were tied on.

The guests were escorted by the Red Cross hostesses to chairs lined up on one side of the club, the Scouts in their best uniforms, polished boots, and sleekly oiled hair, massed on the other. The Okinawan elders stared impassively into space, the young ones giggled and hid their faces, the Scouts stared, made probably ribald comments in a dozen dialects, and drooled. Pulido's orchestra played two inviting waltzes through with no results; nobody moved.

Then the Red Cross and the company commanders went into action, persuading the Scouts to show some initiative, while Fiona and the other wives pried the bashful butterflies away from their fearful, tolerant, or amused chaperones. A half-dozen couples began stumbling about the floor, and stumbling is the right word. The Red Cross people had been working on the project for two weeks but, after all, five hostesses just weren't enough to acquaint two or three thousand men in modern dance. But the dam finally began to break. The Scouts surged forward and the scene began to resemble the sack of Rome by the Vandals, with the Filipinos tugging the reluctant young ladies toward the floor, pairs and triads of Scouts heatedly discussing the possession of the fearful girl in the middle, and embarrassed maidens fleeing to the doubtful safety of the row of chaperones.

But it really wasn't nearly so bad as it looked. The reluctance, foot-dragging, fear, face-hiding, and giggling was merely the proper conduct that was expected of well-reared Okinawan ladies, and these girls were earnestly trying to behave correctly. The Scouts weren't afraid of the women—the Filipino doesn't exist who is. But they had been told so forcefully that the Okies were off limits, that they simply couldn't believe their eyes and ears when Miss Domingo and her cohorts pushed them forward with the exhortation, "Go get girl—dance."

The evening settled down to a very enjoyable party. I exchanged bows with seven mayors and 160 chaperones. The Red Cross directed a platoon of Scouts in serving the elder citizens with ice cream, cookies, and Coca-Cola while the young fry went through lines to get their refreshments.

After four hours of mild carousing by all hands, "Army Blue" signaled the end of the evening, numberless bows were exchanged, and in controlled chaos the native Cinderellas, assembled and checked off by their elders, mounted their two-and-a-half-ton pumpkin coaches, and were trundled back to their thatch-roofed fire-hole hearths.

A number of us gathered at the officers club for a well-earned nightcap of a few pain-killers—334 Japanese bows make a long, hard evening, to say nothing of the mental stress. It had been worse than a battle where you expect and can take a few casualties. As we were about to break up the victory celebration an alarmed Filipino lieutenant and a deadly grim mayor burst into the club.

"Sir, I have to report that one girl is missing. When this man checked his people in Minamiueborue we found that Mitziko Takada was not there."

"But didn't he check her aboard before they left?"

"He thought her uncle checked her but he does not know, sir. I think he was confused."

This was a sweet situation. I couldn't care less about the missing Mitziko. After all, these Okies had been selling their darling daughters and their virtue to their Chinese and Japanese overlords for hundreds of years. But my well-laid plans for interracial unity had just been shot to quivering bits. And I could visualize the hastily triumphant scene that Craig would put on tomorrow. Most important, I had assured General Hayden that nothing like this could possibly occur, not in my outfit.

What to do? Search the Red Cross club? Search the camp? Search the woods and countryside? These solutions ranged from fruitless to foolish but they were all that occurred to me at the moment.

Just as we were leaving for headquarters to map out a king-sized search another agitated young officer appeared, leading the tearful Mitziko Takada who had been rejected by the mayor of Nakagasuku. A lively conversation ensued between her and the mayor. Her defense against his increasingly harsh accusations, loosely translated by Lieutenant Zialcita, was that she had boarded the Tomai bus by mistake, while the mayor charged that she had done it on purpose to stay with a friend named Shibato.

Whoosh!

Fiona and I had another nightcap.

Seventeen.

Deputy Commander and Chief of Staff

Admiral's Quarters

After four months on Okinawa, I was well satisfied with the mental and physical condition and training of the Forty-fourth Scouts and was looking forward to another pleasant year with them. Then during the last week in May my plans were radically changed. General Hayden called me for an interview at Rykom. There was no preamble to the blow—he led with trumps.

"I'd like to have you take over here as deputy commander and chief of staff of Rykom."

"I appreciate the compliment, general, but I've never been a deputy, executive officer, or chief of staff, and God willing never will be. There are several colonels on the island who are senior to me and who would be much better at it. Jenkins, for example, is a natural for the job. Also I'm still needed in the Forty-fourth. So I thank you very much but I ought to stay with the Scouts."

"I can't agree with you. The Forty-fourth is a fine regiment. It won't be hurt by a new commander and I've got a good one on the way, Colonel Waddell. But I do need a deputy commander badly. Crowe is leaving next week and I want you to take the job."

There was no doubt about it, I was going to be busted from a big frog in a small puddle to a small frog in a big pond. I could gracefully assent to a request or I could obey an order. But I still might be able to do something for the Forty-fourth.

"All right, general, I'll take the job. You're losing a hell of a regimental commander and getting a damned poor chief of staff. But the Scouts have one peculiarity that you should know about. They lay great stress on people and personalities. They have a personal loyalty to their commanders, officers whom they have known for some time, to a much greater degree than do American troops. Whether the officer is good, bad, or average is immaterial, they know him and his peculiarities. A new man will win their confidence only after a long, hard pull."

"But you just said you'd take the job."

"I will. But what I'm getting around to is this—Lieutenant Colonel Stangle has been with the Forty-fourth ever since it was formed. They know him, he's their companion. He still scares the hell out of them but they're completely loyal to him. If you were to charge Stangle with murder you'd never convict him. There'd be three thousand eye-witnesses who would get together and swear before your court that he was somewhere else at the time you found him hacking at the body. They wouldn't do that for a new officer. So I recommend that you leave Stangle in command of the Forty-fourth and find some other job for your new colonel."

"I'm afraid I can't do that; Waddell's MOS is infantry commander and there just isn't any other slot for him."

"Sorry to hear that, sir. Stangle's a damned good man."

"By the way, I'd also like to have you take over the admiral's quarters in Tengan. It's the best house on the island—should be, it was built by a battalion of Seebees for a three-star admiral. I'd take it myself except it's too far from headquarters."

I thought of putting up an argument about leaving my oversized quonset home in Napunja, especially since Fiona had just completed her transplanting and landscaping. But it would be obviously inappropriate for me to continue to live in the regimental area like a divorcée living with her ex-husband and his new wife so I accepted the admiral's quarters. The general was right—it was the best house on Okinawa.

About a week after my summary reduction from regimental to deputy Ryukyus commander Colonel Waddell reported to Rykom headquarters as my replacement. He was a large, imposing man, about seventy-two by forty-eight inches, at one time darkly handsome. He was five years my senior both in age and rank and maintained a dour, supercilious, discontented expression throughout our interview.

The general was out so after welcoming him and the usual "How was your trip?" I started to tell him some of what I considered to be the most important facts about Filipinos, the Scouts, and the Forty-fourth in particular.

For three minutes he listened to my monologue with obvious impatience, then brought me to an abrupt halt.

"Colonel," he cut in with an inflection that made it sound like "Lieutenant" or rather *Lieutenant,* "I have commanded regiments before and have had a great deal of experience with Philippine Scouts. When will the general be available?"

So ended my briefing, which most new commanders would welcome and require. I made an appointment for him to report to the general that afternoon and he took his leave.

Once more Fiona and the family moved, this time into quarters that were comparatively magnificent. The basic components of several Butler buildings had been put together with the ingenuity commonly found among the navy's construction battalions. The full-length flagstone porch was screened and fronted with a flagstone patio and walks. The garden, forty by sixty yards, bordered by a low, curving stone wall, was terraced and planted with local flowers and shrubbery. Floodlights mounted on each end of the roof were available to illuminate the garden at night. The admiral had really done himself proud.

Beyond the garden wall, precipitous slopes and cliffs dropped off to Chimu Bay, across which could be seen the large fishing village, Ishikawa. Behind the house abrupt formations of volcanic rock gave the impression of Chinese landscape paintings. It was a delightful house in a magnificent setting. So Fiona promptly forgot her grief about her outsized quonset and hand-selected and transplanted vegetation that we had left.

The main road through the Tengan supply base lighted at night by street lamps to obviate thievery ran half a mile from the main gate directly toward our quarters and ended just short of the volcanic rock ridge immediately behind the house. The light arrangement was the direct cause of a lively moment a month after we moved in.

It had been a gloomy day and a thick cloud ceiling persisted at five hundred feet. We had guests for dinner and I had turned the floodlights on to display the garden for our visitors. About 2100, Colonel Alley was playing the piano in the living room. Fiona, Lee, and Mrs. Alley were gossiping on the porch, and I was listening in. Betty and Catherine were in bed.

Then the clouds across the bay started to brighten in one spot and a large airplane, with landing lights on, dropped down out of the overcast, flying directly toward us, probably a B-29. It continued to drop in a steep glide until my rough calculations indicated that he would touch down on my porch roof. Fiona and Lee began fluttering hither and yon around the porch like a pair of newly caged canaries trying to find the door.

"Bill! He's going to hit us! Bill! Do something!"

If there had been anything to do I would have been briskly at it, but for the moment I couldn't think of anything useful. The floodlight switch was too far away and around the corner—the plane was probably making 150 miles an hour and that was ten times as fast as I could have moved even twenty-five years before. The wingspread—the splash of flaming gasoline—the kids in bed—the people on the verandah—oh nuts! I stubbed my cigarette out as the only reasonable precautionary action I could take. I don't think I was frozen, I was just overwhelmed with the futility of all human endeavor. Mrs. Alley evidently agreed with me and sat calmly observing the approaching disaster.

When the blinding landing lights were two hundred yards distant, Fiona swears they were over our garden wall, all four motors roared out on full emergency power and the pilot evidently hauled his control column back into his umbilical. The plane cleared our roof, it cleared the volcanic ridge behind us, and roared away into the night.

Next day Betty came from school with a thrilling tale. Her teacher's boyfriend had been piloting his B-29 through heavy weather from Japan the night before. His radio and direction finder had gone out of action.

They found their way by stellar navigation and let down through cloud, about the only way to find Okinawa. What luck! There were the lights of Kadena air field right in front of them. Only in the last split second had the pilot seen that it wasn't Kadena, it was Tengan. Only due to his fast reflex and prompt action did he miss landing on my roof, the rocky ridge, or the main service road in Tengan.

With my palace in Tengan, I had inherited a family of rats that lived, thrived, and multiplied inside the beaverboard walls. They had gnawed a few holes here and there in the kitchen area and ate or removed everything edible that was left out overnight. Their rustling and squealing in the walls of the bedrooms caused enraged insomnia and nightmares on the part of the ladies of my family.

Fiona took action by close supervision of Takuda, seeing that he thoroughly sanitized the kitchen to surgical standards every night, and stowed all conceivably edible items in the refrigerator. The rats then moved farther afield, ate soap, candles, cold cream, and wool sweaters, and the sounds of chase, fighting, and multiplying in the walls increased.

One evening as we were entertaining General Beiderlinden and a trio of his staff from Japan a particularly daring and hungry rat sallied out into the living room to see what he could snitch from the hors d'oeuvres. Somewhat to the horror of the star-spangled VIPs and the surprise of all present I jerked a looted German saber off the wall and halved him on the first pass with a right forward moulinet. Couldn't have done it sober.

But that did it. I called the civilian pest control expert in for a consultation and described the situation.

"What can you do about them?" I asked.

"Well, we can poison 'em if you want."

"All right, poison 'em," I decided.

"Of course if we poison 'em chances are they'll die in the walls and you'll have to get the engineers to rip everything out to get at 'em when they start to smell."

"Oh no. But can't you trap them?"

"Sure we can set traps. We'd get one or maybe two. But rats are mighty smart and after we get one or two we could bait them traps with caviar and wouldn't get a nibble. And you'd have forty educated rats in the walls."

"One thing we sure can do," I went on. "We can plug up those holes so they'll have to go outside to make a living."

"I'm afraid that won't do it. They'll just chew out new holes—right through beaverboard most anywhere in fifteen minutes. You'd wind up with your walls all patches and new holes."

This pest control expert was civil service at its worst, a true defeatist drawing the pay of a brigadier general and couldn't whip a family of rats. I suggested cyanide gas—no, same effect as poison, die in the walls. How about king snakes? No king snakes in the Orient, only snakes in Okinawa are Habus and they'll kill you quick as a cobra.

"Well, you're the expert, Mr. Collins, what do you suggest?"

"I'll tell you, colonel, unless you want to move out for a month while the engineers tear up and rebuild your quarters I suggest you leave 'em alone. They don't eat much and if you just put out a couple pieces of bread every night they won't run around through the rest of the house. I figure that's a lot easier and cheaper than getting rid of them."

I was naturally outraged at the idea that I should not only live with rats in the house but feed them as well. But the more I thought about it the more reasonable it seemed. Finally I instructed Takuda to pay tribute, two slices of bread or a similar amount of table scraps to be placed in the Rat's Plate on the floor under the sink every night.

It worked. During the next year of occupancy we occasionally heard the rustlings and squeaks of fights and frolics in the walls but in spite of the obvious increase in numbers we never saw a rat.

In May 1948, I received my orders to return to the United States for reassignment. Colonel Jenkins who was replacing me as deputy commander was entitled to take over my quarters, but since he was well dug in at the Awase housing area declined. So the new Rykom quartermaster, a very correct, pompous, and supercilious young colonel on his first foreign tour, won the quarters by default.

So Colonel Gates, QMC, came over to inspect the layout as we were packing. I showed him around.

"Here's the switch for the floodlights but don't turn 'em on during cloudy evenings or you'll have lost B-29s making emergency landings on your roof—looks to them like the end of the runway."

He made a skeptical note.

"And here's the switch for the house lights. In case the Visayans are making trouble again, for instance if you think you have prowlers, pull this switch first and put the floodlights on."

An audible sneer. I guess they hadn't had Filipinos on the warpath at the quartermaster school.

"And by the way, see that hole and that one? That's where our rats live."

"Rats! Do you have rats here?"

"Oh yes but they don't eat much. Just put out a slice of bread and a few vegetable peelings every night. That's their dish under the sink. Give 'em enough garbage and they won't bother you. They like meat scraps, chicken bones, candle ends, toilet soap, anything you can spare."

"I'll be damned if I feed any rats—I'll poison them."

"I wouldn't advise it. It's a lot cheaper and easier to feed 'em. Poison 'em and they'll die in the walls and then you'll have a real problem."

Again he emphatically stated his clear-cut policy along the lines of "Millions for defense but not one cent for tribute," and I dropped the discussion as unprofitable. Argument with a fool only confirms him in his own foolish opinion.

Fiona and I moved our brood into the Rykom guest house for ten days pending the arrival of the transport to Japan, and Colonel Gates occupied the palace at Tengan. About a week later a small convoy of three sedans and a one-fourth-ton truck unloaded Colonel Gates, their numerous brood, and a mountain of luggage in front of the guest house.

"Hi, Gates, going on leave?" I inquired courteously.

"Hahn!" he replied discourteously—hadn't heard that since leaving France.

Yep, he had poisoned the rats.

Problem I

After the Battle of Okinawa was concluded, a goodly part of the island had become military dumps for the assembly of thousands of tons of ammunition, tanks, artillery, bombs, trucks, and spare parts. Okinawa had been intended to be the springboard and supply base for the final assault on Japan. There were square miles of ammunition and weapon dumps and acres of tanks. Since the atom bombs had interrupted the war, this material was slowly deteriorating due to the lack of ordnance personnel to care for it.

As D/C and C/S, I learned that one of our missions was to support Chiang Kai-shek in his fight to hold the Chinese mainland. Brigadier General Djo and fifteen hundred officers and men of the Kuomintang army were engaged in shipping such material help as we could give them, via four LSTs, to Shanghai.[1]

General Djo wanted small arms, mortars, tanks, and the appropriate ammunition. He had little or no use for heavy artillery or airplane bombs. I visited him and assured him of our all-out support.

Our aid, however, proved to be far less than wholehearted. There were evidently too many people in our government who were in sympathy with or afraid of the Red Chinese and their Russian backers. Successive directives from Washington through FEC and AFWESPAC reduced the scope of what we could do. Some quotes follow:

"Automatic weapons will be retained."

"M4 medium and M5 light tanks may be released to the Chinese, provided that the breechblocks are removed and the cannon destroyed by blowing the barrel off at least four feet from the muzzle."[2]

"Ammunition dumps will be turned over to the Republican Chinese with the proviso that all material (except automatic and semi-automatic weapons) is removed."

Each such directive was the subject of a conference with the understandably distressed General Djo.

"But why do we want two thousand pound airplane bombs? We have no airplanes. All we can do with them is melt out the TNT and use it to make hand grenades. And we already have more than enough TNT." I had no answer.

"What can we use the tanks for? As tractors, as armored command posts?" I was embarrassed.

"And we have to take all the material from each area except what we really need." In this case I was able to say something constructive.

"We are not going to inspect the material you take out of the dumps and no American is going to check on your loading at the dock. If you happen to pick up a few cases of machine guns and auto-rifles by mistake I'm sure that we don't want to know about it. And you get all the mortars you need with unlimited ammunition for them. As far as that directive about barring semi-automatic weapons is concerned, I do not consider that the limitation includes the rifles, pistols, and submachine guns that you want. I'll make it right with ordnance.

"I'm sorry about the requirement that you take the bombs but if you leave them they will be too obvious and it may endanger the rest of the program. And we can't do anything about the tank guns."

So under the erosion of a continuous flow of hampering directives from on high and the consequent useless labor involved in carrying them out, our flow of aid to the Kuomintang army dwindled to a trickle. The Red Chinese advance gained momentum. General Djo was recalled and replaced by Colonel Ho.

He was a neat, pleasant, nice little man who was understandably depressed by the restrictions placed on his activities. He must have encountered the same foot-dragging, halfhearted type of resistance in his own government, however, for he accepted the situation in good spirit and did the best he could.

Hearing that he liked to play Mah Jong, I asked him over for a Sunday afternoon of the ivories. Fiona was the Mah Jong champion of Okinawa, Lee wasn't far behind, and I was damned good at the game, so we agreed between us that we ought to let him win now and then in the spirit of American hospitality.

We did—let him win, that is. During two hours of clacking ivories Fiona said "Mah Jong" twice, Lee triumphed once, and I just admired Ho's technique. He never looked at his tiles, he just "read" the Chinese characters carved on the underside with his sensitive fingers and immediately discarded or added them to his hoard according to their value. If we had been playing for money the Triplet ménage would have been in debt well into the next decade.

After dinner while the girls played the piano Ho and I retired to the verandah and talked about tanks, weapons, ammunition, and dumps. I outlined in full all of the concessions we could make without having my buttons pulled off and General Hayden busted to permanent lieutenant colonel. He left at a late hour, filled with bourbon, quite happy about the Mah Jong and depressed over the American support of the Republic of China.

President Truman must have noticed the Far East situation about the time Colonel Ho was clobbering the Triplets at Mah Jong.

Next morning my bourbon-bleared eyes focused on a telegraphic order that in effect directed all-out aid to the Kuomintang. I phoned Colonel Ho and asked him over to Rykom and called in the ordnance officer, Colonel Winningstedt.

"Good news, Colonel Ho. We just received this wire. Quite a change from what I was telling you yesterday. We're to let you have anything we've got that is surplus to our needs."

Ho blinked, absorbing the good news cautiously, and reiterated their basic requirements. Winningstedt took notes and designated a dump that contained the weapons and several hundred tons of ammunition. Ho said his crews would start picking up the material at dawn the next morning. Both left in high spirits, Ho to arrange his labor details and Winningstedt to try to find the paperwork among the cubic yards of inaccurate records that were rotting in his rusting files.

About 2000 that evening my telephone rang.

"Winningstedt. We have a fire in the south dump area, the dump we're turning over to Ho. My fire-fighting crew got on it right away. I'll let you know when we get it under control."

"How will that affect Ho's job?"

"Ho probably won't be able to get in there today."

"How about another area for him?"

"Can't do it—the paperwork—it'll take another day to—"

"OK, let me know."

But as I put the phone down I thought I've seen a lot of ammunition fired and I've seen tanks explode but I've never seen an ammunition dump burn, might be instructive and I wouldn't have to rely on third-hand telephonic reports.

A second thought, tomorrow was a holiday and the young ones would probably enjoy the show. I'd take them along. Fiona showed no interest in a nocturnal jeep ride but approved the outing for the rest of the family.

"Lee, B'Ann, Cat, get your coats on. We're going to see a fire."

The four of us made a jeepload so I told Konasura to go back to bed and drove myself. B'Ann was the Japanese-speaking expert of the family, but when I got lost (as I always do) her queries of a native about the road to Chinen were not useful. He understood what she wanted but she couldn't understand the directions. The arcing red flares and the faint stutter of a brisk battle in the distance, however, gave us the information we needed, so we declined his apparent offer to ride with us and marched to the sound of the cannon.

I immediately learned one thing—Winningstedt's "fire fighting crew" was a misnomer. One does not fight an ammunition dump fire. One halts at a respectable distance and tries to contain it or just watches the fireworks.

All of the dumps on Okinawa were extremely vulnerable to fire. The ammunition was in open storage, there were miles of it separated into city-block-sized dumps, and the manpower available to the ordnance officer during this postwar period was not sufficient to keep it free of vegetation. The uncut grass, weeds, and brush had grown up thickly around the stacks and the weather was dry.

The grass fire was advancing steadily across the area, fanned by a moderate night breeze. Tracers of .30 caliber to 20-mm. were arcing in all directions like an antiaircraft defense of the Remagen Bridge, while the irregular rattle of exploding small-arms cartridges was punctuated by an occasional sharp explosion of medium artillery magnitude.[3] Sounded like a heavy infantry-tank engagement. I asked Lee to run the jeep back a bit, clear of the falling bits and pieces.

I admired the courage of the fire-fighting crew—two tank-dozer crews who were bulldozing firebreaks wide enough hopefully to prevent the spread of the fire to the neighboring dumps. The outsized Negro sergeant who parked his machine nearby explained the situation.

"Yes sir, there's some five-hundred-pound stuff over on the other side. But there ain't much chance of it blowing. It ain't fused and most likely the TNT'll just burn. Same with the mortar shells. All we really got to worry about is the cases of fuses and detonators *(whoosh!)*—that was one of 'em. And the small stuff, of course. The .30s generally won't do more than break the skin but I sure don't want to get hit by one of them .50s. And the 20-mm. cannon shell are fused."

He drank a prodigious amount of water and readjusted helmet and goggles.

"If I was you, colonel, I'd move back a little. One of them chunks taking off in the right direction won't do you any good."

He remounted his tank, snugged down in the turret until only his eyes were exposed as he directed the driver back into the danger area. I hoped he was right about the bombs and shell. But somewhere I did read that under certain conditions of heat and pressure TNT would explode. And recalling his advice I moved back with the family to enjoy the show as well as I could under the circumstances.

Next morning I had another conference with Ho and Winningstedt. We agreed on another suitable dump and Colonel Ho diverted his crews accordingly. By 1000 the work was under way and truckloads of automatic weapons were pulling out to the piers.

By a strange coincidence that area caught fire that night. And again. In spite of secrecy in our plans, guards, and patrols, three ordnance dump fires hampered our efforts and caused serious damage. Others were discovered and extinguished early enough to cause no delay.

It appeared to me that someone in Colonel Ho's organization or on our own ordnance staff did not agree with President Truman's policy of all-out aid to the Kuomintang. But in spite of the opposition we got four overloaded LSTs off to Shanghai.

Then Stalin's man in Washington again took control of the telegraph key, and amendments to the all-out aid telegram began to arrive.

"Reference to TWX _____, tanks furnished Chinese will have breech-blocks removed and cannon barrels blown off four feet from muzzle."

"Reference TWX _____, automatic weapons will not be released."

Problem II

I don't like but am not shaken by the sight of dead men; in the infantry one sees a lot of them. Such sights are merely serious wounds. And after rigor mortis has set in they're easier to handle. But I'll never willingly be in the neighborhood of bodies after they have softened, swelled, and started to decay. And to dig them up—unthinkable.

Undertakers do not have my sympathy. During a bivouac I once overheard one of my young men discussing his past and future careers.

"Come the end of this hitch I'm going back in the undertaking racket. I worked a year for an undertaker and know the game. Take a stiff, straighten him out, shoot in two bits' worth of formaldehyde, and there's fifty bucks right in your hand for embalming. Pine coffin costs maybe eight dollars but you can always con the sucker, I mean the bereaved, into buying that same box with black sateen tacked over it for two hundred dollars. A little talcum powder and rouge and 'Don't he look natural!' It's easy money. Only trouble is you have to talk soft and wear that come to Jesus look all the time. And I mean all the time. Hard to keep a straight face when the old lady decides on mattress (fifty dollars) stuffing instead of straw for the comfortable rest of the dear departed throughout eternity. Eternal rest, hah! Dig him up a couple of years later and see what you find."

Neither was I in accord with the movement to repatriate the dead at the end of World War I. The men who were killed or died in France had been decently buried in French military cemeteries and assured of permanent care. But the Association of Undertakers had seen a great opportunity and began their propaganda and political lobbying campaign to bring the boys home.

Their efforts were successful. A wave of hysteria swept the nation. The unthinking relatives got solidly behind the movement, politicians seeking votes in the elections of 1920 mounted the platform, and we brought the boys home. Bodies were recovered, the bones placed in new coffins, and the feelings of bereaved relatives and friends were torn a second time by the volleys of military funerals. The undertakers as receiving and arranging agents were delighted to receive the shower of treasury checks for their small part in the show.

So it was with no great enthusiasm that I received Captain Harding who commanded the graves registration detachment. He was a capable-looking middleweight with a strong-boned brunet face but spoke in the hushed tones and wore the devout, downbeat expression appropriate to a civilian undertaker. He took my VIP chair as I waved him to it and produced a large photograph album from his bulging briefcase.

"My detachment is responsible for the exhumation, preparation, and return to their homes of all of our men who fell on the battlefield during the Ryukyus campaign," he explained.

"You have quite a chore in front of you, captain. I understand that there are twelve thousand bodies on the islands buried in many dispersed locations."

"That is quite true, sir, but the numbers are comparative to those in the Philippines that are dispersed from Luzon to Mindanao. Here we have less than a hundred miles to search. My crews are all experts at their jobs and I've requisitioned 12,500 bronze coffins, so the work should go right along." He opened his photograph album, rose, and placed it on the desk, oriented so that I could miss nothing.

"I have our operations in sequence in these pictures, colonel, and I'd like to show you what we do."

He had lost his low-voiced, graveyard approach, sounded now more like an automobile salesman. I could think of several other things I'd rather be doing but he evidently took such pride in his work that I hadn't the heart to cut him off.

"We locate the initial burial sites by a study of unit records, by personal observation, and frequently from reports of natives. We then exhume the bodies and place each individual in a waterproof body bag, shown here, here, and here." He displayed a series of pictures.

The sharply focused, glossy finished signal corps photographs showed every gruesome detail. There was a pair of gas-masked and rubber-gloved figures digging, another of a trio, one leaning on a spade in the background, another holding open a long black bag, while a third shoved an undefinable bulk of things into the opening. I looked closer.

"My God! They come apart, don't they?"

"Well, yes, they do. They've been buried a year or more, and decomposition is well advanced. But I assure you that my men are very careful to recover the complete body and the identification tag."

"Do you always get all the pieces? Under conditions like that? But what if the head is blown off and the tags with it? And I know that some men in Europe would take their tags off before an action. What about them?"

"I know, colonel, we do have problems like that in a few cases. And at times two or three bodies or partial bodies were hastily buried in the same grave, so identification is difficult. But I have a very capable identification team. They measure the bones and match them up. They can sometimes find an identifiable fingerprint. They study the missing list, service records, dental charts, and operations reports. They make sure that the bodies are correctly assembled and identified. It takes time, of course, but—"

"I see." I was still skeptical, recalling the horror story of the family that disregarded the caution to leave the coffin sealed. They opened it for a last look on the dear departed and found the parts of a fairly complete skeleton of the right size topped by an undersized skull. But Harding had turned another page of his pictorial record.

"Here is our processing laboratory. The body is laid out on these tables where our technicians remove the flesh from the bones. They are then washed and reassembled to be sure that they are complete and compatible."

"That they fit, I take it." My brief view of the pair of masked, gloved, and aproned ghouls stripping the putrescence and slime from—I just couldn't take it—pulled my nauseated eyes away.

"Must be a smelly job," I commented.

"Yes, it is," he admitted. "But our crews are highly dedicated and we use powerful deodorants. Their masks are also deodorizing and scented so that they—"

"Ah yes, I imagine so."

He turned a page.

"The body is then placed in a new bag and tagged—"

Another page.

"And placed in the bronze coffin for shipment."

"Why do you use a full-sized six- by three- by two-foot coffin? Those bones don't weigh over thirty pounds and they could be fitted into medium-sized suitcases."

"Oh, the full-sized coffin has dignity and the bereaved think of it as containing the complete body. We could not—"

"Seems to me that the Japanese system is better—stack up five hundred bodies on a pile of firewood and send five hundred small white boxes home with a cubic foot of ashes in each box. No, captain, I'm not at all in sympathy with your program. I'd rather let them rest where they drop. But once the return of the bodies is required I'm very glad to have you and your detachment here to do it. Please let me know if there is any further help you need from the engineers or transportation. And I thank you for your most interesting briefing."

As Captain Harding left with his briefcase and advertising portfolio, I noted that my watch stood at 1200 and started for the mess. At the door I paused and after a moment of meditation returned to the desk to attack the pile of paper in the overflowing in-basket.

Just didn't seem to care for lunch.

A score of correspondents from leading newspapers and magazines descended upon Rykom. Orders from AFWESPAC were to "give them everything they want." They wanted whiskey and geishas but we hoarded our whiskey and had no geishas. We did show them everything else we had: the failing, food-spoiling refrigerator banks, Suicide Cliff, Nakaga-suku Castle, a review of the Forty-fourth Scouts, the quonset quarters, the overgrown ammunition dumps, even the hospital. But not the cemetery.

The Rykom program for the repatriation of the dead was not going well. Captain Harding's graves registration detachment was proceeding with the exhumation, cleaning, and rebagging of bodies, but the requisitioned 12,500 bronze coffins had not appeared. The storage of ten thousand bone-filled body bags for an indefinite period pending appropriation of funds, procurement, manufacture, and shipment of bronze coffins had become a major problem.

I don't know the reason for the decision or who gave the order—I stayed as far as possible from Harding's activities and problems—but he was presently engaged in reburying the bodies in what was hoped to be a temporary national cemetery in his area south of the ammunition dumps. At his request I had furnished engineer units with ditch-diggers, bulldozers, graders, and grass seed for the job.

The site, three hundred yards square, was first leveled, then dug with parallel ditches four feet deep, two hundred and fifty yards long, and eight feet apart. Allowing six feet per grave, which was more than ample for a body bag, this area would accommodate the 12,500 corpses that were expected to be assembled. The area was cross-surveyed, marked, plotted, and registered so that the exact location of any individual grave could be immediately determined.

Eighteen hundred temporary burials had been made. The body bag had been placed in its private six feet of trench, the name, number, and point of burial registered, the earth bulldozed over it and graded, and the grave marked by temporary wood markers. About nine hundred more bodies had been placed ready for covering.

A typhoon had brushed by close to Okinawa on its way to Japan and the outrider clouds had dumped a foot of water on the islands. Captain Harding consequently had informed me that the cemetery was not in condition to be seen by the press at this time.

When I had given him the warning order to stand by for inspection he had begged off.

"I really don't think you should bring them down here if you can avoid it. We just can't make it. We're drowned out."

That was all right by me. I didn't think his operations were suitable for public viewing at any time, so I gladly deleted his unit from the show-and-tell agenda. But the spokesman for the press had another idea.

"We want to see Ernie Pyle's grave," he announced with the arrogance of his seniority and the assurance of his official backing.

The correspondent Ernie Pyle had been killed on Ie Shima and his body was among those recovered.[4] He was somewhere among those now being processed in the storage building or resting in the temporary cemetery pending the arrival of coffins. But as Captain Harding had indicated, his area was not in condition for viewing.

General Hayden and I tried to deflect their morbid curiosity by inviting them to take a tour showing the Kuomintang compound and the aid to Chiang Kai-shek activities. But in vain; the press people smelled a story.

"No. We want to see Ernie Pyle's grave, and this letter from MacArthur says—"

"OK, Bill, take them down there," said Hayden resignedly. "I have an appointment and won't be able to go with you, gentlemen."

It was the first time I'd been to the cemetery. I'd seen the photographs and just wasn't masochist enough to want to see the real thing.

A light breeze that was blowing from the processing building informed us at a range of a mile that something awful was going on upwind. Like a Chicago slaughterhouse only much worse. The visitors wondered what it was. I knew, I'd seen the pictures.

We dismounted, mercifully on the windward side of a large Butler building, and were greeted by Captain Harding. He seemed a bit nervous, torn between pride in his work and apprehension, but he did well under pressure. I introduced him.

"Gentlemen, this is Captain Harding, the officer in charge of the Rykom graves registration program." Harding caught the ball and ran with it.

"Good morning, gentlemen. The general has just informed me that you wish to see the grave of Mr. Ernest Pyle. Unfortunately—"

"Yes, and while we're at it we want to see everything," announced the spokesman in a tone that implied "especially what you are trying to hide."

Everything? Captain Harding was no longer apprehensive or nervous. "Very well, gentlemen (meaning "you asked for it"), follow me." He led off toward the wide door of the Butler building, starting his lecture en route. His voice was no longer hushed and his bearing was that of a line officer rather than an undertaker. I heard the beginning of his spiel but stayed where I was—I'd heard it before.

"The bodies are exhumed from their initial burial points in the field and placed in body bags. They are brought to this building and temporarily stored pending—" and he led the party into the building. Yes, I stayed out there in the windward breeze.

Ten minutes later Harding reappeared, followed by the gaggle of pale but still determined note takers. He led them into the processing laboratory where masked, gloved, aproned, and rubber-booted apparitions were working on decomposed human debris at metal tables with water jets, scrapers, and body bags.

He did not lead the tourists out of this area—he followed them. They entered bravely but reappeared immediately in pairs and trios, pale, gasping, retching, and the more fortunate vomiting. Their remarks indicated that they had seen everything.

"They just fall to pieces."

"Good God."

"That made me a vegetarian."

"How do they get men to do that?"

"I'll never eat creamed chicken again."

"I'll never eat again!"

There ensued a period of deep breathing of the clean windward air while Harding explained the layout and construction of the cemetery. He was going into detail about the possibly temporary reburial, covering, marking, and grass-seeding when the senior correspondent interrupted.

"We still want to see Ernie Pyle's grave, captain."

"So I understand, please follow me," and Harding led off toward one of the cross paths between the markers. The first four rows of graves had been sown and the young grass had a good start. It occurred to me that Harding had buried Pyle in this well-finished area or had switched markers on receiving the general's warning call—that's what I would have done. Show them the nicest, levelest, grassiest grave in the place. But he was too honest, or was he just feeling vengeful on account of the verbal beating he'd been taking?

Captain Harding paused at the far edge of the grassed area. Beyond that point there was nothing but hock-deep clay with row on row of markers.

"Gentlemen, you understand that we have just had a typhoon pass through here, which dropped so much rain that we're flooded out. We haven't been able to get the machines in to recover and grade promptly. But you want to see Mr. Pyle's grave. I'll show you."

We pushed on through the thoroughly soaked clay until Harding stopped at the first open trench and pointed.

"Gentlemen, Mr. Ernest Pyle."

The press lined the trench and stared, grimly silent, at the black bag anchored to a stake and semi-floating in the foot of clay-colored water.[5]

Eighteen.

Murder in the Forty-fourth

Killings

Shortly after Colonel Waddell took command of the Forty-fourth, Captain Gardner of the cannon company preferred charges against one of his men for failure to obey an order and "insolence to a noncommissioned officer." He sent the charges to regiment, recommending a summary court-martial conducted by one senior officer. Colonel Waddell directed that the charges be referred to a special court of three or more officers and that the entire cannon company attend the trial for their instruction in military law.

Two mistakes had been made. The charge did not warrant the power of a special court with three members, a trial judge advocate, a defense counsel, and recorder—the lower summary court of one experienced officer could have heard both sides of the case and like King Solomon awarded the small fine and restrictions appropriate to the offense. But this error was comparatively unimportant. Requiring the entire cannon company to attend was fatal.

Private Bacawan, the accused, was a Visayan from the island of Visaya, settled centuries ago by immigrants from India. Visayans have great pride, both as individuals and as Visayans. This pride gave them a reputation among the Spaniards, Americans, and other Filipinos for being troublemakers.

As the court proceeded through the formalities of the trial the two dozen Visayans in the audience were deeply chagrined to see one of their race publicly exhibited as a criminal and the accused was hopelessly humiliated by being exposed to the ridicule of his company mates and his Visayan companions.

The man was found guilty and sentenced to forfeit fifty pesos and to be restricted to his company area for one month. The sentence was appropriate, but that was of no consequence to Bacawan. He had lost face and his pride and reputation could be restored only by blood.

On leaving the courtroom he went immediately to his company supply room, picked up a hammer, and knocked the supply sergeant unconscious. He then unlocked the arms racks, selected two carbines and a pistol, loaded them, and filled a belt and pockets with ammunition.

Bacawan had made an understandable error. He had the fixed idea that the public spectacle of his trial had been ordered by his company commander; after all, Captain Gardner had formed the cannon company and marched them to the court. In fact Gardner had vigorously protested the idea when Colonel Waddell had ordered the show.

So Bacawan proceeded to the orderly room, waved the unarmed orderly and clerk aside with his pistol, burst into the office, and put five bullets through the center of Captain Gardner's chest. He then dashed out, ran down the company street, and disappeared.

At that point things became confused and stayed confused for the next twenty hours. The guard was called and began beating the bushes where Bacawan had disappeared. The cannon company drew arms and ammunition and took up the trail of their former companion. Colonel Stangle telephoned me, I alerted the provost marshal, Lieutenant Colonel Momyer, and he deployed the military police in radio-equipped jeep patrols. I notified intelligence and Lieutenant Colonel Patton put the CIC on the job. Captain Gardner's body was dispatched to the hospital so the medical wizards could determine whether or not he was dead.

Radio reports came in on Bacawan's progress from MP patrols who were informed by gesturing natives that "the wild man went thatta way." Pursuing Scout units were assembled, loaded into trucks, and unloaded at the scene of the latest sighting on an average of once an hour.

Mrs. Gardner went into a serious state of shock when notified and was ambulanced to the hospital where eager medicos who intended to specialize in forensic surgery were enthusiastically disassembling her husband to learn what had killed him.

I was delighted that General Hayden was in the hospital undergoing treatment for his chronic blood pressure and heart troubles and advised the surgeon that he was to be told nothing. The situation would probably have killed him.

I have always hated to conduct an operation by telephone or radio—could have done much better during the Civil War days before the damned things had been invented. You just can't project personality or urgency over a telephone wire and shielded by distance it is easier for the other fellow to exaggerate his difficulties and disagree with the plan of action. Further, being aurally slow-witted, it is difficult for me to understand the rapid gabble of the excited lad on the other end of the wire. For those reasons, while in Europe, I had always stayed up with the advance guard and sabotaged or disregarded my radio, leaving the executive to deal with the highest echelons who were demanding progress reports or cheering us on over the ether waves.

But in this situation I was stuck with it, a telephone connected through switchboards operated (and monitored) by Filipinos and Okinawans, radio orders and reports via the communications section, and a large-scale map of Okinawa and offshore islands studded with colored pins indicating the last reported positions of the fugitive and pursuing units. It was like fighting a ghost. A verbal report from Okie farmer to Okie mayor, sign language and dirt-drawn sketch from mayor to MP patrol, radio to provost marshal to communications and telephoned to me would come in an hour or more late. Waddell had apparently gone into seclusion so I'd get Stangle through the Okinawan-Filipino switchboards and he would transfer the cannon company or F Company to the new front. They would assemble, entruck, arrive two hours late, inspect the farmer's trampled compote patch, and take up the fresh trail. It was hopeless.

Bacawan was moving fast and in no predictable pattern or we could have cut him off from his probable objective. The search parties were trailing, and in spite of the stories put out by Hollywood and other fiction writers a trail is not followed at a run. The trailers lose ground.

But at last a report came in that we could get our teeth into. At Ishikawa, Bacawan had spotted the landing craft that military government had loaned the village for fishing. It had just beached with the morning catch. Bacawan took charge, ordered the skipper to take him to the Philippines, and waved the other fishermen back to the village. When the MP jeep patrol skidded to a halt on the scene the landing boat was putt-putting away at full speed a quarter mile out and the muscle-powered boats available on the beach would have had no chance in pursuit.

I called the First Air Division at Kadena and got their timid, ineffectual chief of staff on the phone.

"Triplet here. You have an armed fighter up, don't you?"

"Yes, we keep a hot fighter patrolling day and—"

"OK, there's a landing craft heading from Ishikawa out of Chimu Bay. There's a man aboard just murdered his captain. He's kidnapped the Okie skipper and ordered him to steer the craft to the Philippines. We'd like to have your pilot buzz him, shoot across his bow, and force him back to the beach where the MP patrol can pick him up. Shoot up the front end of the craft if you can't stop him any other way."

"I'll notify the general and let you know."

A long wait ensued during which I called the navy commander and explained the situation.

"I'd like to borrow one of your small craft to transport a platoon of MPs or Scouts to run the poor devil down."

"OK, we've got a tugboat and a mine sweeper both at Buckner Bay wharves. You can have either or both."

"We'll take both. I'll have the troops there within the hour."

"I'll have 'em fired up."

"Thank God we've got a navy."

Back to First Air Division and the chief of staff.

"Have you turned him back yet?"

"Our pilot has spotted him. He's heading for the pass between Heanza and Taka. We've buzzed him but we can't turn him."

"Well, shoot in front of him, closer every time. Riddle the front of the boat if he won't turn. Sink him. We'll pick him up."

That would be the ideal solution; a fugitive who'd been soaking in sea water for ninety minutes wouldn't be near as much of a problem as a man with a carbine in a boat or on land. But it wasn't to be.

The C/S First Air objected to my solution.

"The pilot says he won't take the responsibility of shooting. Neither will General Hegenberger. We might hurt somebody."

Having been shot at a couple of times by the fighters of the Eighth Air Force in Europe, I could see his point—the pilot had no more confidence in his marksmanship than I had. The hot shots just weren't accurate enough to fire warning shots without probably sprinkling the boat from end to end.[1] But I still wanted to turn that boat back to the MP reception committee on the Ishikawa beach.

"Listen, Scott, that man is heavily armed and dangerous. If he gets ashore on one of the islands our people will have to go in and get him out of that jungle. If he holes up for a shootout he'll probably kill several of our men before they get him. Would General Hegenberger rather have our men killed than take a chance of your flyboy hitting him or the Okinawan?"

"We can't take the chance. General Hegenberger feels that it's entirely the army's problem."

"Well, thanks for your cooperation and give General Hegenberger my best wishes."

Phone calls to the provost marshal and Stangle. A platoon of military police aboard the navy tug and the F Company Scouts cram aboard the mine sweeper.

"The surgeon is on the phone, colonel," reported my secretary, flashing her teeth.[2] Our chief medico was still apparently sober. His report was bad.

"We have Mrs. Gardner here in a private room, colonel. Sedatives don't seem to have any effect and the psychiatrist is afraid she may lose her reason. She insists that she does not want us to perform an autopsy and of course the autopsy to determine the cause of death has been—"

"What do you mean 'of course'? Are you people so stupid you can't figure that a handful of bullets in the chest—Never mind, I'm coming down there."

I called in Colonel Jenkins, the operations officer (G-3), brought him up to date, and turned the remote-control of the hunt over to him while I took off for the hospital.

Lieutenant Colonel Kranz was surprisingly sober and considerably concerned about the autopsy.[3] His crew had stepped out of line before with near disastrous results. A Mohammedan Chinese of the Kuomintang army detachment on Okinawa had been found by an MP patrol with his throat cut and the body was brought to the hospital. The students of anatomy had immediately sawed open his skull, removed the brain, and opened chest and abdomen so they could pull out all the internal organs to determine the cause of death. They had then done a very crude job of hemstitching him together before releasing the corpse to the Chinese. General Djo had arrived at Rykom headquarters in a stormy mood to protest our desecration of the body. We had learned that the Chinese Mohammedans have the belief that the soul of the departed must endure eternity in the same condition as the body when it is buried. It was therefore understandable that the Moslem half of the Chinese brigade was outraged to the point of mutiny. General Djo had been distressed by the incident and its consequences.

So was I and had discussed the matter of unnecessary butchery with Kranz at some length. He had quoted medical custom and army regulations and stated that surgeons had the right as well as the duty to do an autopsy on every corpse to determine the cause of death.

I disagreed and told him that there would be no more autopsies in cases where the cause of death was obvious. Further, under no circumstances would the surgeons cut up any Chinese corpse. As an afterthought I had extended the proscription to include Mohammedan Filipinos. An outbreak of Moro juramentados would be as serious as a war with Chiang Kai-shek's outfit.[4] Now it looked like I'd have to add devout Catholics to the surgeon's list of exemptions.

But for the present I just asked if Mrs. Gardner had been informed that the autopsy had been done.

"No, in view of her condition I thought it best not to let her know."

"Good. I want to see her now."

I found the poor girl sitting on a cot in a dark, dusty, windowless cubicle that the surgeon had described as a private room. In spite of her overload of tranquilizers she was still crying and understandably looked terrible.

She recognized me at once and folded herself into my arms like a small child seeking comfort after a bump on the head. Reminded me of my daughters who when very young would come to me with a pinched finger or bumped shin so I could "ho'd it." I'd clamp an anesthetizing squeeze on and above the injury that seemed to have a soothing effect, practicing psychosomatic medicine without a license. I've never been good at talking so I just held her till the sobbing ran down. Finally she was able to talk.

"Please take me out of here. I want to see him. Don't let them do an autopsy—I've got to see him." That was a large order.

"Is this all you have?" I asked, picking up her bag. It was, still unpacked.

I led her out to the jeep and went back into the office for a brief phone call.

"Fiona, Mrs. Gardner is in bad shape and I'm taking her out of the hospital. How about bringing her home? It would do her a lot of good to have you to talk to."

"That's a wonderful idea. I'll take care of it, and ask Father Mulvaney to come over right away."

I delivered the girl to Fiona's welcoming arms and went to the phone that was distant enough to obviate overhearing. I rang graves registration. Captain Harding had left an hour before and was probably at his quarters. I was surprised to note that it was that late, 1845, and tried his quarters.

"Captain Harding." He was obviously chewing and swallowing his dinner.

"Colonel Triplet, Harding. I've got an outsized problem on my hands. You know about Gardner getting killed. Well, Mrs. Gardner is staying with us and is about to lose her mind. She's dead set against an autopsy for religious reasons and I've assured her that we won't permit it. Now she wants to see him and you have an idea what those interns have done. What can you do to get me off the hook and keep her out of the psycho ward?"

There was a twenty-second pause while he considered the impossible situation and evidently choked down a tough piece of stew.

"Can you get me his best uniform, with ribbons if possible, and a garrison cap, delivered to the cemetery chapel, and give me an hour?"

"I'll give you two hours, or rather, take your time and call me at my quarters."

I seriously breached the chain of command by phoning a married lieutenant who lived next door to the Gardners.

"Lieutenant Ryan."

"Colonel Triplet. Listen, Ryan, graves registration wants Captain Gardner's Class A uniform with cap at the cemetery chapel right now. Break into Gardner's quarters, find the uniform, and deliver it to Captain Harding at the chapel right away. Don't forget to see that his ribbons are on the coat and never mind the speed limit. Got it?"

"Yes sir. Gardner's Class A, ribbons, and cap to the cemetery chapel right now."

It's good to have men like Harding and Ryan grab the ball and run with it, make the goal or tear a leg off trying.

I moped around in the hinterlands of the Butler, barely hearing the murmur of the voices in the living room where Captain (Father) Mulvaney had joined the group.

At 2000 the phone rang.

"Captain Harding, colonel. We're all set."

Mulvaney had just left and Fiona wanted no part of cemeteries or morgues, so Mrs. Gardner and I jeeped off into the night. We arrived at the chapel about 2030. Harding was waiting alone by the door to the viewing room and waved us in, silently. As I followed he caught my sleeve for a moment and whispered, "Don't let her shake him."

He had wrought miracles. The chapel was dimly lit. I learned later that he had substituted fifteen- and twenty-five-watt bulbs for the normal seventy-fives. Captain Gardner lay at rest in a silk-lined bronze coffin in full uniform with garrison cap, ribbons, and polished shoes. He had never looked better in life. I was reminded of tombs in Westminster.

She was quite calm now, standing by the head of the coffin and whispering to him, reached out and touched his cheek, finally kissed him, a sign of the Cross, and at long last she turned away.

As we left, Harding was still standing just outside the door. I gripped his hand, couldn't say a word. I've been blessed by knowing a lot of good men, the type who rise to emergencies, and Captain Harding was one of the best. I'd sure see that his next efficiency report was a straight perfect rating right down the line.

Got back to the office where Colonel Jenkins was running the show and found that Bacawan had given up the idea of sailing to Cebu in the landing craft. He had directed the kidnapped skipper to beach him on Taka. He jumped ashore with his little arsenal and disappeared into the jungle of second-growth bushes and weedy vegetation that had grown up on the nearly uninhabited island.

He awoke and scared hell out of a two-man post that was maintained by military government. He made them lie down, "boca al mundo," while he selected a supply of food. Then he took their carbines and disappeared into the night.

The mine sweeper and tug loaded with MPs and Scouts had met the released Okie fisherman who had pointed out the beach where he had delivered his captor. The MPs and Scouts had landed and bivouacked. At first light the hunt would be resumed.

Bacawan was next seen as the skirmish line of MPs was approaching the beach on the southern tip of the island. He was wading out, chest deep in the mild surf, apparently intending to swim to Heanza or Cebu. He glanced over his shoulder, saw the pursuing patrol, and raised the single carbine that he had retained. He missed. The MP didn't. The undertow took Bacawan and the sand swallowed the carbine.

Aftermath

Conferences about returning Mrs. Gardner to her family and in-laws, evidently a close group living in Washington State, ensued. The next sea transport was due in three weeks. This delay was not acceptable.

Although Fiona and Father Mulvaney had done wonders we felt that the best treatment for such a brutal bereavement would be her own families. The Trans World Airlines had established its infant service in the Pacific—Philippines-Japan-Guam-Hawaii was the schedule of the next plane, due to touch down in three days.

Communications arranged a radio-ham radio-telephone link to her own family and the senior Gardners, the Forty-fourth Scouts officers club loaned her two thousand dollars in scrip, finance changed it to greenbacks, and transportation made the reservations.

At 2115 on the appointed date the plane touched down at Kadena. A heroic figure in a four-striped powder-blue uniform came down the boarding ramp and was introduced to Mrs. Gardner. He'd been well briefed and expressed his condolences. Final hugs and blessing and the pilot escorted her up the ramp while the coffin was being loaded into the baggage compartment. The plane taxied, turned, and took off toward Japan. As the running lights disappeared I felt like a boil that had just been lanced, still painful but the pressure relieved.

Next morning my Medusa dropped an official envelope on top of the pile.

"This came from the Forty-fourth Infantry message center, sir. I didn't open it because it's marked 'personal.'"

It was, the typed address was "Colonel Triplet (PERSENEL)" so I opened it first. Nothing inside but a blank three by five card. I turned it over. A crude drawing of a skull mounted on a pole. A poor joke by some fun-loving young idiot. I tossed it in the wastebasket and started through the pile of plaints, plans, and reports.

Lieutenant Colonel Patton (intelligence) barged in, excited as usual, just before noon. In addition to his usual shoulder-holstered .45 he had an M-3 submachine gun slung on his bulky frame in the ready position.

"Morning, Patton. Going to war?"

"Colonel, I've got something here that's hotter'n a firecracker."

The situation was evidently normal; everything that came within Patton's sphere of action or attention was verbally reported as hotter'n a firecracker.

"What now? Are the natives restless again?" I asked without much interest.

"I found this card pinned to my door this morning, a death's head." He laid the card on the desk, skull up. "And Momyer got one in the mail."

I fished around in the wastebasket.

"I'll join the club," I said, handing him my "persenel" billet doux.

"You too? That confirms it. Yes sir, this one's really hot. I had CIC check it out with their man in the Scouts and he says there's a lot of talk in the Forty-fourth about killing every officer that had anything to do with running down that man in the Gardner case. Not all the Scouts, just the Visayans. Seems the man that was killed was a Visayan and the rest of them are out for blood."

"Doesn't sound reasonable, Patton. If that was so, why aren't we dead? If they intend to kill anybody, why should they warn their target? Scaring a man just makes him dangerous. No, I think it's a practical joke by some clerk with a poor sense of humor."

"You may be right, colonel, but our agent thinks it's real. By the way, did your card come in an envelope?"

I looked through the wastebasket again and retrieved "Colonel Triplet (PERSENEL)." Patton stowed it and both cards in a large envelope.

"Good. I'll stay right on top of it. I'll get a sample from every typewriter in the Forty-fourth, a list of every Visayan, have CID try to develop fingerprints from these cards. Then I'll match everything up with some Visayan that's doing a lot of talking. In the meantime, colonel, if I were you I'd be careful, keep loaded for bear and sleep light."

He charged out to do his sleuthing. He was having a wonderful time.

Couldn't seem to focus on my job. Kept thinking about that card. Quite possible that the Visayans were out for blood and that they were trying to scare their targets. Soften us up before the slaughter. I recalled Major "Machete Pete," a veteran of the Philippine Insurrection, who was marked for execution by a Filipino secret society. He wore two revolvers in tied-down holsters in bed and could be safely approached at night only with a lot of noise. He had been careful and slept light for twenty years, a rather miserable existence.

I became increasingly careful, started carrying the M-3 in the jeep, had the ancient Smith & Wesson in holster or pocket at all times, and slept very light. Bessie, our Okinawan dog, was a nice pet, too nice. Sure wished I had Chow now.

Found myself resembling Machete Pete more and more every day. Got to be careful not to shoot one of the family or one of the maids by mistake. Remembered Captain Lane's story:

"Went to Camp Perry in 1929 for the rifle match. I was in one of those rooms in the BOQ with Captain Potts, Jerry Potts.[5] One Sunday afternoon I went out for a walk, left Potts in his bunk, bald head just sticking out from under the blanket. While I was out it snowed. Not much, just enough for me to make a snowball. Went down the hall and eased open the door. Yep, there he was, bald head sticking out from under the blanket. I let him have it. Right on his shiny pate.

"Man, that bunk just erupted and there was this bare naked, bald-headed wild man there in the center of the room with two double-action .45s on my belly button and the hammers sort of weaving back and forth.

"I said, 'I'm sorry, major, I think I'm in the wrong room.' He said, 'I think you're in the wrong world!'"

Oh well, at least I wasn't sleeping in a belted, tied-down holster rig. I just kept my hand on the gun under the pillow. Fiona began to notice things.

"Bill, why do you keep turning off the lights?"

"Oh, it's nice and relaxing here in the dark."

Or:

"Let's play Mah Jong. Betty Ann and Cat can make up the foursome."

"Uh-uh. Hard day at the office. I just don't feel like Mah Jong."

Or:

"Well, come out of that corner and let's walk around the garden. It's pretty with the lights on."

Go out at night under those floodlights? No way!

"I really would rather just sit here and sog."

"Bill, what in the world is the matter with you?"

So I swore her to absolute secrecy and told her why I preferred to sulk in dark corners and move fast and erratically when caught in the light. With great interest she also began observing the bushes behind the garden wall and scanning the volcanic ridge that rose sharply behind the house.

I was confident that there would be no ambush between Tengan and Rykom headquarters; the time and route was predictable but the run took place at a time when every Scout would be present and accounted for. There'd be no danger in my daily travels either, too irregular in timing and direction. Night was the time to be careful when the men were off duty, arms racks could be broken, and the target in place. The ridge was out, too steep and a limited field of fire. That left the garden side, the three-foot stone wall fronting the verandah at a poisonous forty yards with a good bush-covered approach up the steep slope from the beach of Chimu Bay. That was the only place to be concerned about. This rationalization of the situation didn't help much—it just concentrated the phobia. I was badly scared.

After three evenings of this I'd become fed up, and turned on all the lights and the floodlights that lit up the garden and left the verandah in black shadow. Bessie was out on her nightly prowl, suddenly started barking, rearing up, front feet on the wall. Yes, she was calling for help, the same hysterical bark she'd used when she found the Habu in Napunja. She had something or somebody.

I started for the door, intending to step to the left against the dark wall and start combing the bushes beyond the stone wall with a few bullets. Was hampered by Lee who shoved past and started out the door in front of me. I grabbed her arm and pulled, courteously murmuring "Git inside!" and jumped into the shielding shadow.

Changed the plan of action and moved down the dark verandah to the left where the wall curved in to the kitchen area so I could deliver flanking fire. By that time Bessie had stopped barking and bounced over to join me. If there had been anyone out there they'd pulled out.

As I mulled it over I realized several great truths:

Our visitors if any were merely window-peepers. They'd had too good a chance during the confusion at the door, couldn't have missed and didn't even fire.

Fiona had not kept the situation secret—no, that's unfair. Lee could have heard headquarters gossip. Patton sure couldn't keep quiet.

Lee evidently had unwarranted faith in Filipino chivalry.

And/or even more nerve than ever I had given her credit for.

On the next alarm take the time to think. Pick up the M-3 with sixty rounds and slip out the kitchen door—no more of this berserking out the front door with a six-shooter.

The flap over the death's head cards, initially hotter'n a firecracker, fizzled out. Nobody got shot, Patton reported that the envelopes were not typed on a Forty-fourth machine (or any other that he could locate) and Momyer's fingerprint expert found only unidentifiable smears on the cards. Bessie and I found crushed-down vegetation just beyond the garden wall but I suspected that they were traces of annoying but harmless peeping toms. If they'd been dedicated snipers I'd have been long since sniped.

Nineteen.

Atkinson-Jones

As soon as the troop housing was in livable condition we threw a good deal of effort into the completion of a hangar-sized Red Cross club-theater, a post exchange–beer garden building, and the conversion of a Butler building into an officers club at Napunja.

The club, being practically our only means of entertainment for officers and families, was well patronized and most successful. Old Army customs were followed in many respects. Guests were most welcome, provided they were accompanied by a member of the regiment who introduced his guests to the senior officer present on arrival. Dress uniform was worn after Retreat.

One evening I dropped in to the club early, just at dusk, and found three obese civilian laborers in their soiled undershirts bellied up to the bar, unshaved, and covered with the cement, grease, and grime of their various professions. The Scout bartender was purple with suppressed rage.

"Excuse me, gentlemen, who is your sponsor?" I asked.

"That's what this gook asked, and I'll give you the same answer. We don't need no sponsor."

"In that case, if you'll toss down those drinks real fast and leave at once it will save us all a lot of embarrassment."

Somewhat to my surprise and relief they did and stomped out with the fattest one remarking, "To hell with you, Chicken Colonel Highpockets, we're going to see the general and we'll be back."

Their jeep took off from the front of the club like a P-38 on a strafing run and buzzed around the corner toward the main gate. Three carbine shots rang out.

"Omigod, they've tried to run the guard."

I left for the main gate at a gallop and arrived to find the indignant sergeant of the guard castigating the weeping sentry. "Wassa marrer you? Esshoot tree time, no man, no jeep, no blood. You jerk trigger. Gotta squeeeze."

I took over. "Anyone hit, sergeant?"

"No sar. Thees recruit he mees every time. Esshould I pool hees belt?"

An inefficient sentry was normally relieved from his duty, disarmed, and his cartridge belt removed, hence the phrase "pull his belt."

"Sar," interrupted the tearful sentry, "they have come by veree fast, do not halt, do not show treep teecket, no lights, veree dark, I try hard but I mees. I am essorree." And he showed signs of weeping again.

"Yes, sergeant," I said, "without lights they would be very hard to hit,

256

maybe even I could not hit them in the dark. He did the right thing, and in the daylight I expect that he would hit them every time. So we will not pull his belt. Just see that he does better next time."

Next morning the chief of staff telephoned, asking that I come over to Rykom at once. On my arrival the aide showed me in to General Hayden's office where Hayden was confronted by three grim-looking fat civilians, my acquaintances of the evening before. In honor of the occasion they were wearing their Sunday best with neckties under their clean-shaven jowls. As I reported they transferred their glowering from Hayden to me.

"Have a seat, Colonel Triplet." I joined the semicircle facing his desk.

"These gentlemen have made a complaint, two of them in fact. They say you forced them to leave your club yesterday evening and, second, that your sentry fired on them as they left."

"Both statements are correct, general. I directed them to leave the club because they were not sponsored by a member of the regiment and in any case they were unsuitable in appearance for the club. As for the shooting, when they failed to halt at the gate the sentry fired according to my standing orders. Fortunately for them the light was bad and he missed."

"That's a lie," interrupted the fattest character. "There's two holes in my windshield and one through the fender to prove it. It's a wonder we weren't killed. We demand that you take the rifles away from that gook outfit, general. They shoot right at people."

"Well, colonel," prompted Hayden.

"Yes, general, our sentries do shoot right at people. They are posted to protect life and government property and to secure the post against intruders. And anyone who attempts to enter or leave our camp without halting on demand of a sentry is certain to be fired on."

"That is so, gentlemen," agreed the general. "That's the way it has been since long before Julius Caesar and probably the way it always will be. The answer is very simple—when a military sentry orders you to halt you stop and you will be safe. If you do not stop he is required to fire at you. I'm sorry but I can do nothing to change this basic requirement of guard duty."

There was a rumbling, whispered consultation between the trio of complainants. Then Fat Boy took up the cudgels again.

"But you can't laugh this club business off, general. It says in the contract that Atkinson-Jones has with the government that any employee has the rights and privileges of members of any club, mess, or place of entertainment on Okinawa, and it says the same thing right here in my contract," and he shook a folded paper like a sword.

"He's quite right about that, colonel. Any civilian employee of the government or of a government contractor does have the stated right to enter and be served in any officers club as a guest or as a member. In this case I will have to request that you receive these gentlemen and any other members of the contractor's organization as guests at any time."

I was stunned. I had no intention of permitting the only recreational facility we had to be overrun by such riffraff as the Atkinson-Jones lot. They had pulled the Rykom club down to the level of a bowery barroom. I would close the place before I would permit their entry in our regimental area. But that gave me an idea.

"Very good, general. These gentlemen and any of the other civilian contractor's people may attend our club any time they are in Camp Napunja. But unlike the Rykom club, theater, and the other clubs that front on public roads the Forty-fourth club building stands two hundred yards inside our camp boundary. And in the interests of the security of the post I cannot permit the indiscriminate entrance of persons who are not specifically authorized or on official business.

"So I will put it this way—if these gentlemen can come in by parachute and leave the same way we will welcome them as guests at any time. But they will never be allowed to cross the boundary of the post without permission."

General Hayden leaned back, steepled his fingers, clenched his jaws, pursed his lips, and reddened to his scalp. I was beginning to worry about his blood pressure when finally, with great control, he addressed the plaintiffs.

"I regret to inform you, gentlemen, that the colonel's point is quite valid. You will be welcome in his club at any time, just as you are welcome in any other club on the island. Napunja is a military reservation, however, and in the interests of security persons may enter the post only on official business or with the express permission of the commanding officer. I am sorry that I cannot help you further."

I recognized the moment to take my leave and did so, with impassioned threats of letters to Congress ringing in my ears, and like old times in the Eighty-sixth Division.

As I halted at the Napunja gate the same crestfallen sentry called, "Turn out the guard, commanding officer." I saluted him to waive the ceremony but asked him to call the sergeant of the guard.

"Never mind the guard, sergeant of the guard, number one."

When the sergeant reported I told him in a voice that would fully inform eavesdroppers within fifty yards, "I have just talked to the general about the shooting last night. This man shot very well. He hit the jeep three times. It was just bad luck that he did not hit the men."

And I drove on, leaving the sixty-two-inch sentry standing nine feet tall.

The morning after my initiation as DC & CS, I became aware of a hole in the tarmac pavement in front of headquarters. In fact I almost lost a wheel when I hit it too fast. I mentioned it to the engineer during the morning staff meeting.

"Colonel Cowper, there's a chuckhole at the entrance that ought to be repaired. It not only strains sacroiliacs and spinal discs, it's a disgrace to the command. Please get one of your young men to fill it in."

"Yes, colonel, I'll do what I can do. Of course I'll have to get Atkinson-Jones to work on it. They have the contract for all roads and road maintenance. But I'll go over and put in a request right away."

I left it at that, being somewhat awed by the rarefied atmosphere of the Ryukyu command, and simply dodged the hole for the next three days while the negotiations were going on. Requests, approvals, priorities, work orders, and the processing thereof took time, of course.

Then the following Monday, Atkinson-Jones rose to the rescue. Five men, a dump truck, a truck-mounted compressor, an air-driven jack hammer, a tar boiler, and a road roller appeared on the scene. Barriers were set up. One man occasionally used the jack hammer or pecked at the hole with a pick. Four men rested. This awesome assembly of men and equipment was apparently going to become a permanent landmark. Friday morning I asked the engineer to call the American labor off.

"Just withdraw your work order, all they're doing is enlarging the hole. I'll ask the Forty-fourth to send over Lieutenant Apeles and a couple of Scouts. They'll have it filled in a couple of hours."

"Well, sir, they've almost finished now. They say they'll pour this morning and have it rolled for traffic by quitting time tonight."

He was almost right. They poured tar and gravel Saturday morning, getting one day of overtime pay, the barriers were removed, and traffic over the patch was resumed. The job had taken six days.

I did some calculating concerning the cost of material (very little), cost of machines (considerable), cost of five men (outrageous), volume of hole (3.1416 x radius squared x average depth); the specific gravity of silver and the volume of a pound of silver. I reached the startling conclusion that we could have more economically repaired that pothole by filling it with silver dollars and solidifying the mass of coins with a few gallons of molten silver solder. I could have been finished in a day's time—and what a status symbol.

The American Army engineers had built an astonishingly adequate road net of crushed coral throughout the southern half of Okinawa. These roads were good but not speedways. In order to reduce the number of useless casualties General Hayden had imposed a most reasonable speed limit of thirty-five miles per hour for all vehicles. The military police patrolled to ensure compliance and I appointed Lieutenant Colonel Williams, the Rykom headquarters commandant, as summary court officer to deal with the few offenders who were brought in.

Williams was a tall, middleweight, crop-haired blond, a very sound and efficient young man who would carry out a mission or tear a leg off trying. He also had a temper that was normally under firm control.

He had very little difficulty in dealing with military misdemeanors; a five-dollar fine meant a lot to a fifty-dollar soldier. And even the Atkinson-Jones civilian laborers became cautious drivers after they were charged fifty dollars for suicidal or murderous speeding; that was a day's pay.

But Mr. Anders, an American who was on contract with General Djo's Chinese force, was in a category by himself. He was drawing one thousand dollars a month for keeping the Chinese heavy equipment and trucks moving, and was an important person. He was by his own account too important to be delayed by any speed limit.

So having received several warnings, Mr. Anders led a military police patrol a very merry chase one afternoon during which he was alleged to have reached the improbable speed of seventy-five miles per hour in a sixty-five mph jeep on the curves of a thirty-five-mph road.

"First time I ever got air-sick in a jeep," remarked the pursuing MP who had been a motorcycle speed cop in civilian life as he testified before the court.

Mr. Anders was quite voluble in his defense. And virulent.

"I'm a civilian and I can't be tried by any pipsqueak military court. I don't have to pay attention to any speed limits put out by the goddamned military brass. I'm under contract to Chiang Kai-shek and the American Army can — — —." He was very indelicate but most positive about what the American Army could do in his case.

Colonel Williams took a firm grip on himself before he spoke.

"Mr. Anders, all personnel of any nationality, affiliation, or condition of servitude with the Ryukyus command are subject to the military law of the United States, and—"

The enraged culprit interrupted Williams's calm explanation.

"Colonel, you can take your military law, your MPs, and the whole goddamned United States Army and — — —." He closed his defense with another improbable and unacceptable recommendation.

That did it. Williams opened the manual and carefully studied the stated limits of monetary punishment that could be imposed by a summary court. Then he passed sentence.

"Mr. Anders, the court finds you guilty of exceeding the speed limits of the Ryukyus command and guilty of reckless driving and fines you two-thirds of your monthly pay for one month."

"What? Why that's — that's over six hundred dollars! I won't pay it. I'll see you in hell first."

"You will remain in the custody of the provost marshal until it is paid, Mr. Anders. Sergeant, remove the prisoner."

The pair of MPs, aggregating .22 tons, removed the prisoner and placed him in the scantily furnished maximum security cell of the stockade. After a miserable night, in a chastened mood, he asked that he be taken before the court to pay his fine.

"I want to pay the fine, colonel, but I'll have to get it from the compound. If you could—"

"I will release you on your own cognizance, Mr. Anders, to go to the Chinese compound and return with $668.67 before 1200."

On reaching the compound Mr. Anders's Christian attitude suffered a relapse. He did not return. Instead, until past midnight he supported himself on most of the bars in Okinawa, loudly proclaiming his extraterritorial immunity, his diplomatic above-the-law status, and describing in vivid detail what the United States Army could do about it. Early the next morning the provost marshal removed the profanely protesting Mr. Anders from the Chinese compound. This time he brought the money with him, in U.S. greenbacks.

The mere possession of American "green money" in the scrip-paid occupation area was a high crime and would normally be good for a further fine and months in the stockade. The court, after a moment of shock, decided that Anders had been hurt enough and accepted the money.

This yarn, illustrating that crime does not pay, had an ending that was not altogether happy. I suspect that General Djo got into the act in behalf of his high-powered hired man and made a sub rosa plea to General Hayden. At any rate there ensued a series of conferences between Hayden, myself, the finance officer, the judge advocate general, the inspector general, and the provost marshal regarding the ex-patriot (misspelling intentional) Mr. Anders, the size of the fine, and what to do about the illegal greenbacks that had probably traveled from President Truman to Chiang Kai-shek to General Djo to Anders.

The JAG ruled that the fine was legal.[1]

The finance officer wanted to crucify someone about the U.S. cash.

The IG stated that no one had been unjustly treated.[2]

The PM recommended that Anders be deported.

I was with the provost marshal and further recommended ten days in the stockade for contempt of court.

After a good deal of lively discussion the general directed that the fine should not be reduced or remitted and the money should be quietly turned in to the treasury by the finance officer. He further directed me to appoint another "more mature" summary court officer to deal with future traffic offenses. As an immature chief of staff I protested this action as tantamount to relieving a loyal subordinate on the field of battle immediately after he has won a hard fight. But in vain, I was overruled. I couldn't give Williams the reason for his relief but hoped that the next efficiency report I would give him would have a healing effect on his wounds.[3]

"Mr. Wilson from Atkinson-Jones would like to see you, sir," announced my secretary with her customary correct coldness.

"Please ask him in."

Mr. Wilson, a former combat engineer and now a top-flight employee of Atkinson-Jones Construction Company, entered, "good morning sirred," shook hands, and dropped into the indicated best visitor's chair. He was a very decent type for AJ, about thirty-five, a well-muscled brunet middleweight, wearing a distrait, embarrassed expression—nervous about something.

"And how is Atkinson-Jones doing this fine morning?" I inquired. Doing damned little, I knew, but it was polite to ask.

"Oh, AJ is doing fine, colonel. But I came to see you on a personal matter. Ah—"

"Yes? What's the problem?"

"Hmmm, you knew the *Brewster* brought in some dependents for the company last week."

"Yes, six wives and seven children, I think it was."

"Right, and my wife was one of them."

"Congratulations."

"Well, I don't know. She just isn't the same woman I left in Oklahoma six months ago. In fact she doesn't even seem to like me any more."

"Hmmm—" What the hell was I getting into now? The bleeding hearts business? Way out of my depth.

"There's talk going around, you know how women are, talk about my wife and a colonel that came out on the *Brewster.* He went on to Manila. Seems they saw a lot of each other during the trip, too damned much. These other women—"

"I see." I didn't of course, just stalling.

"Well, I had to talk to somebody about it and sure can't talk to anybody in the firm, so what would you think? What would you do?"

Dear Lord! This is what they have chaplains for. But there weren't any chaplains on the spot and I was. So I leaned back, put on my "deeply concerned" mask, and said nothing for a full minute. I hadn't any ideas, but the silent concentration act frequently fools the other fellow into believing that I'm thinking constructively. Long enough. I came to, leaned forward, and donned my serious advice face.

"OK, let's start at the beginning. How long have you been married?"

"Almost a year, next Sunday would have been our anniversary."

That "would have been" sounded tragic.

"Is your wife pretty?"

"She's a living doll."

"Well, that explains it. A two-week trip on a ship, penned up in a cabin with three other older women. Women have a compulsion to talk and they'd naturally rather talk to a man than to other women. And women always hate each other. I'd bet that your wife is the prettiest of the lot that came over on that ship."

"She sure is."

"And women especially hate women that are younger and prettier than they are. Why? Because the men cluster around the best-looking women. I know, because I've always had that trouble myself. But I got over being jealous when I saw that it was really a compliment."

"Hmmm—"

"And you sure can't blame the colonel for being attracted to the prettiest girl in sight. You would be too."

"Well, I guess not, you're right, I would be—"

"And women are always jealous and spiteful. So when your wife and this colonel were standing elbow to elbow at the rail day after day while these other wives couldn't even get the time of day out of him they naturally want to cut her down. That's female nature. So I read this talk that's going around as just so much poisonous, jealous gossip."

"I don't know, she just isn't—"

"Let me finish. You came over on the *Brewster,* didn't you?"

"That's right, February this year."

"Then you know she isn't any cruise ship. And with four-bunk cabins full of families, four men, or four women, always with somebody seasick in every cabin, did you ever get any chance for serious hanky-panky with any of the wives or nurses?"

"Hell no—crew, stewards, children everywhere. All I ever got was a little something on the boat deck, damned little."

"Well, so that's off your mind. Finally, I haven't seen this Don Juan that went on to Manila but he's a replacement, noncombat type. Spent the war in a swivel chair in CONUS, about forty-five or fifty-five years old.[4] That's the type that's coming over here now. And do you think that any woman in her right mind could yearn after an overage wreck like that when she already has a man like you?"

"No, I guess not. But what can I do about it? She doesn't—"

Another period of "serious consideration" ensued. I was beginning to enjoy this. Have to be careful, don't want to louse it up.

"The way I read it you might have been jealous long before she ever got off the boat and she felt it, something in the way you acted or talked that put her off. They're awfully sensitive that way. Seems to me that you ought to go back to the beginning again, act the same way as when you caught her in the first place. Go to the post exchange and bring her the best box of chocolates in the place, send out some Okinawan kids for flowers and give her a bouquet, especially for next Sunday, take her to Chang's Restaurant and the Rykom club. You know, make a fuss over her."

"By god, colonel, maybe you're right. I'll sure try it. And thanks for talking to me."

Ten days later I was walking through the AJ compound with the company chief of police discussing his current troubles concerning whiskey, knives, and blackjacks on weekend nights. We approached a trio of white-collar employees who were walking to the mess for the lunch break. One of them dropped slightly behind the group, gave me a broad grin, and waved a "thumbs up" sign. Oh yes, it was Mr. Wilson.

Sure hoped that it didn't get out. I can take the title "Marrying Sam" and smile. But Ann Landers? Never.[5]

Colonel Momyer, factual and unaffected by human frailties as befits a provost marshal, appeared at 0830 one Monday morning and stated that he had a case that should be brought to my attention.

"That rumor about a motorized cat house—the CIC brought them in last night. We've got Lieutenant Clarice Rutledge, Master Sergeant Shrum, and two customers in the stockade. Rutledge is ANC, Shrum is MC.

"Shrum had this ambulance fitted out like a Turkish harem: bed, cushions, curtains, and Christmas tree lights. He contacted the customers, the AJ boys, and drove the ambulance. Lieutenant Rutledge was putting out on a sliding scale, fifty dollars an hour to two hundred a night.

"We kept them in the stockade overnight to get them in a good frame of mind. No confessions, but I mentioned deportation to the AJ customers and they're anxious to testify, want to hold onto their jobs.

"Question is what do you want to do about this nurse and the sergeant?"

"Hmmm, pretty good pay for moonlighting jobs."

"I'll say it is. The going rate in Frisco is ten bucks. But she's quite a dish in her working get-up, a Marilyn Monroe about ten pounds overweight, and you've got to figure on overseas prices and what Atkinson-Jones is paying the hands. But what I was thinking was that this isn't doing the reputation of the army any good. Should I turn them over to Colonel Kranz or do you want to draw up the charges?"

What to do? A court-martial for unbecoming conduct with dismissal wouldn't do anybody's reputation any good. Unauthorized use of government transportation? A ridiculous evasion and the whole business would come out in the trial anyway. I chickened out.

"We'll see the general and Kranz right after the staff meeting, Momyer. Let them figure it out."

General Hayden did nobly. After hearing the charge and Momyer's précis of evidence he dumped the entire can of worms on Kranz's plate.

"Colonel Kranz, you are clearly the responsible party in this case. You will see that Lieutenant Rutledge submits her resignation from the army immediately, place her in arrest in quarters, and see that she is aboard the first transport out of here.

"You will reduce Master Sergeant Shrum to the grade of basic private and assign him to menial duties commensurate with his grade.

"If either of them object to this summary treatment, refer them to the chief of staff who will explain the alternatives such as a public trial covered by reporters from the *Okinawan* with copies mailed to hometown newspapers, dismissal, dishonorable discharge, and confinement at hard labor."

I was proud of him.

So Master Sergeant (motor pool maintenance chief) Shrum became a broom and mop operator and Miss Clarice Rutledge played hell with the morals of the officers, crew, and passengers of the UST *Brewster* throughout the next long homeward voyage.

Twenty.

Miscellany

The Forequarter Crisis

Mr. Chang, a Filipino citizen of Chinese ancestry, had been granted a concession to operate a restaurant on Okinawa for the benefit of the garrison. He had taken over a surplus Butler building and imported a dozen relatives to do the work while he played the genial host. He had further been authorized to buy meat and other supplies from the quartermaster to feed the affluent soldiers who wanted a change from the mess or home cooking.

He and his Chinese cohorts were now well set up in their garishly redecorated building and by the time I was settled into my new job Mr. Chang was entertaining a steady stream of customers.

"Mr. Chang to see you, sir," announced my beautiful secretary with a glare that added "and I wish you were in hell with your back broken."

I rose to greet him. He was a neat, well dressed, well fed little man of indeterminate age, reminded me of a cattle dealer I'd known in Tientsin, so I greeted him the same way.

"Min-na hao pu hao, Lao Chang?" shaking hands with myself. "Min-na chirr fan mu?" Which was a silly question, asking a restaurant owner if he had eaten.

He looked puzzled. Of course he didn't understand Mandarin. I switched to English.

"Come in, Mr. Chang. Have a seat. And how is the restaurant business going?"

He flashed a gold tooth in a brief smile, very brief, then looked slightly unhappy.

"The business is very good, colonel. Customers every night. Plenty of people come. But we lose too much money."

"How is that, if you have plenty of customers?"

"Everybody want steak, all the time steak. I have many of Chinese, Japanese, Filipino dishes with other meat but everybody want steak."

"I see." Did he want me to put out a Rykom order changing the preferences of the customers? He went on to explain.

"I buy beef from the quartermaster. I must buy half beef, front and back part. Cannot just buy back part for steak. Front part only good for sukiyaki, Chinese vegetables with beef, hash, stew. Everybody want steak—I must throw away too much."

OK, I had the problem. Cows have four legs, two in front and two behind. Being new on the job I went into high gear. Even used the telephone, and how I hate to do business on the telephone.

266

Learned from the G-4 and the quartermaster that beef must always be issued or sold in halves, when a hind quarter (steak) left the refrigerator a forequarter (stew) must go with it. As Major Epstein put it, "You want our boys should have only stew unless they pay for steak in the restaurant?"

His argument had merit; it was not only regulation but also right. But if I could find an outlet for stew meat, some market for forequarters and spare parts—

I called my favorite foe, Colonel Craig, at military government. He had three hundred thousand Okinawans to feed. From experience I knew that his answer to any constructive idea would be negative, especially if it came from me. It was.

"Our funds are appropriated only for the purchase of rice. There are no funds available for the purchase of meat. Also I would not favorably consider the introduction of meat into the Okinawan diet. It would upset their digestive systems, and the taste of meat might build cravings that they could not afford to gratify."

Oh well, I had to try.

Then I remembered, every morning Takuda made up a package of sandwiches for B'Ann and Cathy to take to school. I'd be glad to lay out thirty cents a day to get hot lunches for them and felt that every other parent would too. Twenty school days a month, fifteen cents a day per kid, three dollars a month would be a small price to get away from the cheese–jelly–peanut butter grind.

"Mr. Chang, would you cook up beef stew and deliver it to the school at noon, enough to feed three hundred children for fifteen cents each? That would come to forty-five dollars a school day, say nine hundred dollars a month."

"Oh yes, three hundred bowls of nice fat stew for forty-five dollars. Oh yes. That will help us much." He showed his gold tooth and rose to leave.

"Just a moment, Mr. Chang."

A second idea had struck home. The Kuomintang troops were not authorized to draw or buy our ration supplies. But if Mr. Chang bought beef then he as a civilian and a Filipino citizen should be able to sell any leftovers to the Chinese. I thought of calling the judge advocate general or the inspector general to get an opinion. But no, in case of any shadow of a doubt it is always too easy to say no, especially over the telephone. It might be illegal but it wouldn't be criminal, so I'd do it.

I called the Chinese compound, got General Djo, and explained Chang's problem.

"So Mr. Chang has more forequarters and stew meat than even three hundred hungry children can eat. Now if the Kuomintang can buy the rest from Mr. Chang for cash it would help him and would save you trying to bring fresh meat from Shanghai on those slow LSTs."

Djo's reaction to the proposal seemed to be favorable.

"Thank you for your consideration, colonel. Please ask Mr. Chang to visit me at my headquarters."

Settling the crisis of the four-legged steers was not the most important action I took as DC/CS, but it was certainly the most successful. Everyone concerned or affected seemed to be happy.

Djo and Chang struck a mutually agreeable bargain. Djo invited Fiona and me to a wing-ding in the Kuomintang compound where we were regaled with a plethora of exotic Chinese dishes made from the forelegs, brisket, and chuck of U.S.-inspected corn-fed cattle.

The dependent school children grew sleek, fat, and frisky on a rather restricted diet of rich stew, hash, and more hamburgers than they could possibly eat, a diet that would give a professional dietitian a nervous breakdown.

The parents of said children were happy to send Mr. Chang a check for three dollars each month per child and get the little monsters out of their hair during the psychologically fragile breakfast-preschool period.

Mr. Chang was delighted to deliver his daily offerings to the school and sell surplus forequarters to the Kuomintang in exchange for real money.

Chang's customers were pleased to be able invariably to have steaks done to order (overlapping the platter, two inches thick, and medium, rare, or raw).

And Fiona was puzzled but pleased when Mr. Chang (whom she had not met socially) presented her with a beautifully carved Cantonese chest. Chang knew that no army officer could accept a present. But Fiona was a civilian, so she could.

Hospital

"Bill," said the general on his return to duty, "I'd like to have you inspect the hospital."

During the period of Captain Gardner's murder General Hayden had been resting in the hospital with high blood pressure and a slight heart attack. He was evidently not pleased with the place.

"Yes sir, but I'll feel a bit silly criticizing operating rooms and hospital wards. The inspector general can—"

"I don't want you to inspect medical treatment or surgical techniques. Just get them up to the same standards of decent living that you required in the Forty-fourth." That put it on a reasonable basis.

"Yes sir."

A telephone message was sent to the hospital, "Stand by for working inspection at 0930," and I was on my way. Found a master sergeant in the colonel's office.

"Sergeant Flint, sir," he reported. "Hospital sergeant major."

"I want to see Colonel Kranz, sergeant."

"He'll be here right away, sir. I gave him the message about the inspection."

"Where is he?"

"In his quarters, sir."

Eight minutes later Lieutenant Colonel Kranz arrived, dressed and shaved, but still bleary-eyed and slack-faced. He'd probably had to take a stiff "hair of the dog" to get on his feet.

Accompanied by the sergeant major we started a tour of the command.

The hospital was not the worst unit I'd ever inspected. The Bulucan guerrilla regiment holds that position. These medicos used their latrines. Never cleaned them up, but at least they used them. In general the hospital reminded me of the first day I saw the 342d. I finally stopped commenting, just pointed at, pushed, and pulled out trash with my stick. Sergeant Flint made notes.

Unswept wards and quarters, piles of dirty linen and clothing, unmade beds; a bed-bound patient calling desperately and in vain for a "duck"; half-eaten sandwiches, beer cans, and Coke bottles stowed in operating room cabinets, and flies everywhere.

Our last stop was the mess, where I casually discussed the deficiencies with the CO over a cup of coffee. The mess was a large Butler building originally painted olive drab, dark and gloomy. With age the interior had acquired a patina of soot, dust, and cobwebs that gave the place the impression of a monstrous black cave. The tables had obviously never been scrubbed and the menu for the last several meals could be deduced by a study of the fragments, splashes, and debris on the unswept floor. And flies. I stopped, just didn't have the courage to look at the kitchen. And the usual cup of coffee? Unthinkable.

"Well, Colonel Kranz, no point in going any farther. I'm reminded of the British consul who was ordered to write a report on the morals, habits, and customs of the natives in his area. He wrote, "Morals—none, habits—nasty, customs—disgusting.""

Kranz didn't even twitch, just maintained that blank, slack-faced, uncomprehending mask. Couldn't get through to him, but I tried again.

"Your sergeant major has notes on deficiencies up to this point. Now about this mess hall, it's filthy, depressing, and damned poor psychosomatic medicine for the patients who have to eat here. The effect on your own people who have to eat here for years is worse.

"You are to paint everything in sight in bright, cheerful colors. The quartermaster salvage people have hundreds of colored parachutes. Get a couple of dozen and deploy them overhead from the rafters. Scrub the floor and tables, and use tablecloths. Your storerooms are full of more sheets than you'll ever use—use sheets for tablecloths.

"And the flies. Get thirty fly traps and two hundred fly swatters in action and eliminate them. And mend your screens.

"I'll be back in one week to check on your progress. Questions?"

Kranz blinked and showed signs of returning to consciousness.

"I don't think there are any fly traps or swatters on Okinawa, colonel. I don't see how we—"

"There ain't. You make them."

"Make them?"

"Yes. A four-by-six-inch piece of screen wire tacked to any eighteen-inch stick makes a fly swatter. And I'll have Lieutenant Apeles bring you one of the Forty-fourth Scout fly traps that he invented. Just have your people copy it thirty or forty times."

The general heard my report on the ghastly condition of the hospital with interest and complete understanding. After all, he'd spent ten days in that fly-cursed sweat box and even in one of those "private" cubbyholes it must have been bad. But he hadn't seen the mess and was inclined to recommend Kranz's relief as the sovereign cure for the hospital's ailments.

"No, we'll wait and see how he shapes up."

The following week as scheduled I arrived at the hospital at 0900. Sergeant Flint reported Colonel Kranz to be sick in quarters.

"I see—in that case call in the second in command."

"That's Captain Blumberg, sir. He's in surgery."

"It looks like you're it then, sergeant. Let's go."

Sergeant Flint had done wonders during the past week. And I say he had done wonders against odds, considering the quality of his officers. The beds in quarters and wards were made, the laundry was caught up, floors were swept and where appropriate scrubbed. Screens were mended or replaced, the Apeles-designed fly traps strategically spotted and buzzing with imprisoned flies. The Forty-fourth Scout–type fly swatters were in use or hanging at the head of every bed, convenient for a quick draw by the annoyed patient. The fly population had been considerably reduced to an almost acceptable level. Flint was obviously Old Army and had needed only a bit of backing to sharpen up the outfit. I was feeling quite kindly until I entered one of the operating rooms to see if the moldy sandwiches and beer cans had been removed. They had been.

But it was there that I found Captain Blumberg "in surgery." A de-gutted corpse lay on the table with heart, lungs, liver, and lights tastefully arranged on each side, while Captain Blumberg was skinning and pulling the scalp back from the forehead. He apparently didn't notice our entry.

"What's this, captain?"

"Sailor washed ashore this morning," he mumbled reluctantly, without looking up from his scalping job.

"Seaman First Class Weatherby, sir," volunteered Flint, "lost overboard from Destroyer 212 during the storm last Wednesday."

"What was his religion, captain?"

"Religion? I don't know. In forensic medicine we are not concerned with the superstitions of the subject."

"Forensic—report to me in Colonel Kranz's office in fifteen minutes, captain, at 1040."

"Can't make it, I"ll be busy here for at least—"

"At 1040, captain. Your patient will wait."

We entered the mess. I noticed that Sergeant Flint looked somewhat grim as he opened the door. He'd lost his enthusiastic bounce.

As throughout the rest of the hospital a lot of work had been done here. The floor was clean, the flies were few, colored silk parachutes concealed the black, yawning space above the rafters, and the walls and supporting posts were painted in red and white. The tables were covered by sheets decorated by large maroon-colored splotches, streaks, and spatters, operating room sheets that had probably been laundered in hot water, indelibly fixing the bloodstains. Imagine trying to swallow a dinner in this charnel house.

"Sergeant, you have hundreds of sheets that have never been used. Why in God's name do you have this corruption in the dining hall?"

"I know, sir. I tried to get them but the colonel said he didn't want to waste new sheets in the mess."

Again I didn't have the courage to enter the kitchen.

"I'll see the colonel now, sergeant."

"Mmmm, ah, he's sick in quarters, sir."

"I know. Show me to his quarters."

Flint led the way reluctantly to the colonel's hut.

I knocked, no result, harder, dead silence. Sergeant Flint remained tactfully outside.

Yes, Colonel Kranz was beyond a doubt sick in quarters. The empty bottle and the shattered glass on the floor by his bunk gave me the diagnosis for his illness and his snoring gave proof that he was not dead.

Back to the office. Flint appeared embarrassed, downcast, ill at ease, discouraged. He had no reason to be anything but proud of his work.

"Sergeant Flint, you are to be commended. You've done a wonderful job in straightening your outfit up in the past week. Keep it up. Now let's get those sheets in the dining hall changed before the next meal."

"Yes sir!" and he stomped out, bright-eyed and bushy-tailed.

The medico slouched in, sogged into the chair across the room, and sulkily studied his shoes. I thought very briefly of requiring him to stand up, pull in his ponderous belly, get his eyes off the ground, and report properly. But what the hell, it would take too much time and effort to make a man of him. He was just another of those government-subsidized, draft-deferred students who were resentfully serving their internship in the army instead of the Mayo Clinic.

"Captain Blumberg—"

"Doctor Blumberg," he corrected.

"In accordance with military custom I will address you as Captain Blumberg and you will address me as Colonel Triplet, colonel, or sir. Now, did Colonel Kranz tell you that no more autopsies were to be performed on Catholics, Chinese, or Moros?"

"Hmmm yes, colonel. But according to regulations a surgeon has to sign the death certificate and to be sure that no crime has been committed he—" This guy just enjoyed cutting up bodies.

"Just a moment, captain. The criminal investigation people are responsible under the provost marshal for the detection of crime. Get your eyes up and listen very carefully, captain.

"In case there is any suspicion of crime in connection with a death in this command the provost marshal will notify me that an autopsy should be made. If the general approves I will direct the surgeon to conduct an autopsy and report the findings to me.

"If you without my order touch another corpse with your scalpel you will be transferred to the Rykom special staff as latrine inspector for the rest of your tour of duty. Do you understand?"

"I understand what you said, sir," he sulked, resuming the study of the toes of his shoes.

"Good. Please remember that I am keeping the job open for you, captain. Thank you for coming in."

Captain Blumberg slowly pulled his broad tail out of his close-fitting chair, hesitated, gave me a glare of undying hatred, and oozed out. But at least he had raised his eyes and looked at me.

This time the general was persuaded that if the housekeeping of the Rykom hospital was to be brought up to the level of a line regiment Lieutenant Colonel Kranz had to go. On the next transport he went. He was last reported to be drying out in Letterman General Hospital where the psychiatrists were finding him to be a most interesting case, a case of combat fatigue who had never been within six thousand miles of a hostile gun.[1]

His replacement was a good man, almost as good as Master Sergeant Flint.

May Day

About 1100 on May 1, 1948, Colonel Patton, armed to the teeth, burst into my office in more than his usual state of red alert.

"Colonel, I'm onto something big. This is hotter'n a firecracker. All the natives have disappeared. Nobody in sight in the villages and you won't see anyone in the fields. The few Okinawans you do see are on the road, all going toward Naja. They're going to hold a big communist demonstration with riots and maybe outright rebellion. We've got to—"

"Wait a minute, Patton. I know of five Okinawans that haven't disappeared. My house crew were all on the job this morning. Isn't the rest of the labor force working?"

It gave me to think. A large number of the labor force reporting yesterday, in effect, that they planned to be sick today; no farmers hoeing their camotes; villages deserted; all movement toward Naja; the number of ex-PWs indoctrinated and recently released by the Russians; and it was the sacred day celebrated by the proponents of world revolution. It appeared that Patton might have something there. Maybe I should have—

I ought to consult the general but he was in the hospital having high blood pressure and heart palpitations again. He couldn't be put under stress so it was my baby. Maybe I'd better—I did. I asked Miss Medusa to get Colonel Waddell on the phone.

"Colonel Stangle speaking."

"Triplet here. Is Colonel Waddell available?"

"He's in the field just now but I can get him for you in twenty minutes."

"Never mind. Just give him this message—'Yellow alert for riot control. Stand by for further orders. Report when ready to move out.' Got it?"

"Yes sir. 'Yellow alert for riot control. Stand by for further orders. Report when ready to move out.' " A pause, then, "Can you give us any idea about where we're to move or who we're going to control?"

"Not yet. Just get your trucks lined up, ammunition issued, and your men ready to load up and roll. I'll give you the mission later."

The phone rang. "Colonel Waddell for you, sir," said the Gorgon.

"Waddell speaking. The Forty-fourth Infantry is ready to move out on riot control duty. What is the objective, where is the riot, when do we move out?"

"Can't give you anything further for the moment, colonel. Just stand by."

I shuddered to think of how the Scouts would enjoy practicing their riot control methods on a mob of Okinawans—bayonet and butt in the line, shoot anyone with a weapon or throwing a rock, snipers posted in rear to pick off agitators, it would be a bloody brawl.

Colonel Patton having dispatched two jeeploads of Nisei spies joined me in jittering through the next hour.

A stocky, toil-worn, grim Okinawan farmer in holiday-clean shapeless cotton trousers, bottomless sashed-in jacket, thonged sandals, and conical straw hat entered the office, slapped his sandals together, and saluted. Patton figuratively pounced on him.

"What did you find out, Koriyama? Any of them armed? What are they planning?"

"Sir, it's the Okinawan championship baseball game. Final playoff between Naha and Yonabaru starts at 1300. Odds are running five to two on Naha, sir."

Twenty-One.

Departure

General Changes

General Hegenberger, commander of the First Air Division, was a surly, disagreeable, noncooperative type feared by his subordinates and disliked by all others who had any dealings with him. His physique and appearance could be covered by the description "medium," except for the perpetual appearance of cynicism, scorn, and dissatisfaction that he presented to the rest of the world.

He was obsessed with the concept of "operational" and to hell with the comfort, entertainment, mental welfare, or morale of his troops or their dependents. They led a grim life.

The First Air Division barracks and housing areas were consequently military slums, basic quonsets or Butlers surrounded by bleak areas of mud or dust with buildings connected by untrustworthy duckboard walks. Decorative or protective paint was applied only to planes, hangars, or shops. Everything else, being nonoperational, received no support, material, or effort.

When the Department of Defense was formed in 1947 with three combat arms, both Hegenberger and I were delighted. He was thrilled with the idea of belonging to a separate arm no longer subordinate to the army. I was relieved that we were at last rid of the air corps and the dangers inherent in air corps support. We could call on the marines and navy air; they had a reputation for hitting the right targets and flew low and slow enough to identify and miss their friends.

But the idea of an independent air force really pushed the general off the deep end. When requested to cooperate on a project or mission where his men or planes would be useful his answer used to be, "I consider that to be purely a problem for the support troops." After independence the phraseology changed to, "that's purely an army problem." When General MacArthur directed that all units under his command take small-arms training the order was ignored by the First Air Division on the grounds that "that's purely the army's problem. The only function of the army is to support the air force in its fight to win the war three hundred miles away." That to me was a new concept. Formerly every arm and service had the mission of supporting the infantry. I was quite relieved to hear that in the future I'd be a safe three hundred miles from combat.

I was delighted to get a call from Hegenberger's whipped-down, non-committal chief of staff, Colonel Scott.

"General Hegenberger has orders to return to CONUS and will leave

275

from Kadena at 1300 next Wednesday. I suggest that General Hayden may want to see him off. And you are also invited."

"We'll be there, Scott. Can't think of anything I'd enjoy more." Let him figure that one out. Hegenberger had not notified Hayden nor invited him but I was sure that Hayden would be glad to see him leave.

We arrived at Kadena Air Field at 1230 on the happy occasion but could not locate the general among the brass milling around the waiting plush-lined converted B-29. Scott told us "the general is in conference with General Simmons." Simmons was the brigadier, assistant division commander. So we waited.

At 1258, Hegenberger's sedan drove up to the boarding ramp. He couldn't miss us as he shook hands with his wing commanders and reservedly with us. Both Hayden and I perjured ourselves, violating the code ("An officer shall not lie, cheat, or steal"). Both of us with barefaced duplicity said, "Sorry to see you go, general."

The plane roared down the runway and disappeared into the overcast in the direction of Kyushu.[1] Hayden and I were on our way back to our sedan when Colonel Scott caught us.

"General Hayden, General Simmons would like to have you both come over to the club for refreshments, sir."

We went. Found a goodly number of the officers and wives from both the fighter and bomber wings as well as the staff assembled for the occasion. The bar was open, the orchestra playing, refreshments flowed freely, and merriment was unrestrained. The hitherto reserved and uncooperative staff reminded me of the bodyguard of the Wicked Witch of the West when Dorothy melted the old girl down with a bucket of water. Even C/S Scott seemed to be a nice guy after all.

Hayden and I excused ourselves before the party got rough and started back to Rykom.

"Odd," mused the general, "giving the CG a farewell party like that after he's gone. Never seen such a thing before."

"Hmmm," I noncommittaled. He knew damned well why; he'd never seen a CG like Hegenberger before.[2]

General Hayden was having his blood pressure taken and his pulse monitored every morning, and was finally spending more time in the hospital than out of it. It made very little difference to me, since I was doing everything anyway. Saved a lot of time, actually, because I didn't have to brief him daily on what was going on.

Finally he was ordered to Letterman General Hospital for evaluation of his condition and better treatment than he could get in the Orient.

We gave him a very nice farewell party and as he left after saying what a nice party and how he'd enjoyed serving with us, Hayden added the goddamnedest remark I've ever heard.

"You are the most immature chief of staff I have ever known or heard of."

I must admit that it really took me by surprise since I'd been running Rykom for almost a year with little help from him. Maybe it was his one drink of whiskey talking but in vino veritas. The only comeback was, "Well, general, as I told you a year ago you were making a serious mistake, I had no staff experience and you were reducing the best regimental commander in the Pacific theater to be a damned poor chief of staff."

A Major General Eagles was ordered in to replace him. On the day of his arrival I went to Kadena to meet his plane. The weather was cold, wet, and miserable.

Somehow the Okinawans had gotten word of the arrival of the new commander. All schools on the islands had been closed and the road between Kadena and Rykom was lined with the schoolchildren equipped with their hand-made and colored cloth and paper American flags. They'd been out there since eight o'clock, hopefully waving their flags at every sedan coming from Kadena. I was horrified to think of the epidemic of colds, pneumonia, and sudden death that was going to strain our medical resources. But the Okies are a hardy race and perhaps most of them would survive conditions that would kill a human being.

I'd looked up General Eagles. He had commanded a division and in addition to two Distinguished Service Medals (a general's Good Conduct Ribbon) he had a Bronze Star and a Purple Heart so I was delighted that we were getting a soldier instead of a clerical type.

I was sadly disappointed. Eagles came down the ramp from the plane, a skinny, medium-sized, scrawny-appearing type with a slight protuberance at the belt line. A sallow visage with a sharp, red-tipped nose, a slit mouth with a downturn at the corners, and approving suspicious eyes made me wish we had Hayden back. This one was a bilious liver case and would be harder to live with than high blood pressure and fibrillating heart. Oh well, I was leaving in a month anyway.

Following the general down the ramp was the prettiest, sweetest-smelling, curliest-haired aide I'd ever seen. He was a pleasantly plump five feet six inches, rosy complexion, curly blond hair, and I think carried a cloud of "Blue Moon" perfume.

I reported to the general—"Sir, Colonel Triplet, deputy commander, Rykom."

"Colonel," with a suspicious glare and a disgusted "Rykom!" followed by "Okinawa!"

Aha, that was it. Eagles hadn't wanted to come to Rykom and was disgusted with the idea of such a minor command under such pioneering conditions.

I led them to the sedan and took the left seat, while Quelque Fleurs sat with the driver. We were followed by a second sedan because Rykom's vehicles still broke down frequently and I wanted to be sure the new commanding general would arrive without walking or waiting for help.

We started to Rykom and as soon as we had left the Kadena base there were the schoolchildren lining the road, waving their American flags and smiling in spite of the wind-driven rain. Between squalls I rolled my window down and heard the Banzais and from some groups "Gorbress Merika." Those little lads and the cute chicks leading them were really putting on a show. I just can't understand the Okies. If one out of four of my relatives and friends were killed by the indiscriminate shelling, shooting, and bombing of Japanese invaders, I certainly wouldn't stand out in the weather for five hours to yell "Three cheers for Hirohito."

General Eagles noticed the efforts the kids were making in his behalf and made a comment.

"Filthy natives." His liver or gall stones must be giving him hell.

One might get the impression that I didn't like General Eagles. You are perfectly right; I disliked him and loathed Lieutenant Chanel No. 5. I was breaking in Colonel Jenkins as C/C and CS at the time so I let him deal with the general whenever possible.

Two Parties

Fiona and I showed at the Rykom club (New Year's) party as required by protocol but since the festivities showed no signs of getting off the ground we made our escape as soon as decently possible and went to the Forty-fourth Infantry (PS). The Scouts' club was always entertaining.[3]

We were disappointed. In place of the usual uninhibited revelry there was formality and restraint. We paid our respects to Colonel Waddell, who glumly sat in lone majesty, and receiving no invitation to join him took a table across the room. Fiona spent the evening on the dance floor as usual while I made the rounds of the wives.

We missed Colonel Stangle and learned that he was sick in quarters. So along toward the end of 1947, Fiona had a good idea—we would pay the poor, sick, lonely man a visit. Armed with a bottle of medicinal whiskey and followed by a platoon of Fiona's Anglo and Filipino admirers we burst in on the invalid. There he was, a great ugly, beaming bear-like figure, in pajamas and bed true enough. But sick no. Or the cure was instantaneous. He was up, bathrobed, and joined us immediately.

There was only one chair and one glass for two dozen guests so most of the time we sat on the floor around the overheated oil stove, passing the bottle from hand to hand around the circle. Stangle broke out another bottle, and another.

Apart from a Conga line by the younger set around the seated ring of elders I cannot recall any particular incident or conversation that took place; neither can anyone else. But it was agreed that it was a wonderful party.

Early in 1948, I did note that Stangle was showing signs of a relapse. He was having trouble with his balance when he stood up to get another bottle, so I advised him to go to bed and Fiona and I took our leave. So did everyone else, shouting good wishes and farewells from the stoop in front of the hut.

My fun-loving Fiona, feeling faint from the fast transition from the heated hut to the cold fresh air, felt for the first step with her foot, failed to find it, and flailing frantically fell flat on the fairest face in the Far East. With one accord the officers and ladies of the FFFFFT turned their backs, and chatted with animation about this and that until I had assisted her to her feet. Never be it said that the "Mather of the Regiment" couldn't hold a pint of Panther Sweat with dignity. A very nice lot of people in the Forty-fourth.

Next morning I awoke rather late to find Fiona foggily regarding her hand, which bore a distinctly printed big blue heel mark.

"I thought someone stepped on my thumb last night."

During the spring of 1948, I received orders to proceed by water transport via Japan to Fort Lewis and await reassignment. My request for another year in Okinawa was promptly disapproved.

One Saturday afternoon in April my favorite guerrilla, Carmela Domingo, called at our quarters in company with a couple of her winsome colleagues and asked Fiona and Lee for their dress sizes. They then produced tape measures, made notes of the vital statistics, and among other chit-chat asked that we be home on the next Saturday afternoon. Some of our friends in the Forty-fourth would like to call on that date.

Came the day. Liquid refreshments and "tung shis" had been prepared for the dozen callers expected, and Takuda, Mitziko, Chioko, and Kanisura had been instructed in their duties.

About 1600, Miss Domingo and her friends arrived and presented Fiona and Lee with gorgeous, heavily embroidered mestiza costumes and insisted on fitting them. I was surprised to receive a Barong Tagalog, the Filipino evening dress shirt of the thinnest linen with twenty copies of the Philippine seal embroidered on the front. It was a staggering amount of needlework that the Filipino ladies of the Red Cross and special services had accomplished in an impossibly short time.

I had always assumed that mestiza costumes designed for and by Filipinas would look right only on the Filipinas. How wrong that was; Fiona and Lee looked luscious in their barbaric splendor.

Felt sorry for B'Ann and Catherine. Those poor little deprived waifs just hung wistfully around the outskirts of the activities and got nothing but kindly conversation and an occasional pat on the head.

At 1700 the dam broke. A truck and several jeeps roared up to the back lot and our garden was invaded by a horde of officers and ladies of the Forty-fourth with a sprinkling of mestiza-costumed representatives of the Red Cross and special services. They were putting up a long sawhorse-plank table, covering it with sheets, and laying out an imposing array of viands and drinkables. The latter were of the usual variety—whiskey and soda for the Anglos and beer and Coca-Cola for the Filipinos.

We joined the party. And what a party it was! Fiona and I were introduced to our own individual roast pig, one of which was placed at each end of the table. We were told that as the guests of honor it was our duty to carve. Carving has never been one of my best points and roast (or rather ground-baked) pig is too well done to carve neatly. Don't know how Fiona made out but although my efforts were applauded my pig soon looked like the victim of an enthusiastic ax murderer.

I like Filipinos. They wear their hearts on their sleeves. Contrary to our Anglo reserve or inhibitions their emotions are right out in the open, and when a man is your friend (or enemy) you have no doubt about his feelings. We apparently had a lot of friends among the Scouts, which as an ex-regimental commander amazed me. Fiona reported a heart-to-heart outburst by Lieutenant Filoteo Apeles. "Meeses Treeplet, we are all loyal to thee new colonel. But Colonel Treeplet ees thee fawther and you are thee mawther of thee regiment."

There was I fear a good deal of hidden meaning behind that remark. As Colonel Waddell had told me during our first meeting, he had had a great deal of experience with Philippine Scouts. But according to my observation he did not like Filipinos, knew little about them, and did not try to learn. He was not simpatico with the Scouts and they felt it. The new colonel due to a previous engagement had been unable to attend our fiesta. Understandably so; we couldn't stand each other.

We were pleased with the attendance but I also regretted that our guests were possibly endangering their military careers by their presence.

I know that Fiona enjoyed the evening. She gets all choked up when she mentions it thirty years later. So do I.

Notes

One. The 342d Infantry Regiment

1. There was talk in Germany of continuing resistance through partisans who would fight on for years, even decades, rising out of the forests like wolves.

2. The nationally syndicated columnist Pearson was especially active in soliciting criticism of the military for attempting, as he described the situation, to hold troops and sailors in service against their will.

3. Stationed at Fort Benning in 1940–1942, Triplet served under the then Lieutenant Colonel Melasky as a member of the test section of the Infantry Board. The latter, composed of field grade officers of long service, was seeking to discover and test new weapons, vehicles, and equipment, and to certify them for employment with troops if they passed the testing. Triplet had enjoyed his connection with the board and found Melasky an admirable taskmaster.

4. A member of the class of 1924, Triplet was promoted to first lieutenant in 1930.

5. The tent was invented by General Henry H. Sibley, a West Pointer who served on the Confederate side during the Civil War.

6. Like the other attacking divisions in the Meuse-Argonne, the Thirty-fifth did well on the first day or two and then found itself up against murderous machine-gun and enfilading artillery fire, the latter from the heights of the Meuse on the east, the Argonne Forest on the west.

7. Not long after he was assigned to the regiment Triplet received the task of flying a heavy out-sized American flag from the weakened flagpole, assigned the task by Manila army headquarters; the flag had come from an American Legion post in Rochester, New York, the members of which desired a flag flown on Corregidor. "The flag was a monster, of heavy wool, forty by twenty-eight feet, and weighing two hundred pounds. We unwrapped the bundle, the size and weight of a folded general purpose tent, and were impressed. . . . On December 22 the weather wizards prophesied a flat calm for the next day, so the flag raising was scheduled for 1600 and the . . . [Manila command] public information officer was notified to have the press and his platoon of reporters and photographers at the ceremony. . . . Just as the flag reached the top, a slight gust of wind fluttered and raised it clear of the mast. There was

an ominous creaking of straining metal, and the top third of the mast slowly leaned over five degrees. . . . I had cautioned the . . . [command] chaplain (as a light colonel he ranked my chaplains out of the job) to keep his dedication brief. That was very stupid of me—from long experience I should have known that it is impossible for any chaplain to be brief. During the fourth paragraph of his exhortation a vagrant puff lifted and flapped the flag, strained steel screeched and cracked, and the weakened portion of the mast leaned another ten majestic degrees while cameras clicked to record the tragedy for the *Daily Worker, Pravda,* and posterity. Since his eyes were reverently closed the chaplain remained unaware of my frantic 'cease firing' signal, and droned on for three more sonorous paragraphs while the mast quivered and squeaked. But due no doubt to his influence with the Almighty the calm settled in again and held. . . . That evening I had two aspirin and three nightcaps for dinner."

8. Army Forces in the Western Pacific.

9. Because the post–World War I officer corps was heavy with veterans, Congress in 1936 passed legislation allowing for generous retirements.

Two. Morale Building

1. In one month of fighting during the U.S. conquest of the city, four-fifths of the capital were razed. "Manila was a quagmire in the rainy season; and in the hot season the red dust above the city, thrown up by heavy army traffic, made it look, from a distance, afire. The city was full of jerry-built shelters, and its hasty bazaars were full of gimcrack goods. Soldiers, sailors, and peddlers jammed its sidewalks; whores and pimps and pickpockets, confidence men and influence mongers; ex-guerrillas still in jungle uniform, and throngs of common men and women, tired and unemployed. To one observer who had loved the old city, the new Manila looked like a carnival in hell." Theodore Friend, *Between Two Empires,* 263–64.

2. In the case of Pershing, Triplet wrote from hearsay.

3. Petty and Vargas were well-known illustrators of the time.

4. The Thirty-fifth was a National Guard division.

5. Francis Cardinal Spellman, archbishop of New York, was vicar of U.S. armed forces in World War II. The *Pacifican* was the newspaper of AFWESPAC published in Manila. Its B-Bag column was named after the second of the bags belonging to soldiers. The first, the A-Bag, the men usually carried, a rounded bag with clothesline drawstrings, just the thing to carry up a wobbling gangplank, for it had a tendency to roll off one's shoulder. In the movements of troops the B-Bag, which was supposed to follow them after storage or bulk transportation, often became lost.

6. The vaudeville comedian Chic Sales was the author of a thin volume

entitled *The Specialist,* much admired in the 1920s, concerning construction of outhouses.

7. The CID was counterintelligence.

8. The USO was United Service Organizations.

9. The performers were Ingrid Bergman and Jack Benny. CCA was Combat Command A, Triplet's command in the Seventh Armored Division in Europe.

10. Styer was commanding general of AFWESPAC. Ben Lear was commanding general of army ground forces. For the issue involving the generals see chapter 8.

11. "Hinton was a sour-pussed and mean-dispositioned old Indian fighter, and my declared enemy. His athletic teams clobbered mine regularly, and his unit newspaper wrote editorials about Prussianism, the 342d brass, fascists, and *me.*" For such good reasons Triplet did what he could to Hinton, overlooking no opportunities. "On Christmas Eve the bandmaster had told me of his secret plan to play Christmas carols at dawn, in place of the Reveille that I had cancelled. I never like to discourage such commendable initiative, but Christmas carols at *dawn?* I compromised. I agreed, providing the band spread the good cheer wider, and played the first carol in front of Colonel Hinton's quarters in the 341st Regiment area next door. . . . As I pointed out to the bandmaster it would be a friendly gesture appropriate for Christmas morning. My plans for sleeping late were in vain. The hearty strains of 'Good King Wenceslaus,' beaten out by an enthusiastic twenty-eight-piece military band, even at a range of half a mile, brought me up all standing just as the pearly gray dawn brightened into day. What it did to Colonel Hinton at a range of thirty yards I shuddered to contemplate. At noon I approached the division commander's reception expecting the usual barbed remark or poisonous exchange, but evidently my opponent was puzzled; was the pre-dawn serenade a genuine Yuletide peace offering? Or was it a malicious joke? But there were no comments—just the customary dour, suspicious glare."

Three. Settling In

1. Gai's rank was Technician-5, equivalent to corporal.

2. "Chow was sick. In spite of a prodigious appetite he became thinner. His nose was hot and his fur lost its luster. He would still give the alarm when an unknown approached our quarters, but instead of dashing about begging to be let out to eat the intruder he would make sure that I was awake, and obviously was content to let me cope with the situation while he stayed in bed.

"I called the veterinarian in Manila and described the symptoms.

" 'Sounds like worms,' said the doctor. 'Don't feed him today and bring him in tomorrow at 1000.'

"I did. The telephone diagnosis was confirmed. 'This dog has a beautiful case of worms,' said the young man, expertly tossing three pills down Chow's visibly resisting throat, while two muscular orderlies expertly held him. 'Now you can take him back and in four hours give him a dose of Epsom Salts—one tablespoon in a half glass of water. He has to get a full dose or the worm medicine will burn his stomach out.' The vet ladled out a generous quarter pound of the white powder.

" 'And just how do you give a dog Epsom Salts?'

" 'Oh, it's simple. Just hold his head sidewise, hold his muzzle closed, pull down the side of his lower lip to form a cup, and pour the mixture in. Stroke his throat to make him swallow.' The three medics gave a successful demonstration with a glass of water. It looked easy.

"I should have waited four hours and insisted on professional assistance, but stupidly accepted the doctor's advice and took the patient back to camp.

"When the four hours were about up I stirred up the half glass of water and a tablespoonful of salts and asked the Scout orderly to hold the dog while I poured it. That did it. Chow had become fairly tolerant of Filipinos in uniform and didn't even attack Japs unless they entered his current domain. But to lay hands on him—he exploded into motion and bit us both, retreated to a corner, and dared us to come and get him. I called for reinforcements and resumed the battle.

"At the end of a quarter hour Chow had bit me, the adjutant, Colonel Stangle, two Japs, and three Scouts, and was still defiantly crouched in his corner, sick and drooling from the nauseous stuff poured in our fifth futile attempt. Our uniforms were drenched with blood and the floor was puddled with a mixture of blood and Epsom Salts. But Chow still hadn't swallowed a drop and was apparently quite able and willing to resume the fight at any time at our pleasure. My cohorts were a bit worn, and marked for life, but were still game. About one dose of the salts remained. Then I chickened out and had a second thought that might save us all a lot of grief and skin.

" 'Ramierez, will you go to the headquarters mess and ask the cook for three pieces of raw meat, about so big?'

"I then called the dispensary.

" 'Major Gomez, please send me three Caesar's Pills.'

" 'Three Caesuras sir? But they should be taken with great caution. Do you have any pain in the right upper quadrant?'

" 'No, major. The pills aren't for me, they're for Chow, to help him get rid of the worm medicine.'

" 'But three CCs for your dog would be dangerously excessive. One pill would be a dose of normal amplitude for a sixty-pound person *or dog*'

" 'Just send me the pills, major, and I'll take it from there. I'll probably need the spares.'

"This was not a normal case, so I compromised. Two chunks of beef were punctured and a pill inserted in each. . . .

"About 2000 he frantically demanded to be let out and promised to tear the door down if I didn't open it NOW!

"I didn't see much of Chow next day—just occasional glimpses of him trotting over the hills around the outskirts of camp trying to find new places to squat. Perhaps Major Gomez had been right, one pill would probably have been the correct dose, and I feared I might have overdone it.

"But my bodyguard was back on duty again that night, weak but bright-eyed, alert, unusually good-humored, and very hungry.

"I must get a letter off to the chief of the veterinary corps describing my technique. It might save lives."

3. Peiping, meaning "northern capital," so designated for Peking by General Chiang Kai-shek when his revolutionary forces occupied Nan-king in 1927, underwent a name change, back to Peking, when the Communist Chinese occupied it and organized their government in 1949. Colonel Triplet of course had been in Tientsin during the Nationalist era.

4. Most of the men were from Officers Candidate School, coming from the enlisted ranks.

Four. Thieves

1. Triplet was en route to his regiment in Tientsin.

2. Paul V. McNutt was U.S. high commissioner to the Philippine Commonwealth, which came to an end with Philippine independence on July 4, 1946.

3. In central Luzon the communist-led Huks controlled the country-side. In 1942 peasants and communist mayors had united in a popular anti-Japanese, anti-landlord movement, political and military. The Huks abolished rents and redistributed land, and after the war established local governments to the provincial level. And yet their wartime and postwar tactics had been difficult to admire. During the war the other guerrilla groups could not cooperate with them. The Huks may have killed as many as five thousand Japanese but killed twenty thousand of their countrymen, presumably landlords and collaborationists but also, doubtless, creating a reign of terror that supported their own cause. They received advice on propaganda and organizing from the Chinese communists, and financial support from the Philippine Chinese. They possessed an army of ten thousand and claimed a militia backing of ten

times that number. George E. Taylor, *The Philippines and the United States,* 121–22.

4. Triplet did not understand that Secretary of the Treasury Henry Morgenthau, Jr., had arranged for the Soviet Union to possess plates for printing occupation currency, and that any Soviet-printed currency turned in to the treasury for redemption was a charge on U.S. taxpayers. Hence General Eisenhower's attempted intervention.

Five. Japanese

1. COMO is communications officer.

2. Colonel Triplet attributed the story to the paper but the prose resembled his and so appears here.

3. CIC is counterintelligence corps.

Six. Guerrillas

1. Despite an estimated guerrilla strength at V-J Day of 188,000, 260,000 Filipinos received back pay. Friend, *Blue-Eyed Enemy,* 241. Triplet and his fellow officers assuredly had analyzed the situation correctly. What they perhaps did not always understand was that the organization of guerrilla units traced back to a situation that lay far into the past. "A man of little standing could appoint himself a guerrilla rank and enlist his friends and neighbors in his company. The Filipino sociopolitical system aided him. In pre-Spanish times local control was in the hands of a *datu,* or boss. Spaniards found this system compatible with their own and called the boss the *cacique.* Unhappily this *caciqueism* was inherited by the Americans, and was too embedded to be eradicated by their attempts to enforce democratic voting. In guerrilla outfits the *cacique* usually gave himself brevet rank in grade from captain to colonel. The arrogance of one transferred easily to the arrogance of the other." William A. Owens, *Eye-Deep in Hell,* 57. This author, a technical sergeant, later a second lieutenant, in the counterintelligence corps, holder of a Ph.D. in English and an erstwhile college and university teacher, concluded that "The Army from the Commanding General down, for political or other reasons, was too soft on the guerrillas."

2. S-2 was intelligence.

3. Triplet could become too suspicious. "I noticed a man approaching who seemed to be wearing a Purple Heart slung on a leather thong around his neck. It *was* a Purple Heart without the ribbon. Aha! A thief or bandit wearing part of his loot. I stopped him. 'Where did you get this?' I asked accusingly. 'Not spik mooch Eengleesh,' he replied, but he understood me. He pulled out a well-worn leather folder and produced an honorable discharge from the Philippine Army. Then, opening his shirt, he showed a nine-inch purple scar slanting across his abdomen, and said,

'Boom!' He couldn't have had better credentials. I provided cigarettes, and heard what I believe was a vivid, blow-by-blow account of the Battle of Bataan (which he correctly pronounced Bat-ah-ahn) in a mixture of Eengleesh, Illocano, Spanish, and sound effects. So I complimented him on being authorized to wear the Purple Heart, the Bronze Star (v), and a Combat Infantry Badge on a string around his neck if he wanted, left him the pack of cigarettes, and took my embarrassed leave."

Seven. Twenty-first Replacement Depot

1. S-3 was operations.

2. Camp Blackjack received its name from General John J. Pershing's army nickname. In the 1890s he commanded black troops.

3. G-4 was transportation and supply. "G" designations applied to divisions or higher commands, "S" to the others.

Eight. The New Army and the Old

1. A major point of irritation for U.S. soldiers in the Pacific Theater was the extra time necessary for passage back to their homes, as compared with men in Europe. They failed, of course, to calculate the much longer distance.

2. Columnist Walter Winchell also had a national radio program.

3. MOS was Military Occupation Specialty.

4. EM, or enlisted men, was a misnomer as many of the men were drafted, and was a holdover from Regular Army days.

5. Seeking to determine the state of army morale, General Eisenhower as chief of staff made an inspection tour of the Pacific, during which he inquired of innumerable soldiers what they liked and disliked about the army. "At 1400, I was at the main gate of the area when the procession of six jeeps arrived. Generals Eisenhower and Kramer dismounted from the lead vehicle and fifteen camera men and reporters boiled out of the next five, unslinging their gear and notebooks. I saluted, gave my name, and shook hands with the chief of staff. 'And now I'd like to introduce my commanders and staff.' 'No,' said Eisenhower in a carrying voice, with a disgusted, discarding, downward flap of the hand. 'I've met too many officers!' The press sniggered and scribbled. *That* was good for a headline. Glancing about for a suitable subject Eisenhower walked over to my jeep, which was parked on the right of the staff line, threw his arm around the shoulders of my startled driver T-5 Fong, and briefly bared his teeth to the clicking of the cameras. All cameras having clicked, he dropped his arm and his pleasant personality and strode back to his jeep, leaving my bewildered driver surrounded by the gentlemen of the press who were demanding his name, address, and vital statistics apparently in vain—they couldn't understand him any better than I could. That

was, in brief, the story of the inspection. The general privately ignored my very solid officers, other than the bare acknowledgment of their reports. He posed with many privates and corporals, and even a few sergeants. He grabbed each confused subject with a shoulder clasp or a handshake, flashed his fangs at the cameras, and then dropped the whole act with a sudden thud." In an unpublished portion of his memoirs that followed the above, the colonel related that Eisenhower was running for the presidency. Triplet had discovered in his 201 file that he had come close to promotion to brigadier general during World War II, with his promotion held up by Eisenhower, who had scribbled a brief note that there already were enough generals in Europe to win the war—it was near the end of the fighting. It is also worth mentioning the experience of the historian Robert Allen Rutland, biographer of James Madison, who after World War II had been banished by his Philippine commanding officer to Okinawa and there met Eisenhower during the latter's tour. The general spent an hour and more with Rutland and a friend, the group having drinks, inquiring about morale, as hospitable as he could be. Before undertaking the tour the chief of staff had received an inquiring letter from President Truman, equally concerned about the riotous behavior in Manila and the many other contemporary evidences of downturns in discipline, especially those of men writing to Pearson and other columnists.

Ten. The FFFFFT
1. S-1 was personnel.
2. Fiona was the colonel's wife, Lee his eldest daughter.
3. Upon the fall of the dictator Ferdinand E. Marcos, General Ileto in 1986 became minister of national defense in the cabinet of Cora Aquino.

Eleven. Cultural Differences
1. A scourge of white settlers in the Southwest, Chief Red Sleeves was captured and killed in 1863 while allegedly attempting to escape.
2. "Two years later when I was assigned to command the 182d Special Regiment at West Point, I found a copy of the piano score among my papers. I turned this over to Captain Resta, the bandmaster, who was interested in music of all types. A month later Captain Resta invited Fiona and me to the rehearsal room where the West Point band was assembled. A signal with his baton and the band swung into the Forty-fourth Infantry march! Like paleontologists rebuilding a dinosaur from a thigh bone Captain Resta and his musical geniuses had made a perfect reconstruction of the march from the piano score, complete even to the chimes of the glockenspiel."

Twelve. Gardner, Mertel, and MacLaughlin

1. "In Saigon in 1962, I heard of the exploits of Lieutenant Colonel Kenneth D. Mertel who commanded one of the newfangled helicopter battalions flying close support or landing troops in the then current actions against the Vietcong. I was not able to see him but heard his praises sung by the junior officers and a buck sergeant of his battalion. He had evidently continued his mastery of new and strange manuals. Between Korea and Vietnam he had graduated from the Infantry School, Airborne School, Ranger School, Flying School, Helicopter School, and the Command and General Staff College. Now he was making a reputation for flying more close support missions while losing fewer men and machines than any other battalion commander in the business. As the sergeant said, 'He's a ring-tailed sonofabitch on discipline. Makes us fly in tight formation whether we're taking off, landing, or plastering the Congs at a hundred feet. Mutual support all the time, and God help you if you break formation.'"

2. After departure of General Douglas MacArthur for Australia, Lieutenant General Jonathan M. Wainwright was in command of all American and Filipino troops.

Thirteen. Housekeeping

1. Seabees were navy construction battalions.

2. ANC was the army nurse corps.

Fifteen. Acquaintance

1. Interestingly, the ambitious Perry, en route to Japan, had written from Madeira in favor of seizing the Ryukyus: "Now it strikes me that the occupation of the principal parts of those islands for the accommodation of our ships of war, and for the safe resort of merchant vessels of whatever other nation, would be a measure not only justified by the strictest rules of moral law, but, what is also to be considered, by the laws of stern necessity; and the argument may be further strengthened by the certain consequences of the amelioration of the condition of the natives, although the vices attendant upon civilization may be entailed upon them."

2. "But it worked. No more inflammatory letters in the public press. Don't know how the lads put the pressure on but I was delighted with the results."

Sixteen. Accommodations

1. As all members of the U.S. Army during World War II and after remember, field rations came suitably labeled according to the alphabet. The C-ration was a can of spam or hash, slimy if eaten cold, attractive if heated. The D-ration was a chocolate bar, hard as a rock, worth three

or four thousand calories, tasty on the first bite but overwhelming after half eaten. The K-ration had its moments, as the food inside the box often was almost good and the box included surprises in the form of candy; men often opened a K-ration for the surprise.

2. Buckner Bay was named for Lieutenant General Simon Bolivar Buckner II, commander of the invading American troops, killed on the island of Ie Shima.

Seventeen. *Deputy Commander and Chief of Staff*

1. The LST, landing ship tank, was a sizable vessel, well above destroyer tonnage, shallow draft, with huge opening doors at the bow, and possessed seagoing qualities, as its use on the Okinawa-Shanghai run demonstrated. See *A Colonel in the Armored Divisions,* 69–87, for Triplet's experience with an LST while training with amphibious tanks off the California coast in 1943–1944. The LST's shallow draft produced stories, such as a tale Triplet overheard in the regimental club, related by a navy lieutenant to an army nurse: "You remember that big rain day before yesterday? Well, my ship, the LST 497, was anchored in Manila Bay. Fully loaded with eight hundred tons of tanks and trucks we draw only four feet forward and seven feet aft. Empty, as we were, we float right on the surface. When that rain from the west hit us it was so dense that the 497 floated right up in it, dragging her one anchor inshore. Then the rain stopped all of a sudden and we dropped two hundred feet right into the middle of the Old Spanish Market inside the Walled City. Hell of a jolt! Damn near broke m'ankle!"

2. The M-4 was the Sherman tank, the M-5 the Stuart.

3. The partly destroyed railroad bridge at Remagen, captured in March 1945, allowed the U.S. Army to cross the Rhine.

4. Pyle, a native of Indiana, covered the experiences of common soldiers in an attractive, down-home way, and gained a large readership, making his death and grave a subject of popular interest.

5. "They had evidently expected to see a pink marble monument with a suitable inscription in gold. General Hayden expected a rush of Pulitzer Prize–winning exposés. But never a word about Ernie's final resting place was seen in the public press."

Eighteen. *Murder in the Forty-fourth*

1. As a commander of tank-infantry-artillery forces on the ground, Triplet had come under friendly fire from the air—one instance involving the dumping of bombs on a village that clearly, he believed, stood apart from the town he desired bombed. On another occasion the "flyboys" bombed his own positions, despite markings on his vehicles and laying out of panels.

2. As chief of staff to General Hayden, Triplet inherited an unfriendly secretary.

3. Kranz gave trouble later; see chapter 20.

4. Moro insurrectionists, or juramentados, had bedeviled Americans since shortly after conquest of the Philippines in 1898, and such officers as the then Captain Pershing (whom President Theodore Roosevelt in 1906 raised to brigadier general) made their military reputations by putting them down.

5. BOQ was bachelor officers quarters.

Nineteen. Atkinson-Jones

1. Judge advocate general.

2. Inspector general.

3. "It didn't. Eighteen years after the case of the demon driver was closed I met Colonel Williams in Germany and learned that the lack of support by higher authority still rankled. I'm on his side. It wasn't right."

4. Continent of the United States.

5. Ms. Landers dispensed marital advice in a nationally syndicated newspaper column for a half century.

Twenty. Miscellany

1. Letterman General Hospital was in San Francisco.

Twenty-One. Departure

1. Kyushu is the southernmost of the Japanese home islands.

2. "A year later I was in Walter Reed General Hospital for a checkup and learned that General Hayden was over in the heart ward. Dropped in to see him and diagnosed his trouble as malingeritis, acute. Nothing wrong with him that a few games of volleyball wouldn't cure. After a bit of chitchat about the good old days in Okinawa he mentioned Hegenberger. 'You ought to go up and see him. He's in the room right overhead.' 'Right overhead? On the next floor? Why, that's the psychiatric ward.' 'That's right,' he smirked."

3. "The Rykom party evidently did get off the ground after all. At General Hayden's New Year's reception both the members of the receiving line and the guests seemed pale and distrait. The most outstanding individual was Colonel Winningstedt. His normally ruddy countenance was a pale chartreuse. His eyes had lost their luster. His usually alert and aggressive manner had changed to flaccid indifference. His condition was quite normal to the occasion. What caught my attention was three imposing rows of campaign and decoration ribbons raggedly pinned over the right pocket of his uniform."

Bibliographical Essay

For American military history of the years since the end of World War II the best resort is to the U.S. Army Military History Institute at Carlisle Barracks, not far from Harrisburg, Pennsylvania, where the army has gathered personal collections of papers and many oral histories. The Institute was founded a third of a century ago and has relied on personal donations of materials, and so there are wide gaps in its holdings. But they are the easiest sources. Its papers are organized by military units—divisions, and within them brigades and regiments and attached organizations. The other principal arrangement of materials is by name—the papers of this or that individual.

After exploring the holdings of the Institute a researcher may wish to investigate holdings of the National Archives in Washington and College Park, Maryland, easy commutes from Carlisle, this for official papers.

The post–World War II service of Colonel Triplet in the Philippines and Okinawa unfortunately does not offer a wide background of materials either in personal papers (the Institute) or the Archives, and beyond occasional accessions, which the investigator would have to discover by name or unit, there is a thin crust of books pertaining to the occupations of the Philippine Islands and of Okinawa. Devastation in the islands, especially the virtual destruction of Manila at the end of the war, precluded the survival or even collection of records, and on Okinawa, as Triplet learned after a quick reconnaissance prior to taking his Scout regiment there, almost every building on the island had been pulverized.

Books on the American reoccupation of the Philippines, for such it was, nonetheless are of surprisingly high quality. It is true that the early post–World War II period has had less attention than the initial American occupation in 1898 and after (for which see the splendid book by Glenn A. May, *Battle for Batangas: A Philippine Province at War* [New Haven, Conn.: Yale University Press, 1991]) or the rise and fall of the dictatorship of President Ferdinand E. Marcos (Richard J. Kessler, *Rebellion and Repression in the Philippines* [New Haven, Conn.: Yale University Press, 1989]). Such early post-1945 publications as Garel A. Grunder and William E. Livesay, *The Philippines and the United States* (Norman: University of Oklahoma Press, 1951) are remarkably thin on what happened in the Philippines at the end of World War II and immediately thereafter. But the later literature has been impressive. An excellent survey is George E. Taylor, *The Philippines and the United States: Problems of Partnership* (New York: Praeger, 1964); Taylor's judgments have stood the test of time. See also the hauntingly eloquent memoir of a member of the army's counterintelligence corps, William A. Owens, *Eye-Deep in Hell: A Memoir of the Liberation of the Philippines 1944–1945* (Dallas: Southern Methodist University Press, 1989). Despite its lurid title it is a remarkable book, well written, highly emotional, about the army's return to the Philippines. There is much about the Huks here, for this author saw Luis Taruc many times. It is very much anti-MacArthur. And see another similarly eloquent book by the Philippine expert Theodore Friend, *Blue-Eyed Enemy: Japan against the West in Java and Luzon, 1942–1945* (Princeton, N.J.: Princeton University Press, 1988). The author of the authoritative *Between Two Empires: The Ordeal of the Philippines, 1929–1946* (New Haven, Conn.: Yale University Press, 1965), Friend in his later book compares the occupations of Java and Luzon, showing the enormous loss of life and especially the depredations of the Kenpeitai, the Japanese military CIC, which controlled the highest-ranking army officers. Douglas I. Macdonald, *Adventures in Chaos: American Intervention for Reform in the Third World* (Cambridge, Mass.: Harvard University Press, 1992) has two chapters on the Philippines that begin in 1950. Special for its topic is Nick Cullather, *Illusions of Influence: The Political Economy of United States–Philippines Relations, 1942–1960* (Stanford, Calif.: Stanford University Press, 1994), ably done. Another special study is Davis J. Steinberg, *Philippine Collaboration in World War II* (Ann Arbor, Mich.: University of Michigan Press, 1967), which offers background for Colonel Triplet's experience; Steinberg relates the fact that the Japanese Army during the war shot ten civilians for every Japanese soldier killed.

Michael S. Molasky, *The American Occupation of Japan and Okinawa: Literature and Memory* (New York: Routledge, 1999) has just a few pages on Okinawa in 1947–1948. For Okinawan affairs the best resort is encyclopedias and newspaper accounts.

Index